REFRAMING ASSESSMENT TO CENTER EQUITY

REFRAMING ASSESSMENT TO CENTER EQUITY

Theories, Models, and Practices

Edited by Gavin W. Henning,

Gianina R. Baker, Natasha A. Jankowski,

Anne E. Lundquist, and Erick Montenegro

STERLING, VIRGINIA

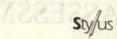

COPYRIGHT © 2022 BY STYLUS PUBLISHING, LLC.

Published by Stylus Publishing, LLC.
22883 Quicksilver Drive
Sterling, Virginia 20166-2019

Library of Congress Cataloging-in-Publication Data
The CIP data for this title has been applied for.

13-digit ISBN: 978-1-64267-256-5 (cloth)
13-digit ISBN: 978-1-64267-257-2 (paperback)
13-digit ISBN: 978-1-64267-258-9 (library networkable e-edition)
13-digit ISBN: 978-1-64267-259-6 (consumer e-edition)

Printed in the United States of America

All first editions printed on acid-free paper
that meets the American National Standards Institute
Z39-48 Standard.

Bulk Purchases

Quantity discounts are available for use in workshops and
for staff development.

Call 1-800-232-0223

First Edition, 2022

CONTENTS

PART THREE: HOW?

PART FOUR: NOW WHAT?

LIST OF FIGURES AND TABLES

This book is the result of a collaborative effort among five editors. It is about making the case for positioning assessment of student learning as a vehicle for equity in higher education. It was our intention in this book to provide a conversation aggregator, bringing together in a shared space the different discussions and dialogues on equity, cultural responsiveness, and socially just assessment, among others. To do so, the book offers a foundation to assist higher education faculty and staff to perform equity-centered assessment that can enable equitable student outcomes and experiences. The book is written for assessment professionals but is relevant for a wider audience that is involved in supporting student learning throughout institutions of higher education. In order to provide a foundation for practice while also advancing the scholarship and dialogue on equity and assessment, various authors from different institution types, positions, perspectives, backgrounds, and approaches were invited to be a part of this edited volume.

As editors, we were involved in writing various chapters, reading and providing feedback on chapters throughout, and we also invited a variety of authors to join in the journey. While more will be said momentarily on how to read this book and what is in it and why, this section begins with an introduction to the five of us who edited this book. As editors, we strongly believe it is necessary to offer statements of our positionality that in turn directly impacted the focus, direction, and nature of this book and required each of us to engage in acts of self-reflexivity (for those interested in reading about all the authors in this book, please see the Authors and Contributors section at the end of the text). What follows is a brief positionality statement for each of the editors with the caveat that our ideas, perspectives, assumptions, and approaches have all been influenced, formed, and curated by those who came before us and by those who are not found in the pages of this book. To each of you, a great debt is owed, and we thank you for your companionship on this equity journey.

Who We Are

Since this book regards equity, the editors thought it was critical for us to discuss our backgrounds, identities, and privileges as these impact how assessment is implemented and how we approached this book.

Gavin W. Henning

White, heterosexual, cisgender, man; husband, son, uncle; first-generation college student, working class, hearing disabled—these are the key elements of my identity. As I have become aware of the unearned power and privilege I garner from my identities, they have become more salient.

Not only have I benefited from my identities, because of them I have had relatively few challenges in my life. I have never been tracked while shopping in a store. I have rarely feared walking at night. When holding my wife's hand in public I have never been concerned about jeers, ridicule, or even attack. For many years, I have taken these basic everyday acts for granted. I constantly struggle with my privilege, as I should, especially when writing and talking about equity-centered assessment. I wonder what credibility I have as a White, cisgender, heterosexual man. I wonder about whose voice is not heard if I am speaking. These questions are juxtaposed with the acknowledgment that because of my multiple privileged identities, I have a responsibility to use that power to dismantle the systems of power and oppression from which I have benefited.

White, heterosexual, cisgender, man; husband, son, uncle; first-generation college student, working class, hearing disabled—these are the identities, the perspectives, and the privilege I brought to this project.

Gianina R. Baker

I identify as a Black, heterosexual, cisgender female whose scholarship and practice are informed by my studies in counseling and educational organization and leadership, with a specific focus on higher education, as well as personal experiences of my own and other family members navigating educational systems. In fact, out of four grandparents, only one, my maternal grandmother, graduated high school. The inequitable experiences in education my family faced serve as my reason why I engage in work to identify equitable solutions throughout our educational systems. My lived experience helps inform conversations I have professionally with presidents, provosts, faculty and staff, and other professional organizations nationally about learning, specifically, assessing student learning on college and university campuses.

In an effort to dig deeper, using a worksheet from a recent Racism Untaught workshop on campus to help understand our positionality in how I as a person of color uphold systems of oppression, I identified with the following privileges: gender identity and expression; class, educational level, religion/spirituality, national origin; ableness, use of English, marital status, parental status, athleticism, and geographic region. It was a helpful exercise as I often move in and out of such spaces with both privilege and marginalization. This juxtaposition of privilege and marginalization is often where I sit and is, ultimately, what I brought to this book. I hope this book helps those with similar experiences identify ways of healing ourselves, our students, and our colleges, thus transforming our educational systems.

Natasha A. Jankowski

I identify as a White, heterosexual, cisgender woman. I am a mother, sister, aunt, wife, mentor, confidant, and colleague. I am midwestern in attitude (mostly), the youngest of two siblings, and first in my family to acquire a PhD. I served as executive director of the National Institute for Learning Outcomes Assessment, balancing the need to push the field of assessment with being responsive and supportive of current and ongoing needs of the field. As a faculty member at a research-intensive doctoral institution, I took seriously the preparation of the future leaders of U.S. higher education.

The positionality that I brought to this book is multifaceted. As a constructivist with a background in continental philosophy, it was necessary to do the writing of this book with others. As someone aware of their position at a national institute, there was a responsibility in the writing of this book to bring in varied voices and perspectives from throughout the national landscape. As a faculty member, it was necessary to provide those new to the publishing process opportunities to engage in a safe and supportive experience. As a White woman with a graduate education, it was necessary to use the privilege afforded me to make way for others, model how to engage in equity conversations, and make the business of equitable education part of my daily practice; in part because privilege means there is a choice to look away. That choice is not the lived experience of my colleagues of color nor is it their burden to educate others. To solve educational challenges and position education to attain the ascribed status as a public good, my position is to lift others up while calling out the historical inequities within the systemization of assessment and the choices made to perpetuate inequities within higher education. Such a positionality stance also meant that in reviewing chapters, I had to lead with grace, understanding, and be mindful of ways in which the review process can limit and silence voices. I am on an equity journey, it is not done, nor am I an expert, but I brought belief in humanity and the power of evidence-based storytelling to the writing of this text.

Anne E. Lundquist

I identify as a White, cisgender, currently able-bodied, heterosexual, neurotypical woman. I also identify as a mother to a biracial son, a grandmother, widow, poet, yogi, practicing Buddhist, and a social justice advocate and activist. I am learning about the impact of my privileged identities. Particularly salient for me is my Whiteness (and how I have been shaped by and benefited from White supremacy culture) and my third-generation educational privilege (where even though I worked hard to graduate from college and obtain my PhD, I have educational and economic benefits I did not earn). It is my responsibility to continuously reflect on those privileges, and to use them where I have power and influence to lift up and center voices of those traditionally marginalized and to speak up and take action when I witness injustice.

Reflecting on identity, privilege, and place has made me increasingly aware of my colonized perspective on education and work. I am aware that as I progressed through increasingly higher-level positions at colleges and universities, I was rewarded (and hence continued to cultivate and emphasize) individualistic, cognitive, goal-oriented, objective ways of knowing and being. I see how much and how often I split my body, mind, heart, and spirit, viewing them—and often experiencing them—as if they are separate. I'm practicing compassionately cultivating an embodied awareness which moves me toward integration, toward trusting my lived experience, toward relationships, and toward wiser action in every aspect of my life.

Erick Montenegro

I am a Latinx, heterosexual, cisgender male focused on exploring the concept of equity-mindedness and what that means for broader assessment practice. I am the youngest of three siblings, an immigrant—born in Durango, Mexico before moving to the southside of Chicago—an English language learner, first-generation high school graduate, first in my family to go to college, and the first in my family to earn a doctorate.

I carry these elements of my identity—and many others—into this book. There are many aspects of my identity that have served to marginalize me in the past (and likely will again in the future), but there are many others that have and will continue to serve as points of privilege. Continuous awareness and contextualized reflection of these facts are instrumental for my approach to life and for equity-minded assessment work.

My perspective on equity-mindedness is an unwavering bias toward calling it a "need." It is not a "want" or a luxury, but a *need*; and a pressing one at that. I also strongly believe the field of assessment has much to learn from Minority Serving Institutions, especially regarding how the postsecondary education system supports students who identify as Black, Indigenous, and People of Color (BIPOC). Lastly, the voiceless need a voice if equity is to be achieved, and students (especially BIPOC students) are often voiceless when it comes to assessment. This needs to change. These three affinities of mine, along with elements of my identity, strongly guide my writing and review of works in this book.

How to Read This Book

What is in this book and why? This book follows a framework of "why, what, how, and now what" in presentation of material The opening chapters outline why an entire book focused on the intersection of equity and assessment is needed, presenting the case for infusing equity into assessment (chapter 1) and arguing that assessment professionals can and should be activists in their practice in order to advance equity (chapter 2). For those still unconvinced on the "why," chapter 3 presents lenses through which to consider equity work in assessment and offers a brief overview of the history of assessment as a systemic blockade to educational access and attainment for historically marginalized populations. In order to understand "why" equity and assessment conversations are needed today, it is important to understand past conversations on equity in fairness, bias, and testing such that current conversations can be grounded by the past while engaging with the present and looking to the future.

The next grouping of chapters focuses on the "what" of equity and assessment. In chapter 4, an introduction and overview to the different fields of scholarship within equity and assessment are presented, serving as a foundation for later chapters and offering definitions for different terms widely used and those that are emerging. Chapter 5 discusses where equity appears in stories of student learning, if at all, through considering the narratives of equity in evidence of student learning. Positioning the assessment professional as a storyteller, counter-stories, students as storytellers, and Indigenous ways of knowing are discussed in relation to assessment and equity. Chapters 6 and 7 present models and approaches to promote equity in higher education as well as the relationship between knowledge systems and assessment practice. Together, chapters 4–7 lay out the landscape of assessment scholarship and work in relation to equity.

Chapters 8–16 provide examples of the "how" in regard to equity and assessment. The chapters are intentionally leveled, meaning they start within classrooms, sharing examples of equity practice and approaches to addressing equity in assessment that unfold within classrooms in the form of assignments (chapters 8 and 9). Carrying the assignment focus forward but moving up a level, chapter 10 presents an example of how assignments can be utilized at a program level to examine equity gaps, while chapter 11 shares how programs can engage the voices of students and faculty in culturally responsive assessment. Chapters 12 and 13 move beyond the program level to share examples from student affairs, providing practices from outside the classroom that support equity-minded assessment. The remaining chapters in the "how" section of the book tackle organizational-level issues considering the problem of equitable access to STEM fields (chapter 14), culturally responsive practices within the context of community colleges (chapter 15), and the ongoing work of culturally situated assessment practices in Historically Black Colleges and Universities (chapter 16).

The final three chapters in the book address the "now what" content of the structural outline. In chapter 17, the role of technology enabled assessment is explored as a possible tool for equitable assessment. Chapter 18 provides a way forward for assessment professionals to develop individual awareness within their practice and lived experiences as a next step in the equity journey, while chapter 19 provides a conceptual framework to anchor equity work along with an invitation into future conversations and collaborations.

A Note on Reading the Book

While readers are welcome to start and stop anywhere in the book and/or use the text as a reference book throughout their equity and assessment journey, it is easy to jump into the "how" section to simply get to doing the work. A word of caution is offered here, because part of the doing of the work is understanding "why" equity and assessment efforts are needed as well as "what" such efforts might mean or entail. In addition, work is needed internally as argued in chapter 18 (and various others throughout the book) to ensure that equity work also does no harm. Further, while readers are invited to engage with the book in any order of chapters desired, we do encourage readers to explore each chapter because each chapter adds something unique of value regardless of institutional context to thinking about how to engage in equity work.

As editors, we hope you might consider this book your companion on an equity journey, referring to it when needed, arguing with it at times, and returning to it to reset and recharge. If assessment is truly about student learning and improving student learning, understanding institutional effectiveness, and ensuring that institutions of higher education deliver on the promise and potential of education, then whether we may like it or not, action is required to address systemic inequities in educational systems, processes, and practices. Through the pages of this book, authors share the ways in which they are taking up the charge and answering the call. Each chapter provides lenses and perspectives to interrogate processes and practices, ask hard questions, and consider ways in which we, in our everyday spaces and places, can enact system change. Thank you for joining us in this journey.

PART ONE

WHY?

WHY THE INTERSECTION OF ASSESSMENT AND EQUITY?

Erick Montenegro and Gavin W. Henning

Horace Mann, the influential American educator and architect of the country's public education system, once said that education—beyond all other devices—is a great equalizer. This was true in 1848 when he uttered these words, and it remains true today. Now, and perhaps more than ever, the importance of an education—specifically of holding quality higher education credentials—can determine entire families' futures and future generations.

But what happens when the promise of education remains unmet for some, generation after generation? When learning outcomes attainment varies by student demographics? When the return on investment in a college education is disproportionately less for some student populations over others? The answer is that inequities grow. Society continues to further divide and stratify instead of equalize.

This chapter begins to merge the conversation of equity—specifically the ways it manifests in higher education through graduation rates, campus climate, norms, assumptions, and the uneven return on educational investment—with the purpose of assessment. The goal is to create a wider understanding for why assessment practitioners need to approach their work through an equity lens so that we may serve as a vehicle for just educational experiences and equality through equitable assessment praxis.

The Inequitable Value of Higher Education

The majority of existing high-paying jobs and jobs that will be created in the near future require education beyond high school or a college degree (Lumina, 2020). Employers are seeking applicants with advanced credentials including short-term credentials and certificates offered by quality education providers. Less opportunity for social mobility exists—and will continue to exist—for those with only a K–12 education (Araki, 2020), with huge disparities regarding who currently has quality credentials beyond high school. The Lumina Foundation (2020) reported that only 43.2% of Americans between ages 25 and 64 had such credentials in 2018: 63.8% of Asian Americans, 47.9% of Whites, 31.6% of Blacks, 24.6% of Native Americans, and 24.5% of Latinx. The disparities in attainment among racial/ethnic demographics are stark and offer cause for reflection regarding what these disparities mean for future income inequality and other social inequities by race and ethnicity.

The good news is that the student population attending college is diversifying and will continue to diversify in the coming years. According to the National Center for Education Statistics (NCES), the diversity of college enrollment will continue to increase in the next 5 years with an increase of 20% Black, 26% Latinx, 12% Asian and Pacific Islander, and 37% for students who are of two or more races (Hussar & Bailey, 2018). White students are expected to increase by 1% in that same time span, with an expected and unfortunate decrease of 3% enrollment among the Native American and Alaskan Native population (Hussar & Bailey, 2018). Diversifying the college-going student population offers an opportunity to close the attainment gap between student populations, but in order to do that, colleges and universities have to first be ready to properly support diverse students through to completion.

The college graduation rates of students of color are dismal compared to those of White students. While 74% of Asian students and 64% of White students graduated college in 2016 within 6 years of enrolling, only 54% of Latinx, 51% of Pacific Islander, 40% of Black, and 39% of Native American/Alaskan Native students did the same (NCES, 2019). Diverse learners are walking through college doors but are not graduating in similar numbers as their White and Asian peers. We have to ask "why?" We have to understand how and which systems operating within colleges and universities contribute to these disparate attainment rates by marginalized student populations.

Students enroll in college with very different needs, levels of preparation, expectations, and supports. Institutions, programs, those conducting assessment, and those using assessment data to make decisions should be expected to meet students where they are, provide welcoming spaces where students feel as if they belong, and help students succeed regardless of differences.

Systemic Issues Undermining Equity in Higher Education

At its core, "equity" means being mindful of fairness and giving everyone their fair share in specific situations. It is also the process that provides us with the underlying principles to reach equality—equity is equality turned into action (Smith & Gorard, 2006). Equity means acting to remedy injustices. As a concept, equity allows practitioners to foster social justice by creating the needed considerations for institutions to have positive impacts across social groups by being mindful of how policies and norms create disadvantages, account for historical inequities, and create social change to reach equality (Pasque et al., 2012). It involves interrogating, reflecting, and improving practice, policy, and perspectives. It necessitates intentionality and commitment. Through being ever mindful of equity, assessment practitioners can make inequities visible and demonstrate where and when injustice and differential experiences create and sustain inequities within institutions (hooks, 1998; Pasque et al., 2012). But to even do equity work, we need to identify where those inequities take place, how they manifest, and for whom. We have to go beyond the conversational layer on issues of access, retention, and graduation among different student groups toward dismantling the environments and customs that create these metrics. Equity requires using this knowledge and data to change the status quo.

Assessment practitioners need to explore how the policies, norms, traditions, assumptions, representation (or lack thereof), and influences that comprise our assessment approaches along with elements which can be regarded as tangential that permeate academia—such as the campus climate—can impact student achievement and our assessment data. By being mindful of equity, this chapter argues that assessment can give voice to students who are often marginalized en masse in higher education by addressing systems of power and oppression and interrogating any underlying Western paradigms for assessment. The goal is to use equity in assessment—implementing the various lessons in this book—to inform and create more inclusive, evidence-based learning environments.

To do so, we first have to recognize that assessment is not free of bias. It is planned and carried out by people and conducted within social institutions guided by norms, policies, assumptions, and preferences, which means bias is inherently a part of the process because assessment is socially situated. Sue et al. (2007) introduced the idea of environmental microaggressions—or invalidations, whether intentional or otherwise, that communicate negative, offensive, or evidently hostile racial slights and insults to a specific group or population. Environmental microaggressions are not person-to-person but instead occur through organizational policies, practices, and norms that can send both c/overt messages to students of color that they do not belong, are unwanted, and/or are unappreciated. In institutions and programs, these environmental microaggressions can manifest through:

- a lack of cultural houses or spaces on campus;
- having few to no student organizations operated by students of color;
- hyper-criminalization of students of color;
- lack of representation among faculty and staff;
- seemingly segregated undergraduate housing;
- lack of representation within college majors;
- lack of culturally representative content both in classrooms and the cocurricular;
- lack of faculty and administrator responses to instances of racism on campus;
- a sense of pressure for students of color to conform and assimilate instead of be themselves;
- unrepresentative, nonculturally relevant, and/or noninclusive campus imagery; and
- low expectations of intellect from certain student groups by faculty and/or administrators.

The impacts of these can be either partially remedied through assessment that is mindful of equity or exacerbated by assessment that ignores these realities.

The reality is that students are experiencing environmental microaggressions in our colleges and universities. Students of color who experience racial microaggressions and negative campus climates are more likely to suffer academically, and often drop courses, change majors, or drop out of college entirely (Lewis et al., 2019; Solórzano et al., 2000; Yosso et al., 2009). Some students may also suffer negatively from the assessment choices we make; from what we choose to count as evidence of learning; from the voices and perspectives we choose to include in the assessment process. If students of color are suffering academically due to institutional policies and practices, then higher education is not serving diverse students. If assessment practitioners are not using assessment data to uncover, explore, and understand these realities so that viable solutions can be found, then we are contributing to the problem.

Often, deficit models are utilized to blame students and actively divert fault and/or responsibility, effectively subverting the conversation from institutional policy and practice solutions (Clycq et al., 2014; Tewell, 2020). The issues that contribute to the disproportionate and inequitable returns for students of color on their college education are systemic issues embedded within the fabric of academia. That there is a hidden curriculum (Sambell & McDowell, 1998) has been known for years, and yet it still continues to affect first-generation students, students from low socioeconomic backgrounds, and students of color (Mthethwa-Sommers, 2013; Valderama-Wallace & Apesoa-Varano, 2020). Simply being aware of an issue does not mean it is resolved. We know students are affected by inequities in the learning environment of which assessment is a part.

How much longer can we continue to ignore these inequities and pretend assessment does not have a role in their permanence? Or do we expect inequities to not wreak havoc on the very students that higher education swore to serve—at no fault of the students themselves, nonetheless? These systemic issues are systemic *barriers* that negate a fair opportunity to succeed for certain student populations. These issues are issues of *equity*. And the various chapters in this book demonstrate just why and how assessment can help create more equitable learning outcomes for all students.

Equity and Assessment

Assessment can be a valuable tool in either addressing and solving inequities on campus or perpetuating them. Assessment—the systematic "gathering and use of evidence of student learning in decision-making and in strengthening institutional performance and public accountability" (Kuh et al., 2015, p. 2)—can help identify areas where student populations are experiencing inequitable outcomes attainment, inform decision-making to address identified inequities, and explore how changes have impacted students. But conducting assessment to uncover and remedy inequities requires intentionality and conviction at every step of the assessment process, even in the purpose of undertaking assessment in the first place. An equity lens can give assessment practitioners cause to reflect on the assessment process as a whole to ensure we do the following:

1. Check biases and ask reflective questions throughout the assessment process to address assumptions and positions of privilege.
2. Use multiple sources of evidence appropriate for the students being assessed and the assessment effort.
3. Include student perspectives and take action based on perspectives.
4. Increase transparency in assessment results and actions.
5. Ensure collected data can be meaningfully disaggregated and interrogated.
6. Make evidence-based changes that address issues of equity that are context-specific. (Montenegro & Jankowski, 2020, p. 13)

Purposes of Assessment

Assessment in higher education has been used primarily for two purposes: accountability and continuous improvement which can also be seen as summative and formative types of assessment, respectively (Ewell, 2009). The goal of accountability is to ensure that colleges and universities are achieving their espoused goals and student learning outcomes. In other words, are colleges and universities "doing what they say they are doing?" Accountability has two thrusts. External accountability arose in the early 1980s when constituents outside of higher education, primarily regional accrediting boards and the federal government, were concerned that colleges and universities were not supporting student learning and the cost of higher education was not consistent with the value received or the investment made (Ewell, 2009). Internal accountability is similar to external accountability in that the end result is ensuring goal achievement. However, internal accountability is driven by college and university faculty, administrators, and staff rather than external stakeholders.

The goal of continuous improvement is to find opportunities to improve courses, programs, and services to advance learning. The focus for improvement can be on an individual course, an academic program, a cocurricular program or service, or the institution. Regardless of level of focus, ideally, assessment processes are embedded in everyday practice providing critical feedback about what is working well and what needs to be improved.

Ewell (2009) argued that while accountability and improvement are two main purposes of assessment, they can be in tension with one another. Resulting from state and federal performance mandates, accountability requires an organization to use evidence to demonstrate achievement of expected standards or outcomes "in a posture of institutional compliance, or at least appearance of it" (Ewell, 2009, p. 9). Improvement, however, centers on making changes to processes to increase student learning, development, and success (Ewell, 2009). Not only are these purposes incentivized differently, but each uses data differently. Thus, while both accountability and improvement seem worthy goals of assessment, they may conflict with each other. Despite this encumbrance, both roles are critical in effective functioning of colleges and universities and both can further equity and inclusion.

Paradigms—Limitations of and Opportunities for Assessment

Approaches to assessment are undergirded by systems of assumptions, beliefs, and theories regarding the construction of reality and knowledge, which in turn affect how assessment is implemented. These systems or paradigms, often unconscious, are philosophies or worldviews for making sense of the world (Patton, 2014) or a set of beliefs that guides action (Lincoln et al., 2011). These paradigms influence the extent to which equity can be integrated into assessment.

Paradigms have their foundation in research, but those research paradigms are relevant to assessment work. Kivunja and Kuyini (2017) argued that there are four research paradigms that can be applied to educational contexts: positivist, interpretivist/constructivist, pragmatic, and critical/transformativist.

The positivist paradigm includes a number of assumptions including the tenet that knowledge is objective, measurable, and generalizable (Egbert & Sandeen, 2014). Another belief is that there are universal, unchanging facts, and to comprehend these facts researchers must be external to that which is being researched (Taylor & Medina, 2013). Additional assumptions are that results of inquiry can be quantified, research should follow the scientific method of investigation, and the goal of research is to develop theory to account for behavior (Kivunja & Kuyini, 2017). The main theme of positivism is objectivity—the belief that knowledge can only be generated by unbiased observation of the phenomenon from a distance. A subcategory of positivism is postpositivism that contends that while objectivity is not fully possible, it is still an important state to which one should strive (Mertens, 2019). A positivist paradigm applies criteria such as internal validity, external validity, reliability, and objectivity (Burns, 2000). These criteria are achieved through the use of quantitative methods of data collection and analysis that center on the ability to generalize from a sample to a population, which unintentionally minimize attention to variation in a sample. The underlying assumptions of positivism and the procedures built upon it have implications for equity. Data gathered through quantitative methods are aggregations of individual responses with a goal of discovering what is common among participants. In an attempt to be objective, the results of a positivist approach are general, not specific; lifeless, not robust; blunt. Quantitative assessment results do not take into account students' subjectivity of their experience and thus only provide limited understanding of a phenomenon. Assessment built upon a positivist paradigm is often inequitable because individuality and the context for data is not part of the assessment process.

The goal of the interpretivist/constructivist paradigm is to understand the subjective element of the human experience (Guba & Lincoln, 1989), providing the context that a positivist approach cannot. Emphasis is placed on the individual and their interpretation of their experience and world around them (Kivunja & Kuyini, 2017) and an important belief is that reality is socially constructed (Bogdan & Biklen, 1998). There is an assumption that the researcher (or assessor) is connected to and engaged with the phenomenon rather than "objectively" distanced from it as in the positivist paradigm. Additional assumptions include that realities are multiple rather than being singular and immutable, knowledge and findings are value laden, there is a need to understand the individual in relation to the phenomenon being studied, and contextual factors need to be considered when interpreting findings (Kivunja & Kuyini, 2017). Assessment emanating from an interpretivist/constructivist paradigm utilizes qualitative data collection and analysis methods. As such, there is a value placed on individual interpretation of reality, and culture and context are paramount to understanding. This focus on individuality and context makes assessment based on this paradigm more equitable than one based on a positivist paradigm.

A pragmatic paradigm bridges positivist and interpretivist/constructivist paradigms in an effort to implement methods that are most appropriate, or practical, for the phenomenon being studied (Kivunja & Kuyini, 2017), whether they be quantitative or qualitative. Assumptions of this paradigm include rejection of the notion that a study must be situated in either a positivist or interpretivist/constructivist paradigm, focus on using the methodology most appropriate for the topic of study, and search for points of connection to facilitate understanding (Kivunja & Kuyini, 2017). This paradigm further supports the integration of equity and assessment as it is not beholden to any one set of assumptions regarding reality and knowledge and multiple methodologies can be employed providing a more complete picture of complex phenomenon from various vantage points. Pragmatism breaks free from a traditional objective or subjective stance to broaden the set of assumptions underlying assessment practice.

The main foci of a critical paradigm are the roles of power and oppression in understanding reality. There is recognition of the impact of power and oppression on individual interpretation and social construction of a phenomenon (Bronner, 2011). Key assumptions within this paradigm include concern with power relationships and social structures that perpetuate them, acknowledgment that some versions of reality are privileged over others, and an emphasis on construction of reality rather than discovery of reality (Kivunja & Kuyini, 2017). When a critical paradigm involves action to change systems of power and oppression it is sometimes called a transformative paradigm (Hurtado, 2015; Kivunja & Kuyini, 2017; Mertens, 2019). A goal of assessment using a critical paradigm is to understand the role of power in regard to the interpretation and construction of reality and moving toward social justice to dismantle systems of power and oppression. This approach supports the use of both qualitative and quantitative methods of data collection and analyses to expose the social structures that perpetuate oppression and to identify strategies to dismantle these structures. Assessment based on this paradigm has the most promise for integrating equity and assessment. It builds on interpretivist/constructivist assessment to take into account subjectivity but recognizes that power affects reality and thus equity. It affords the use of multiple methods for a more complete understanding of a phenomenon. Equity-centered assessment cannot be undertaken without acknowledgment of the role that power and oppression play in student learning, development, and success and recognition that assessment can be a vehicle to address power and oppression when it is used to identify solutions.

An emerging research paradigm being applied to assessment is an Indigenous paradigm. An Indigenous paradigm is rooted in four axial assumptions: responsibility, respect, reciprocity, and rights and regulations (Snow et al., 2016). Assumptions of this paradigm include the belief that people are connected to each other, the earth, and the cosmos; that knowledge is relational, constructed, shared, and cannot be discovered or owned by any one person; equity, equality, and inclusion are key values (Wilson, 2008). Assessment rooted in this paradigm emphasizes the role of participants as equitable partners with assessors in the assessment process as cocreators of knowledge as part of an inclusive, connected, collaborative process. Since knowledge is shared, not owned, understanding the relationships of those who share knowledge is integral to understanding. Indigenous and critical paradigms complement each other in their underlying beliefs.

Each paradigm has a set of beliefs, a perspective, and a lens that is applied to the assessment questions and unconsciously affects methods, data collection systems, policies, and the institutional structures put in place to implement and support assessment processes and practices. Thus, recognizing and scrutinizing the paradigms that undergird assessment is needed if we are to intentionally integrate equity into assessment practice. To fully realize the benefits of assessment as a vehicle for equity, traditional assessment approaches must be interrogated with a critical lens to make unconscious beliefs conscious to effectively attend to them. Assessment as inquiry is a broad approach to assessment that can accommodate nontraditional paradigms. Table 1.1 offers a summary of the paradigms discussed.

Shifting assessment from accountability and improvement to inquiry provides another way to answer key questions in higher education. Inquiry seeks to answer "why" questions rather than "what" questions. "Why" questions attempt to understand the reasons for something happening rather than simply describing a phenomenon. Inquiry takes into account the relational nature of reality, acknowledging that student experience and learning does not occur in a vacuum, but takes place in institutions of higher education that are steeped in centuries-old systems of power and oppression.

TABLE 1.1
Research Paradigms and Equity

Paradigm	Characteristics	Connection to Equity
Positivism	Knowledge is objective, measurable, and generalizable; a single truth	None
Postpositivism	Knowledge is measurable and generalizable, but not fully objective; a single truth	None
Interpretivism/ Constructivism	Emphasis on individual and their interpretation of their experience; multiple truths	Considers individual context and culture
Pragmatic	Focus on methods most appropriate and practical for the phenomenon being studied, not underlying philosophy of knowledge	Allows for flexibility in use of appropriate methods and is not constrained by specific philosophy
Critical	Considers the role of power and oppression on individual interpretation and social construction of phenomenon	Power and oppression play a central role
Indigenous	Rooted in Indigenous knowledge systems and includes four axial assumptions: responsibility, respect, reciprocity, and rights and regulations	Eschews Western ways of knowing and values decolonization

An example could be with graduation rates across student identity groups. An assessment approach that tries to answer a "what" question would identify that there are differences in graduation rates for White students compared to Black/African American, Latinx, Asian/Asian American, and Native students. San Diego State University took an inquiry approach to this issue by trying to answer "why" questions to understand why these differences exist in order to improve these achievement gaps (Montenegro, 2020).

Until underlying paradigms are understood, assessment methods rooted in these beliefs cannot address inequity in higher education. Without change, higher education is destined to continue to perpetuate societal inequities. Moving beyond a focus on accountability and improvement, implementing assessment as inquiry with equity in mind can be a powerful tool for change.

The Intersection of Assessment and Equity

Assessment data can be a valuable tool to explore inequities on campus and in our assessment approaches to inform appropriate ways to remedy them. While it can be easy to think that assessment is free from the concerns of environmental microaggressions or won't feed into the effects of a negative campus climate, the reality is that not disaggregating data, not involving the perspective of students in assessment, using language in outcomes and assignments that is not easily understood by students, lacking transparency in grading, and so forth are examples of the same negative practices that contribute to inequities. Assessment is not apolitical. Assessment is not fully objective. Assessment happens within a campus context that is situated within a larger society, and assessment is conducted by human beings with specific preferences, perspectives, experiences, dispositions, and so on. Those conducting assessment need to be well versed on the issues of equity that impact students in their classroom, in their program, and in their institution.

In assessment, environmental microaggressions take the form of using aggregate data, eliminating small sample sizes, and not including students' voice—these are systematic issues and systems of power and subjugation that turn assessment into a tool for the perpetuation of inequities. Using aggregate data, doing surface-level data disaggregation, or simply identifying gaps in data analysis is not in itself equitable assessment. Equitable assessment requires a deeper dive into the data, disaggregated by different student populations, its subpopulations (e.g., further analyzing Latinx populations by comparing the outcomes of Mexican Americans and Cuban Americans), and intersection between different student characteristics (e.g., first-generation Mexican American students who also identify as female and are commuter students; Montenegro & Jankowski, 2020). Failing to take this deeper dive into the data can lead to false understanding and missing potential inequities—not to mention the issues that arise when populations are continuously disregarded due to small sample sizes (Montenegro & Jankowski, 2020). If assessment practitioners continuously do assessment in ways that are not mindful of inequities, then we are doing our students a disservice.

There also cannot be equitable assessment without purposefully including the student voice in the assessment process (Montenegro & Jankowski, 2017, 2020). Nothing sends a clearer message of not being valued than to be excluded from processes that ultimately have a direct impact on students' own success. Meaningful student involvement in assessment can help mitigate issues created when assumptions are made about students without evidence, can help make the assessment process more relevant for different student populations, and can inform changes that minimize negative unintended consequences while strengthening their intended impacts (Montenegro & Jankowski, 2020).

Assessment can help institutions meet their goals, set benchmarks, and make evidence-based changes to improve. It is a process that helps institutions be at their best and be accountable, but institutions cannot do this when there are inequities happening on campus. Equity ensures that students of color are in the best position to succeed, attain the learning outcomes set forth by their institutions, and ultimately graduate. Assessment and equity work together to more effectively help institutions and students achieve their goals.

Conducting more equitable assessment is not a radically different way of doing assessment. In fact, it relies on a sound assessment process already being in place and adding an intentional focus on equity throughout. Equitable assessment involves more instances of reflection to interrogate the assessment process in place, to consider how the assessor's identity impacts the assessment, to identify which perspectives are missing from the assessment process, and act accordingly to address any and all issues.

Conclusion

It should go without saying, but equitable assessment does not mean we use assessment to *only* identify and close equity gaps (Montenegro & Jankowski, 2020). However, seeking to identify and fix equity gaps should be part of the purpose of assessment. Without conducting assessment from an equity perspective there is a risk of further contributing to the marginalization of students of color, failing on the promise of education for an ever-growing number of college students. These issues will worsen if higher education does not act now. With the continued diversification of college enrollment, and the expected reliance of the American economy on ensuring these diverse populations attain quality credentials, the ramifications of failing to right the course can be widespread. It is a moral and practical imperative to conduct equitable assessment, and it begins by interrogating our own practice. We need to look inward and ask: what role do higher education assessment processes have in either perpetuating or remedying the inequities affecting students?

The chapters in this book interrogate the role that assessment processes and practices can play in fixing the inequities that impact students' learning outcomes attainment. The chapters provide an overview of why assessment must be conducted equitably, what is currently being done in the field to advance such an approach, and how these practices can be tailored to fit the context and needs of different programs and institutions. The goal is to help you look inward at your practice and identify examples that can help you implement more equitable approaches, so that individual and institutional competencies can be built and scaled to advance equitable assessment that can truly support and drive the success of diverse learners.

References

Araki, S. (2020). Educational expansion, skills diffusion, and the economic value of credentials and skills. *American Sociological Review, 85*(1), 128–175. https://doi.org/10.1177%2F0003122419897873

Bogdan, R., & Biklen, S. K. (1998). *Qualitative research for education: An introduction to theories and methods.* Allyn and Bacon.

Bronner, S. E. (2011). *Critical theory: A very short introduction.* Oxford University Press.

Burns, B. (2000). *Introduction to research methods* (4th ed.). Pearson Education.

Clycq, N., Ward Nouwen, M. A., & Vandenbroucke, A. (2014). Meritocracy, deficit thinking and the invisibility of the system: Discourses on educational success and failure. *British Educational Research Journal, 40*(5), 796–819. https://doi.org/10.1002/berj.3109

Egbert, J., & Sandeen, A. (2014). *Foundations of education research: Understanding theoretical components.* Routledge.

Ewell, P. (2009, November). *Assessment, accountability, and improvement: Revisiting the tension* (Occasional Paper No. 1). University of Illinois and Indiana University, National Institute for Learning Outcomes Assessment (NILOA).

Guba, E., & Lincoln, Y. (1989). What is this constructivist paradigm anyway? In D. M. Fetterman (Ed.), *Qualitative approaches to evaluation in education: The silent scientific revolution* (pp. 89–115). Praeger.

hooks, b. (1998). *Teaching to transgress: Education as the practice of freedom.* Routledge.

Hurtado, S. (2015). The transformative paradigm: Principles and challenges. In A. M. Martínez-Alemán, B. Pusser, & E. M. Bensimon (Eds.), *Critical approaches to the study of higher education* (pp. 285–307). Johns Hopkins University Press.

Hussar, W. J., & Bailey, T. M. (2018). *Projections of education statistics to 2026* (45th ed.). U.S. Department of Education's Institute of Education Sciences. https://nces.ed.gov/pubs2018/2018019.pdf.

Kivunja, C., & Kuyini, A. (2017). Understanding and applying research paradigms in educational contexts. *International Journal of Higher Education, 6*(5), 26–41. https://doi.org/10.5430/ijhe.v6n5p26

Kuh, G. D., Ikenberry, S. O., Jankowski, N. A., Cain, T. R., Ewell, P. T., Hutchings, P., & Kinzie, J. (2015). *Using evidence of student learning to improve higher education.* Jossey-Bass.

Lewis, J. A., Mendenhall, R., Ojiemwen, A., Thomas, M., Riopelle, C., Harwood, S. A., & Huntt, M. B. (2019). Racial microaggressions and sense of belonging at a historically White university. *American Behavioral Scientist*, 1–23. https://doi.org/10.1177/0002764219859613

Lincoln, Y., Lynham, S., & Guba, E. (2011). Paradigmatic controversies, contradictions, and emerging confluences, revisited. In N. K. Denzin & Y. S. Lincoln (Eds.), *The SAGE handbook of qualitative research* (4th ed., pp. 97–128). SAGE.

Lumina Foundation. (2020). *A stronger nation: Learning beyond high school builds American talent.* https://www.luminafoundation.org/stronger-nation/report/2020/#nation

Mertens, D. (2019). Introduction to research and ethical practice. In *Research and evaluation in education and psychology* (5th ed.). SAGE. https://www.sagepub.com/sites/default/files/upm-binaries/29985_Chapter1.pdf

Montenegro, E. (2020, June). *San Diego State University: Supporting commuter students through equity-driven and student-focused assessment.* University of Illinois and Indiana University, National Institute for Learning Outcomes Assessment, Council for the Advancement of Standards in Higher Education, and Anthology. https://www.learningoutcomesassessment.org/wp-content/uploads/2020/10/EquityCase-SDSU.pdf

Montenegro, E., & Jankowski, N. A. (2017, January). *Equity and assessment: Moving towards culturally responsive assessment* (Occasional Paper No. 29). University of Illinois and Indiana University, National Institute for Learning Outcomes Assessment. https://www.learningoutcomesassessment.org/wp-content/uploads/2019/02/OccasionalPaper29.pdf

Montenegro, E., & Jankowski, N. A. (2020, January). *A new decade for assessment: Embedding equity into assessment praxis* (Occasional Paper No. 42). University of Illinois and Indiana University, National Institute for Learning Outcomes Assessment. https://www.learningoutcomesassessment.org/wp-content/uploads/2020/01/A-New-Decade-for-Assessment.pdf

Mthethwa-Sommers, S. (2013). Reading beyond research results: The hidden curriculum in a college and urban high schools partnership. *Journal of Community Engagement and Higher Education*, 5(2), 45–55.

National Center for Education Statistics. (2019). *Indicator 23: Postsecondary graduation rates.* NCES. https://nces.ed.gov/programs/raceindicators/indicator_red.asp.

Pasque, P. A., Carducci, R., Kuntz, A. M., & Gildersleeve R. E. (2012). Qualitative inquiry for equity in higher education. *ASHE Higher Education Report*, 37(6), 1–15. https://api.taylorfrancis.com/content/books/mono/download?identifierName=doi&identifierValue=10.4324/9781315619392&type=googlepdf

Patton, M. (2014). *Qualitative research and evaluation methods* (4th ed.). SAGE.

Sambell, K., & McDowell, L. (1998). The construction of the hidden curriculum: Messages and meanings in the assessment of student learning. *Assessment and Evaluation in Higher Education*, 23(4), 391–402. https://doi.org/10.1080/0260293980230406

Smith, E., & Gorard, S. (2006). Pupils' views of equity in education. *Compare*, *36*(1), 41–56.

Snow, K., Hays, D., Caliwagan, G., Ford, D., Jr., Mariotti, D., Mwenda, J., & Scott, W. (2016). Guiding principles for Indigenous research practices. *Action Research*, *14*(4), 357–375. https://doi.org/10.1177%2F1476750315622542

Solórzano, D., Ceja, M., & Yosso, T. (2000). Critical race theory, racial microaggressions, and campus racial climate: The experiences of African American college students. *Journal of Negro Education*, *69*(1/2), 60–73. http://www.jstor.org/stable/2696265

Sue, D. W., Capodilupo, C. M., Torino, G. C., Bucceri, J. M., Holder, A. M., Nadal, K. L., & Esquilin, M. (2007). Racial microaggressions in everyday life: Implications for clinical practice. *American Psychologist*, *62*(4), 271–286. http://dx.doi.org/10.1037/0003-066X.62.4.271

Taylor, P., & Medina, M. N. (2013, January). Educational research paradigms: From positivism to multiparadigmatic. *International Journal of Meaning Centred Education*, *1*. https://doi.org/10.13140/2.1.3542.0805

Tewell, E. (2020). The problem with grit: Dismantling deficit thinking in library instruction. *Portal: Libraries & the Academy*, *20*(1), 137–159. https://doi.org/10.1353/pla.2020.0007

Valderama-Wallace, C. P., & Apesoa-Varano, E. C. (2020). 'The problem of the color line': Faculty approaches to teaching social justice in baccalaureate nursing programs. *Nursing Inquiry*, *27*(3), 1–12. https://doi.org/10.1111/nin.12349

Wilson, S. (2008). *Research is ceremony: Indigenous research methods*. Fernwood Publishing.

Yosso, T. J., Smith, W. A., Ceja, M., & Solórzano, D. G. (2009). Critical race theory, racial microaggressions, and campus racial climate for Latina/o undergraduates. *Harvard Educational Review*, *79*(4), 659–691. https://psycnet.apa.org/doi/10.17763/haer.79.4.m6867014157m707l

2

THE ASSESSMENT ACTIVIST

A Revolutionary Call to Action

Divya Samuga_Gyaanam+Bheda

I write this chapter as a call to action to all my higher education colleagues as it applies to you (i.e., to assessment professionals, staff, faculty, student employees, and administrators). Please delve deep into social justice theories and scholarship to be able to fully engage with this chapter. I write this chapter recognizing that we, as assessment professionals, staff, faculty, student employees, and administrators, are working within a capitalistic, patriarchal, and colonial system where certain labors are privileged over others, where time is money, culture is money, and knowledge is money. My intention is to subvert this system and way of being (even as I, ironically, participate in it) where we privilege certain types of knowledges and certain means of knowledge production and transmission (such as publishing) that then privileges only those of us who have the time and the access to these privileged opportunities, excluding numerous others.

In this chapter, I am honoring the Indigenous, decolonized reality that knowledge is generated, shared, and preserved collectively. Hence, the Samuga_Gyaanam+ (community knowledge/wisdom in Tamil) before my name. My work is but an evolution of a collective's work. My writing draws upon ways of being, thinking, and maxims that have forgotten origins or origins told generation after generation, community after community—each time getting new flavors, ownerships, and edits based on the historical situation and the positionality of the storyteller. I draw from and build on generative knowledge, lived experiences, conversations, and thinking that are occurring among various social justice and people-of-color communities that I participate in. So, I write this chapter humbly, recognizing that the ideas I espouse are not only my own, but instead, are the culmination of exchanges and actions as are real for me at this point in time, and are subject to change as

I learn, grow, and evolve. In this chapter, I ask you, my colleagues, to engage in concrete action to advance equity and social justice within your various spheres of influence in and beyond higher education—as an activist, as an ally, and as someone committed to equity and social justice.

Where Does Social Justice Fit Within the Assessment Context?

There is a fundamental question that needs to be answered as we connect assessment and equity; a conflation of purpose that needs clarifying. Are we primarily trying to achieve and advance equity *in* assessment or equity *through* assessment? When I talk about equity *in* assessment, I am referring to whether our assessment practices, processes, methods, tools, frameworks, and so on are equitable in design. When I reference equity *through* assessment, I am alluding to equity being the goal and assessment practice being the means to achieve it. I offer that no matter what our goal is, equity *in* assessment and/or equity *through* assessment, (i.e., for either or both goal[s] to be achieved, realized, or pursued), a robust theoretical and historical understanding of equity founded on social justice awareness, and a skilled and continuous deployment of reflexivity need to occur for assessment to connect and engage meaningfully with equity.

I must note that I use social justice as much as equity as verbiage throughout this chapter because equity is a part of social justice (please see chapter 4 for definitions). I begin my chapter making a case that for both—equity *in* assessment and equity *through* assessment—social justice awareness and understanding is the starting point. This constitutes the first half of this chapter. I continue and end my chapter by inviting you into activism, explaining what I mean by it and how I believe we must engage in it.

Equity Through Assessment versus Equity in Assessment

If we, as higher education and assessment professionals, are trying to advance and achieve equity as a goal (i.e., equity *through* our assessment practice rather than *in* our assessment practice), we need a foundational understanding of the goal we are aspiring for so that the tools we use to get there do not subvert the very goal we are working toward. As Audre Lorde (1984/2007) put it, it is impossible to dismantle the master's house with the master's tools. In fact, in her work, she makes a couple of statements that readily serve as a great analogy for assessment: "What does it mean when the tools of a racist patriarchy are used to examine the fruits of that same patriarchy? It means that only the narrowest perimeters of change are possible and allowable" (pp. 110–111). This means that if our assessment practice in and of itself is framed and built within parameters that make privilege, bias, and oppression invisible, we will be unable to achieve our goal of equity and social justice, and what is worse, we will not even realize it because, in essence, our assessment actions will only reify the very systems we are trying to transform because our impact will be subverted by the inequity of our approach.

Similarly, for us to be able to engage in equitable assessment as a process (i.e., advance equity IN our assessment practice), a sound foundational understanding of the various invisible and ubiquitous historical and systemic social justice issues permeating our practice of higher education today must occur (Carlson & Sorrell, 2020). We need to first evaluate the efficacy of our practice and examine/take stock of how equitable our current practice is to further engage in equitable assessment. After all, without examining current practice, how can we improve on it? We need to train ourselves to interrogate our practice where issues of inequity and social justice are so rampant and so unconscious that they influence our questions, our process, our findings, our recommendations, our decisions, and our follow-up actions without us realizing the extent to which they do so (Bensimon, 2012; Jones & Phillips, 2020; Patton, 2014).

Critically Examining Practice

Let me offer one example to highlight this issue: climate surveys. How did we decide that a climate survey with a 15–25% response rate is an adequate foundation for decision-making? How did we decide that inferences can be made, or actions can be dictated by just the data with that response rate (because often, while I have seen the climate survey reports say that more investigations needed to be done, how often are they really done before ill-informed decisions are made and actions are undertaken)? Thus, that one survey often seems to be the answer and the end for institutions until the next compliance requirement cycle kicks in. Additionally, my social justice championing colleagues in higher education and I have mostly experienced these surveys as the justification behind inaction rather than action around social justice and equity issues. Krause (2019) and Echo Hawk's work (as cited in Secaira, 2019) around equitable data and decolonizing data speaks to this very issue.

Digging deeper on the issue of climate surveys, when less than 1% of survey respondents raise institutional climate and culture concerns, I have often seen climate survey reports whitewash out these issues (often raised by people of color or other minoritized groups) due to small response sizes. How often have we seen such issues of gravity minimized and inaction justified and defended because of the claim that the data cannot be generalized and acted upon due to low Ns? I also consistently see and hear colleagues' experiences of language (and have lived this myself) that pathologizes and/ or dehumanizes our minoritized students or colleagues who do share their own discontent and concerns around social justice and equity issues in our climate surveys. Those with power often make "reasonable" and "logical" statements that ascribe and allude to ill intentions of those folx who offer critical or negative feedback, thus successfully calling into question the credibility and validity of the data. Those in power often use direct anecdotal evidence or hearsay to justify why said folx are not "truly" reflective of the overall campus experience. They offer authoritative alternate interpretations or excuses to ensure these folx's feedback can be ignored or their responses on a survey dismissed. These folx (who have been brave and vulnerable enough to share negative lived experiences and concerns) are often afforded no power at the decision-making table. Thus, our current climate survey practices often lead to perpetuating and normalizing a deficit-thinking way of dismissing feedback from anyone who shares that all is not well at our institution or program.

Additionally, in the previous example (and this is just one example of practice), a positivist philosophical ideology and epistemology often underpins the survey design approach in a climate survey assessment context (i.e., that there is one neutral, objective truth out there that can be measured). When we begin to question this epistemological foundation, we can begin to examine systematic and structural issues of social justice and equity. We can begin to ask questions such as "why are survey responses reviewed in a manner where all responses have equal weight?" Why doesn't a student or colleague's intersectional identity and minoritized status and lived experience of oppression have a greater weight during the data-analysis process?

We need a rethinking of how we collect, analyze, and report out data. Lynner et al.'s 2020 case study is one example of a different way to approach a climate-study endeavor. They used a critical theory approach to frame their entire investigation that then mediated and transformed various assessment actions undertaken that better reflected and aligned with social justice values from intent to action to impact. Their work only reinforces my belief and efforts—we must examine and revisit whose voices and perspectives we unconsciously privilege and whose voices we silence by utilizing an equalizing "unbiased" lens in the assessment endeavor. Similarly, as Jones and Phillips (2020) point out, mostly, the theories utilized behind the design of climate surveys lead to questions focused on the comfort level of White students with diverse "others." When those surveys are used to compare peer groups of institutions for baseline purposes, institutions that are not predominantly White institutions are disadvantaged with a survey that is meaningless to them about their campus climate. As is evident, the ripple effect of the negative impact of the lack of social justice values and theories underpinning such climate survey efforts (again, as just one example) is beyond one institution—it impacts the field of practice, and higher education as a whole.

All these aforesaid thoughts are just some questions and issues to consider deeply especially given the fact that students or colleagues of color experiencing an unsafe, oppressive, or biased climate are baring their souls every time we survey them and yet we demonstrate no commitment to acting on their feedback (let alone sharing it back with them) because it is not the "majority" perspective. It is the *bridge that is their backs* (Moraga & Anzaldua, 1983) that is taking the brunt of our lack of a deep and authentic social justice understanding. There is a negative impact when we do not deeply interrogate our assumptions, processes, behaviors, and conclusions. We *are* actively causing harm by not realizing the gaps in our practice and we *are* inflicting pain. Our inequitable practices do have a tremendous cost.

Almost all critical, feminist, woman of color scholars (whose many works serve as the foundation of my thinking and actions as an assessment professional and equity champion) have addressed this issue one way or another in their work. From Chandra Mohanty to Audre Lord, and from bell hooks to Chela Sandoval—every single one of these scholars has grappled with the pervasiveness of oppressive ways of being that influence how we function as a society and people today in various spaces and in different professional and personal contexts. The field needs to look to critical feminist theory and epistemology using the works of Black, Latinx, Indigenous, and other womxn of color and immigrant scholars like Gloria Anzaldua, Patricia Hill Collins, Kimberlé Crenshaw, bell hooks, Audre Lorde, Beatrice Medicine, Chandra Mohanty, Vandana Shiva, and many *many* others.

They draw attention to the fact that even our interrogation of our practice is influenced by various hegemonic forces that we have normalized, that we must even more deeply and critically interrogate because these numerous problematic ways of being have become so ubiquitous and embedded in who we are and how we do things that they have become invisible.

We need to fully dig into, discover, and comprehend the harm our current practices can cause or are causing by exploring how the institutional, historical, and systemic hegemonic forces of racism, ablism, capitalism, colonialism, patriarchy, sexism, cultural imperialism/appropriation/erasure, and various other forces operate in taken-for-granted ways that are implicit, normalized, affirmed, and compliance instilled into our ways of being in U.S. higher education. We need to assess our assessment efforts and the goals we are trying to achieve. Assessment and higher education professionals need to be able to take ownership of the fact that our current assessment practices may be inherently inequitable or unintentionally perpetuating inequity.

Consider the fact that research has shown how unintentionally inequitable standardized tests are and how they often disadvantage communities of color, collective cultures, or certain gender groups (see chapter 3, this volume). The 2021 articles and conversations in the *Chronicle of Higher Education* and *Inside Higher Ed* news portals around not requiring SAT scores for higher education student selection and admission considerations because it disadvantages students of color is one example of a single practice that has decided the lives of millions of students over the years that has been exposed to be faulty and detrimental, and yet still stands. Similarly, consider how faculty are asked to own assessment and yet, faculty are often only trained in their discipline and hardly ever in effective teaching and learning, curriculum design, or assessment practice. And most importantly, any training barely skims the surface, if at all, of how to work for equity and social justice in our education endeavors. How are faculty going to be effective educators or assessors of learning if they have no training in the same? How can we get past being graders to being true assessors of learning? How can faculty engage in equitable assessment practices when there is no training or curriculum for the same that they are required to master before becoming educators themselves? What are we valuing and privileging (answer: capitalism and monetary revenues of research) over teaching and helping our students learn?

Thus, I would offer that we should all be proactively setting up pathways for graduate students to learn about social justice and assessment and set up centers of teaching and learning as institutional orientation offices for faculty development (i.e., preemptive, possibly required[?] resources and support offices that offer educational programming rather than the current remediation centers they often are), for educators to be trained to be effective social justice-focused educators so that we can engage in equitable assessment of our students and champion equity in our teaching and learning contexts. Important practices such as transparent assignment design (Winkelmes, 2013), backward design (Wiggins & McTighe, 2005, 2011), culturally responsive teaching (Ladson-Billings, 2009), and culturally responsive, socially just, and equitable evaluation and assessment practices (Dean-Coffey, 2018; Hood et al., 2015; Montenegro & Jankowski, 2017, 2020) need to become part of the higher education mainstay rather than the fringe conversations they are at present.

Social Justice Comes First

Overall, I hope I have made a strong case that for both equity *in* assessment and equity *through* assessment, social justice awareness and understanding is the starting point. It is the foundation upon which we must gain assessment training. Applying the chicken and egg reference to assessment and social justice, my position is that social justice comes first. There is no question because methodology is premised on epistemology, axiology, and ontology, and assessment is methodology. Social justice theory is foundational to our assessment work if we are truly committed to social justice and if we do want to answer the call of this racial reckoning we are in the midst of (Zerquera et al., 2018).

I call us into action to be about social justice because if we, as assessment and higher education professionals, are simultaneously striving to advance equity in our practice *and* through our practice, we are trying to *achieve* and *live* social justice as assessment professionals. Thus, social justice comes first. This dual expectation of social justice in and through assessment requires us to clearly see the full scope of the problem we are facing and addressing, including our roles in perpetuating it. As professionals engaging in assessment, we need to practice reflexivity (see chapter 19, this volume; and Bheda & Jones, 2020 for an overview of the same). Only then can we tackle the critical challenges we face with commitment. Else, as Oluo (2019) put it, we may end up becoming the oppressors in our social justice efforts. It is for this reason that I call us into activism as assessment professionals in the rest of this chapter.

The Call to Action

As folx committed to social justice in our respective lived contexts, we must learn how to expose, navigate, and/or dismantle oft-hidden, insidious, systemic, and institutionalized forces of oppression to truly advance our equitable practice of assessment. Simultaneously, we must unlearn the ways in which we reinforce or collude with these forces to retain power, privilege, and control as they play out in our different realities.

I offer that this learning and unlearning needs a collective energy and spirit, and hence this call to action to be activists; to become *social justice* or *equity* assessment professionals. Today, given our COVID-19 realities, restorative approaches (built on relationships and accountability) have become extremely important because they humanize, decolonize, and center lived experiences and social/societal/collective good and harmony over stopgap, band-aid, punitive, and/or compliance solutions that problematize people rather than problem-solve oppressive and hegemonic, problematic systems and ways of being because they often do not recognize, address, and/or change systemic, root cause problems and circumstances. We need a collective spirit and community to proactively help us grow, hold us accountable, and nurture us as social justice activists in assessment. So, what do I mean by calling on you as a higher education or assessment professional to be an activist? What will it mean for you if you choose to engage with me and answer this call to action in your own contexts? I share my expectations as follows as one frame to consider in your decision to answer this call.

As I call you into activism, let me define what it means to be an activist. The *Oxford English Dictionary* defines an *activist* as, "a person who campaigns to bring about political or social change." When we look up the definition of *campaign*, it then states that it is, "work[ing] in an organized and active way toward a particular goal, typically a political or social one." Using these common, nonscholarly definitions, I offer that with this invitation to be an activist, I am asking us to take on the following five responsibilities:

1. Intentionally be in community or create one.
2. Organize.
3. Act.
4. Accept that social justice activism is a recursive exercise.
5. Own being an activist.

I expand on each of the five expectations or responsibilities as follows.

1. Intentionally Be in Community or Create One

As professionals in higher education in the United States, we are often forced to subscribe to a framework of individualism. We are judged and our advancement is based on self-promotion—How many articles or research studies did I publish? At how many conferences did I present? How much grant money did I bring in? How often have I been cited? How many awards did I receive for my contributions? How much change/improvement did I bring about? What can I list as my achievements for my performance appraisal? And the list goes on. This imposition of an individualistic success and recognition worldview often results in us seeking power for our own personal success even if the intent is for a collective good. Thus, I offer that within the higher education space, and as higher education professionals, activism and having a collective, community orientation does not come naturally to us. We are primed to be individual contributors with individual metrics for success.

I do not think what I am saying is new. The push–pull between individual motivations and accolades that is systemically produced, perpetuated, and maintained as meritocracy and our collective well-being is real and I have come to realize that this individual way of being imposed on us takes away from the collective possibilities we could and should explore. After all, my thinking and ask in this section and throughout this chapter are an evolution of the activism and knowledge creation I have personally gained from through my own community networks and activism and yet, I am possibly the sole beneficiary of this chapter's creation (the irony of publishing).

We need to come together to push each other. When we come into community, we get exponentially further than going at it alone. Coming into community means intentionally finding folx working toward similar social justice goals, building trust, lifting each other up, raising awareness of problems, and exploring solutions together. Of folx recognizing each other's humanity first and foremost, building on relationships, trust, and hope, and pushing each other further than we think is possible and at times comfortable and uncomfortable. It means intentionally creating a safety net that allows for difference but ensures accountability to social justice principles of disrupting internalized and transferred oppression as much as external systems of oppression. It means creating a space for authentic engagement and purpose-building. I ask you to choose community that could be in the form of a community of praxis or a collective network or some other form of sustained, engaged, coming together.

When we come into community, there is validation we gain from each other. This validation of who we are and what we are striving for helps us name and address our lived experiences of visible and invisible oppression or microaggressions even as we arrive upon creative and subversive ways to deal. It helps us affirm our reality, excellence, power, and achievement rather than letting us give into the negative narratives and stereotypical perceptions that surround us that many a time force us to be silent or complicit in injustices. And we need this affirmation to create and sustain activism.

There is critical, courageous vulnerability and tremendously freeing power that can better be nurtured in the safe spaces of inclusive friendship and trust. There have been times in my graduate journey that the only way I survived and got through the Carnegie credit hour time expectations was by a group of us divvying up the readings and teaching each other the key concepts. I couldn't have succeeded without my village. That is one easy example of the power of the community approach. Being in community allows us to talk through problems being faced, vent feelings that need to be heard and understood, and brainstorm plans of action to deal with the situation(s) we need to address.

When I call us into activism, it is a call to be part of a community. We can create it or join existing ones. An activist is not a lone ranger. Activism requires us to seek out community and connection to learn and nurture—ourselves and others. Activism thrives in community. It is about the collective good and about collective action. Activism, by its very definition, cannot just be a single individual's personal endeavor. Rather, that individual's activism (even if it is personal) is built on or framed by a collective philosophy, ideology, or a paradigm. Activism is about coming together and being accountable to each other because many a time a social justice actor who is not centered in community often, unknowingly and unintentionally, reifies the very systems they are trying to dismantle. *We need community to help us recognize our flaws, to help us become aware of our privileges, and to possibly help reveal and assert our agency and power to ourselves.* Being in community is about being in a relationship with each other. It is about starting with trust, building trust, and always going back to trust. It is about staying engaged even when we want to disengage.

So, when I call on us to each be an activist, I am requesting that we build or participate in a community of praxis around social justice even as we ensure oppressed voices are centered, privileged, and given credit in this community. Being in community is essential because (a) it facilitates our learning in a supportive environment where we push and nurture each other's growth, and we can learn from and with each other; (b) it helps us maintain our accountability toward our purpose in a strategic and courageous environment by breaking down the walls we may hit up against and be stumped by (that we will all experience at one time or another in this equity praxis); and (c) it forces us to recognize the importance of self-care and offers us a safe space to do so. We can engage in creative problem-solving in a compassionate space to advance our purpose. Being in community helps us alleviate our possible exhaustion so that we can replenish our reservoirs and gain the required rejuvenation to sustain the energy needed in this work. The role of community in providing space to advance as a collective is well documented in communities of practice efforts (Dennen & Burner, 2008; Wenger, 1998).

In practice, being in community or creating a community for equity and assessment could mean actively partnering with diversity and equity offices or colleagues in our institutions. It could mean inviting centers for teaching and learning folx into this equity work. It could mean actively searching for and finding like-minded people in our institution (through faculty and staff resource/affinity groups or even student groups). It could even mean seeking and/or creating such a community in our professional organizations or other spaces outside our institutions. It would require us to get together and set an intention to work together to advance social justice.

2. Organize

Activism requires strategizing. Activism demands effectiveness and efficiency planning. It is proactive in its purpose. It requires creative and subversive tools and techniques to be ideated, employed, and deployed to achieve the goals of social justice—as journey or destination. Activism in assessment requires intentional designing and preparation of structures, policies, processes, and so forth so that we can fulfill our purpose of embodying the social justice values we are attempting to achieve. Activism requires the community we create or participate in to do all the above or, in other words, to organize.

Organizing entails coordinating, collaborating, cocreating, and healing together—intentionally. That is the organizing that is involved. Organizing is planning. Organizing as part of activism involves agitation, advocacy, and some amount of agony. As Frederick Douglass put it in his speech on August 3, 1857,

> Those who profess to favor freedom and yet depreciate agitation, are people who want crops without plowing the ground; they want rain without thunder and lightning; they want the ocean without the roar of its many waters. The struggle may be a moral one, or it may be a physical one, or it may be both. But it must be a struggle. Power concedes nothing without a demand. It never did and it never will. (2015, pp. 133–134)

Social justice activism is about organizing and organizing takes effort. There is toil involved. There is struggle. Organizing in a manner that reflects our intention and values is essential to it. It is about us coming together to shape a space, engage in a dialogue, and be intentional as we plan our actions (Sachs, 2000). It is about sharing labor through relationship-building and this organizing is my invitation to you.

An example of what this organizing looks like for assessment and other higher education professionals is to begin with a question, any one of these for example—how do you plan and intentionally shift the power in who takes on assessment as their responsibility at your institution (so that it is not folx with the least power to effect real change because they have been voluntold to take on assessment)? How do you plan to ensure committee and leadership meetings advance social justice beyond tokenism? How will you magnify dissenting voices that are often silenced? How will you ensure integrity and accuracy in representation when your institution or leaders want to paint a rosy picture of the current climate for all stakeholders or minimize the horror of the lived experiences of the minoritized few? How do you plan to influence-up or influence around you to make assessment about equity rather than about compliance? How do you strategize interrupting microaggressions? How do you change policy for proactive social justice training for all faculty, staff, students, and leaders? How will you begin to ask critical questions of the curriculum, policies, or taken-for-granted expectations within your program or institution to effect substantive change? How will you strategize (and with whom) to figure out best practices to answer all the previous questions and more? You need strategy and planning with the help of the community you are a part of. So, organize. So that you may be prepared to act.

3. Act

Activism is about doing. It is about acting—now. Activism asks us to engage in concrete action in the service of social justice that goes beyond us saying we "care about" equity and social justice. As Nel Noddings (1984) put it—we need to demonstrate that we "care for" rather than "care about" this issue. To care for social justice rather than care about it means asking ourselves every day what did I do today to embody and enact my social justice commitments? It means our actions must impact us as much as those we think we act for or on behalf of. We cannot engage in armchair activism anymore. It is not enough. Acting ensures we do not give in to the insidious draw of indifference or, for that matter, hopelessness. *If we are not invested and impacted, if we do not face consequences for our actions (good and bad), our actions may be too far removed from us to be meaningful activism or to even be considered activism.*

By acting, or in "caring-for," I rely on Chela Sandoval's (2000) "loving" approach. She asks us to engage in critical, decolonized, social justice-framed action that does not take a savior approach but rather an anti-oppressive one that builds on our fluid identities, clarifies, and reconciles our complicity as participants in hegemonic spaces (such as our various roles as participants in our higher education environments), and moves us to break down barriers to strengthen our agency and our actions toward a particular purpose. With this call, I invite us into loving action and caring for social justice. We must be careful about taking on a savior mantle and we must be real with ourselves about our intentions as we act. It requires introspection and reflexivity. Acting also requires a community we must invite in to call us out on our BS.

A few examples of this for assessment professionals include how are you going beyond report writing as an assessment professional to directly, positively impacting student learning and success? How are you practicing what I call "data-use accountability" or "data-use validity"? How are you sharing back with your stakeholders how you used their feedback in the climate survey, for example? How comfortable are you for your students or stakeholders to read your student learning outcome reports and gain useful information from them? How are you interrupting deficit-narratives and the silencing of voices? How are you actively investigating the ways in which you, your program, or institution are perpetuating inequities in your ways of being, operating, review, and reporting? How often are you disaggregating the data? How are you advocating for social justice? How are you centering the voices of your colleagues and students of color? As you attempt to respond to these questions, you will become aware of the actions you are undertaking. Or not. These are just some low hanging fruit—easy examples and guidelines/suggestions for actions you can undertake to be courageous. To act.

4. Accept That Social Justice Activism Is a Recursive Exercise

Make peace with the fact that social justice activism is never done, but always in need of action. If one chooses to be an activist, one is committing to living as one. We must embed the values of social justice into our very being and choose to live our values every single day. Activism does not constitute a one and done action. It is a continuous process of evolution—of the self, a community, and society—of life itself. Engaging in social justice activism makes social justice as much a journey as a destination just like life. And just like life, the success or failure of one action does not mean you give up or stop. It is not done, because it is a way of being. Ups and downs are part of activism and one must ride them as one would our life.

I offer that social justice activism is a discursive praxis; it is never perfect and never done. It requires critical exploration, examination, and investigation of the issues at hand, the solutions we think we have, and our own complicity in the problems we see. It is about going deeper and like an onion, each time we peel a layer there may be more tears and a redefinition of the whole issue. Thus, in a particular context, whatever we may frame as the socially just solution or action may be a false trope that only gets exposed once we push ourselves and our boundaries to engage with social justice more critically and authentically.

With the invitation to be an activist, I offer that we must practice our activism and live our values by embodying social justice to the best of our ability. As much as we try to achieve social justice as a goal, we must engage in social justice as a process in and through our activism—missteps and all. With discomfort. Courageously. Vulnerably. Continually. Possibly never achieving the goal of social justice but always striving toward our best version of it. Embodying it. Living it. I must note there are whole bodies of work around activism (follow any of the histories of any movements such as Black Lives Matter, or Me Too, or civil rights to just name a few), and a lot of scholarship on living courageously and vulnerably (Brené Brown's work on shame, vulnerability, and courage). These are great places to start.

An example of this recursive nature of social justice praxis is the idea that many of us, as assessment professionals, see ourselves as student success champions. However, our focus on learning outcomes assessment and rubrics may mean that we do not focus on graduation and retention rates or the student experience at all. This is a result of simple human resource bandwidth/capacity limitations and once again the ontological, epistemological, axiological, Western, positivist approach limitations that frame assessment methodology. We emphasize going deep and narrow in framing an issue and studying it rather than recognizing the irrevocable interconnectedness of multiple issues. Thus, many of us, with accreditor blessings, see our role as assessing student learning outcomes only or primarily rather than a more holistic student lived experience function. Our existing "objective" frameworks often do not allow for us to go broad and all-encompassing in one's research/assessment endeavor because it cannot be valid, reliable, and/or generalizable with that breadth.

Thus, while we try to ensure student learning as learning outcomes-focused assessment professionals, we may miss our student needs around their negative lived experiences of their educational journey that can impact their learning and success too. We may positively impact one sphere of policy or practice but not another which could be just as important, if not more. That latter policy or practice may be more critical than the one we ended up focusing on. When we realize this, we need to take corrective action and change course. We can't rest on our laurels as changing one policy isn't enough. We must take responsibility and always try to do more; do better. Hence the recursive, discursive nature of this work. As we peel back the onion layers, we may have to implement an assessment project yet again because the reflexive, social justice focused-approach opens our eyes to something we didn't consider before—a depth that now means we have to reassess our approach and destination to achieve our goals of social justice. So, instead of student learning, we may have to focus on student retention and assessing the quality of our students' lived experiences. This change in focus may require us to challenge our own assigned roles and responsibilities within the institution and, once again, organize and act around it. We need to be able to pivot as needed. Grow. Evolve. And help those around us do the same. That is continuous improvement as we know it. That is discursive praxis. And with all the barriers we will face in trying to effect continuous change, the question is—are we ready for this life?

5. Own Being an Activist—Own It

I believe (based on my lived experience) that one must identify and call oneself an activist to be an effective one—at least in the safe space of our activism community. There is a certain amount of negativity around the term "activism" or "activist" as a label because of negative perceptions of being a problem personality that needs to be managed. We need to stop worrying about others' perceptions of us to the extent that we feel we can function and fulfill our responsibilities. If we are apologists as activists, we are once again reifying the very trope we are trying to dismantle with our activism. On the flip side, some of us (including myself many a time), wonder if we have the right to call ourselves activists. Are we doing enough? The answer: Keep trying to live our principles and values in community, continually as we are able, in an intentional manner, and with growth and accountability. We can only try.

The activist self-identity will recharge, reenergize, and reinforce the strength of our work and contributions. Some call it being a warrior. Some call it being a survivor. Some call it being a leader. Some call it being brave and courageous, and some call it being radical or revolutionary. Owning this label or identity, I believe, is and will be a self-fulfilling prophecy. It is also one of the toughest actions to undertake (something even I struggle with every other day). In what spaces can I out myself as an activist? How will I be perceived? Will I get that job or promotion if they see me as an activist? Will they perceive me as a troublemaker or "not a good fit" for a role, team, or institution? This journey is something we all go through as activists—and many of us deal with these questions constantly in the various spaces we find ourselves in. I am going through the risks and worry, and hope and optimism right now writing these very words in this chapter. However, I do believe there is true power in claiming an identity. It is freeing. It is naming. It is sustaining. As mentioned before, even if it is just in the spaces of safety, claim your identity; claim your stance. When I call us in to be activists, I ask us to own it, not for anyone else but for yourself. The advantage is also that when we claim our identity, we are more likely to find our allies or activist communities or be found by those in need of us.

These previous five expectations or responsibilities frame my call to action for us to be activists and I hope you answer this call—in your own way, for yourself.

Conclusion

Being social justice revolutionaries in assessment work means keeping a constant eye on how we can be different or do things differently from how it is assumed it should be done. How can we be the champions of our students? How can we be change agents or catalysts in our institutions and in our personal–professional contexts? How can we be colleagues who truly see each other and lift each other up? How can we reimagine who is successful and who deserves to be successful? How can we coalesce learning, success, opportunity, and lived experience in a way that is truly meaningful, transformational, and joyful for all of us? How can we be enablers instead of gatekeepers—at every opportunity and every time? These are hard questions and there are no easy answers. But these are the questions we should be grappling with as equity assessment professionals every single day.

Higher education is in such a state of flux given the realities of COVID-19. This pandemic has only further exposed and exacerbated the structural and systemic inequities at play that have long disadvantaged many of our students and colleagues as we strive to learn, teach, and make a difference. To practice equity in assessment and to achieve equity through assessment, we need a foundational understanding of oppression, power, privilege, intersectionality, implicit bias, and so on. We, as assessment and higher education professionals, have some of the greatest power and greatest responsibility to make a difference in advancing equity and social justice. We need to look at ourselves and our actions just as much as our institutions' structures, processes, and policies at play.

We must have an interest if not a deep understanding of social justice and equity. Not equality but equal opportunity to succeed. We must use reflexivity like a muscle and be metacognitive in our thinking and practice. We need to always keep at the forefront—where is power; where, when, and how is oppression playing out; where and what is our agency; and who are our allies that we can call upon to support our social justice efforts.

Assessment is complicit in either exacerbating the equity problem already existing in higher education today or mitigating it. It is not a value neutral exercise. Whether assessment is seen as grading, as various continuous improvement efforts, as program reviews or evaluations, as meta-analysis of student learning, or as strategic planning and progress monitoring, any effort we undertake is blended with power or the lack thereof, skewed by positionality, and stuffed with implicit bias, privilege, and oppression. Given the invitation I have shared—to be an activist—I hope that we can begin to responsibly and responsively (if we aren't already) advance social justice in higher education and beyond as assessment and education professionals, as a community of like-minded souls. As a reader engaging with this book and chapter, I ask you to reflect on your power and agency to make a meaningful difference in the lives of those who are impacted by your actions and decisions every day—whether you know it or not. I make this call to action. I invite you to be an assessment activist—a revolutionary one—because, together, we can make a difference. For. The. Better.

Acknowledgments

Natasha Jankowski, for the invitation and for being a true enabler. Julie Wilhelm and Annabelle Goodwin, for critical eyes and detailed, invaluable input. Catherine Wehlburg, for good perspective. ALA Cohort X, The

Mavens, and the Feminist Evaluation Regenerative Network, for being cheer-leaders, problem-solvers, and my activism communities. Gavin Henning, for the rich feedback, questions, and your never-ending patience. Britt Nichols and the ExamSoft team, for creating an environment where work is pleasure, where I can thrive, and where writing is part of my job. Aruya, Bhuv, Irya, and Jani, I could not have done this without your constant strength, support, love, and understanding. To all intergenerational activists doing the work and not publishing. I see you. The Samuga_Gyaanam+Bheda byline (Bheda building on community knowledge/wisdom) is to do justice by you because my work relies on (y)our existence and effort—many-a-time co-opted, unac-knowledged, unattributed, and undervalued in print and beyond. Thank you for your inspiration and perspiration!

References

Bensimon, E. M. (2012). The equity scorecard: Theory of change. In E. M. Bensimon & L. Malcolm (Eds.), *Confronting equity issues on campus: Implementing the equity scorecard in theory and practice* (pp. 17–44). Stylus.

Bheda, D., & Jones, A. (2020, November 16). FIE TIG week: Reflexivity and the importance of practicing it in evaluation. *AEA365 Blog*. https://aea365.org/blog/fie-tig-week-reflexivity-and-the-importance-of-practicing-it-in-evaluation-by-divya-bheda-alissa-jones/

Carlson, C., & Sorrell, M. J. (2020, June 20). Higher ed's reckoning with race. *The Chronicle of Higher Education*. https://www.chronicle.com/article/higher-eds-reckoning-with-race

Dean-Coffey, J. (2018). What's race got to do with it? Equity and philanthropic evaluation practice. *American Journal of Evaluation*, *39*(4), 527–542. https://doi.org/10.1177/1098214018778533

Dennen, V. P., & Burner, K. J. (2008). The cognitive apprenticeship model in educational practice. In M. J. Spector, M. D. Merrill, J. van Merrienboer, & M. P. Driscoll (Eds.), *Handbook of research on educational communications and technology* (pp. 425–439). Routledge.

Douglass, F. (2015). Frederick Douglass, from West India emancipation. In J. Kaufman-McKivigan & R. Levine (Eds.), *The heroic slave* (pp. 133–137). Yale University Press. https://doi.org/10.12987/9780300210569-021

Hood, S., Hopson, R. K., & Frierson, H. T. (Eds). (2015). *Continuing the journey to reposition culture and cultural context in evaluation theory and practice*. Information Age.

Jones, S. M., & Phillips, G. A. (2020). Re-imagining campus climate assessment at HBCUs. *Research and Practice in Assessment*, *15*(2), 32–44. https://www.rpajournal.com/dev/wp-content/uploads/2021/01/RPA_VOL15_Iss2.pdf

Krause, H. (2019, March 9). FIE TIG week: Data is not objective: Feminist data analysis. *AEA365 Blog*. https://aea365.org/blog/feminist-tig-week-data-is-not-objective-feminist-data-analysis-by-heather-krause/

Ladson-Billings, G. (2009). *The dreamkeepers: Successful teachers of African American children* (2nd ed.). Jossey-Bass.

Lorde, A. (2007). The master's tools will never dismantle the master's house. In *Sister outsider: Essays and speeches* (110–114). Crossing Press. (Original work published in 1984)

Lynner, B., Ho, W., Narui, M., & Smith, J. (2020, July). *Capital University: Pilot campus climate assessment through critical race theory.* National Institute for Learning Outcomes Assessment, Council for the Advancement of Standards in Higher Education, and Campus Labs. https://www.learningoutcomesassessment.org/wp-content/uploads/2020/07/EquityCase-CapitalUniversity.pdf

Montenegro, E., & Jankowski, N. A. (2017, January). *Equity and assessment: Moving towards culturally responsive assessment* (Occasional Paper No. 29). University of Illinois and Indiana University, National Institute for Learning Outcomes Assessment (NILOA). https://www.learningoutcomesassessment.org/wp-content/uploads/2019/02/OccasionalPaper29.pdf

Montenegro, E., & Jankowski, N. A. (2020, January). *A new decade for assessment: Embedding equity into assessment praxis* (Occasional Paper No. 42). University of Illinois and Indiana University, National Institute for Learning Outcomes Assessment (NILOA). https://www.learningoutcomesassessment.org/wp-content/uploads/2020/01/A-New-Decade-for-Assessment.pdf

Moraga, C., & Anzaldua, G. (1983). *The bridge called my back: Writings by radical women of color* (2nd ed.). Kitchen Table/Women of Color Press.

Noddings, N. (1984). *Caring, a feminine approach to ethics & moral education.* University of California Press.

Oluo, I. (2019). *So you want to talk about race.* Seal Press.

Patton, M. Q. (2014). *Qualitative research & evaluation methods: Integrating theory and practice* (4th ed.). SAGE.

Sachs, J. (2000). The activist professional. *Journal of Educational Change, 1*(1), 77–94. https://doi.org/10.1023/a:1010092014264

Sandoval, C. (2000). *Methodology of the oppressed.* University of Minnesota Press.

Secaira, M. (2019, May 31). Abigail Echo-Hawk on the art and science of "decolonizing data." *Crosscut.* https://crosscut.com/2019/05/abigail-echo-hawk-art-and-science-decolonizing-data

Wenger, E. (1998). *Communities of practice: Learning, meaning, and identity.* Cambridge University Press. https://doi.org/10.1017/CBO9780511803932

Wiggins, G., & McTighe, J. (2005). *Understanding by design* (2nd ed.). ASCD.

Wiggins, G., & McTighe, J. (2011). *The understanding by design guide to creating high quality units.* ASCD.

Winkelmes, M. (2013). Transparency in teaching: Faculty share data and improve students' learning. *Liberal Education, 99*(2), 48–55. https://www.aacu.org/publications-research/periodicals/transparency-teaching-faculty-share-data-and-improve-students

Zerquera, D., Reyes, K. A., Pender, J. T., & Abbady, R. (2018). Understanding practitioner-driven assessment and evaluation efforts for social justice. In D. Zerquera, I. Hernández, & J. G. Berumen (Eds.), *Assessment and Social Justice: Pushing Through Paradox* (New Directions for Institutional Research, no. 177, pp. 15–40). Jossey-Bass. https://doi.org/10.1002/ir.20254

3

EQUITY AND ASSESSMENT

A Storied Past

Natasha A. Jankowski and Anne E. Lundquist

In a National Institute for Learning Outcomes Assessment (NILOA) survey of provosts regarding institution-level assessment practices, equity was listed as a driver of assessment efforts and important to assessment work but underemphasized in data use—meaning assessment data were rarely used to address equity gaps in learning (Jankowski et al., 2018). Campus Labs, now Anthology, conducted a survey of assessment professionals about knowledge and practice regarding the intersection of equity, inclusion, and assessment. Of the survey respondents, 55% indicated that they thought the effective intersection of diversity, equity, and inclusion efforts on their campus was very important, and 51% somewhat agreed they had the necessary background and training to engage in related practices. And in a survey of assessment professionals regarding the spring 2020 pivot to remote instruction due to COVID-19, 30% of respondents strongly agreed that concerns about equity drove decisions, with professional development around issues of equity high on a list of needs (Jankowski, 2020a). What this collection of data points may suggest is that while equity remains a concern, it is not being addressed systematically in assessment practice and assessment is not yet viewed as a vehicle for addressing equity gaps. This might raise the question: Where does equity fit within assessment?

Lenses of Assessment and Equity

Conversations on equity and assessment are not new (Gipps, 1995; Sacks, 1997); what is unique to current conversations is where equity fits into assessment and how it is being discussed in relation to assessment. Some of where equity in assessment is viewed as fitting can be attributed to lenses of assessment that guide and inform different purposes, forms, and functions of assessment. For the purposes of this chapter, assessment is focused on the assessment of *student learning*, or the systematic collection, review, and use of information about educational programs/courses/experiences—undertaken for the purpose of improving student learning and development (Jankowski & Baker, 2019). Elsewhere, four such lenses about the purposes, forms, and functions of assessment are presented as a heuristic to understand the different ways in which equity fits into assessment conversations (Jankowski, 2017). These four lenses are not all encompassing and are presented here very briefly at a macroview of generalization to guide discussion. The four most common are measurement, compliance, teaching and learning, and student-centered.

- Measurement concerns instrument or assessment design and is built upon the scientific principles of empirical research that are post-positive, objective, rational, valid, and reliable. It is most often focused on good assessment as good measurement or measuring; involves standardization, comparisons, pre/post approaches, and entails the most familiar assessment type—the standardized test. Equity within measurement is focused on fairness via use of the same measures or standardization, reduction of bias, comparison, and disaggregation of data.

- Compliance regards putting in place reporting systems to document, collect, archive, and report upon institutional quality assurance and effectiveness. It is viewed as overly bureaucratic, time consuming, and divorced from teaching and learning. There is a fair amount of data collection, but minimal use beyond report submitting. Equity within compliance entails completing a question on a reporting form about equity needs, goals, or equity issues within the data.

- Teaching and learning concern a desire to understand the student experience by interrogating offerings, programs, and practices. The question is asked: Is what we are doing working for students? Assessment here is embedded within praxis experiences, focused on improvement, designed to be formative, and adaptive to changing student, faculty, and staff needs. Equity in teaching and learning entails examining practices for differential impacts on learning by different student populations and modifying practice to close equity gaps in learning.

- Student-centered is a concept about individual students and involves students as active agents in their own learning. Transparency of design is clearly shared with students, assessment is for learning, and student self-reflection and transference of learning are ongoing foci of assessment efforts. Equity in student-centered assessment involves transparency in design and student agency—ensuring students are clear on expectations for learning and related demonstrations as well as future plans for success.

Depending on which lens(es) is dominant impacts if, where, and how equity is viewed as connected to assessment. While each of the lenses is required in assessment in part because institutions are accountable to external bodies and measurement matters, it is important to understand the dominant operating lens within a particular institution to determine the path forward of equity conversations. Further, the lenses help explain the history of assessment and equity conversations thus far. To assist in exploring assessment lenses within a program, unit, or institution, two activities were developed; one for student affairs and one for academic affairs in order to bolster and support productive dialogue and conversations (Jankowski, 2020b, 2020c). Student affairs lenses differ slightly including a focus on cocurricular learning, measurement of participation/satisfaction, compliance/reporting, and student-centered.

Current equity and assessment conversations cross the various lenses by examining bias in design and measurement, using multiple sources of evidence to inform teaching and document learning, including student voice in the process, increasing transparency, interrogating learning data, and making evidence-informed, context-specific changes that address issues of equity (Montenegro & Jankowski, 2020). But why are equity and assessment conversations that examine equity throughout the entire process of assessment only happening now?

This chapter presents a brief overview of the history of equity and assessment beginning with work that was undertaken within the lens of measurement, followed by more recent conversations on teaching and learning and student-centered dialogues. The connections between equity and assessment are presented to provide a historical grounding in prior conversations that share the current equity and assessment space. Due to the broad coverage of this chapter, it is necessarily not comprehensive, and elements and areas are missed, the history of equity and measurement is limited, but we hope it serves as a starting reference point for the reader's equity and assessment journey.

Assessment as a Blockade

There is a long ancestry of equity work in evaluation, measurement, K–12 assessment, pedagogical approaches, and the like, but in assessment in higher education, the focus historically has been a measurement one—disconnected from related conversations in evaluation and K–12. In part, this is because of a distinction made in assessment regarding assessment that happens *inside* institutions of higher education once a student is enrolled, attending classes, and going to events as separate from assessment that occurred prior to enrollment—such as SAT/ACT or standardized testing in K–12. Assessment processes and practices within institutions of higher education are just that, cycles and processes that happen annually *within* an institution as though it is a closed system. However, assessment as a process employed in education writ large has served as a long-standing sorting function and is most widely known outside of assessment scholarship as standardized testing due to the prevalence of testing, the use of testing for tracking, and for student placement based on "academic preparedness" (Dowd & Bensimon, 2015; Ford & Helms, 2012; Kohn, 2000; Sacks, 1997).

Accountability and assessment are so intertwined because of the use to which assessment has historically been put. By the time a student from K–12 enrolls in an institution of higher education they "are numb with all these criterion referenced tests" (Gallagher, 2007, p. 66). However, the function of assessment as a sorting mechanism is often forgotten in the dualistic debate between improvement and accountability (Kohn, 2000). Assessment stood as a means to determine standards for allowing entry and access to higher education (Gipps, 1995; Sacks, 1997; Stowell, 2004). This is accomplished through the use of assessment to provide "a rationale and legitimacy for the social structures and power relations of modern-day societies and for one's place within these" (Leathwood, 2005, p. 307), making it normalized that some will succeed and some will not. This "extensively paper-based bureaucratic game seems to bear little relation to learning" (Leathwood, 2005, p. 309), filtering opportunities to fewer and fewer students deemed by the system to be more or less likely to succeed and/or be successful. Understanding assessment within a social, political, and historical context helps to move the gaze away from simply refining and improving the technique of implementing assessment. If the game is rigged, "doing it better" will still occur within a rigged game, one designed to require privilege and connection as well as insider knowledge in addition to demonstration of learning (Gallagher, 2007; Kohn, 2000; Leathwood, 2005).

Curriculum and learning experiences are socially constructed, as are assessments designed to document the resulting learning. What that social construction means is that standards, quality, and assessment are not neutral or value-free but socially constructed as well (Stowell, 2004). Standard assessment approaches have silenced the experience of students of color (Zerquera, Reyes et al., 2018), causing additional stress which in turn leads to a lack of academic motivation and subsequent disinterest in assessment (Chilisa, 2000; Dorimé-Williams, 2018; Francis et al., 2020). This loss of identity, disconnect from learning, and detachment from the institution means that "nothing could be as unjust as an attempt to achieve equity through sameness" (Dowd & Bensimon, 2015, p. 13) because students of color do not have the same experience as White students. It also means assessment data might not measure learning alone, but something else entirely, based on the constant, negative impacts on learning experienced in lower participation in class, discomfort in learning experiences, and perceptions of intelligence experienced by students of color in higher education (Harrison & Hatfield Price, 2017). This is in part because as Zerquera, Hernandez et al. (2018) argued, "while colleges and universities often align with social justice ideals through discourses, they simultaneously struggle in achieving alignment in policy and practice" leading to "superficial responses that do not fully confront systemic inequities" (p. 7).

It is well documented that students of color experience an environment in traditionally White institutions punctuated by "lack of caring, cultural sensitivity, and support sensed from the professors" which "results in students' loss of interest, vigor, and trust" (Koshino, 2016, p. 107). Further, students are less likely to put forward their best examples of what they know and can do in an assessment when feeling disconnected from the learning environment (Chilisa, 2000; Kohn, 2000). Assessment should not add to such disconnect but instead actively work to support students' sense of belonging. Instances such as requiring students to cite work when there are not any references due to the silencing of particular traditions, cultural positions, and methodologies reinforces and maintains outsider status for students within assessments—there is no space for their authentic self in the answer (Koshino, 2016).

If higher education strove to gather data on learning, then ensuring learner success and positioning learners to best demonstrate their learning should be a goal. However, if assessment is about measurement, then the evidence collected should ideally be focused on the best means students have to demonstrate their learning as opposed to assessing privilege or how well a student is able to repeat a majoritarian story in an assignment, thus reducing potential noise in the data on learning by measuring discrimination instead. For instance, Taras (2006) found that undergraduate students are not afforded the opportunity to engage in formative feedback writing processes when refinement of writing was what was being assessed. The luxury of revision was only allowed at the graduate level. The inconsistency of forbidding working on a paper from one semester to the next, juxtaposed with the perpetual complaint of students' inability to write, and concerns that working together equates with cheating, all while faculty regularly engage in collaborative revision processes, reinforces a "two-tier system of feedback that promotes injustices, especially if one tier promotes learning while the other acts as a covert selection procedure" (Taras, 2006, p. 373). The denial of students a luxury afforded to faculty to engage in iterative feedback and drafting, coupled with the lack of opportunities to develop standards and criteria to evaluate good work, positions undergraduate students to be unable to make judgments needed to improve their work and their learning (Taras, 2006). As Taras (2006) argued, "These inconsistencies show a lack of equity towards undergraduate students. What does this situation say about us as teachers and the way we view and treat our students?" (p. 374).

Students of color have to navigate hidden curriculums (Margolis, 2001), the years of stress and psychological harm caused by constant racism and unrelenting requests to continuously prove themselves (Kohn, 2000; Pierce, 1989; Sacks, 1997), and structural gaps and cultural practices that collectively work to "impose a self-worth tax on students" (Dowd & Bensimon, 2015, p. 163). Further, that entire experience occurs within institutions not designed with students of color in mind (Dean et al., 2007; Shotton et al., 2013). Yet rarely are experiences of students of color validated. Dowd and Bensimon (2015) attested

> many White Americans do not acknowledge that educational practices can be discriminatory in the absence of conscious, overt, interpersonal acts of racial discrimination. They do not realize that racism can be embedded within organizational structures and routine operations . . . the current state of affairs in postsecondary accountability practice and policy is characterized by historical amnesia about higher education's role in the racialization of educational opportunities and outcomes. (p. 3)

For students, assessment can be simply another place of stress, anger, and anxiety due in part to the embedded structures and routines mentioned by Dowd and Bensimon (2015). As an example, a study by Falchikov and Boud (2007) explored the impact of assessment on students through student's autobiographical stories about the experience of being assessed. Students reported feelings of distress, and in some cases, experiences were so negative the emotional impact lasted years "affecting career choices, inhibiting learning, and changing behavior towards teaching situations" (Falchikov & Boud, 2007, p. 144). Such a finding places assessment not simply as a measurement exercise, but one with the potential to cause lasting harm if not student-centered.

Students reported lingering effects with assessment intimately connected to their identity, not simply as learners, but as people within a larger society. Palucki Blake et al. (2012) also interviewed students who described sensations of monitoring themselves and their behavior, language choices, and movement for "fear of being stereotyped or viewed as less intelligent by professors and peers" (p. 105) which in turn affected students' academic development and success. The stress of double consciousness and stereotype vulnerability hindered learning, particularly when students were aware their ability was being assessed in a domain in which members of their group were generally thought to perform poorly, subsequently interfering with performance (Palucki Blake et al., 2012). The collective experience serves to make the classroom places where students with minoritized social identities feel invisible and excluded (Georges, 2020; Shotton et al., 2013), unable to be their authentic selves (Vaccaro & Newman, 2016), leading to de-identification from their academic self (Verschelden, 2017). How can assessment data gather accurate pictures of student learning within such an environment? And if the classroom experience is so negative, can student affairs support truly serve to fill the disconnect for learners?

In student-centered assessment, the work of Winkelmes (2016) has focused upon making assessment instructions clear and transparent to learners, which was found to have an impact on the success of students of color. The approach involves faculty working to "increase students' understanding of the purposes, tasks, and criteria for their academic work *before* they begin working" (Winkelmes, 2019, p. 19). Such clarity in conversations on what is intended may also involve varied forms of assessments or assignments focused on inclusion and cultural alignment (Koshino, 2016). Maki (2017) offered a possible solution in the form of real-time assessment at the institution and program levels, which requires faculty and staff to consider how well they are functioning as part of a team to prepare students for their next learning experience. Real-time assessment helps faculty and staff ask questions such as "How well prepared are all students at the end of my course or education experience for the academic demands and expectation that lie ahead of them" (p. 79) and "How well prepared are all students at the end of my course or education experience to continue to progress toward attaining high-quality exit-level institution- and program-level outcomes?" (pp. 79–80). Asking these questions positions faculty and staff to make changes to immediately stop a gap from starting, but it does not negate the long-standing history of exclusionary practices and negative impacts of assessment *prior* to a student's entry to higher education.

In teaching and learning, students benefit in the learning process from bringing their culture with them to the learning environment—which includes how they are assessed in the learning environment—making more meaningful connections between their lived experience and the content of a course (Bolitzer et al., 2016). Instead of asking students of color to assimilate to historically White learning spaces (Shotton et al., 2013) through curriculum and assignments that can "invalidate the knowledge and experiences of racial/ethnic minority students, which are rarely present in any form in the higher educational setting" (Quaye et al., 2009, p. 161), learning can be assessed in various ways. Quaye et al. (2009) stated that the use of multiple assessments enables students to demonstrate proficiency in different ways and for faculty and staff to rethink how learning is evaluated.

Yet, while educators reinforce the importance of authentic assessment and a fair amount is occurring in classrooms and cocurriculum experiences across the United States, tests are still the predominant means by which learning is assessed throughout the course of someone's educational journey. The persistent use of tests is increasingly problematic, especially due to the long-standing knowledge of bias and unfairness in tests (Sacks, 1997) as well as documentation that such tests are inaccurate and cause harm (Dais, 1993). Yet the use of tests persists. If the main purpose of standardized testing is efficiency in sorting students, the cheapest and easiest means to do so is the multiple-choice test (Sacks, 1997), a decision which is reinforced by an over-reliance on quantitative data to inform decisions about learning, all at the expense of equity (Francis et al., 2020).

Bias and Fairness in Assessment: A Brief History of Inequities

Testing is an institution in its own right which has actively impacted the lives of students in the United States in various ways (Sacks, 1997). Children are categorized, labeled, monitored, and sorted by standardized tests. The further into opportunities for future education a student moves, the more consequential the tests become (Ford & Helms, 2012). Green and Griffore (1980) argued that "Testing is pervasive and powerful in its influence on modern life. Testing is also difficult to check and control even when its influence appears to be unfair and/or counter-productive to the welfare of those being tested" (p. 239). The negative impacts of tests can be seen with respect to racial minorities where tests become a "convenient tool for rationalizing discriminatory practices" (p. 239). Instead of addressing years of discrimination in education, health care, housing, and employment that impacts test scores, judgments are made on the innate "intellectual abilities of racial and ethnic minorities" (p. 239). Nor are any of these practices recent developments but instead threads of long-standing systemic inequities.

Due to pervasive discrimination, the experience of growing up as part of a minority population is quantitatively and qualitatively different from that of growing up White (Ford & Helms, 2012; Francis et al., 2020), meaning extreme caution should be employed in interpreting disparate score results. Thus, given the different lived experiences of students of color, the notion that tests are colorblind, neutral, and unbiased measures is a fallacy (Ford & Helms, 2012). The problem of test interpretation related to students of color even led the American Psychological Association to release guidelines on interpreting test results of individuals with cultural, linguistic, or economic backgrounds that differ substantially from the majority population, and of individuals with disabilities (Sandoval et al., 1998).

The answer to these issues has been a focus upon fairness and equality of opportunity. A basic notion of fairness is often employed, where everyone is treated in the same way unless there is a particular case where an alternative version of a test is provided, such as in offering an audio version of a test for a blind test taker (Kane, 2010). In standardized testing, equity was viewed as access to equal opportunities, not compensatory education for disadvantaged groups, and standardized tests were positioned as fair because everyone took the same test (Gipps, 1995). But what knowledge is deemed valuable? Who gets to determine and define what counts as achievement? On the grounds of equity, all groups must be offered *actual* equality of access to the curriculum and examinations; and assessment must be made as fair as possible to all groups (Gipps, 1995) otherwise the fairness argument does not hold.

Arguments about addressing bias through equality of opportunity are infused with individualism, concepts of competition, and conceptions of fairness which in turn drive student blaming because "if it was equal and fair then there is something about the student which is the problem" (Gipps & Murphy, 1994, p. 14). Yet, the purpose of assessment is to "help rather than sentence the individual" (p. 15). Further, most tests reinforce elements of cultural value to the White middle class. Individualism and questioning authority are generally presented as White and middle-class values, while interdependence and respect for authority is "often a cultural value in working-class communities, so constant messaging about independence can alienate low-income students" (Harrison & Hatfield Price, 2017, p. 153) which subsequently reinforces perceived underperformance in college classrooms where faculty often place a premium on critical thinking and questioning ideas. While African Americans exert little influence over the structure and content of tests, they are expected to perform as "if they are White middle-to-upper class, monolingual Americans" (Ford & Helms, 2012, p. 187). One might ask, how is that fair?

Validity and Equity

When assessment is viewed as a fair means to sort students, then a system is built upon some being successful and perhaps a majority who fail (Taras, 2006). But excellence does not always look the same, whereby if "excellence means excelling on multiple-choice tests . . . then only a few will be deemed interested or excellent" (Smith, 2015, p. 240). If equity in opportunity to learn material is not possible, and the purpose of the assessment is to examine how much has been learned in a particular program, an issue of validity is now raised. Kane (2010) described,

> if low scores indicate a home environment that does not promote develop-
> ment of the skills (i.e., a lack of opportunity to learn), keeping the child out
> of school for another year would seem to be counterproductive. In this sec-
> ond case, the use of the test to make admission decisions is inappropriate/
> invalid and unfair to those children who have not had an opportunity to
> learn the skills. If most of the children for whom counterproductive deci-
> sions are being made are in a particular subgroup within the population
> (defined by socioeconomic class, race, or gender), the decision procedure is
> arguably unfair to that subgroup. (p. 79)

Thus, validity and fairness are closely connected. An assessment that is unfair, in the sense that it systematically misrepresents the standing of some individuals or some groups of individuals on the construct being measured or that tends to make inappropriate decisions for individuals or groups is, to that extent, not valid for that interpretation or use. Similarly, an assessment that is not valid in the sense that it tends to generate misleading conclusions or inappropriate decisions for some individuals or groups will also be unfair (Kane, 2010). In the case of standardized entry and placement tests in higher education, variance is explained mostly by noninstructional factors (Kohn, 2000). But tests are widely used because they are believed to "objectively measure something of importance about the person, such as cognitive abilities, academic abilities, and employment skills that generalize to or will be useful in other situations" (Ford & Helms, 2012, p. 186). When students of color have an entire life span of virtually never obtaining the same scores as their White counterparts in the same settings, the score disparities are more likely to mean that students of color are excluded from a variety of academic and vocational experiences and domains in society because there is not equality in opportunities of learning, which leads to more exclusion, contributing to low achievement overall (Ford & Helms, 2012).

The idea that validity should be considered a property of inferences, rather than of assessments, has developed slowly over the past century.

In early writings about the validity of educational assessments, validity was defined as a property of an assessment. The most common definition was that an assessment was valid to the extent that it assessed what it purported to assess (Garrett, 1937) and this definition has had a long reach (Brasel et al., 2004; Cohen et al., 2004). The problem with such a definition is that an assessment does not actually purport to do anything. The purporting is done by those who claim that a specific assessment outcome has a specific meaning—a test simply tests (Wiliam et al., 2010).

By moving validity from being viewed as an intrinsic quality of a particular measure to one that examines the consequence or uses to which assessments are put, validity was repositioned to include uses and decisions made based on instrument results. It further allowed that a test could be valid for some purposes but not others and that a test could be valid for some students but not others (Caines & Englehard, 2012; Gallagher, 2007; Kane, 2010; Wiliam et al., 2010). Yet, decisions regarding achievement and attainment continue to be made from assessments that are viewed as "the objective quantitative indicator" (Gipps & Murphy, 1994, pp. 14–15), a puzzling point since Thorngate's postulate claims an instrument cannot be general, accurate, and simple all at the same time, a point often overlooked in the uses to which test results are put.

Test Bias

Unfairness in a test or test bias means that the test does not measure the same achievement across different groups. Green and Griffore (1980) argued this is due to three types of test bias: (a) bias due to content factors, (b) bias due to norms, and (c) bias due to the testing situation (p. 240). Content bias occurs when items are more familiar to one group of test takers, such as by upper-class socioeconomic status than lower socioeconomic status, a bias which aligns with the creators of test constructs who have been White and upper class. The test items are piloted with a particular sample to detect items out of place, but how the sample is chosen and what feedback is received or not temper this step. Language differences can impact content validity including dialect differences. Further, students may be test naive in how to navigate tests, experience test anxiety, and if compared to future GPA are being compared to a historically agreed upon unreliable number. When results of biased tests are used to place students into less rigorous learning trajectories than their "more ready" peers, at the end of the educational journey those in the less rigorous learning trajectory do not surprisingly achieve as much, which is taken as proof that they were indeed not ready to begin with. That is bias at play.

Biases are embedded within unconscious cognitive processes, making intention rarely the issue. The issue is a lack of examination of unconscious bias, anchoring bias, or hindrance of correspondence bias. For illustration, this excerpt from Carnevale et al. (2020) in their book the myth of meritocracy explained bias.

> People tend to attribute positive traits to themselves and their own group, even at times when that group is arbitrarily and artificially defined, as in the context of a psychological experiment. When told that there is a link between eye color and character, many will start thinking up virtues that those with eye color possess. People will project their own characteristics, or their group's, onto a prototype that connotes merit and predicts success. They'll credit the successes of members of their own group to permanent, personal, and pervasive causes. Their own kids' success in business will be cheered as the result of brains and hard work, the Smiths' kids' to being in the right place at the right time. The reverse holds true for failure. They'll say their son is simply lazy. College admissions officers will almost naturally blur judgements of applicants' qualifications with judgments of applicants' ability to "fit in," favoring traits common among those already on campus. (p. 98)

In fact, Carnevale et al. (2020) pointed out that

> For all of the controversy surrounding race-conscious admissions, it's the white beneficiaries of various admissions preferences who account for the largest share of students who fall below the standards that colleges claim to follow. One analysis of admissions and student data from 146 of the nation's most selective colleges determined that 15 percent of their students were white students whose presence on campus was tough to justify. Their grades, test scores, teacher recommendations, and high school extracurricular records all were well below those of other students. They were statistical outliers that could not be accounted for in analyses charting the relationship between applicants' academic qualifications and chances of acceptance. (p. 112)

Rankings, stats of the incoming or graduating class, and admission criteria all help to perpetuate the continued use of standardized measures to examine and compare students (Carnevale et al., 2020). In essence, practice is "stuck working within a system that's defined by its own biases" (Carnevale et al., 2020, p. 92) where "college leaders are well aware that college rankings are based heavily on criteria linked to students' socioeconomic status, such as average SAT or ACT scores, alumni giving rates, and university financial resources" (p. 94) but are remiss to change the structure due to efficiency in choice and motivators to increase rankings. This leads to the use of standard-ized tests and their results being normalized within higher education and seen as outside the purview of *within* institution assessment processes and practices. Thus, assessment professionals can argue that inside the institution, the assessment processes are separate from the storied history of inequity in testing and K–12 and may forget the connections between and structures that support both. However, what a history of testing does is provide a "way for colleges to dodge accounting for racial and socioeconomic inequality. They're mechanisms for laundering race and class behind a scientific façade of quantitative metrics" (Carnevale et al., 2020, pp. 102–103).

Viewing solutions as one of making a better test or a test fairer sees the issue of equity and assessment as only a measurement issue instead of engaging in a larger conversation of student-centered educational practices, limiting reporting structures and processes, and pedagogical concerns that lead to the instance of demonstrating learning captured within an assess-ment. But if as Gipps and Murphy (1994) argued "there is no such thing as a fair test, nor could there be" (p. 2), and tests are part of a larger system of discrimination, then the question is raised: Do higher education practi-tioners have a responsibility to engage in equitable assessment that actively works to dismantle the long-standing biased, sorting testing systems; or work to actively embed equity within institutions in an attempt to make learning amends?

Connecting Lenses

In the opening of the chapter, we presented four lenses as a means to explore the history of equity and assessment. In some ways, equity and assessment conversations are fresh to higher education because diversity, equity, and inclusion conversations and work have moved through different foci over time. From adding more numbers of students to reach critical mass to decol-onizing or diversifying curricular offerings, from adding specific diversity focused courses as opposed to reimagining readings or assignments across the entire curriculum to revamping hiring and promotion processes, and from surveying campus climate about faculty, staff, and student interactions to listening to students about their lived experiences (Denson & Chang, 2009; Smith, 2015). The work moved from tolerance, to statements, to inclu-sion, to involvement, but the work has not examined the everyday myriad ways in which students are subtly and not so subtly told they do not belong. Assignments and assessments are two means by which institutions and those within them affirm or deny students entry and access to higher education success and to being their full selves in higher education. But they would not have been seen as such from a measurement or compliance lens. It necessarily requires a student-focused gaze to the educational enterprise.

In a similar way, the benefits of diversity in terms of student body and numbers of students have long been justified based upon the educational benefits accrued by White students focused on an "Anglo way of knowing—*saber*—that focuses on formal learning, measurement, and objectivity" (Smith, 2015, p. 76). In such institutions, excellence is defined by "who succeeds, what is taught and what research is thought to be important, who feels as if they matter, and whether the institution has sufficient resources of people, ideas, and policy to successfully function in a diverse context" (Smith, 2015, p. 87) but excellence will not always look the same. Assessment is a necessary component of an equitable curriculum, program, or learning experience because simply focusing on adding numbers of diverse faculty and students is not enough. Equity-minded approaches to assessment require engaging in alternative assessment processes and practices (Gansemer-Topf et al., 2019). It is a call to reexamine the existing lenses for how practice might view the work of assessment through a lens of equity as opposed to measurement, compliance, or even teaching and learning. In a study of faculty member views about the value of diversity in the classroom, faculty members reported that diversity of the student body did not lead them to make any changes in classroom practice (Maruyama & Moreno, 2000). A teaching and learning lens does not necessarily mean equity was considered. Such findings serve as a reminder to employ an equity mindset in the work of assessment (Roberts, 2019), remove bias in alignment (Tkatchov, 2019), rethink what data are collected and how (Tharp, 2019), employ different theoretical frameworks and research methodologies (Hanson, 2019; Logli, 2019), and critically examine narratives about numbers (Gansemer-Topf et al., 2019). Through such modification of practice we can align with accountability as justice where accountability in this case refers to the responsibility of educators and policymakers to hold themselves and one another responsible for creating and sustaining just, caring, equitable, and effective postsecondary learning environments in America's colleges and universities. (Dowd & Bensimon, 2015, p. 1).

To truly address equity, the four lenses of assessment need to shift to one of equity. There is a storied history of underplaying or ignoring equity in assessment, there is not a lens for it, and the perception that assessment *inside* institutions of higher education is somehow protected from prior inequities does no justice to students. A lens is needed that critically examines and dismantles processes and practices, assumptions, and biases that if continued unchecked, serve to ensure that when learning is examined, data are actually gathered on the persistent nature of educational inequities. The brief historical overview in this chapter serves as a reminder of the prevalence of inequity. The remainder of this book serves to illustrate means to address it.

References

Bolitzer, L. A., Castillo-Montoya, M., & Williams, L. A. (2016). Pursuing equity through diversity: Perspectives and propositions for teaching and learning in higher education. In F. Tuitt, C. Haynes, & S. Stewart (Eds.), *Race, equity, and the learning environment: The global relevance of critical and inclusive pedagogies in higher education* (pp. 23–43). Stylus.

Brasel, K. J., Bragg, D., Simpson, D. E., & Weigelt, J. A. (2004). Meeting the accreditation council for graduate medical education competencies using established residency training program assessment tools. *Surgical Education—Core Competency, 188*(1), 9–12. https://doi.org/10.1016/j.amjsurg.2003.11.036

Caines, J., & Engelhard, G., Jr. (2012). How good is good enough? Educational standard setting and its effect on African American test takers. *The Journal of Negro Education, 81*(3), 228–240. https://doi.org/10.7709/jnegroeducation.81.3.0228

Carnevale, A. P., Schmidt, P., & Strohl, J. (2020). *The merit myth: How our colleges favor the rich and divide America.* The New Press.

Chilisa, B. (2000). Towards equity in assessment: Crafting gender-fair assessment. *Assessment in Education: Principles, Policy & Practice, 7*(1), 61–81. https://doi.org/10.1080/713613318

Cohen, L., Manion, L., Morrison, K., & Wyse, D. (2004). *A guide to teaching practice* (5th ed.). Routledge.

Dais, T. A. (1993). An analysis of transition assessment practices: Do they recognize cultural differences? In T. Dais, N. Meier-Kronick, P. Luft, & F. R. Rusch (Eds.), *Selected readings in transition: Cultural differences, chronic illness, and job matching* (pp. 4–21). Transition Research Institute, University of Illinois Urbana-Champaign.

Dean, K., Moore, D., Peters, K., Jojola, T., & Lacy, A. (Eds.). (2007). *How it is: The native American philosophy of V. F. Cordova.* University of Arizona Press.

Denson, N., & Chang, M. (2009). Racial diversity matters: The impact of diversity-related student engagement and institutional context. *American Educational Research Journal, 46*(2), 322–353. https://doi.org/10.3102/0002831208323278

Dorimé-Williams, M. (2018). Developing socially just practices and policies in assessment. In D. Zerquera, I. Hernández, & J. G. Berumen (Eds.), *Assessment and Social Justice: Pushing Through Paradox* (New Directions for Institutional Research, no. 177, pp. 41–56). Jossey-Bass. https://doi.org/10.1002/ir.20255

Dowd, A. C., & Bensimon, E. M. (2015). *Engaging the "race question": Accountability and equity in U.S. higher education.* Teachers College Press.

Falchikov, N., & Boud, D. (2007). Assessment and emotion: The impact of being assessed. In D. Boud & N. Falchikov (Eds.), *Rethinking assessment in higher education: Learning for the longer term* (pp. 144–155). Routledge.

Ford, D. Y., & Helms, J. E. (2012). Overview and introduction: Testing and assessing African Americans: "Unbiased" tests are still unfair. *The Journal of Negro Education, 81*(3), 186–189. https://doi.org/10.7709/jnegroeducation.81.3.0186

Francis, P., Broughan, C., Foster, C., & Wilson, C. (2020). Thinking critically about learning analytics, student outcomes, and equity of attainment. *Assessment & Evaluation in Higher Education, 45*(6), 811–821. https://doi.org/10.1080/0260 2938.2019.1691975

Gallagher, C. W. (2007). *Reclaiming assessment: A better alternative to the accountability agenda.* Heinemann.

Gansemer-Topf, A. M., Wilson, J., & Kirk, M. (2019). Numbers may not lie, but they can hide: Critically examining our "number" narratives. *AALHE Intersection,* 5–10. https://www.aalhe.org/assets/docs/Intersection/AAHLE_fall_2019_ Intersection_final.pdf

Garrett, H. E. (1937). *Statistics in psychology and education* (2nd ed.). Longmans, Green.

Georges, C. T., Jr. (2020, April). Establishing culturally responsive pedagogical practices via 'storytelling'. *Feature on Research and Leadership, 5*(3), 1–7. University of Illinois, Office of Community College Research and Leadership. https://occrl .illinois.edu/docs/librariesprovider4/briefs---non-project/establishing- responsive-pedagogical-practices-via-storytelling.pdf

Gipps, C. (1995). What do we mean by equity in relation to assessment? *Assessment in Education: Principles, Policy, & Practice, 2*(3), 271–281. https://doi .org/10.1080/0969595950020303

Gipps, C., & Murphy, P. (1994). *A fair test? Assessment, achievement and equity.* Open University Press.

Green, R. L., & Griffore, R. J. (1980). The impact of standardized testing on minority students. *The Journal of Negro Education, 49*(3), 238–252. https://www.jstor .org/stable/pdf/2967240.pdf

Hanson, J. M. (2019). Feminist evaluation: A theoretical framework for culturally responsive higher education assessment. *AALHE Intersection,* 28–32. https:// www.aalhe.org/assets/docs/Intersection/AAHLE_fall_2019_Intersection_final .pdf

Harrison, L. M., & Hatfield Price, M. (2017). *Interrupting class inequality in higher education: Leadership for an equitable future.* Routledge.

Jankowski, N. A. (2017). Moving toward a philosophy of assessment. *Assessment Update, 29*(3), 10–11. https://doi.org/10.1002/au.30096

Jankowski, N. A. (2020a). *Assessment during a crisis: Responding to a global pandemic.* University of Illinois and Indiana University, National Institute for Learning Outcomes Assessment. https://www.learningoutcomesassessment.org/wp- content/uploads/2020/08/2020-COVID-Survey.pdf

Jankowski, N. A. (2020b). *Activity: What is your student affairs philosophy of assessment?* University of Illinois and Indiana University, National Institute for Learning Outcomes Assessment. https://www.learningoutcomesassessment.org/ wp-content/uploads/2020/11/Philosophy-Activity_SA.pdf

Jankowski, N. A. (2020c). *Activity: What is your philosophy of assessment?* University of Illinois and Indiana University, National Institute for Learning Outcomes Assessment. https://www.learningoutcomesassessment.org/wp-content/uploads/2020/05/Philosophy-Activity.pdf

Jankowski, N. A., & Baker, G. R. (2019). Movement afoot: Fostering discourse on assessment scholarship. In S. P. Hundley & S. Khan (Eds.), *Trends in assessment: Ideas, opportunities, and issues for higher education* (pp. 19–32). Stylus.

Jankowski, N. A., Timmer, J. D., Kinzie, J., & Kuh, G. D. (2018, January). *Assessment that matters: Trending toward practices that document authentic student learning.* University of Illinois and Indiana University, National Institute for Learning Outcomes Assessment. https://www.learningoutcomesassessment.org/wp-content/uploads/2019/02/2018SurveyReport.pdf

Kane, M. (2010). Validity and fairness. *Language Testing, 27*(2), 177–182. https://doi.org/10.1177%2F0265532209349467

Kohn, A. (2000, September 27). Standardized testing and its victims. *Education Week.* https://www.alfiekohn.org/article/standardized-testing-victims/

Koshino, K. (2016). Campus racial climate and experiences of students of color in a midwestern college. In F. Tuitt, C. Haynes, & S. Stewart (Eds.), *Race, equity, and the learning environment: The global relevance of critical and inclusive pedagogies in higher education* (pp. 98–111). Stylus.

Leathwood, C. (2005). Assessment policy and practice in higher education: Purpose, standards and equity. *Assessment & Evaluation in Higher Education, 30*(3), 307–324. https://doi.org/10.1080/02602930500063876

Logli, C. (2019). Culturally responsive assessment 2.0: Revisiting the quest for equity and quality in student learning. *Research and Practice in Assessment, 14,* 19–31. https://www.rpajournal.com/culturally-responsive-assessment-2-0-revisiting-the-quest-for-equity-and-quality-in-student-learning/

Maki, P. L. (2017). *Real-time student assessment: Meeting the imperative for improved time to degree, closing the opportunity gap, and assuring student competencies for 21st-century needs.* Stylus.

Margolis, E. (Ed.). (2001). *The hidden curriculum in higher education.* Routledge.

Maruyama, G., & Moreno, J. F. (2000). *University faculty views about the value of diversity on campus and in the classroom.* American Council on Education and American Association of University Professors. https://files.eric.ed.gov/fulltext/ED444409.pdf

Montenegro, E., & Jankowski, N. A. (2020, January). *A new decade for assessment: Embedding equity into assessment praxis* (Occasional Paper No. 42). University of Illinois and Indiana University, National Institute for Learning Outcomes Assessment. https://www.learningoutcomesassessment.org/wp-content/uploads/2020/01/A-New-Decade-for-Assessment.pdf

Palucki Blake, L., Vallejo Peña, E., Akiyama, D., Braker, E., Maeda, D. K., McDonald, M. A., North, G., Swift, J., Tamada, M., & Yoshino, K. (2012). Faculty learning and reflection from student interviews. In E. M. Bensimon & L. Malcolm (Eds.), *Confronting equity issues on campus: Implementing the equity scorecard in theory and practice* (pp. 96–116). Stylus.

Pierce, C. (1989). Unity in diversity: Thirty-three years of stress. In G. Berry & J. Asamen (Eds.), *Black students: Psychological issues and academic achievement* (pp. 296–312). SAGE.

Quaye, S. J., Tambascia, T. P., & Talesh, R. A. (2009). Engaging racial/ethnic minority students in predominantly white classroom environments. In S. R. Harper & S. J. Quaye (Eds.), *Student engagement in higher education: Theoretical perspectives and practical approaches for diverse populations* (pp. 157–178). Routledge.

Roberts, J. (2019). An argument for employing an equity mindset in higher education assessment. *AALHE Intersection*, 11–15. https://www.aalhe.org/assets/docs/Intersection/AAHLE_fall_2019_Intersection_final.pdf

Sacks, P. (1997). Standardized testing: Meritocracy's crooked yardstick. *Change: The Magazine of Higher Learning, 29*(2), 24–31. https://doi.org/10.1080/00091389709603101

Sandoval, J., Frisby, C. L., Geisinger, K. F., Scheuneman, J. D., & Grenier, J. R. (Eds.). (1998). *Test interpretation and diversity: Achieving equity in assessment.* American Psychological Association. https://psycnet.apa.org/doi/10.1037/10279-000

Shotton, H. J., Lowe, S. C., & Waterman, S. J. (2013). Introduction. In H. J. Shotton, S. C. Lowe, & S. J. Waterman (Eds.), *Beyond the asterisk: Understanding Native students in higher education* (pp. 1–24). Stylus.

Smith, D. G. (2015). *Diversity's promise for higher education: Making it work* (2nd ed.). Johns Hopkins University Press.

Stowell, M. (2004). Equity, justice and standards: Assessment decision making in higher education. *Assessment & Evaluation in Higher Education, 29*(4), 495–510. https://doi.org/10.1080/0260293031000168905

Taras, M. (2006). Do unto others or not: Equity in feedback for undergraduates. *Assessment & Evaluation in Higher Education, 31*(3), 365–377. https://doi.org/10.1080/02602930500353038

Tharp, D. S. (2019). Cultural consciousness in data-driven efforts: Why it matters and how to do it. *AALHE Intersection*, 20–23. https://www.aalhe.org/assets/docs/Intersection/AAHLE_fall_2019_Intersection_final.pdf

Tkatchov, M. (2019). Equity in "authentic" assessments: A closer look at defining and assessing learning outcomes in competency-based education. *AALHE Intersection*, 16–19. https://www.aalhe.org/assets/docs/Intersection/AAHLE_fall_2019_Intersection_final.pdf

Vaccaro, A., & Newman, B. M. (2016). Development of a sense of belonging for privileged and minoritized students: An emergent model. *Journal of College Student Development, 57*(8), 925–942. https://doi.org/10.1353/csd.2016.0091

Verschelden, C. (2017). *Bandwidth recovery: Helping students reclaim cognitive resources lost to poverty, racism, and social marginalization.* Stylus.

Wiliam, D., Klenowski, V., & Rueda, R. (2010). What counts as evidence of educational achievement? The role of constructs in the pursuit of equity in assessment. *Review of Research in Education, 34*(1), 254–284. https://doi.org/10.3102%2F0091732X09351544

Winkelmes, M. (2016). *Helping faculty use assessment data to provide more equilearning experiences.* University of Illinois and Indiana University, National Institute for Learning Outcomes Assessment. https://www.learningoutcomesassessment. org/wp-content/uploads/2019/08/Viewpoint-Winkelmes.pdf

Winkelmes, M. (2019). Why it works: Understanding the concepts behind transparency in learning and teaching. In M. Winkelmes, A. Boye, & S. Tapp (Eds.), *Transparent design in higher education teaching and leadership: A guide to implementing the transparency framework institution-wide to improve learning and retention* (pp. 17–35). Stylus.

Zerquera, D., Hernández, I., & Berumen, J. (2018). Editor's notes: Introduction. In *Assessment and Social Justice: Pushing Through Paradox* (New Directions for Institutional Research, no. 177, pp. 7–14). Jossey-Bass. https://doi.org/10.1002/ ir.20253

Zerquera, D., Reyes, K. A., Pender, J. T., & Abbady, R. (2018). Understanding practitioner-driven assessment and evaluation efforts for social justice. In D. Zerquera, I. Hernández, & J. G. Berumen (Eds.), *Assessment and Social Justice: Pushing Through Paradox* (New Directions for Institutional Research, no. 177, pp. 15–40). Jossey-Bass. https://doi.org/10.1002/ir.20254

PART TWO

WHAT?

4

CURRENT STATE OF SCHOLARSHIP ON ASSESSMENT

Gianina R. Baker and Gavin W. Henning

All education is political; teaching is never a neutral act.

—Paulo Freire, *Pedagogy of the Oppressed* (1968/1970, p. 19)

Equity-minded or equity-centered assessment is an evolving concept in higher education. With the evolution of the concept comes evolution in the terminology used. Language for equity-minded and related types of assessment include antiracist assessment, bias-free assessment, critical assessment, culturally relevant assessment, culturally responsive assessment, culturally responsive evaluation, decolonizing assessment, deconstructed assessment, equity-centered assessment, Indigenous assessment, mindful assessment, socially just assessment, and universal design for learning (UDL) assessment. These terms comprise a constellation of similar concepts, which all have nuanced differences, and ultimately work toward justice in our postsecondary education systems.

In this chapter, the authors synthesize the current scholarship regarding equity-minded related assessment to provide a landscape of the current literature in the field. Each topic is listed in alphabetical order and readers may choose to focus on specific sections or read the chapter in its entirety.

Antiracist Assessment

Antiracist assessment, informed by critical race theory, incorporates antiracist pedagogy and "focuses more in-depth on the analysis of structural racism, power relations, and social justice" (Kishimoto, 2018, p. 540). Antiracist assessment mutually uses and centers the negotiation of learning and knowledge production between faculty and students. Instead of the banking philosophy as described by Freire (1968/1970), antiracist assessment forces us to ask, "what counts as legitimate truth" (Collins, 2009, p. 230) and pushes into questions of "whose knowledge counts, and who has access to the knowledge" (Kishomoto, 2018, p. 546). This scholarship builds on foundational work of studying and researching antiracist educational systems which has over a 15-year history and used Whiteness studies and concepts such as colorblindness to help define principles, elements, and so forth of antiracist education (Niemonen, 2007).

Antiracist teaching, also used interchangeably with antiracist pedagogy, allows for antiracist assessment. Antiracist pedagogy as acknowledged by Kishimoto (2018) "focuses on the process of learning, not necessarily making students reach a uniform and prescribed outcome" (p. 546). Further, "[a]nti-racist teaching challenges the Eurocentric curriculum and the apolitical and ahistorical approaches to education, discipline, and course materials" (p. 546) by encouraging faculty to coconstruct syllabi, assignments, and assessment with students in the hopes of diminishing the historical power differential between the two groups. Thus, for faculty to engage in antiracist pedagogy practice, self-reflection is necessary; however, as Chew et al. (2020) described, "[r]eflective journaling or discussion alone will not provide the comprehensive historical, sociopolitical economic, and cultural context required to engage more broadly in anti-racist discussion" (p. 21) for students and faculty. Additionally, Chew et al.'s (2020) antiracist discussion pedagogy guide centers the antiracist practices and policies of three faculty members of which include:

> setting clear communication guidelines and discussion intentions for students, planning reflective writing assignments that help students engage with their own ideas before class, thinking through how to respond to possible scenarios that might come up—like a student using an anachronistic or offensive term—as well as readying themselves to model vulnerability by sharing personal stories when relevant. (Weissman, 2020)

Antiracist pedagogy is necessary for antiracist assessment to be an effective indicator of learning for various student populations. Many of the practices used in antiracist pedagogy are applied to antiracist assessment.

Inoue (2019), in working toward an antiracist assessment process specific to the discipline of writing, describes seven elements that create a "writing assessment ecology, or living network," used to formatively assess student work (p. 377). These elements include power, purposes, processes, parts, products, people, and places (Inoue, 2019). As Inoue (2019) explains

> To make a writing assessment ecology antiracist, then, we must find ways to see, critique, and use the dominant, white, middle-class discourse of the classroom for the benefit of all students in the classroom, which means it cannot be the standard against which all are measured. (p. 377)

Or another way is to help students to "see, critique," and explain the "compounded effects of various dimensions of oppression" (Inoue, 2019, p. 374). Inoue's focus on power, purposes, processes, parts, products, people, and places is informative to antiracist assessment with specific attention paid to critiquing dominant, White, middle-class discourse in higher education and using this as the standard for comparison.

Bias-Free Assessment

Bias-free assessment is rooted in assessment of student learning, particularly in primary and secondary education and is focused on bias in testing. Popham (2012) defined *assessment bias* as the presence of "one or more items on a test that offend or unfairly penalize students because of those students' personal characteristics such as race, gender, socioeconomic status, or religion" (p. 6). For Popham (2012), the two main components of bias-free assessment include test items that do not offend and test items that do not penalize students. By eliminating bias in testing, measurements and interpretations of student learning are more accurate (Popham, 2012). However, Popham warned readers that disparate scores on tests for different racial/ethnic student groups does not necessarily suggest bias in the testing instrument. Rather, disparate outcomes could be a result of poor instruction for certain student populations. While there may still be bias and discrimination, this results from the education students receive, not the testing instrument.

Lundquist and Henning (2020) defined bias-free assessment similarly to Popham (2012) with the attention on surveys and similar data collection tools, but expanded assessment to be of student learning, program effectiveness, or some other type of assessment. Bias-free assessment removes cultural and contextual biases so that these do not affect the assessment process (Lundquist & Henning, 2020).

Popham (2012) and Lundquist and Henning (2020) identified a handful of strategies for bias-free assessment. Popham's (2012) tactics center on bias detection in tests of student learning. Bias can be reduced through test review panels using experts or peers or empirical analysis test items. Lundquist and Henning (2020) suggested that data collection instructions be clear and the data collection itself ideally should take place in a neutral location. In addition, survey response options should be inclusive. Lundquist and Henning (2020) also identified the use of student, expert, or peer reviewers can reduce bias in surveys, similar to Popham's (2012) bias detection process. In sum, bias-free assessment relates specifically to tests, surveys, and similar data collection tools with the goal of reducing bias in those instruments to ensure fairness for participants.

Critical Assessment

Critical assessment literature and practice is grounded in disciplines of "library information science, student affairs assessment, institutional and educational research, feminist and indigenous methods, and critical data studies" (Magnus et al., 2018, para. 6). Critical assessment centers critical theory, or crit theory, which is used by researchers and scholar practitioners to question, critique, and, hopefully, emancipate our assumptions of various parts of the systems in which we live (Magnus et al., 2018). According to Benjes-Small et al. (2019), critical assessment "pushes us to consider the roles of power and privilege in the design of our learning measurement methods, and to give voice to the people involved with the assessment" (para. 1) where such practice "perceives everyone involved with assessment—from the people designing and performing the assessment to those who are being assessed—as individuals affected by social, political, and economic drivers, and seeks to account for those factors in societal change" (para. 1).

While critical assessment is still being defined, some scholars have started to outline its concepts, both in academic and student affairs. For instance, DeLuca Fernández (2015) acknowledges four principles of critical assessment:

- expose and address power, privilege, and structures;
- consider thoughtfully histories and contexts;
- make explicit assumptions and intentions; and
- eschew colorblind and ideological neutral claims (p. 5).

Realizing that traditional power dynamics between faculty and students continue to exist and oppress those for whom the educational system was not designed, critical assessment explicitly centers on the faculty/researcher and if done well "become[s] transformative for all students by considering the positionality of the evaluator, recognizing agency of the participants, employing methodological diversity, and extending analysis strategies" (Heiser et al., 2017, pp. 2–3). If, like teaching, assessment is viewed as social and political as Freire (1968/1970) argues, it is inherent that the power and privilege of approaches, practices, and so forth be unhidden and lay bare. And if equity-focused assessment is the goal, critical assessment of approaches, practices, and so forth is necessary work.

Culturally Responsive Assessment

Culturally responsive assessment (CRA), often interchangeable with culturally relevant assessment, has roots within culturally responsive evaluation (CRE), a space ripe with research and literature. CRE has beginnings in Stake's (1975) early work on program evaluation but has been more fully defined through the years. CRE, as defined by Hopson (2009), is:

> a theoretical, conceptual, and inherently political position that includes the centrality of and [attunement] to culture in the theory and practice of evaluation. That is, CRE recognizes that demographic, sociopolitical, and contextual dimensions, locations, perspectives, and characteristics of culture matter fundamentally in evaluation. (p. 431)

Evaluation elements of context, purpose, audience, questions, design and methods, criteria for judging program quality, judgments and recommendations, reporting, and utilization are central to conducting and implementing CRE with fidelity (Hood et al., 2015).

Montenegro and Jankowski (2017) began to aggregate literature and examples of assessment practice to begin defining CRA. Several practitioners responded to the paper to help further describe and refine CRA around principles, assumptions, definitions, and frameworks (Felder, 2017; Levy & Heiser, 2018; Roberts, 2019; Rudnick, 2019). For instance, Laird and BrckaLorenz (2017) proposed culturally responsive principles that include the following:

- CRA accounts for students' multiple cultures.
- CRA uses varied techniques sensitive to the varied ways students describe and demonstrate their experience, knowledge, and learning.
- CRA seeks just judgments based on collected information.

Further, Singer-Freeman et al. (2019) proposed a *Theoretical Matrix of Culturally Relevant Assessment* which has been tested for cultural relevance in college classrooms.

It is negligent to not discuss culturally relevant teaching/pedagogy and its influence on current work in this discussion of CRE and CRA. Ladson-Billings (1995a, 1995b) coined the term culturally relevant pedagogy, and has since built on its original framework to encompass a new term, culturally sustaining pedagogy, where faculty and scholar-practitioners

> layer the multiple ways that this notion of pedagogy shifts, changes, adapts, recycles, and recreates instructional spaces to ensure that consistently marginalized students are repositioned into a place of normativity—that is, that they become subjects in the instructional process, not mere objects. (Ladson-Billings, 2014, p. 76)

To do this work, whether it be culturally relevant pedagogy and/or CRA, requires strong cultural competence of faculty and staff (Hood et al., 2005; Hopson, 2003; SenGupta et al., 2004). For example, this work involves

> question[ing] yourself about whether your assessments are responsive to students' learning in the classroom and respectful of their culture . . . collaborating with families and inviting them in to creat[e] assessments . . . invit[ing] your peers to talk about the assessments that you are using . . . [to] learn from one another and best aid in the growth and development of our students. (Gibson, 2020, para. 12)

Culturally relevant and responsive assessment, with its roots in CRE, has laid the scholarly and praxis foundation for equity-centered assessment.

Decolonized and Indigenous Assessment

Decolonized and Indigenous assessment requires the exploring of how to decolonize higher education as well as integrate Indigenous perspectives including Indigenous ways of knowing and Indigenous knowledge systems.

Colonization, Decolonization, and Indigenization

Much of the scholarship regarding decolonized and Indigenous approaches refers to research and evaluation. Since assessment is influenced by research and evaluation, this scholarship can and has been applied to assessment.

Before understanding decolonization and Indigenization, colonization must be defined. Chilisa (2012) described colonization as an attempt by the Western world to order the whole world according to Western culture, politics, and economic structures and policies. Queens University Centre for Teaching and Learning (n.d.) stated that colonization involves one group taking the lands, resources, languages, cultures, and relationships of another group. Western philosophical paradigms dominate colleges and universities and devalue Indigenous ways of knowing (Louie et al., 2017). The colonial oppression that has taken place in larger society also exists in research methodologies (Louie et al., 2017) that are applied to assessment practice. If colonization is the dominance of Western values and culture, decolonization is the removal of Western influences. Indigenization takes decolonization one step further through the addition of Indigenous elements to assessment, research, and evaluation practices (Queens University Centre for Teaching and Learning, n.d.) and adapting of conventional research approaches by including paradigms and methods that have been colonized and marginalized rather than dismissing these conventional approaches (Chilisa, 2012).

Decolonization and Indigenization centers Indigenous ways of knowing, which value interconnectivity, reciprocity, and taking ecology and place into account (Eizadirad, 2019). Kawakami et al. (2007) stated that decolonizing methodologies recenter Indigenous peoples within their own lands. Wilson (2008) contended that ideas and people are connected to each other, the earth, and the cosmos; that knowledge is relational and shared and cannot be owned or discovered by any one person; and equity, equality, and inclusion are key tenets of Indigenous paradigms. These tenets are key elements in Indigenous approaches to assessment and evaluation.

Applying an Indigenous lens to assessment and evaluation practice challenges understanding of knowledge creation and the effect of a given cultural context on knowledge creation (Hood et al., 2015). Furthermore, using Indigenous approaches requires critiques of traditional concepts of validity, which is a mainstay of research, assessment, and evaluation. While there are more complex definitions and explanations of validity, Cushman (2016) succinctly stated that validity is an assumption regarding what is valid or credible evidence and is rooted in colonialism and imperialism. Colonizing populations employed validity as a tool for oppression by determining what knowledge was acceptable (Cushman, 2016) because knowledge from dominant populations was valid while knowledge from colonized populations was not. Because validity is a requirement of rigor in research, the concept has reified social, linguistic, and knowledge hierarchies that perpetuated power and oppression (Cushman, 2016) and its use as a controlling mechanism is present today.

To dismantle systems of power and oppression in research methodologies, which influence assessment methods, the concept of validity must be interrogated and Indigenous ways of knowing must be validated. However, Lopez (2020) suggested strategies for Indigenous data collection that support post-positivist paradigms while still centering Indigenous voices. A primary challenge in quantitative data collection with Indigenous populations is the sample size. To address this challenge, Lopez (2020) suggested combining tribes with similar creation stories into one sample for collection and analysis. He argues that tribes having similar creation stories have similar values and customs, making it appropriate to combine the two tribes into the same sample. Combining two tribes to address issues in quantitative approaches to research and assessment supports Indigenous ways of knowing.

Indigenous Knowledge and Ways of Knowing

Brant-Castellano (1997) described three types of Indigenous knowledge: traditional knowledge handed down through generations; revealed knowledge acquired through dreams, visions, and spiritual protocol; and empirical knowledge gained through careful observation from multiple perspectives. Grenier (1998) extended the concept by identifying six characteristics of Indigenous knowledge: (a) Indigenous knowledge is cumulative over generations; (b) it is dynamic with new knowledge being added and adapted to local contexts; (c) all members of a community (elders, women, men, and children) have Indigenous knowledge; (d) the quantity and quality of Indigenous knowledge that an individual possesses varies by age, gender, experiences, and roles; (e) Indigenous knowledge is stored in memories and expressed through stories, songs, dances, rituals, and language; and (f) Indigenous knowledge is shared and communicated orally and by example through cultural practices and rituals. Indigenous knowledge and ways of knowing provide enlightening perspectives on the world that complement and provide contrast to Western perspectives. However, these Indigenous viewpoints have rarely been incorporated into Western research and assessment paradigms.

White supremacy permeates assessment and evaluation systems (Beriont, 2020) and ignoring the role of imperialism and colonization in the construction of knowledge is a shortcoming of Western research (and assessment) paradigms (Chilisa, 2012). A decolonizing approach to assessment acknowledges equity among all people and values multiple ways of knowing (Cushman, 2016). Assessment and evaluation utilizing an Indigenous paradigm must address power and imbalance resulting from colonization (Hood et al., 2015). To use assessment and evaluation for equity, evaluators and assessors must reflect on what knowledge is privileged and understand the politics and oppression of knowledge creation (Cram, 2016).

Indigenous and Decolonizing Assessment

Ways of knowing inform assessment methods and the process of data gathering and must allow participants to share their experiences in their own terms (Chilisa, 2012; Hood et al., 2015). Scholars have identified how Indigenous and decolonized evaluation and assessment can be implemented. To begin, assessors must take a critical colonial worldview (Cram, 2016) examining the lasting impact of colonization on society and higher education. Second, assessors must acknowledge the sovereignty of Indigenous peoples (Cram, 2016; LaFrance & Nichols, 2010) and reflect upon whose agenda is being served by a particular assessment with the population being assessed having ownership in the process (Chilisa, 2012; Cram, 2016; LaFrance & Nichols, 2010). Assessors must also recognize their insider/outsider status and the power and motivations assessors bring to assessment and evaluation (LaFrance & Nichols, 2010). Indigenous or decolonizing assessment must center on the root causes of the issue being assessed (Cram, 2016) as context for the evaluation is critical to understanding the phenomenon (Chilisa, 2012; Kawakami et al., 2007).

To decolonize means to use the standards of good assessment practice that are defined by local values and protocols, not Western paradigms and expectations (Hood et al., 2015; Nelson-Barber & Trumbull, 2017). Sense of place is vital to Indigenous assessment because knowledge arises out of people's relationships and interactions with their particular environment (Cushman, 2016). The concept of time is treated differently in Indigenous assessment (LaFrance & Nichols, 2010) as such an approach to assessment requires looking forward and backward, beyond the present moment and this nonlinearity influences data collection (Hood et al., 2015). In addition, prayer and ceremony play a critical role in Indigenous assessment (LaFrance & Nichols, 2010). Wilson (2008) described research as ceremony and used this metaphor to define his Indigenous research paradigm.

Assessment, evaluation, and research in higher education are rooted in colonized paradigms that ignore Indigenous ways of knowing. Decolonizing and Indigenizing assessment leverages Indigenous ways of knowing and methods to validate non-Western paradigms and expand the approaches and methods assessors have.

Deconstructed Assessment

Deconstructed assessment is assessment used as a vehicle to dismantle systems of power and oppression and is built upon poststructuralism, which is a philosophical paradigm extended from critical theory (Henning, 2019).

The central tenet of poststructuralism is that systems of power and oppression in society are perpetuated through social structures (Peters & Burbules, 2004) which include policies, practices, norms, social institutions, and so on. Deconstruction exposes the social structures that advance oppression as a first step in dismantling them (Agger, 2003). By applying this concept of deconstruction to assessment, deconstructed assessment is thus an approach that uses assessment to expose these social structures (Henning, 2019) with a focus on what phenomena are being assessed, not just how they are assessed.

There are five tenets of deconstructed assessment:

1. Assessment as inquiry (Bourke, 2017) is the first characteristic of deconstructed assessment. Inquiry requires reflection.
2. A second characteristic of deconstructed assessment is an activist/social change approach to assessment to uncover power and relation issues inherent in social structures that impact various phenomena but also to effect change to dismantle oppression through assessment.
3. Third is an increased emphasis on the use of qualitative assessment methods.
4. A fourth characteristic of deconstructed assessment is student involvement in the assessment process.
5. A fifth characteristic of deconstructed assessment is what Montenegro and Jankowski (2017) call cultural responsiveness, a pedagogy where instructors use an asset-based approach to teaching that includes students' cultures. (Henning, 2019)

While deconstructed assessment was originally conceived as a stand-alone concept, Lundquist and Henning (2020) incorporated it as one step in their equity-minded assessment continuum as a transition point between socially just assessment, which is assessment implemented in an equitable manner and the final step of the continuum, assessment for social justice in which assessment is a method to further social justice.

Socially Just Assessment

Many authors apply Bell's (2007) definition of social justice to assessment arguing that socially just assessment is both process and product (Henning & Lundquist, 2018; McArthur, 2016; Zerquera et al., 2018). The argument continues that assessment should be implemented in an equitable manner so that it does not perpetuate oppression, but also that assessment can be a vehicle for promoting social justice if implemented with the goal of dismantling systems of power and oppression. While McArthur (2016) and Zerquera et al. (2018) combined both prongs of process and product into a single definition of socially just assessment, Henning and Lundquist (2018) separated out these two goals in their continuum of equity-centered assessment. Socially just assessment is the implementation of assessment in a just and equitable way whereas assessment for social justice (a separate step in the continuum than socially just assessment) regards assessment being a vehicle for equity. For Henning and Lundquist (2018), socially just assessment is a broad umbrella approach to assessment that does not necessarily apply to specific types of assessment such as student learning or program evaluation. Broadly, socially just assessment is a transformative approach to assessment that seeks to dismantle the systems of power and oppression in higher education (Dorimé-Williams, 2018; Henning & Lundquist, 2018; McArthur, 2016).

A Framework for Equity-Centered Assessment

In the previous sections we summarized the individual concepts and approaches to address equity in assessment. In this section, we outline the current landscape of scholarship by discussing the ways in which scholars are pulling together individual concepts, making sense between and across them. We conclude the section with emerging concepts.

In their second of two occasional papers, Montenegro and Jankowski (2020) moved from what they term CRA to equity-minded assessment. Using CRE and equity-mindedness, the authors thus conceptualized that equity-minded assessment centers the term *equity-mindedness* coined by Bensimon (2018) who explained equity-mindedness "requires explicit attention to structural inequality and institutionalized racism and demands system-changing responses" (p. 97).

In the many conversations that ensued after their first occasional paper, Montenegro and Jankowski (2020) built on the previous concept of CRA to conceptualize equity-minded assessment to include the following:

- "Check biases and ask reflective questions throughout the assessment process to address assumptions and positions of privilege.
- Use multiple sources of evidence appropriate for the students being assessed and assessment effort.
- Include student perspectives and take action based on perspectives.
- Increase transparency in assessment results and actions taken.

- Ensure collected data can be meaningfully disaggregated and interrogated.
- Make evidence-based changes that address issues of equity that are context-specific." (p. 13)

The authors argue that equity-minded assessment employs an equity lens through which to view assessment. Equity-centered assessment is just that—where equity is at the center of assessment—as a goal for assessment that works toward addressing inequity and changing systems that perpetuate oppression. The authors are not arguing that all assessment should be equity-minded or equity-centered assessment as there are other types of assessment that are critical in higher education. However, assessors should consider how they can employ assessment to address inequity.

Building on the work of Montenegro and Jankowski (2017), Popham (2012), McArthur (2016, 2017), and Henning (2019), Lundquist and Henning (2020) developed a framework for understanding different types of equity-centered assessment to help them understand and organize the various concepts. This six-component continuum of equity-centered assessment ranged from minimally doing no harm through assessment to using assessment for social justice. The steps are:

- *do no harm assessment*—where the focus is on not doing harm through the assessment process
- *bias-free assessment*—in which assessors reduce bias in the assessment process
- *CRA*—which considers students' culture and backgrounds (Montenegro & Jankowski, 2017)
- *socially just assessment*—where the focus is on implementing assessment in a socially just manner
- *deconstructed assessment*—in which assessment is used to expose social structures that perpetuate oppression
- *assessment for social justice*—in which assessment is used as a strategy to advance social justice

As noted earlier, many authors apply Bell's (2007) definition of social justice to assessment arguing that socially just assessment is both process and product (Henning & Lundquist, 2018; McArthur, 2016; Zerquera et al., 2018). While McArthur (2016) and Zerquera et al. (2018) conceptualize socially just assessment as both process and project, Henning and Lundquist (2020) separate these functions into steps in their continuum. *Socially just assessment* is the act of implementing assessment in an equitable way whereas *assessment for social justice* is the use of assessment to advance equity. As new forms of equity-centered assessment emerge, Lundquist and Henning's (2020) model should be revised. While traditional assessment approaches place responsibility on the student, the approaches focused on in this chapter center the positionality of the assessor. To understand more about what is meant here, see chapter 18, (this volume), on developing individual awareness.

Future Directions

There are a few emerging topics related to equity-centered assessment that provide further opportunities to integrate equity into assessment. These topics include feminist assessment, healing-centered assessment, mindful assessment, and UDL.

Feminist Assessment

There is little scholarship surrounding feminist assessment currently. An article from 1996 written by Elana Michelson discussed assessment of prior experiential learning in relation to feminist epistemology and gendered natures of knowledge. Michelson posited that by privileging certain experiences over others and accepting theories and epistemologies as facts as opposed to critiquing, we do not acknowledge "that experience is gendered and that knowledge is differently valued when produced by women and men [which] can be applied concretely across the full range of current assessment activities, up to and including the awarding of credit" (p. 647). Shapiro (1992) outlined nine principles to help conceptualize feminist assessment:

1. Feminist assessment questions almost everything related to evaluation.
2. Feminist assessment is student-centered.
3. Feminist assessment is participatory.
4. Feminist assessment is deeply affected by its context or institutional culture.
5. Feminist assessment is decentered.
6. Feminist assessment approaches should be compatible with feminist activist beliefs.
7. Feminist assessment is heavily shaped by the power of feminist pedagogy.
8. Feminist assessment is based on a body of feminist scholarship and feminist research methodology that is central to this interdisciplinary area.
9. Feminist assessment appreciates values.

Similarly, Brisolara and Whitmore (2002) outlined the tenets of feminist evaluation. In their chapter in a special edition of New Directions for Evaluation titled *Feminist Evaluation: Explorations and Experiences*, the tenets they offered included the following:

- Feminist evaluation focuses on gender inequities.
- Gender discrimination and inequality is systemic and structural.
- Evaluation is a political activity, and the perspectives of evaluators lead to a particular political stance.
- Knowledge is a powerful resource that serves explicit and implicit purposes and should be a resource shared.
- Knowledge and values are contingent upon culture and time.
- There are multiple ways of knowing.

In *Feminist Evaluation and Research: Theory and Practice* (2014), Brisolara et al. provide a more comprehensive coverage of the topic. With a foundation in feminist scholarship, feminist pedagogy, and feminist research methodology, despite the limited literature, feminist assessment certainly has merits in such equity-centered assessment conversations. In fact, recent conversations pushing on feminism to that of intersectional feminism may lend itself even more to acting on data and power in the field of assessment (D'Ignazio & Klein, 2020).

Healing-Centered Assessment

Healing-centered assessment is a relatively new concept in assessment. Healing-centered assessment builds on the concepts of trauma-centered and trauma-informed assessment as they are much more researched and documented in the literature, especially K–12 (Carello & Butler, 2014; Crosby et al., 2018; Reeves, 2019). Using trauma-informed pedagogy as a reference point allows for a wider literature base to inform healing-centered assessment, including concepts, frameworks, practices, and so on. That said, Ginwright (2018) encourages educators to reframe trauma to that of healing. Moving from a trauma-centered to a healing-centered approach allows us to

> view trauma not simply as an individual isolated experience, but rather highlights the ways in which trauma and healing are experienced collectively. The term healing centered engagement expands how we think about responses to trauma and offers [a] more holistic approach to fostering well-being. (para. 10)

Most recently, Jankowski (2020) conceptualizes how the two work together:

> Coupled with trauma-informed and healing-centered pedagogy and assessment, faculty and staff can partner with students as producers of content, experts of their lived experience, and be active partners in solving the problem of demonstrating complex learning during a pandemic. (p. 27)

That said, we are currently imagining and creating what healing-centered assessment could look like in postsecondary education during this pandemic and hope that assessment practitioners, faculty, and staff are documenting healing-centered practices that work for their students and their needs.

Mindful Assessment

Mindfulness as a concept has become more popularized over the past decade in a variety of disciplines. The field of assessment is no exception and has benefited from such conversations. Consilio and Kennedy (2019) describe the relationship between mindfulness and assessment as one where "[m]indfulness, or present-moment awareness, and its associated qualities of calm/relaxation, nonjudgement, intentionality, concentration, and compassion, are increasingly being used to help cultivate self-awareness, attention, and optimal learning experiences" (p. 28).

Cocreating such learning experiences, as Consilio and Kennedy (2019) did with their Mindful Grading Agreement Process, assists students in their reflection or inquiry process while also assisting faculty in evaluating writing across disciplines. It has been well-studied that reflection is considered an authentic assessment practice, thus, any attention minded to such work can only amplify the benefit. If assessment is viewed as inquiry, then reflection, or mindfulness, is inherent to this process

Thus, the term mindful assessment is in the beginning stages of conceptualization for assessment practitioners and scholars. Using mindful assessment to promote creative learning (Watts, 2016), there is much to be learned from national and international contexts if we are insistent and intentional in transforming learning environments to be meaningful, compassionate, calm, and nonjudgmental.

Universal Design for Learning

UDL arose from the universal design movement in architecture but focuses on maximizing learning for all students instead of accessibility to physical spaces. UDL extends universal design from a physical space to a pedagogical space (Dolan et al., 2013). UDL is based on neuroscience research suggesting that individual learners differ in their motivation for learning, how they comprehend knowledge, and how they express what they know (Hall et al., 2003). To further student learning, there are three UDL principles: (a) provide multiple means of engagement, (b) provide multiple means of representation, and (c) provide multiple means of action and expression (Hall et al., 2003; Hanesworth et al., 2019). A distinguishing characteristic of UDL is the perspective regarding assessment of student learning. Whereas assessment of learning in a traditional sense focuses on weaknesses of the learner in an attempt to make improvements, assessment in UDL centers on weaknesses and barriers in design of the educational context itself (Rose et al., 2018). UDL takes into account the capabilities each learner brings to the learning environment with the goal of adapting the learning context for all learners and identifying strategies to further learning for each student (Rose et al., 2018). The focus is on the learning environment and is inclusive of each learner.

Knowledge types exist in hierarchies (Hanesworth et al., 2019) and some types of knowledge are deemed more valuable than others. Through assessment methods and content, assessors educate students as to what types of knowledge are important (Hanesworth et al., 2019). A Western hierarchy of knowledge not only privileges some knowledge over others, but it also advantages some student populations over others, perpetuating underlying systems of power and oppression (Lundquist & Henning, 2020). A UDL approach to assessment is a socially just approach as it considers the abilities of each learner and the deficits in the educational environment and system, not the student (Hanesworth et al., 2019). The goal of UDL is not to customize or individualize learning but remove systemic barriers to learning so that all students can learn effectively (Hanesworth et al., 2018). There is emerging literature that outlines how to utilize UDL for assessment (CAST, 2020; Hanesworth et al., 2019; Johnston and Castine, 2019; McConlogue, 2020; Rose et al., 2018).

Conclusion

In this chapter, we synthesized literature to provide a current account of scholarship to date on various assessment approaches working to center equity. We provided frameworks for thinking about the current landscape of equity and assessment efforts and included some of the emerging assessment approaches and practices, such as healing-centered assessment and mindful assessment. We invite you to think about various practices shared in the coming chapters and which approach to assessment is dominant and why. Think about the students they are serving and why that particular approach was chosen.

Further exploring these various concepts of equity-centered assessment and considering which ones could be integrated into assessment practice will allow assessors to have a much better understanding of how to address inequities discussed throughout the book.

Building out each of these assessment approaches and intentionally practicing them allows assessors to have a much better understanding of the needs of students and assessment practitioners in order to address inequities.

References

Agger, B. (2003). Critical theory, poststructuralism, postmodernism: Their sociological relevance. *Annual Review of Sociology, 17,* 105–131. https://doi.org/10.1146/annurev.so.17.080191.000541

Bell, L. A. (2007). Theoretical foundations for social justice education. In M. Adams, L. A. Bell, & P. Griffin (Eds.), *Teaching for diversity and social justice* (2nd ed., pp. 1–14). Routledge.

Benjes-Small, C., Seale, M., Hodges, A. R., & Meiman, M. (2019, June 11). *Keeping up with . . . critical assessment.* http://www.ala.org/acrl/publications/keeping_up_with/critical_assessment

Bensimon, E. M. (2018). Reclaiming racial justice in equity. *Change, 50*(3–4), 95–98. https://doi.org/10.1080/00091383.2018.1509623

Beriont, L. (2020, May 4). *Decolonizing evaluation.* Emergence Collective. https://www.emergencecollective.org/post/decolonizing-evaluation

Bourke, B. (2017). Advancing towards social justice via student affairs inquiry. *Journal of Student Affairs Inquiry, 3*(1), pp. 1–18. https://drive.google.com/file/d/1yIlaAWxyFtD7h5CN_1OVa28XwkMUgz7F/view

Brant-Castellano, M. (1997, May). *Partnership: The key to ethical cross-cultural research* [Conference presentation]. Canadian Evaluation Society, Ottawa, ON.

Brisolara, S., & Whitmore, E. (2002). Exploring feminist evaluation: The ground from which we rise. In D. Siegert & S. Brisolara (Eds.), *Feminist Evaluation: Explorations and Experiences* (New Directions for Evaluation, no. 96, pp. 3–8). Jossey-Bass. https://doi.org/10.1002/ev.62

Brisolara, S., Seigart, D., & SenGupta, S. (Eds). (2014). *Feminist evaluation and research: Theory and practice.* Guilford.

Carello, J., & Butler, L. D. (2014). Potentially perilous pedagogies: Teaching trauma is not the same as trauma-informed teaching. *Journal of Trauma & Dissociation, 15*(2), 153–168. http://dx.doi.org/10.1080/15299732.2014.867571

CAST. (2020). *UDL tips for assessment*. https://www.cast.org/products-services/resources/2020/udl-tips-assessments

Chew, S., Houston, A., & Cooper, A. (2020). *The antiracist discussion pedagogy guide*. https://www.packback.co/resources/anti-racist-discussion-pedagogy-guide/

Chilisa, B. (2012). *Indigenous research methodologies*. SAGE.

Collins, P. H. (2009). *Black feminist thought: Knowledge, consciousness, and the politics of empowerment* (2nd ed.). Routledge.

Consilio, J., & Kennedy, S. M. (2019). Using mindfulness as a heuristic for writing evaluation: Transforming pedagogy and quality of experience. *Across the Disciplines*, *16*(1), 28–49. https://wac.colostate.edu/docs/atd/contemplative/consilio_kennedy2019.pdf

Cram, F. (2016). Lessons on decolonizing evaluation from Kaupapa Maori evaluation. *Canadian Journal of Program Evaluation*, *30*(3), 296–312. https://doi.org/10.3138/cjpe.30.3.04

Crosby, S. D., Howell, P., & Thomas, S. (2018). Social justice education through trauma-informed teaching. *Middle School Journal*, *49*(4), 15–23. https://doi.org/10.1080/00940771.2018.1488470

Cushman, E. (2016). Decolonizing validity. *Journal of Writing Assessment*, *9*(1). http://journalofwritingassessment.org/article.php?article=92

DeLuca Fernández, S. (2015). *Critical assessment* [Webinar]. Student Affairs Assessment Leaders (SAAL). http://studentaffairsassessment.org/files/documents/SAAL-SC-Critical-Assessment-sdf-9-dec-2015-FINAL.pdf

D'Ignazio, C., & Klein, L. F. (2020). *Data feminism*. MIT Press.

Dolan, R. P., Burling, K., Harms, M., Strain-Seymour, E., Way, W., & Rose, D. H. (2013, April). *A universal design for learning-based framework for designing accessible technology-enhanced assessments* [Research report]. Pearson. http://images.pearsonclinical.com/images/tmrs/DolanUDL-TEAFramework_final3.pdf

Dorimé-Williams, M. D. (2018). Developing socially just practices and policies in assessment. In D. Zerquera, I. Hernández, & J. G. Berumen (Eds.), *Assessment and Social Justice: Pushing Through Paradox* (New Directions for Institutional Research, no. 177, pp. 41–56). Jossey-Bass. https://doi.org/10.1002/ir.20255

Eizadirad A. (2019) Decolonizing educational assessment models. In *Decolonizing Educational Assessment* (pp. 203–228). Palgrave Macmillan. https://doi.org/10.1007/978-3-030-27462-7_10

Felder, P. P. (2017, May). *On the importance of culturally responsive assessment* (Equity Response). University of Illinois and Indiana University, National Institute for Learning Outcomes Assessment (NILOA).

Freire, P. (1970). *Pedagogy of the oppressed*. Herder and Herder. (Original work published 1968)

Gibson, V. (2020, February 26). Working toward culturally responsive assessment practices. *Ways to Change the Conversation About Assessment*. NCTE. https://ncte.org/blog/2020/02/working-toward-culturally-responsive-assessment-practices/

Ginwright, S. (2018, May 31). The future of healing: Shifting from trauma informed care to healing centered engagement. *Medium*. https://medium.com/@ginwright/the-future-of-healing-shifting-from-trauma-informed-care-to-healing-centered-engagement-634f557ce69c

Grenier, L. (1998). *Working with indigenous knowledge: A guide for researchers*. International Development Research Centre. https://www.idrc.ca/en/book/working-indigenous-knowledge-guide-researchers

Hall, T., Vue, G., & Mengel, M. (2003). *Curriculum based assessments*. National Center on Accessing the General Curriculum. http://www.cast.org/products-services/resources/2014/ncac-curriculum-based-assessments

Hanesworth P., Bracken, S., & Elkington, S. (2019). A typology for a social just approach to assessing: Learning from universal design and culturally sustaining pedagogy. *Teaching in Higher Education: Critical Perspectives*, *24*(1), 98–114. https://doi.org/10.1080/13562517.2018.1465405

Heiser, C. A., Prince, K., & Levy, J. D. (2017). Examining critical theory as a framework to advance equity through student affairs assessment. *Journal of Student Affairs Inquiry*, *3*(1), 1–17. https://drive.google.com/file/d/1ksQstiXwP51Edipg dylU7nvdenVpIJA-/view

Henning, G. (2019). Using deconstructed assessment to address issues of equity, civility, and safety on college campuses. In P. Magolda, M. Baxter-Magolda, and R. Carducci (Eds.), *Contested issues in student affairs: Diverse perspectives and respectful dialogue*. Stylus.

Henning, G., & Lundquist, A. E. (2018). *Moving towards socially just assessment* (Equity Response). University of Illinois and Indiana University, National Institute for Learning Outcomes Assessment (NILOA). https://www.learningoutcomesassessment.org/wp-content/uploads/2019/08/EquityResponse HenningLundquist.pdf

Hood, S., Hopson, R., & Frierson, H. (Eds.) (2005). *The role of culture and cultural context in evaluation: A mandate for inclusion, the discovery of truth and understanding*. Information Age.

Hood, S., Hopson, R., & Kirkhart, K. (2015). Culturally responsive evaluation: Theory, practice, and future implications. In K. Newcomer, H. Hatry, & J. Wholey (Eds.), *Handbook of practical program evaluation* (pp. 281–318). Jossey-Bass.

Hopson, R. K. (2003). *Overview of multicultural and culturally competent program evaluation: Issues, challenges and opportunities*. The California Endowment.

Hopson, R. K. (2009). Reclaiming knowledge at the margins: Culturally responsive evaluation in the current evaluation moment. In K. Ryan & J. B. Cousins (Eds.), *The SAGE international handbook of educational evaluation* (pp. 429–446). SAGE.

Inoue, A. B. (2019). Classroom writing assessment as an antiracist practice: Confronting white supremacy in the judgments of language. *Pedagogy*, *1*(3), 373–404. https://doi.org/10.1215/15314200-7615366

Jankowski, N. A. (2020, August). *Assessment during a crisis: Responding to a global pandemic*. University of Illinois and Indiana University, National Institute for Learning Outcomes Assessment. https://www.learningoutcomesassessment.org/wp-content/uploads/2020/08/2020-COVID-Survey.pdf

Johnston, S. C., & Castine, E. (2019). UDL in apprenticeships and career training programs that serve youth with untapped talent: An international perspective. In S. Bracken and K. Novak (Eds.), *Transforming higher education through universal design for learning* (pp. 131–158). Taylor & Francis. https://doi.org/10.4324/9781351132077

Kawakami, A., Aton, K., Cram, F., Lai, M., & Porima, L. (2007). Improving the practice of evaluation through Indigenous values and methods: Decolonizing evaluation and practice—Returning the gaze from Hawai'i and Aotearoa. *Hlili: Multidisciplinary research on Hawaiian well-being, 4*(1), 319–348. https://www.uaf.edu/ces/files/internal/reporting/programevals/improving_the_practice_of_evaluation_through_indigenous_values_and_methods.pdf

Kishimoto, K. (2018). Anti-racist pedagogy: From faculty's self-reflection to organizing within and beyond the classroom. *Race Ethnicity and Education, 21*(4), 540–554. https://doi.org/10.1080/13613324.2016.1248824

Ladson-Billings, G. (1995a). Toward a theory of culturally relevant pedagogy. *American Educational Research Journal, 32*(3), 465–491. https://doi.org/10.3102%2F00028312032003465

Ladson-Billings, G. (1995b). But that's just good teaching! The case for culturally relevant pedagogy. *Theory Into Practice, 34*(3), 159–165. http://dx.doi.org/10.1080/00405849509543675

Ladson-Billings, G. (2014). Culturally relevant pedagogy 2.0: a.k.a. the remix. *Harvard Educational Journal, 84*(1), 74–84. https://doi.org/10.17763/haer.84.1.p2rj131485484751

LaFrance, J., & Nichols, R. (2010). Reframing evaluation: Defining an Indigenous evaluation framework. *Canadian Journal of Evaluation, 23*(2), 13–31. https://evaluationcanada.ca/secure/23-2-013.pdf

Laird, T. F. N., & BrckaLorenz, A. (2017, May). *First and next steps: Moving towards culturally responsive assessment* (Equity Response). University of Illinois and Indiana University, National Institute for Learning Outcomes Assessment (NILOA). https://www.learningoutcomesassessment.org/wp-content/uploads/2019/08/EquityResponse-LairdBrckaLorenz.pdf

Levy, J., & Heiser, C. (2018, March). *Inclusive assessment practice* (Equity Response). University of Illinois and Indiana University, National Institute for Learning Outcomes Assessment (NILOA). https://www.learningoutcomesassessment.org/wp-content/uploads/2019/08/EquityResponse_ LevyHeiser.pdf

Lopez, J. (2020). Indigenous data collection: Addressing limitations in Native American samples. *Journal of College Student Development, 61*(6), 750–764. https://doi.org/10.1353/csd.2020.0073

Louie, D. W., Pratt, Y. P., Hanson, A. J., & Ottmann, J. (2017). Applying Indigenizing principles of decolonizing methodologies in university classrooms. *Canadian*

Journal of Higher Education, 47(3), 16–33. https://doi.org/10.47678/cjhe
.v47i3.187948 https://teachingcommons.lakeheadu.ca/sites/default/files/inline-
files/Applying%20Indgenizing%20Principles%20of%20Decolonizing%20
Methodologies.pdf

Lundquist, A., & Henning, G. (2020). From avoiding bias to social justice: A
continuum of assessment practices to advance diversity, equity, and inclusion.
In T. Simpson & A. Spicer-Runnels (Eds.), *Developing an intercultural responsiveness leadership style for faculty and administrators* (pp. 47–61). IGI Global.
https://10.4018/978-1-7998-4108-1

Magnus, E., Belanger, J., & Faber, M. (2018, October 31). *Towards a critical
assessment practice*. http://www.inthelibrarywiththeleadpipe.org/2018/towards-
critical-assessment-practice/

McArthur, J. (2016). Assessment for social justice: the role of assessment in achieving social justice. *Assessment & Evaluation in Higher Education, 41*(7), 967–981.
https://doi.org/10.1080/02602938.2015.1053429

McArthur, J. (2017, December). *Opportunities for social justice within & through
assessment* (Equity Response). University of Illinois and Indiana University,
National Institute for Learning Outcomes Assessment (NILOA). https://www
.learningoutcomesassessment.org/wp-content/uploads/2019/08/EquityRe-
sponse-McArthur.pdf

McConlogue, T. (2020). Developing inclusive curriculum and assessment practices. In *Assessment and Feedback in Higher Education: A Guide for Teachers*
(pp. 137–150). UCL Press. https://doi.org/10.2307/j.ctv13xprqb.14

Michelson, E. (1996). "Auctoritee" and "experience": Feminist epistemology and the
assessment of experiential learning. *Feminist Studies, 22*(3), 627–655. https://doi
.org/10.2307/3178133

Montenegro, E., & Jankowski, N. A. (2017, January). *Equity and assessment: Moving
towards culturally responsive assessment* (Occasional Paper No. 29). University
of Illinois and Indiana University, National Institute for Learning Outcomes
Assessment (NILOA). https://www.learningoutcomesassessment.org/publica-
tions/occasional-papers/#1580487536940-f2097d9f-3292

Montenegro, E., & Jankowski, N. A. (2020). *A new decade for assessment: Embedding
equity into assessment praxis* (Occasional Paper No. 42). University of Illinois and
Indiana University, NILOA. https://www.learningoutcomesassessment.org/wp-
content/uploads/2020/01/A-New-Decade-for-Assessment.pdf

Nelson-Barber, S., & Trumbull, E. (2007). Making assessment practices valid for
Indigenous American students. *Journal of American Indian Education, 46*(3),
132–147. https://www.jstor.org/stable/24398547

Niemonen, J. (2007). Antiracist education in theory and practice: A critical
assessment. *The American Sociologist, 38*(2), 159–177. https://www.jstor.org/
stable/27700497

Peters, M., & Burbules, N. (2004). *Poststructuralism and educational research*.
Rowman and Littlefield.

Popham, W. J. (2012). *Assessment bias: How to banish it* (2nd ed.). Pearson.

Queens University Centre for Teaching and Learning. (n.d.). *What is decolonization? What is indigenization?* https://www.queensu.ca/ctl/teaching-support/decoloniz-ing-and-indigenizing/what-decolonizationindigenization

Reeves, A. M. (2019). Compassion fatigue: Stories/artworks of an art teacher with a trauma-informed pedagogy. *Marilyn Zurmuehlen Working Papers in Art Education, 2019*(1), 2. https://doi.org/10.17077/2326-7070.1517

Roberts, R. (2019, September). *Making culturally-responsive sense of assessment data: Inquiry about equity* (Equity Response). University of Illinois and Indiana University, National Institute for Learning Outcomes Assessment (NILOA). https://www.learningoutcomesassessment.org/wp-content/uploads/2019/09/EquityResponse-Roberts.pdf

Rose, D. H., Robinson, K. H., Hall, T. E., Coyne, P., Jackson, R. M., Stahl, W. M., & Wilcauskas, S. (2018). Accurate and informative for all: University design for learning (UDL) and the future of assessment. In S. Elliott, R. Kettler, P. Beddow, & A. Kurz (Eds.), *Handbook of accessible interaction and testing* (pp. 167–180). Springer International Publishing. https://doi.org/10.1007/978-3-319-71126-3_11

Rudnick, D. L. (2019, November). *Culturally responsive assessment is just good assessment* (Equity Response). University of Illinois and Indiana University, National Institute for Learning Outcomes Assessment (NILOA). https://www.learningout-comesassessment.org/wpcontent/uploads/2019/11/EquityResponse_Rudnick.pdf

SenGupta, S., Hopson, R., & Thompson-Robinson, M. (2004). Cultural competence in evaluation: An overview. In M. Thompson-Robinson, R. Hopson, & S. SenGupta (Eds.), *In Search of Cultural Competence in Evaluation: Toward Principles and Practices* (New Directions for Evaluation, no. 102, pp. 5–19). Jossey-Bass. https://doi.org/10.1002/ev.112

Shapiro, J. P. (1992). What is feminist assessment? In C. McTighe Musil (Ed.), *Students at the center: Feminist assessment.* Association of American Colleges and National Women's Studies Association. https://archive.mith.umd.edu/WomensStudies/Development+Support/StudentsAtTheCenter/chapter-3.html

Singer-Freeman, K. E., Hobbs, H., & Robinson, C. (2019). Theoretical matrix of culturally relevant assessment. *Assessment Update, 31*(4), 1–16. https://doi.org/10.1002/au.30176

Stake, R. E. (1975). *Program evaluation, particularly responsive evaluation.* Center for Instructional Research and Curriculum Evaluation at the University of Illinois Urbana-Champaign.

Watts, L. S. (2016). Toward mindful assessment in higher education: A case study in contemplative commentary on student work to promote creative learning. In L. S. Watts & P. Blessinger (Eds.), *Creative Learning in Higher Education: International Perspectives and Approaches* (pp. 122–141). Routledge.

Weissman, S. (2020, August 25). How can professors bring anti-racist pedagogy practices into the classroom? *Diverse Issues in Higher Education*. https://diverseeducation.com/article/188573/

Zerquera, D., Reyes, K. A., Pender, J. T., & Abbady, R. (2018). Understanding practitioner-driven assessment and evaluation efforts for social justice. In D. Zerquera, I. Hernández, & J. G. Berumen (Eds.), *Assessment and Social Justice: Pushing Through Paradox* (New Directions for Institutional Research, no. 177, pp. 15–40). Jossey-Bass. https://doi.org/10.1002/ir.20254

5

THE VARIED ROLES
OF NARRATIVES AND
STORIES IN ASSESSMENT

Natasha A. Jankowski and Lesley D'Souza

In a book on equity and assessment, the question could be raised, why focus on stories and narratives? The answer is: for a variety of reasons. Assessment practitioners enjoy a unique privilege to explore the experiences, patterns, and impacts related to student learning that occur throughout an institution of higher education. By presenting evidence to decision makers to inform institutional actions and responses, assessment professionals reinforce values and norms embodied within campus culture to community members. This positionality comes with a high level of responsibility to ensure that harmful underlying narrative norms, beliefs, and biases are not reinforced by assessments and subsequent stories about students and institutions derived from assessment data. Indeed, assessment practitioners have an important role to play in actively disrupting harmful power structures through decisions about the design of their assessments, determination of which data are gathered, deciding how data are shared, and with whom. In many ways, assessment practitioners determine which stories get told, by whom, and in what ways. In essence, through the sharing of data on learning, assessment practitioners give voice to some data and silence other data. Further, through the act of making sense of assessment data, assessment practitioners play a prominent role in determining *whose* stories are told—not just faculty, staff, and students, but which faculty, staff, and students. If equity is not a consideration in assessment related stories, stories derived from data can reinforce inequities and serve to perpetuate the status quo.

But what are stories? Setting terminology is important when talking about stories, as terms like story and narrative "have multiplied, merged, overlapped and fragmented" (Gabriel, 2018, p. 65). For the purposes of this chapter, stories are explored as individual accountings of an event while narratives represent the systems of stories relaying an understanding of cultural values and beliefs. For instance, in assessment there may be underlying narratives of improvement or accountability within the specific institutional stories told of supporting student learning. Assessment is storied through the act of combining evidence with an argument about institutional effectiveness is one of merging assessment with storytelling through evidence-based storytelling (Jankowski, 2021). Through the combination of evidence and meaning-making, assessment practitioners tell powerful stories that can incite change.

In this chapter, the potential and power of storytelling is presented, followed by a discussion on the connection between equity and stories. The concept of counter-stories is presented as a means to address inequities and damaging narratives. The authors outline assessment practitioners as storytellers and provide examples of including student voice and stories in the process of assessment. The chapter ends with ideas and suggestions for what assessment practitioners can do to advance equitable stories and disrupt damaging narratives. Throughout, since this is a chapter on storytelling and narratives, direct quotes from cited authors are used to integrate the voices of those whose ideas are shared.

The Power of Storytelling

Storytelling is endemic to every culture on the planet and is a powerful teaching tool (Gabriel, 2018; Rosiek & Snyder, 2018). The human brain craves stories. Humans are social animals, and the use of stories is tapped deep into the recesses of human brain chemistry (Gottschall, 2012). Stories, and the empathy they build, are powerful tools capable of motivating widespread, disruptive change (Thomas, 2009).

Stories also help make sense of the world. hooks (2010) claimed that stories are one of the most powerful ways to educate. Stories can change culture and create new ways of thinking about practice or further entrench existing approaches (Butcher, 2006; Feldman, 1990). Stories create organizational memory about why things are done in a particular way (Abrahamson, 1998; Whyte & Ralake, 2013). Storytelling can serve as a vital tool in the assessment toolkit to shift culture and help communities identify and unlearn harmful norms (Williams, 2016). And while stories do not have to be literal accounts of an event, they provide the space to make meaning of an experience and communicate that experience to others, potentially creating new understandings and framings for why things are the way they are (Lawrence & Paige, 2016).

Thus, in answer to the question "Why focus on stories in a book about assessment?" it is because stories influence the social creation of phenomena, what is seen and categorized and what is not; they change underlying beliefs; frame incentives for change by identifying heroes, villains, or victims; and contain or restrain our thoughts and actions which become codified in policies and practices (Harrison & Hatfield Price, 2017; Shadiow, 2013).

Stories and Equity

In examining the role of stories in equity, it is important to remember that stories are told from a specific point of view and much about storytelling involves determining who gets a voice and when (Boje, 1995; Steslow & Gardner, 2011). Through stories, dominant paradigms can be challenged by sharing different voices about not only *that* something happened, but *why* it happened the way it did (Lawrence & Paige, 2016; Rooney & Heuvel, 2004).

Stories about student learning (or lack thereof) frame issues in particular ways that can cause harm to specific student populations if left unquestioned (Koshino, 2016; Taitz et al., 2010). For instance, stories that present an argument that "there are some students who are just inherently not going to be successful in STEM fields" can result in little supportive action to remedy a situation, based in a narrative about who can learn, but stories that shine light on systemic barriers as limiting student success in STEM fields present a path of action to address inequities. Ensuring that stories from historically marginalized student populations are told through the act of counter-storytelling can be an important contribution of assessment in support of equitable student learning.

Counter-Storytelling

Counter-stories are tools that can further equity. Counter-stories are defined by Solórzano and Yosso (2002) as a method of telling the stories of people whose experiences are often not told in order to expose, analyze, and challenge the majority stories of racial privilege. In assessment, this can be the stories of students in general, since student voices are often removed from the assessment process and are not seen as reliable as more quantitative data. Counter-storytelling helps to expose "race neutral discourse to reveal how white privilege operates within an ideological framework to reinforce and support unequal societal relations between whites and people of color"

(Merriweather Hunn et al., 2006, p. 244) by starting with a particular, individual experience that gains validation through the act of retelling. Creating a prominent place for telling of individual stories helps to counter hidden systematic racism (Williams, 2016). Carnevale et al. (2020) argued in *The Merit Myth* about the hidden experience that

> the message "you don't belong here" resonates with what many low-income and minority students hear repeatedly from selective institutions. When they apply, they face low acceptance rates; if they're accepted, they have to endure whispers of "not up to it" and "affirmative action." The broader message is enveloped in the insistence that selective colleges value inclusivity and reward merit—so students who didn't make the cut are led to believe that they have no one to blame but themselves. (p. 114)

In contrast to hidden narratives of belongingness, a study conducted by Daryl Smith (2015) of special purpose institutions (Tribal colleges, Hispanic-serving institutions, and historically Black colleges and universities) found the institutional ethos conveyed a belief in students' ability to succeed and excel regardless of background, an ethos and saga that was believed and supported by actions. "Through providing places and spaces for voices and issues to be heard without concern of upsetting the majority community" (Smith, 2015, p. 216), the counter-stories were not marginalized, but centered. Assessment practitioners can interrogate processes and practices to determine when and where counter-stories are needed to examine student learning from the students' lived experiences fully.

Counter-storytelling utilizes critical race theory to challenge the traditional stories and claims made by institutions of higher education based on "objectivity, meritocracy, colorblindness, race neutrality, and equal opportunity (Solórzano & Yosso, 2002, p. 26). Critical race theory helps to lay bare racism "disguised in the rhetoric of shared 'normative' values and 'neutral' social scientific and educational principles and practices" (Solórzano & Yosso, 2002, p. 27). Under the guise of objectivity and rationality, marginalization is justified via statistical insignificance and/or small Ns which are sometimes used to justify inaction on the part of the institution, program, or individual faculty. The narrative of Western science is the dominant narrative, not the lived experiences of those behind the small Ns.

As an example, Native students have not been served well, if at all, by mainstream institutions (Shotton et al., 2013), instead they have become the "American Indian research asterisk" (Garland, 2007, p. 612; Lowe, 2005). Shotton et al. (2013) stated that Native students have long been invisible because they are often excluded from institutional data and reporting due to small numbers. Further, they argue that Native students are omitted from the curriculum, absent from research, and "virtually written out of the higher education story" (Shotton et al., 2013, p. 175). In addition, the asterisk mentality concerning Indigenous students, staff, and faculty in academia resulted in serious lack of understanding of and dialogue on appropriate solutions to support Native students. Fryberg and Townsend (2008) explained that invisibility is an intentional act involving an active "writing out" of the story of a particular group, often serving to maintain a status quo that benefits the dominant group. In a counter-story, Bennett (1997) in his personal narrative of his time at Dartmouth College shared, "New Englanders think that 'all Indians are dead'" (p. 137), and when faculty and staff saw him they thought

> I was on welfare and received free lunches. I was a "savage" who killed white American settlers. I was a boogey man, a gut eater, a dog eater. . . . I didn't know the power and strength of the old stories . . . Ignorance was at the root of their misdirected bigotry, as well as my own and my mother's sense of inferiority. . . . I felt overly cautious when my white friends were "causing trouble" because I was the only Indian, I was often signaled out as the trouble maker. In sports I had to be better than the non-Native players and in social situations, I had to be more humble than others to avoid problems. (p. 141)

In Bennett's story, the dominant narrative of Native Americans in U.S. higher education formed the basis of beliefs which in turn influenced how Native students were perceived and how the individual stories of Native students were heard and understood or not heard.

In 2008, Canada formed a truth and reconciliation commission tasked with addressing the country's past policy of forced assimilation of Indigenous children in residential schools by providing a vehicle for survivors to share their stories (Truth and Reconciliation Commission of Canada, 2015a). Over 6,750 survivors shared their stories with the commission and these accounts took years to collect, understand, and translate into new collective knowledge (Truth and Reconciliation Commission of Canada, 2015b). The act of collecting these stories moved the work of the commission beyond data collection toward a healing act to rebuild relationships and center and validate the lived experiences of those who had been taken to the schools. The commission's final report was published in 2015 and included 94 calls to action accompanied by six volumes detailing Canada's history and concluding that the actions taken to eliminate Indigenous culture and language through mandatory residential schooling amounted to cultural genocide. The positioning of the calls to action in relationship with a retelling of history supported cultural healing, but also framed these calls to non-Indigenous people within the context of events that had been erased from their education. This act of telling has been a vital step forward in helping settlers and Indigenous communities form a basis for understanding each other, though there remains much more work to be done.

These examples can serve as reminders to assessment practitioners that there is a story behind every small N, and some may require more attention, care, and telling than others. Without counter-stories, underlying narratives about student populations become majoritarian stories. Merriweather Hunn et al. (2006) stated that "Majoritarian stories are so powerful, and many people feel compelled to reject, ignore, and dismiss the evidence that calls the validity of these majoritarian stories into question" (p. 248) that other stories and other voices get labeled as irrational, explained away, or muted— meaning silenced or mooted—meaning made irrelevant. Thus, without also intervening in the role of what is considered rational discourse, counter-stories will simply be viewed as an interesting anecdote about an outlier experiential story and be heard as simply offering a different perspective instead of as a counterpoint. In higher education and in assessment, practitioners need to intentionally ask what majoritarian stories are informing their worldviews and how these potentially biased stories are distorting and silencing the experiences of others.

Cultural Norms in Stories of Learning

In addition to counter-stories, cultural norms can influence data, stories, and subsequent action related to student learning. Cultural considerations in assessment are important because culture signals to people whether and where they "fit" (Cram et al., 2015, p. 305). Kem et al. (2020) shared the story of oft taken for granted cultural notions of what a "normal" learning environment entails which in turn impacts a students' ability to complete an assessment.

> What he [the professor] failed to realize, however, was that not all students in the class came from families that were able to "just talk to each other at the dinner table." Comments by Mirae's professor and classmates did not take into account the reality that many Asian American students come from families where parents work long hours and [an] intergenerational language barrier makes communication between parents and children difficult. The notion of talking at the dinner table is not culturally universal, but this seemed to be taken for granted by both the professor and the rest of the class. As a result, Mirae did not feel that she could write honestly in her response paper about her own experiences with her family because they deviated from the cultural norms that had been established. (p. 121)

The previous story outlines an instance where classroom cultural norms hindered a student's ability to complete an assignment, meaning her story was lost and the showing of her knowledge and skills was blocked due to the pervasiveness of existing cultural norms. In the end, assessment data that was gathered was not a reflection of learning. In pandemic learning, faculty also found that to ensure learning and a valid demonstration of learning on assessments, the whole person needed to be considered within the learning process (Jankowski, 2020). Cultural norms can impact not only assignment design, but feedback on an assignment to direct future learning as well, as the following story explains.

> In one class, I [the instructor] was discussing issues of style and diction with a Mandarin-speaking student. I pointed out some adverbial use I thought awkward and the repetition of a noun I thought unnecessary. The student stopped me—"These words will help someone translating in their head to Chinese. It makes more sense this way." I did not know the truth of this statement—ultimately, it did not matter if the assertion was accurate. What mattered was that the student solved a problem his imagined audience might have: He was lifting communicative barriers for a wider audience than I had imagined possible. He was demonstrating a truly deeper level of learning than could have even been achieved if the class depended on only the instructor to transmit method and strategy. (Williams, 2020, p. 112)

These two examples also suggest that cultural norms and counter-stories are important elements for assessment practitioners to consider when making sense of assessment related data and considering how to use the data to inform policies and practice.

Assessment Practitioner as Storyteller

One of the many roles of assessment practitioners in higher education is to collect and tell stories about learning—whether stories of individual students, programs, the institution, and/or cocurriculum—and explain the role of the institution in assisting and supporting students in attaining said learning. As Jankowski and Slotnick (2015) identified, there is a professional role for assessment practitioners to be narrators/translators. This role of narrator/translator can take the form of evidence-based storytelling (Jankowski, 2021; Jankowski & Baker, 2019). Evidence-based storytelling asks assessment practitioners to use evidence of student learning in support of claims or arguments made about whether things are improving or whether institutions and those within are being accountable, as told through stories to persuade a particular audience (Jankowski, 2021). This might be through an illustrative first-person account that emphasizes data points found in analysis, through a series of social media posts designed to facilitate knowledge translation of the data to students, or in localized examples that are shared in the context of a report to a decision maker. It moves beyond simply a report of data or telling of a data story, to purposely translating results of assessment into a story designed for a given audience to inform action.

What is required of assessment practitioners is to unpack *why* a particular institution believes that *this* particular change for *these* particular students, within *this* institutional context, will lead to improvements (Jankowski, 2021). In most instances, the default options of what to change and why are based upon majoritarian narratives and assumptions about students and learning. Going through the justification process provides opportunities to explore underlying prejudice.

Thus, in examining institutional stories about learning, assessment practitioners have a responsibility to interrupt cycles of inequity by asking questions about the data and the decisions made on what to *do* about it as well as inquire about whose stories are being told. While this can involve more actively having students tell their stories (more on that in the next section), it can also take more subtle approaches such as examining for which student groups success or attainment is assumed. For instance, success data of White students may not be double-checked, as it is assumed to be accurate as White students are generally thought to be successful in terms of persistence, academic performance, and social integration in predominantly White institutions. But if students of color are assessed and found to be successful along the same measures, especially at high numbers, results may be questioned because something is assumed to be incorrect and data are run again. This assumes that students of color are typically not successful and that finding a trend of success among racialized demographics is an error in the data. The disparity in assumptions carries through to institutional decision-making where, if White students are not succeeding, questions are raised as to what the institution is doing wrong. But if students of color are not succeeding, it is because the students are not trying hard enough (Bensimon & Malcolm, 2012). In this way, data can be used to cause harm to students. Assessment should not be used to reinforce and support negative academic views and should instead help students reclaim cognitive resources lost to poverty, racism, and social marginalization (Verschelden, 2017).

In assessment, interruption means digging deeper into the data and questioning assumptions about how faculty and staff think about students, where they think learning occurs, and what their theory of change involves.

Interruption entails pushing back on engrained narratives and stopping faculty and staff within the institution from stifling student narratives, where instead of listening and hearing students, faculty and staff tell students sharing their stories, "no this is what you experienced."

Student Storytellers

Stories are a valuable tool for improving student learning. Listening to and telling the stories of students is important to ensure equitable learning relationships in higher education (Delgado, 1989). Studies indicate that storytelling promotes learning, relationships, sense of belonging with students, and space for self-reflection in the context of higher education (Georges, 2020). In essence, stories help students establish a sense of identity and definition of relationship to higher education and themselves as learners (Lewis, 2011).

Student voices are incorporated in a variety of ways whether through students leading assessment projects (such as the work done at the University of California, Davis Student Learning Outcomes Assessment Office of Undergraduate Education through the Curious Aggies program, Ryerson University's Student Experience Research Team [SERT], or through the student learning analyst program at Bowling Green State University [Turos, 2020]). Student stories can also be shared through video projects, such as Stanford University's What I Wish My Professor Knew series on first-generation and/or low-income students (https://ctl.stanford.edu/promote-inclusive-learning/flip-video). When working with students, leaders with power and privilege should take steps to actively participate in listening and using their power to create pathways and validated platforms for students to have their authentic stories heard. The following are some examples of ways that students can be more fully brought into existing systems and given space to not only share their experiences, but to influence decisions about how assessment occurs.

Assessment Dashboards

Justin Rose at Southeastern University's Office of Institutional Effectiveness, in partnership with information technology, academic affairs, instructional design and technology, and other campus groups, built and maintains an assessment dashboard that facilitates on-demand access to eight dynamic and filterable reports including longitudinal institutional assessments of learning and student feedback on lived experiences at the university. Each report allows for disaggregation by multiple demographic variables, including race/

ethnicity, gender, and first-generation status. The dashboard was developed in response to increasing calls for the democratization of and ease of access to actionable assessment data from multiple stakeholder units seeking to enhance student success for all learner populations, in addition to an effort on the part of institutional effectiveness to contribute to a campus-wide culture of continuous improvement and the development of a source of information that resists majority culture's normative assumptions.

When campus stakeholders are trained on usage of the assessment dashboard, they are encouraged to make use of the filtering components and shown examples of how disaggregating data problematizes assumptions about the lived experiences of students, especially when analyzing data from historically underrepresented or underserved populations. The result of this practice has largely centered around increased demand for, and consumption of, assessment data related to the success of students whose lived experiences require greater attention and care, especially in the social, cultural, and political contexts in which they must navigate life at college. One of the more significant lessons learned in this process is that student voices should be centered not only in the sharing of assessment data, but in the design and construction of assessment measures in the first place. Many well-established and benchmarked assessments are carriers of residual majority culture assumptions and worldviews that are not conducive to equitable practice. As Rose and colleagues work to maintain and enhance the assessment dashboard, they are endeavoring to work closer with students.

Data Sense-Making

Utica College's Office of Institutional Effectiveness, through the work of Ann Damiano, involves students in discussions and analyses of survey findings in order to give students agency in the assessment process. Students are additionally invited to propose recommendations. This practice conveys the important message that assessment is something the college does *with* students, as opposed to doing assessment *to* students, and it reminds them that when they are asked to complete a survey, their perceptions and their voices matter.

In spring 2019, Utica College administered the National Assessment of Collegiate Campus Climate. The Office of Institutional Effectiveness and the Division of Diversity, Equity, and Inclusion and Student Transitions presented the findings to groups of staff, faculty, and students. Students were included in planning these presentations. They helped select the data that would be shared in order to avoid the presenters' biases from influencing what was shared, and they recommended strategies for engaging different student participants in the conversations.

At the start of each session, attendees were given ground rules, one of which was that the results could not be dismissed as "opinion" or "perception," particularly when, in the case of the climate survey, they resonated with what National Survey of Student Engagement data suggested and what was articulated in open community conversations on racial climate. Students who participated in the analysis of climate survey data offered specific examples of faculty behavior that contributed to students of color feeling disenfranchised at the institution. Students also described the effects on their learning when faculty assess their performance through a deficit-minded lens.

While students felt faculty needed to make changes in their behaviors and curriculum in order to foster a more inclusive learning environment, they also held themselves accountable for being more inclusive. Students spoke about breaking down barriers that divided student groups—not just racial and ethnic groups, but all the different categories and classifications of students—and said that multiple perspectives, even conservative views, should be welcome in safe spaces. They posited that they must learn how and where to report bias incidents and be willing to file a report if they witness something. Students in leadership roles, such as resident assistants, suggested making discussions about campus climate part of their agenda at regular meetings.

A final report summarized the survey data and included an analysis of the findings from each of the three stakeholder groups as well as the recommended action plans from each group. The outcomes of this project were not measured, because shortly after these conversations took place, the college's operations were disrupted by the COVID-19 pandemic. Nevertheless, faculty have begun addressing issues related to curriculum and ways to better prepare students for a racially diverse society. Perhaps the greatest impact of this effort was expressed by a student participant, who wrote in an email,

> I still use the meeting we had in my current conversations with my parents, grandparents, coworkers, etc. It was so powerful to see feedback from my peers about our campus climate presented in a way that made their experiences that were unknown to me so tangible and undeniable.

Understanding the Student Journey

Lucas Schalewski shared an example from the University of Arizona and the Student Data Insights Strategy Team which hosts equity-minded discussions with University of Arizona student leaders, faculty, staff, and administration centered on data to better understand and support the student journey.

The Student Data Insights Strategy Team was developed for three main purposes: (a) to apply an equity-minded approach to institutional data and assessments to develop equity-driven, data-informed recommendations that produce equitable student outcomes; (b) to take a broader comprehensive approach to understand student experiences and outcomes compared to assessing persistence, campus climate, or learning separately; and (c) to support the institution's strategic plan and mission fulfillment.

The strategy was led out of the office of assessment and research within the provost office and accomplished through a process that involved students and 10 different department representatives. The team synthesized existing research and institutional quantitative data across departments and information systems that informed subsequent focus groups to better understand Pell Grant student recipients and communicate data-informed insights to enact change.

Data-informed insights are presented with recommendations to inform the development of equity-driven policy, practices, and services that enhance the student experience and their success. Through the yearlong collaborative process, 40 data-informed insights on Pell students across multiple domains (e.g., retention and completion and financial wellness) were shared. The process resulted in equitable changes to the university designed to better support the experiences and outcomes of lower-income students. Uses of the insights included the incorporation of a recommended "Pell Pledge Bundle" where incoming lower-income students are invited and more intentionally embedded in programs that are known to support their retention and completion on top of their need-based aid, changes to institutional policies and processes that restricted student success, informing of an institutional basic needs coalition, obtaining of external funding for student basic needs, and expansion of financial wellness and literacy efforts.

Given the notable success of using data and assessment results that resulted in equitable actions, it is expected that the strategy will continue moving forward, addressing different student populations or issues each year. Most recently, the process provided a readied model that was able to respond to institutional needs for synthesizing assessments and data focused on student needs and experiences due to COVID-19 disruptions. The strength of the process they plan to enhance in the future is the triangulation of quantitative and qualitative data and assessment results. In particular, the focus groups hear student voices and make meaning of the institutional data (surveys, persistence trends, program participation rates) to better develop recommendations. Students were involved through the process on the strategy team with staff members from various departments which also provided critical perspectives and helped steer the synthesis of information and development of recommendations. Faculty members are planned to be part of future teams to bring in additional perspectives that will create stronger insights and possibilities for use. A visual of the process is included on the Student Data Insights Strategy Team website: https://assessmentresearch .arizona.edu/data-informed-insights/student-data-insights-strategy-team.

What Can Practitioners Do?

Every assessment practitioner and person in the world holds narratives that are or could be limiting. The work of the equity scorecard (modified here for the assessment context) offers questions to consider when reflecting on data, stories, and practice (Bensimon, 2012):

- How is assessment done here?
- In what ways are our practices failing students of color?
- In what ways are my practices, or the practices of this institution, related to racial inequities in outcomes?
- In what ways are institutional practices enabling or reinforcing racial inequities in outcomes?
- Are we perpetuating and reinforcing or seeking to challenge stereotypes?
- What type of student does our assessment process and discourse privilege? (p. 25)

The most important questions that need to be asked as practitioners review their assessment practices relate to how the existing culture makes space for stories to be shared, and how the stories chosen to be shared reinforce the existing culture. Those who work in assessment have a unique power to create space for such stories and should align practices with a clear set of shared values to understand where power and privilege must be spent in order to bring in stories that can positively shift culture. And as student affairs focuses more on the inclusion of evidence-informed practices, there is a danger in adopting a hierarchy between quantitative and qualitative types of data. An overreliance on quantitative ways of knowing may result in erasures of important identity-based stories. Student affairs has estab-lished itself as a leader in moving forward equity and social justice work, but this ethic must also inform how data are collected and shared. This equity ethic likely represents a paradigm shift as to how practitioners view data and what is valued as data or considered credible, including a widening space for the student voice.

Last Words

It is important to understand that storytelling is not a new methodology. It has been a key part of Indigenous pedagogy all over the world and requires skill to collect and craft. Storytelling is something of a superpower and requires competency as well as a commitment to shared values. The social location of the storyteller is vital context to any story, which is in contrast to positivist data collection methods that tend to remove individual context. When handling data, it is the norm to remove first-person language and sanitize the information from any hint that a human handled the data and may have influenced it. This is problematic because it incorrectly implies that it is possible to have completely unbiased data. The choices made by researchers at all levels of assessment will influence how data are collected, analyzed, and interpreted. The inability to eliminate the perception of bias from qualitative data has resulted in a hierarchical valuation on the data type, with data that is perceived to be more objective being most valuable. The question then becomes, how do we as a profession and scholarship respect storytelling as a necessary competency for successful assessment work and train for it in collection and sharing?

References

Abrahamson, C. E. (1998). Storytelling as a pedagogical tool in higher education. *Education, 118*(3), 440–451.

Bennett, R. (1997). Why didn't you teach me? In A. Garrod & C. Larimore (Eds.), *First person first people: Native American college graduates tell their life stories* (pp. 136–153). Cornell University Press.

Bensimon, E. M. (2012). The equity scorecard theory of change. In E. M. Bensimon & L. Malcom (Eds.), *Confronting equity issues on campus: Implementing the equity scorecard in theory and practice* (pp. 17–44). Stylus.

Bensimon, E. M., & Malcom, L. (2012). *Confronting equity issues on campus: Implementing the equity scorecard in theory and practice.* Stylus.

Boje, D. M. (1995). Stories of the storytelling organization: A postmodern analysis of Disney as "Tamara-land." *Academy of Management Journal, 38*(4), 997–1035. https://doi.org/10.2307/256618

Butcher, S. E. (2006). Narrative as a teaching strategy. *Journal of Correctional Education, 57*(3), 195–208. https://www.jstor.org/stable/23282752

Carnevale, A. P., Schmidt, P., & Strohl, J. (2020). *The merit myth: How our colleges favor the rich and divide America.* The New Press.

Cram, F., Kennedy, V., Paipa, K., Pipi, K., & Wehipeihana, N. (2015). Being culturally responsive through Kaupapa Māori evaluation. In S. Hood, R. Hopson, & H. Frierson (Eds.), *Continuing the journey to reposition culture and cultural context in evaluation theory and practice* (pp. 289–311). Information Age.

Delgado, R. (1989). Storytelling for oppositionists and others: A plea for narrative. *Michigan Law Review, 87*(8), 2411–2441. https://doi.org/10.2307/1289308

Feldman, S. (1990). Stories as cultural creativity: On the relation between symbolism and politics in organizational change. *Human Relations, 43*(9), 809–828. https://doi.org/10.1177%2F001872679004300901

Fryberg, S. A., & Townsend, S. S. M. (2008). The psychology of invisibility. In G. Adams, M. Biernat, N. R. Branscombe, C. S. Crandall, & L. S. Wrightsman (Eds.), *Commemorating Brown: The social psychology of racism and discrimination* (pp. 173–193). American Psychological Association.

Gabriel, Y. (2018). Stories and narratives. In C. Cassell, A. L. Cunliffe, & G. Grandy (Eds.), *The SAGE handbook of qualitative business and management research methods: Methods and challenges* (pp. 63–81). SAGE. https://www.doi.org/10.4135/9781526430236

Garland, J. L. (2007). [Untitled review of the book *Serving Native American students*, by M. J. Tippeconnic Fox, S. C. Lowe, & G. S. McClellan]. *Journal of College Student Development, 48*(12), 612–614. https://doi.org/10.1353/csd.2007.0053

Georges, C. T., Jr. (2020). Establishing culturally responsive pedagogical practices via 'storytelling.' *Feature on Research and Leadership, 5*(3), 1–6. https://files.eric.ed.gov/fulltext/ED606052.pdf

Gottschall, J. (2012). *The storytelling animal: How stories make us human*. Houghton Mifflin Harcourt.

Harrison, L. M., & Hatfield Price, M. (2017). *Interrupting class inequality in higher education: Leadership for an equitable future*. Routledge.

hooks, b. (2010). *Teaching critical thinking: Practical wisdom*. Routledge.

Jankowski, N. (2021, January). *Evidence-based storytelling in assessment* (Occasional Paper No. 50). University of Illinois and Indiana University, National Institute for Learning Outcomes Assessment. https://www.learningoutcomesassessment.org/wp-content/uploads/2021/02/Occasional-Paper-50_EBST.pdf

Jankowski, N. A. (2020, August). *Assessment during a crisis: Responding to a global pandemic.* University of Illinois and Indiana University, National Institute for Learning Outcomes Assessment. https://www.learningoutcomesassessment.org/wpcontent/uploads/2020/08/2020-COVID-Survey.pdf

Jankowski, N. A., & Baker, G. R. (2019). *Building a narrative via evidence-based storytelling: A toolkit for practice.* University of Illinois and Indiana University, National Institute for Learning Outcomes Assessment. https://www.learningoutcomesassessment.org/wp-content/uploads/2019/10/EBST-Toolkit.pdf

Jankowski, N. A., & Slotnick, R. (2015). The five essential roles of assessment practitioners. *Journal of Assessment and Institutional Effectiveness, 5*(1), 78–100. https://muse.jhu.edu/article/605247

Kem, P., Boxell, S., & Nien-chu Kiang, P. (2020). Asian American studies and AANAPISI writing initiatives. In D. C. Maramba & R. T. Teranishi (Eds.), *Transformative practices for minority student success: Accomplishments of Asian American and Native American Pacific Islander-Serving institutions* (pp. 116–130). Stylus.

Koshino, K. (2016). Campus racial climate and experiences of students of color in a midwestern college. In F. Tuitt, C. Haynes, & S. Stewart (Eds.), *Race, equity, and the learning environment: The global relevance of critical and inclusive pedagogies in higher education* (pp. 98–111). Stylus.

Lawrence, R. L., & Paige, D. S. (2016). What our ancestors knew: Teaching and learning through storytelling. In C. R. Nanton (Ed.), *Tectonic Boundaries: Negotiating Convergent Forces in Adult Education* (New Directions for Adult and Continuing Education, no. 149, pp. 63–72). Jossey-Bass. https://doi .org/10.1002/ace.20177

Lewis, P. J. (2011). Storytelling as research/research as storytelling. *Qualitative Inquiry, 17*(6), 505–510. https://doi.org/10.1177%2F1077800411409883

Lowe, C. S. (2005). This is who I am: Experiences of Native American students. In M. J. Tippeconnic Fox, S. C. Lowe, & G. S. McClellan (Eds.), *Serving Native American students* (New Directions for Student Services, no. 109, pp. 33–40). Jossey-Bass. https://doi.org/10.1002/ss.151

Merriweather Hunn, L. R., Guy, T. C., & Mangliitz, E. (2006). Who can speak for whom? Using counter-storytelling to challenge racial hegemony. In *Adult education research conference proceedings* (pp. 244–250). https://newprairiepress.org/ aerc/2006/papers/32

Rooney, J., & Hauvel, L. N. (2004). Root cause analysis for beginners. *Quality Progress, 37*(7), 45–53. https://asq.org/quality-progress/articles/root-cause-analysis-for-beginners?id=0228b91456514ba490c89979b577abb4

Rosiek, J. L., & Snyder, J. (2018). Narrative inquiry and new materialism: Stories as (not necessarily benign) agents. *Qualitative Inquiry*, 1–12. https://doi .org/10.1177%2F1077800418784326

Shadiow, L. K. (2013). *What our stories teach us: A guide to critical reflection for college faculty.* Jossey-Bass.

Shotton, H. J., Lowe, S. C., & Waterman, S. J. (2013). Introduction. In H. J. Shotton, S. C. Lowe, & S. J. Waterman (Eds.). *Beyond the asterisk: Understanding native students in higher education* (pp. 1–24). Stylus.

Smith, D. G. (2015). *Diversity's promise for higher education: Making it work* (2nd ed.). Johns Hopkins University Press.

Solórzano, D. G., & Yosso, T. J. (2002). Critical race methodology: Counter-storytelling as an analytical framework for education research. *Qualitative Inquiry, 8*(1), 23–44. https://doi.org/10.1177%2F107780040200800103

Steslow, D. M., & Gardner, C. (2011). More than one way to tell a story: Integrating storytelling into your law course. *Journal of Legal Studies Education, 28*(2), 249–271. https://doi.org/10.1111/j.1744-1722.2011.01091.x

Taitz, J., Genn, K., Brooks, V., Ross, D., Ryan, K., Shumack, B., Burrell, T., Kennedy, P., & NSW RCA Review Committee. (2010). System-wide learning from root cause analysis: A report from the New South Wales Root Cause Analysis Review Committee. *Quality & Safety in Health Care, 19*(6), e63. https://doi .org/10.1136/qshc.2008.032144

Thomas, M. (2009). Transforming "Apathy into movement": The role of prosocial emotions in motivating action for social change. *Personality and Social Psychology Review, 13*(4), 310–333. https://doi.org/10.1177/1088868309343290

Truth and Reconciliation Commission of Canada. (2015a). *Honouring the truth, reconciling for the future: Summary of the final report of the Truth and Reconciliation Commission of Canada / Truth and Reconciliation Commission of Canada.* https://nccdh.ca/resources/entry/honouring-the-truth-reconciling-for-the-future

Truth and Reconciliation Commission of Canada. (2015b). *The survivors speak: a report of the Truth and Reconciliation Commission of Canada / Truth and Reconciliation Commission of Canada.* http://www.trc.ca/assets/pdf/Survivors_Speak_English_Web.pdf

Turos, J. M. (2020, March). *Actively engaging undergraduate students in the assessment process.* University of Illinois and Indiana University, National Institute for Learning Outcomes Assessment. https://www.learningoutcomesassessment.org/wp-content/uploads/2020/03/AiP-Turos.pdf

Verschelden, C. (2017). *Bandwidth recovery: Helping students reclaim cognitive resources lost to poverty, racism, and social marginalization.* Stylus.

Whyte, G., & Ralake, M. (2013). An investigation into the effectiveness of storytelling as means of sharing tacit knowledge. In *Proceedings of the European Conference on Information Management & Evaluation* (pp. 309–317).

Williams, B. C. (2016). Radical honesty: Truth-telling as pedagogy for working through shame in academic spaces. In F. Tuitt, C. Haynes, & S. Stewart (Eds.), *Race, equity, and the learning environment: The global relevance of critical and inclusive pedagogies in higher education* (pp. 71–82). Stylus.

Williams, C. (2020). "Even though I am speaking Chinglish, I can still write a good essay": Building a learning community through critical pedagogy and translingual practice. In D. C. Maramba & R. T. Teranishi (Eds.), *Transformative practices for minority student success: Accomplishments of Asian American and Native American Pacific Islander-Serving institutions* (pp. 101–115). Stylus.

6

MODELS AND APPROACHES TO INCREASING EQUITY IN HIGHER EDUCATION

Karen Singer-Freeman, Linda Bastone, and Erick Montenegro

There is compelling evidence of equity gaps in higher education and a growing consensus that commonly used assessment practices contribute to these gaps (Montenegro & Jankowski, 2017a, 2017b, 2020; Singer-Freeman et al., 2019; Singer-Freeman & Bastone, 2019b). To achieve equity, colleges and universities must be reconfigured to provide every student with the support necessary for success (Bensimon, 2005). One essential step toward the creation of equitable institutions is the development of equitable measures of learning. A recent survey of assessment professionals found that increasing equity in higher education was viewed as the most important challenge currently facing the field of assessment (Singer-Freeman & Robinson, 2020a, 2020b). This chapter provides an overview of models and approaches that can inform efforts to increase equity in higher education assessment, considering the possible applications of current theories to each stage of the assessment cycle (Maki, 2010).

Theories of Equity in Assessment

Theories guide the tactics assessment practitioners adopt as they work to embed equity into their practice. Some theories are broad in scope and others focus tightly on assessment work. This section covers six distinct theories that can support efforts to increase equity in higher education.

Critical Race Theory

Critical race theory strives to eliminate subordination by examining societal structures that maintain white supremacy (Bell, 1987; Martinez-Alemán et al., 2015). Several tenets of critical race theory can inform equitable assessment practice. Interest-convergence describes the observation that those in power only implement beneficial practices for marginalized populations when these practices also benefit themselves (Bell, 1987). To capitalize on this, equitable assessment must be supported by institutional policies that provide explicit outcome goals and rewards for progress so that progress toward equity benefits those in power.

Race and racism are embedded in societal practices and policies that contribute to marginalization (Solórzano, 1998). Colorblind stances preserve the status quo by ignoring implicit forms of racism and accepting norms that perpetuate inequities (Harper et al., 2009). White fragility, or the inability to tolerate race-based discomfort, emerges when the status quo is challenged and prevents individuals from recognizing how positionality influences assessment (DiAngelo, 2018). Seeing their perspective as objective, White individuals may miss the extent to which race influences assessment. To move beyond institutionalized norms, assessment professionals must solicit input from all groups of students at an institution (Heiser et al., 2017). Students from subjugated groups can help assessment professionals examine ways in which norms, policies, and approaches elevate certain ways of knowing and denigrate others.

Because assessment methodology emerged from the field of quantitative research, there is an assumption that objectivity in measurement is optimal and possible (Henning & Lundquist, 2018). Current assessment practices are biased toward the pursuit of an impartiality that is unattainable. Every decision is influenced by the decision maker's positionality which includes their experiences, knowledge, and social position. Positionality influences the creation of learning outcomes, the design of instruments, and the interpretation of findings (Heiser et al., 2017). When the positionality of the assessor overlaps with that of well-served students, assessment findings may be biased in ways that perpetuate inequity: Learning outcomes may reflect dominant cultural values, ignoring values of the oppressed; measures of learning may assume prior culturally specific knowledge; and interpretations of findings may be limited by narrow definitions of achievement. Critical race theory invites a critical view of the status quo and the transformation of the structures that perpetuate inequities.

Socially Just Assessment

Like critical race theory, the social justice approach involves considerations of power, privilege, and identity, followed by the implementation of policies that increase equality (Henning & Lundquist, 2018). Social justice approaches question who has the power to make decisions, how decisions create inequality, and what actions can remedy inequalities. Achieving equity requires more than equal treatment (Zajda et al., 2006). Assessing learning in the same way unilaterally often will not accurately capture what students know and can do. One-size-fits-all assessments privilege certain ways of knowing and perpetuate equity gaps (Montenegro & Jankowski, 2017a, 2017b, 2020).

Knowledge is a social construct and the transmission of knowledge is not a neutral activity (Henning & Lundquist, 2018). To mitigate bias, it is essential to consider positionality and agency at each phase of assessment (Heiser et al., 2017). Life experiences, privilege, and biases influence the questions asked, the responses viewed as correct, and the assessment methods selected (Cumming & Dickson, 2007). To increase agency in assessment, students from marginalized groups must contribute to assessment decisions. Student agency improves the quality of assessments, signals respect for those who are assessed, and creates learning opportunities.

Implicit Bias

Systemic racism unconsciously influences thoughts, shaping responses to spoken and written language (Greenwald & Krieger, 2006; Steinke & Fitch, 2017). The effects of implicit bias extend beyond race to impact students with differing abilities (Kimball et al., 2020). Unconscious negative responses to unfamiliar communicative patterns can bias assessments of student writing and speech (Ross, 2016). Faculty must acknowledge that the presence of implicit biases is independent of beliefs about equity. Having accepted implicit biases as unavoidable, faculty can mitigate bias by using grading techniques such as carefully constructed rubrics to focus on content rather than style.

Culture of Inquiry

To increase equity, it is essential to focus on the readiness of higher education institutions to educate students rather than the preparedness of students to thrive (Smit, 2012). When framing issues around student deficits, the structural issues are often overlooked (McNair et al., 2016). Equity gaps represent a failure of institutions to provide equal opportunities for student success and accurate measurements of student learning (Bensimon, 2005). As such, increased equity requires organizational change. A culture of inquiry involves iterative processes of reflection, uses data for critical analysis of outcome equity, and focuses on institutional responsibility, rather than student deficits, when devising solutions (Witham & Bensimon, 2012). An asset approach values student differences and creates educational environments in which all students benefit from the diverse perspectives and experiences of their peers. The establishment of a culture of inquiry is a promising route away from deficit thinking and toward equitable assessment.

Culturally Responsive Pedagogy

Culturally responsive pedagogy stresses the importance of making all students feel welcome and capable of success at the institution (Gay, 2010). When designing assessments of learning, faculty should couple high standards with communications of confidence that all students have the potential to meet the standards (Morrison et al., 2008). Scaffolded assignments provide students with the support needed to produce high quality work early in a class and provide assessments of learning at multiple points in a semester. Success on early assignments also provides opportunities for faculty to express confidence in students' abilities to succeed on more difficult future assignments. Finally, the material in assessments must be equally accessible to all students (Hill et al., 2017; Singer-Freeman et al., 2019). The use of self-reflective writing can infuse assignments with accessible material in classes that enroll diverse groups of students (Singer-Freeman & Bastone, 2019a, 2019b).

Culturally Relevant Assessment

Culturally relevant assessment is an outgrowth of culturally responsive pedagogy that considers how assessments can be structured to optimize accurate measurement of learning (Hood et al., 2015; Padilla, 2001; Singer-Freeman et al., 2019; Verjee, 2003). Small changes in assessment structure increase equity. For example, frequent testing improved content retention and resulted in a 50% reduction in the equity gap in grades among students of different social classes (Pennebaker et al., 2013). Despite documented benefits of testing, testing can also have negative effects if the testing environment evokes feelings of stereotype threat (Steele & Aronson, 1995). Stereotype threat effects occur when aspects of the situation increase the salience of marginalized identities, increasing anxiety and reducing performance. For testing to benefit marginalized students, efforts must be made to reframe tasks and tests as nondiagnostic of ability; minimize attention to group membership; and reduce pressure resulting from proctoring, time limits, and contribution to final grade (Nguyen & Ryan, 2008; Walton & Spencer, 2009).

Often assessments vary along two dimensions: utility value and inclusive content (Singer-Freeman et al., 2019). Utility value describes the extent to which students perceive work to have worth (Eccles et al., 1983). Students believe assignments hold academic value when they foster skills that will help in future classes, professional value when they provide skills that will be useful in a future career, and personal value when they result in self-relevant insights or products (Singer-Freeman et al., 2021). Experimental and applied work have established that increasing assignment utility value reduces equity gaps in grades (Harackiewicz et al., 2016; Singer-Freeman & Bastone, 2018, 2019b, 2021; Singer-Freeman et al., 2019). Inclusive content describes content that is equally accessible to all students (Singer-Freeman et al., 2019). Providing clear and detailed instructions and grading rubrics increases content inclusivity by eliminating effects of prior preparation or familiarity with similar assignments. Allowing students to select ways of demonstrating knowledge increases content inclusivity because students can select assignment structures that are congruent with their experience (Montenegro & Jankowski, 2017a, 2017b, 2020).

Applications of Theories of Equity to Stages in the Assessment Cycle

To be effective, efforts to increase equity in higher education must be sustained across all stages of the assessment cycle: establishment of learning outcomes, development of measures, analysis of findings, and improvements to learning (Maki, 2010). Equitable learning outcomes direct and coordinate instruction, learning, and assessment across a university. Equitable measures provide all students the opportunity to demonstrate proficiency. To catalyze change, the analysis of findings must occur within a culture of inquiry that identifies the contribution of structural barriers to equity. Identified barriers to equity must be removed to improve learning for all students.

Establishment of Learning Outcomes

When functioning well, learning outcomes drive improvement in teaching and communicate educational priorities to students. To promote equity, learning outcomes must reflect the values of all stakeholders. Culturally inclusive learning outcomes welcome all students by communicating alignment between students' values and those of the institution. Engaging students in the development of learning outcomes supports the reduction of equity gaps in assessment (Stiggins & Chappuis, 2005).

Critical race theory and socially just assessment posit that learning outcomes are social constructs that will perpetuate White supremacy unless nondominant groups participate in their establishment (Inoue, 2019; Tkatchov, 2019). An inclusive process might lead to the development of learning outcomes specifically related to equity such as cultural competence. A learning outcome of this sort helps establish an inclusive educational community that supports the delivery of a high-quality education (Milem et al., 2005). Alternatively, an inclusive process might lead to a shift in the definition of a learning outcome. For example, effective communication might not require the adoption of formal rules of grammar or traditional styles of narrative, crediting evidence of communication independently from dominant cultural norms.

Development of Measures

Dictating how students demonstrate learning privileges certain types of learning over others (Montenegro & Jankowski, 2020). The adoption of differentiated measures allows students to select assignments that best demonstrate their proficiency. Authentic measures require input from members of underserved groups (Heiser et al., 2017). Capital University recently demonstrated how each major tenet of critical race theory informed their development and interpretation of a campus climate survey (Lynner et al., 2020). Inviting students to partner with assessment professionals recognizes participants' agency and limits effects of assessor positionality. Incorporating student voices through feedback or focus groups increases the likelihood that measures are accurate, comprehensible, and viewed similarly by diverse groups (Hood et al., 2015). Once developed, assessment measures should be used as teaching tools. Providing students with opportunities to respond to measures prior to formal assessment reduces anxiety and provides students with performance targets (Gay, 2010).

Implicit bias can also affect measurement (Ross, 2016). Rubrics that are carefully aligned with learning outcomes and include student input limit the impact of unconscious bias in the qualitative assessment of learning (Inoue, 2019; Singer-Freeman & Bastone, 2016, 2021). Rubrics help evaluators apply similar standards across multiple individuals and provide a lasting record of assessments, allowing outcome audits across classes or instructors. Rubrics also focus evaluators' attention on specific concepts, reducing the bias that occurs when evaluators assess nonessential elements of a piece of work. For example, Yancey (2012) reported that a university recruited and retained a more ethnically diverse group of students when rubrics focused the evaluation of admissions essays on critical thinking and reflection rather than grammar or punctuation.

Another way in which implicit bias might create equity gaps is in the extent to which faculty serve as cultural agents by welcoming students and supporting their sense of belonging in higher education. Student aptitude or readiness is not fixed at the point of entry to a college or major, it interacts in a bidirectional way with institutional supports (Arnold et al., 2012). Faculty beliefs about potential improvements in academic aptitude influence the extent to which students improve during college (Schademan & Thompson, 2015). For example, a study of science professors revealed that faculty who believed science abilities are fixed had larger racial equity gaps in their classes than faculty who believed they are malleable (Canning et al., 2019). To remediate inequities that arise from classroom practices, faculty training that promotes nonfixed views of aptitude and describes equitable practices for communication around exams and assignments is essential (Singer-Freeman & Bastone, 2019a).

Regardless of the care with which an assessment is prepared, all measurements are accompanied by error. The use of multiple measures, with consideration of the extent to which measures are influenced by power dynamics, reduces general effects of error and specific effects of bias (Montenegro & Jankowski, 2020). The triangulation of multiple assessments, such as written assignments, tests, and portfolios, provides a holistic understanding of student learning (Maki, 2010). Using multiple assessments decreases the likelihood that a single, flawed assessment determines decisions such as acceptance into a major, funding for a program, or changes to a curriculum. Ideally, when using multiple measures of learning, a measurement of students' beliefs about their learning should be included. Meyerhoff (2020) created a protocol for the authentic engagement of students in assessment by having them transition from reflecting about their experiences in a class, to sharing their experiences with a partner and the class. The exercise culminates with the creation of a visual map depicting the ways in which experiences in the class influenced students and how these influences had effects that went beyond the class.

Finally, an essential component for socially just assessment of learning is the inclusion of exhaustive and not exclusive demographic information (Henning & Lundquist, 2018). The presence of exclusive choices for demographic categories limits the extent to which students are seen accurately or feel their identity is accepted by the institution. Only exhaustive demographic information allows full disaggregation of outcomes. When demographic information is collected directly from students, asking demographic questions after an assessment is completed limits potentially damaging stereotype threat effects.

Analysis of Findings

Authentic faculty engagement in the consideration of findings is essential for learning improvement and the achievement of equity (Bensimon, 2005). Historically, assessment data were reported in ways that mask inequities by aggregating all students' outcomes across instructors. Aggregation of data protects faculty and student anonymity. However, aggregated data provide faculty with little information that can be used to improve teaching, reinforcing the view that assessment is an exercise in compliance rather than an essential activity that can improve learning (Fulcher et al., 2017).

To foster collaborative relationships with faculty and encourage learning improvement, assessment professionals must disaggregate student learning outcome data and grades in ways that consider individual positionality (Harper et al., 2018; Singer-Freeman et al., 2019). Conducting analyses that consider intersecting identities of students reveals important insights into student experiences (Gansemer-Topf et al., 2019). As faculty engage with assessment findings, they should take an asset approach by considering how differences between students contribute to the richness of the learning environment (Henning & Lundquist, 2018).

Finally, critical race theory reminds us to increase transparency by disseminating assessment findings. Broad dissemination supports student agency by including students in the analysis process through focus groups, discussions at the end of a class, or student surveys. Student perspectives provide counternarratives and creative solutions (Heiser et al., 2017). The discussion of findings with students also increases students' awareness of the skills and knowledge they have gained by providing them with an opportunity to reflect on their learning (Singer-Freeman & Bastone, 2019a).

Improvements to Learning

During the final phase of assessment, it is critical to take action to remediate equity gaps. A narrow focus on increasing overall scores or the numbers of students demonstrating proficiency can lead to implementation of practices that reduce equity (Dorimé-Williams, 2018). Socially just assessments examine the effects of individual responses to data on power and privilege in higher education. Iterative examination of disaggregated student learning data leads to faculty-driven improvements in equity because when faculty see evidence of disparities, they are motivated to develop, implement, test, and revise possible remedies. Equity audits can direct effective improvements through an examination of institutional practices and supports available to students from underserved and privileged groups (Bauman et al., 2005; Olson, 2020). For example, institutions may consider access to professors, administrators, writing centers, and counseling services. When considering areas for improvement, an equity audit can examine whether policies and procedures contribute to differential outcomes in learning.

One barrier to the implementation of improvements may be the belief that institutional actions to support social justice should be implemented by designated multicultural centers or initiatives (Zerquera et al., 2018). Dorimé-Williams (2018) suggested that to promote socially just assessment, the goals of assessments must be aligned with the institutional mission and center on improvements in student success. Creating clearly articulated goals and metrics for campus equity initiatives increases accountability, aligning the achievement of equity more closely with the self-interests of those with power (Levy & Heiser, 2018).

Regional accreditation standards might also drive improvements in higher education. Cynthia Jackson-Hammond, president of the Council for Higher Education Accreditation, reported that accreditors are interested in creating stronger standards associated with equity (Busta, 2020). Although it is not yet common to require documentation of efforts to increase equity in learning, several agencies reference the need to increase equity in admission, hiring, retention, and degree completion (Singer-Freeman et al., 2021). Increased attention to the examination of equity gaps in accreditation standards might be a systemic route to increase the application of socially just assessment and reduce the impulse to simply document high levels of overall proficiency.

Conclusions

Equity models can provide a way forward for assessment professionals motivated to increase equity in higher education. We suggest a few guiding principles to direct this work.

Own the Problem

Assessment professionals must accept that equity gaps in achievement are prevalent in higher education. These gaps support and create inequities in society and are caused, in part, by bias in assessment that supports existing power structures.

Actively Work to Become Part of the Solution

Assessment professionals must identify inequitable practices and offer remedies. This work must be an integral part of assessment and accreditation.

Accept That Assessment Professionals Cannot Do It Alone

Assessment professionals can begin the work of identifying bias, improving measures, and conducting more sophisticated analyses. However, genuine change requires cooperation among assessment professionals, students, faculty, administration, accrediting agencies, and state governments. To understand students' needs, assessment professionals must invite them to participate in each stage of the assessment cycle as contributors. To create meaningful change, assessment professionals must communicate nuanced findings effectively to stakeholders and decision makers.

References

Arnold, K. D., Lu, E. C., & Armstrong, K. J. (2012). The case for a comprehensive model of college readiness. *ASHE Report, 38*(5), 1–138.

Bauman, G. L., Bustillos, L. T., Bensimon, E. M., Brown, M. C., & Bartee, R. D. (2005). *Achieving equitable educational outcomes with all students: The institution's roles and responsibilities*. Association of American Colleges and Universities.

Bell, D. A. (1987). *And we are not saved: The elusive quest for racial justice*. Basic Books.

Bensimon, E. M. (2005). Closing the achievement gap in higher education: An organizational learning perspective. In E. Kezar (Ed.), *Organizational Learning in Higher Education* (New Directions in Higher Education, no. 131, pp. 99–111). Jossey-Bass. https://doi.org/10.1002/he.190

Busta, H. (2020). CHEA president: As accreditation rules change, colleges can benefit from choices. *Educationdive*. https://www.educationdive.com/news/chea-president-as-accreditation-rules-change-colleges-can-benefit-from-ch/585940/

Canning, K. M., Green, D. J., & Murphy, M. C. (2019). STEM faculty who believe ability is fixed have larger racial achievement gaps and inspire less student motivation in their classes. *Science Advances, 5*(2), 1–5. https://doi.org/10.1126/sciadv.aau4734

Cumming, J. J., & Dickson, E. A. (2007). Equity in assessment: Discrimination and disability issues from an Australian legal perspective. *Education and the Law, 19*(3–4), 201–220. https://doi.org/10.1080/09539960701762854

DiAngelo, R. (2018). *White fragility: Why it's so hard for white people to talk about racism*. Beacon Press.

Dorimé-Williams, M. D. (2018). Developing socially just practices and policies in assessment. In D. Zerquera, I. Hernández, & J. G. Berumen (Eds.), *Assessment and Social Justice: Pushing Through Paradox* (New Directions for Institutional Research, no. 177, pp. 41–56). Jossey-Bass. https://doi.org/10.1002/ir.20255

Eccles J. S., Adler, T. F., Futterman, R., Goff, S. B., Kaczala, C. M., Meece, J. L., & Midgley, C. (1983). Expectancies, values, and academic behaviors. In J. T. Spence (Ed.), *Achievement and achievement motivation* (pp. 75–146). W. H. Freeman.

Fulcher, K. H., Smith, K. L., Sanchez, E. R. H., Ames, A. J., & Meixner, C. (2017). Return of the pig: Standards for learning improvement. *Research & Practice in Assessment, 11*, 10–40. http://www.rpajournal.com/dev/wp-content/uploads/2017/03/A2.pdf

Gansemer-Topf, A. M., Wilson, J., & Kirk, M. (2019). Numbers may not lie, but they can hide: Critically examining our "number" narratives. *Intersection, Fall,* 5–10. https://www.aalhe.org/assets/docs/Intersection/AAHLE_fall_2019_Intersection_final.pdf

Gay, G. (2010). *Culturally responsive teaching: Theory, research, and practice.* Teachers College Press.

Greenwald, A. G., & Krieger, L. H. (2006). Implicit bias: Scientific foundations. *California Law Review, 94*(4), 945–967. https://doi.org/10.2307/20439056

Harackiewicz, J. M., Canning, E. A., Tibbetts, Y., Priniski, S. J., & Hyde, J. S. (2016). Closing achievement gaps with a utility-value intervention: Disentangling race and social class. *Journal of Personality and Social Psychology, 111*(5), 745–765. https://doi.org/10.1037/pspp0000075

Harper, S. R., Patton, L. D., & Wooden, O. S. (2009). Access and equity for African American students in higher education: A critical race historical analysis of policy efforts. *The Journal of Higher Education, 80*(4), 389–414. https://doi.org/10.1353/jhe.o.0052

Harper, S. R., Smith, E. J., & Davis, C. H. F. (2018). A critical race case analysis of Black undergraduate student success at an urban university. *Urban Education, 53*(1), 3–25. https://doi.org/10.1177/0042085916668956

Heiser, C. A., Prince, K., & Levy, J. D. (2017). Examining critical theory as a framework to advance equity through student affairs assessment. *The Journal of Student Affairs Inquiry, 3*(1), 1–17. https://drive.google.com/file/d/1ksQstiXwP51EdipgdylU7nvdenVpIJA-/view

Henning, G. W., & Lundquist, A. E. (2018). *Moving towards socially just assessment* (Equity Response). University of Illinois and Indiana University, National Institute for Learning Outcomes Assessment (NILOA). https://www.learningoutcomesassessment.org/wp-content/uploads/2019/08/EquityResponseHenningLundquist.pdf

Hill, M. F., Ell, F., Grudnoff, L., Haigh, M., Cochran-Smith, M., Chang, W., & Ludlow, L. (2017). Assessment for equity: Learning how to improve teaching. *Assessment in Education: Principles, Policy & Practice, 24*(2), 185–204. https://doi.org/10.1080/0969594X.2016.1253541

Hood, S., Hopson, R. K., & Kirkhart, K. E. (2015). Culturally responsive evaluation: Theory, practice, and future implications. In K. E. Newcomer, H. P. Hatry, and J. S. Wholey (Eds.), *Handbook of practical program evaluation* (4th ed., pp. 281–317). Jossey-Bass.

Inoue, A. B. (2019). Classroom writing assessment as an antiracist practice: Confronting white supremacy in the judgements of language. *Pedagogy: Critical Approaches to Teaching Literature, Language, Composition, and Culture, 19*(3), 373–404. https://doi.org/10.1215/15314200-7615366

Kimball, E., Abbott, J., & Childs, J. (2020, July). *Cripping equity and assessment: Disability as identity and culture in the context of culturally responsive assessment* (Equity Response). University of Illinois and Indiana University, National Institute for Learning Outcomes Assessment. https://www.learningoutcomesassessment.org/wp-content/uploads/2020/08/Equity-Response-KimballAbbottChilds.pdf

Levy, J., & Heiser, C. (2018). *Inclusive assessment practice* (Equity Response). University of Illinois and Indiana University, National Institute for Learning Outcomes Assessment (NILOA). https://www.learningoutcomesassessment.org/wp-content/uploads/2019/08/EquityResponse_LevyHeiser.pdf

Lynner, B., Ho, W., Narui, M., & Smith, J. (2020, July). *Capital University: Pilot campus climate assessment through critical race theory.* National Institute for Learning Outcomes Assessment, Council for the Advancement of Standards in Higher Education, and Campus Labs.

Maki, P. L. (2010). *Assessing for learning: Building a sustainable commitment across the institution* (2nd ed.). Stylus.

Martinez-Alemán, A. M., Pusser, B., & Bensimon, E. M. (Eds.). (2015). *Critical approaches to the study of higher education: A practical introduction.* Johns Hopkins University Press.

McNair, T. B., Albertine, S., Cooper, M. A., McDonald, N., & Major, T. (2016). *Becoming a student-ready college: A new culture of leadership for student success.* Jossey-Bass.

Meyerhoff, L. (2020, June). *Cornell University: Ripple effect mapping.* National Institute for Learning Outcomes Assessment, Council for the Advancement of Standards in Higher Education, and Campus Labs. https://www.learningoutcomesassessment.org/wp-content/uploads/2020/06/Cornell-Equity-Case.pdf

Milem, J. F., Chang, M. J., & Antonio, A. L. (2005). *Making diversity work on campus: A research-based perspective.* Association of American Colleges and Universities. https://www.aacu.org/sites/default/files/files/mei/MakingDiversityWork.pdf

Montenegro, E., & Jankowski, N. A. (2017a). *Equity and assessment: Moving towards culturally responsive assessment* (Occasional Paper No. 29). University of Illinois and Indiana University, National Institute for Learning Outcomes Assessment. https://learningoutcomesassessment.org/wp-content/uploads/2019/02/OccasionalPaper29.pdf

Montenegro, E., & Jankowski, N. (2017b). Bringing equity into the heart of assessment. *Assessment Update, 29*(6), 10–11. https://doi.org/10.1002/au.30117

Montenegro, E., & Jankowski, N. A. (2020). A new decade for assessment: Embedding equity into assessment praxis (Occasional Paper No. 42). University of Illinois and Indiana University, National Institute for Learning Outcomes Assessment.

https://www.learningoutcomesassessment.org/wp-content/uploads/2020/01/A-New-Decade-for-Assessment.pdf

Morrison, K. A., Robbins, H. H., & Rose, D. G. (2008). Operationalizing culturally relevant pedagogy: A synthesis of classroom-based research. *Equity & Excellence in Education, 41*(4), 433–452. https://doi.org/10.1080/10665680802400006

Nguyen, H. H. D., & Ryan, A. M. (2008). Does stereotype threat affect test performance of minorities and women? *Journal of Applied Psychology, 93*(6), 1314–1334. https://psycnet.apa.org/doi/10.1037/a0012702

Olson, A. (2020, March 25). Equity audits should be commonplace. *Inside Higher Education.* https://www.insidehighered.com/views/2020/03/25/more-colleges-should-use-equity-audits-address-inequalities-their-institutions

Padilla, A. (2001). Issues in culturally appropriate assessment. In L. Suzuki, J. Ponterotto, & P. Meller (Eds.), *Handbook of multicultural assessment* (2nd ed., pp. 5–27). Jossey Bass.

Pennebaker, J. W., Gosling, S. W., & Ferrell, J. D. (2013). Daily online testing in large classes: Boosting college performance while reducing achievement gaps. *PLOS One, 8(11)*, 1–6. https://doi.org/10.1371/journal.pone.0079774

Ross, K. A. (2016). *Breakthrough strategies: Classroom-based practices to support new majority college students.* Harvard University Press.

Schademan, A. R., & Thompson, M. R. (2015). Are college faculty and first generation, low-income students ready for each other? *Journal of College Student Retention: Research Theory and Practice, 18*(2), 1–23. https://doi.org/10.1177/1521025115584748

Singer-Freeman, K. E., & Bastone, L. (2016). *Pedagogical choices make large classes feel small* (Occasional Paper No. 27). University of Illinois and Indiana University, National Institute for Learning Outcomes Assessment. http://learningoutcomesassessment.org/documents/OccasionalPaper27.pdf

Singer-Freeman, K. E., & Bastone, L. (2018). ePortfolio and declarations of academic self: A tale of two contexts. In B. Eynon & L. M. Gambino (Eds.), *Catalyst in action: Case studies of high-impact eportfolio practice* (pp. 84–97). Stylus.

Singer-Freeman, K. E., & Bastone, L. (2019a). Developmental science concepts guide effective support of underrepresented STEM students. *Journal of Biochemistry and Molecular Biology Education, 47*(5), 506–512. https://doi.org/10.1002/bmb.21292

Singer-Freeman, K. E., & Bastone, L. (2019b). Increasing equity in general education using self-relevant writing. *Intersection, Fall*, 24–28. https://www.aalhe.org/assets/docs/Intersection/AAHLE_fall_2019_Intersection_final.pdf

Singer-Freeman, K. E., & Bastone, L. (2021). Incorporating self-relevant writing in a social science general education class. In D. Kelly-Riley & E. Norbert (Eds.), *Improving outcomes: Disciplinary writing, local assessment, and the aim of fairness* (pp. 147–158). Modern Language Association.

Singer-Freeman, K. E., Hobbs, H., & Robinson, C. (2019). Theoretical matrix of culturally relevant assessment. *Assessment Update, 31*(4), 1–16. https://doi.org/10.1002/au.30176

Singer-Freeman, K. E., & Robinson, C. (2020a). *Grand challenges in assessment: Collective issues in need of solutions* (Occasional Paper 47). University of Illinois and Indiana University, National Institute for Learning Outcomes Assessment. https://www.learningoutcomesassessment.org/wp-content/uploads/2020/11/GrandChallenges.pdf

Singer-Freeman, K. E., & Robinson, C. (2020b). Grand challenges for assessment in higher education. *Journal of Research and Practice in Assessment, 15*(2), 1–20. https://www.rpajournal.com/dev/wp-content/uploads/2020/11/Grand-Challenges-for-Assessment-in-Higher-Education.pdf

Singer-Freeman, K. E., Robinson, C., & Bastone, L. (2021). Balancing the freedom to teach with the freedom to learn: The critical role of assessment professionals in ensuring educational equity. In E. Sengupta & P. Blessinger (Eds.), *Teaching and learning practices for academic freedom: Innovations in higher education teaching and learning* (pp. 39–51). Emerald Publishing. https://doi.org/10.1108/S2055-364120200000034005

Smit, R. (2012). Towards a clearer understanding of student disadvantage in higher education: problematising deficit thinking. *Higher Education Research & Development, 31*(3), 369–380. https://doi.org/10.1080/07294360.2011.634383

Solórzano, D. (1998). Critical race theory, racial and gender microaggressions, and the experiences of Chicana and Chicano scholars. *International Journal of Qualitative Studies in Education, 11*(1), 121–136. https://doi.org/10.1080/095183998236926

Steele, C. M., & Aronson, J. (1995). Stereotype threat and the intellectual test performance of African Americans. *Journal of Personality and Social Psychology, 69*(5), 797–811. https://doi.org/10.1037/0022-3514.69.5.797

Steinke, P., & Fitch, P. (2017). Minimizing bias when assessing student work. *Research and Practice in Assessment, 12*, 87–95. https://files.eric.ed.gov/fulltext/EJ1168692.pdf

Stiggins, R., & Chappuis, J. (2005). Using student-involved classroom assessment to close achievement gaps. *Theory Into Practice, 44*(1), 11–18. https://doi.org/10.1207/s15430421tip4401_3

Tkatchov, M. (2019). Equity in "authentic" assessments: A closer look at defining and assessing learning outcomes in competency-based education. *Intersection, 2019*(2), 16–19. https://www.aalhe.org/assets/docs/Intersection/AAHLE_fall_2019_Intersection_final.pdf

Verjee, B. (2003). *Towards an Aboriginal approach to culturally appropriate assessment methodologies.* Kwantlen University College.

Walton, G. M., & Spencer, S. J. (2009). Latent ability: Grades and test scores systematically underestimate the intellectual ability of negatively stereotyped students. *Psychological Science, 20*(9), 1132–1139. https://doi.org/10.1111/j.1467-9280.2009.02417.x

Witham, K. A., & Bensimon, E. M. (2012). Creating a culture of inquiry around equity and student success. In S. D. Museus and U. M. Jayakumar (Eds.), *Creating campus cultures: Fostering success among racially diverse student populations,* (pp. 46–67). Routledge.

Yancey, K. B. (2012). College admissions and the insight resume: Writing, reflection, and students' lived curriculum as a site of equitable assessment. In A. B. Inoue & M. Poe (Eds.), *Race and writing assessment* (pp. 171–185). Peter Lang.

Zajda, J., Majhanovich, S., & Rust, V. (2006). Introduction: Education and social justice. *Review of Education, 52,* 9–22. https://doi.org/10.1007/s11159-005-5614-2

Zerquera, D., Reyes, K. A., Pender, J. T., & Abbady, R. (2018). Understanding practitioner-driven assessment and evaluation efforts for social justice. In D. Zerquera, I. Hernández, & J. G. Berumen (Eds.), *Assessment and Social Justice: Pushing Through Paradox* (New Directions for Institutional Research, no. 177, pp. 15–40). Jossey-Bass. https://doi.org/10.1002/ir.20254

7

EQUITY-CENTERED ASSESSMENT

Varying Approaches and Lenses

Stephanie J. Waterman, Gianina R. Baker,
Gavin W. Henning, and Anne E. Lundquist

The previous chapters in this book discussed the varied dialogues and scholarships across higher education related to the intersection of equity and assessment as well as outlined some overarching models and approaches. In this chapter, we want to elevate the work of decolonization and Indigeneity and provide an example of that in practice as well as share brief examples of equity-centered practices across and within an institution to bring the scholarship to application in the institutional context. Subsequent chapters in this book explore each of these areas in more depth, bringing the voices and lenses of a variety of scholars and practitioners.

Knowledge Systems—How We Think We Know What We Know

How do we know what we know? Knowledge construction and knowledge creation is at the heart of epistemology—the study or theory of knowledge. Using a psychological perspective, people can know things through intuition (gut instinct), authority (someone says something is true), rationalism (logic and reasoning), empiricism (observation and experience), or the scientific method (systematically collecting and analyzing; Cuttler, 2017). These five ways of knowing only capture some of the ways people acquire and create knowledge. Other ways of knowing include language, sense perception, emotion, imagination, memory, and faith (IB Better, n.d.).

Western cultures tend to place more value on ways of knowing that claim to be "objective" and can be proven by evidence such as through/via the scientific method and empiricism rather than more humanistic means such as emotion, imagination, and faith. This focus on objectivity is a result of the scientific revolution (Lundquist & Henning, 2020) where objectivity was considered critical to knowledge acquisition as the knower needed to be separated from the known. But the more humanistic, "subjective" ways of knowing should be considered as credible as other, more scientific, approaches in the academy.

Indigenous Knowledge Systems

> *Knowledge must understand where you are.*
>
> —Chavollo, 2019

Indigenous knowledge systems (IKS) and Indigenous research paradigms (IRP; for example, Chilisa, 2012; Kovach, 2009; Wilson, 2008) existed long before settler systems of higher education occupied Indigenous lands. Despite intentional attempts by settler colonial systems, such as our field of higher education, to erase Indigenous peoples and IKS, these ways are still valued and continue to inform Indigenous peoples. In 1991, Kirkness and Barnhardt published their article, "First Nations and Higher Education: The Four Rs—Respect, Relevance, Reciprocity, Responsibility." Linda Tuhiwai Smith's essential work, *Decolonizing Methodologies: Research and Indigenous Peoples*, was first published in 1999. Indigenous scholars rely heavily upon these early foundational pieces. Their work is relevant today and provides the framework for this portion of this chapter. We include them to challenge standard conceptions of assessment.

The very nature of where knowledge is formed and located (see also Basso, 1996) is centered in Smith's (1999) work. Indigenous and othered communities marginalized by dominant systems are communities that continue and grow, construct knowledge, and are sites of resistance. Foundational principles of IKS include expanding settler colonial notions of educational benefits, such as income and academic promotion, to relationship, "bringing the work home," and benefiting the community, lands (Smith et al., 2019, p. 10) because we are in relation and responsible to all of Creation. Indigenous students often report that their purpose in attaining a degree was to give back to their communities (Reyes, 2019), such as strengthening community relationships, strengthening relationships with Creation, and sustaining vulnerable languages and ceremony. These are endeavors that are difficult to measure beyond colonized criteria. For example, a university graduate may return with a degree in biology to a small coastal community and engage in water restoration that greatly benefits the overall wellness in their community yet earn a relatively small salary without a role or title that is recognized as impactful by institutional ranking criteria. In this example, success cannot be measured within the dominant Western paradigm as it does not value or "count" relational and community success.

That Native students' success is not recognized post-graduation is not surprising because they were not served well, if at all, by mainstream institutions while in attendance (Shotton et al., 2013). They have instead become the "American Indian research asterisk" (Garland, 2007, p. 612; Lowe, 2005). Shotton et al. (2013) stated that

> native scholars and practitioners have long struggled with the invisibility of Native people within the academy; we are often excluded from institutional data and reporting; omitted from the curriculum, absent from the research and literature, and virtually written out of the higher education story. (p. 175)

Fryberg and Townsend (2008) explain that invisibility is an intentional act involving an active "writing out" of the story of a particular group, often serving to maintain a status quo that benefits the dominant group. Furthermore, the "asterisk" mentality concerning Natives in academia has resulted in a serious lack of understanding of and dialogue on appropriate solutions. In part because the Native American student population has remained around 1% of the national student population for about 40 years (McFarland et al., 2017), Native participation in statistical reports, including individual institutional or departmental reports, often uses an asterisk to explain (erase) that there were too few students who identified as Native to be included in the statistical analysis. While sample size does impact statistical analysis, data drives funding which in turn impacts support services and assessment practices. There is insufficient space here to discuss the larger impact of invisibilizing an entire population through colonial constructs of counting (Walter & Anderson, 2013). Suffice it to say that the unquestioned normalization of an asterisk to (dis)count a population normalizes erasure. These issues also apply to the common lumping together students of color or "othered" groups for purposes of statistical analysis.

In addition to being invisible in data sets, IKS and IRP are invisible within higher education decision-making and assessment. Arola (2011) stated that the first "hallmark of American Indian philosophy is the commitment to the belief that all things are related—and this belief is not simply an ontological claim, but rather an intellectual and ethical maxim" (p. 555). All knowing is contextualized and complex within a particular environment and circumstances, so there are no absolutes which close off the possibility of an option that has not yet been experienced. One's views are both "universally applicable but also eminently revisable" (Arola, 2011, p. 558). What is central is the act of relating, and that relating can occur through stories. Pewewardy (2013) stated that there is much to be learned from the oral and written records of the educational history of Indigenous Peoples, including the ancient and traditional forms, where "[t]hese ancient traditions are profound models of culturally responsive excellence in Indigenous education" (p. 148).

The narrative voice in research provides space to capture and lift up the storytelling tradition of Indigenous Peoples (Archibald et al., 2019). Using research methods that allow for the telling of different stories where "the choice of materials and methods are inspired by, and depend upon, the context . . . values diverse forms of knowledge, especially those knowledges that have historically been subjugated" (Kaomea, 2016, p. 100). While Kaomea (2016) offered the lens of bricolage and metaphors of quilting along with the Hawaiian practice of ha'i mo'olelo or "talk story"; Shawn Wilson (2008) provided research methods to reap stories, based in the importance of relationships and relationality, where research is a journey in relationships; and Linda Tuhiwai Smith (1999) offered decolonizing methodologies for research. Minthorn and Shotton's (2018) edited text offers examples of decolonized and Indigenized higher education research. IKS in partnership with research is more than story. Research questions need to come from communities, in partnership with communities, not about or on communities. Variables need to be clearly understood by the researcher and research participants. Indigenous communities have been harmed by research and therefore often distrust academics (Smith, 1999). In documenting and assessing learning, we should not shut down learning where educators are "threatened" that those who had things taken from them "might reclaim it when we are skilled, proficient, and earned degrees" (Bennett, 1997, p. 142).

Kirkness and Barnhardt (1991) spoke directly to the field of higher education critiquing policies that do not increase Indigenous degree attainment. A key critique they offer is considering "coming to the university versus going to the university" (p. 2). Universities recruit students to "come" to institutions "with its own long-standing, deeply-rooted policies, practices, programs and standards intended to serve the needs of a society in which it is embedded" (pp. 2–3) and students are expected to adjust to the system. When students do not adjust to a system not designed for them, they leave and are then counted as dropouts. However, through an Indigenous lens "going to" university recognizes that students do not want to assimilate, they want an education that respects their Indigeneity, one that provides many ways to connect their education to the broader benefit of their community or Indigenous people.

Kirkness and Barnhardt (1991) offer the "4Rs—respect, relevance, reciprocity, responsibility" to frame our understanding of Indigenous university students. Institutions must *respect* Indigenous ways of being and include communities; institutions must develop "inclusive" standards to provide a relevant education that supports spirituality, traditions, place, and other values that Indigenous students can *relate* to (p. 9) and that are important to the community. Learning must be *reciprocal*—institutions have much to learn from Indigenous peoples and ways of being. This "entails honoring each other's roles" (Pidgeon & Hardy Cox, 2002, p. 103); with institutions being *responsible* to support all students. Relationships are key to the 4Rs. In order to support Indigenous students, higher education staff need to engage in respectful relationships to learn a community's traditions, to develop relevant programming and assessment, to expand their knowledge base, and to be responsible in their work. The 4Rs would help any institution work with marginalized groups. The 4Rs inform assessment alone or along with the Indigenous wholistic framework (see, e.g., Pidgeon et al., 2014), which is infused with "perspectives of emotional, intellectual, spiritual and physical realms" (p. 6) with an individual at the center surrounded by family and community.

Examples of Practice

The following example, offered by Stephanie Waterman, Onondaga, Turtle Clan, from the Onondaga Nation and associate professor at the Ontario Institute for Studies in Education/University of Toronto, illuminates an approach to assessment that centers Indigenous ways of knowing.

Indigenous Knowledge and Assessment

Do you know where you are? What does this question mean to you? Do you know the Indigenous people who were removed so that your institution could be built? Do you know what plants are native to where you work and live, or in your own homeland?

I asked these questions at the beginning of a presentation at the ACPA/CACUSS 2019 Assessment Conference in Toronto, Ontario, where we were the guests of the Mississauga of the Credit River, a territory that is subject to the Dish with One Spoon Wampum covenant between the Haudenosaunee and Anishnaabek peoples of the area, as well as the Huron-Wendat, Petun, and other First Peoples. I also asked the audience to consider their responsibility to the land, to think beyond reading acknowledgments, to extend them to how we interact, literally, by recycling, using reusable water bottles, considering our environmental footprint, and respect for the land and peoples.

In my presentation, I also mentioned the hotel policy regarding chair and table placement in the room where I was presenting. Chairs that were not bolted to the floor might as well have been, considering a hotel policy that did not allow them to be moved. Grounding the presentation in this way emphasized my Indigeneity in the context of structures, the hotel, and higher education, and questioned "normalized" ways of being. These largely unquestioned norms in higher education, based on settler colonialism (Coulthard, 2014), inform the practice and foundations of assessment.

Let me connect this discussion to a classroom example. I once had a master's student who was a highly recommended practitioner. Her colleagues praised her, and I never heard a negative comment about her. She was engaging in class, asked thought-provoking questions, brought creativity to the classroom, would casually sum up our class discussion beautifully—without notes—and struggled with her writing. Writing was difficult for her. I feared for her success in the program if she could not write a thesis or pass a written comprehensive exam. When the time came, we sat in my office and I administered an oral comprehensive exam. She answered each question with confidence and accuracy. I had notes. She did not. One could argue that a good student affairs practitioner needs to write proposals, reports, and programming documents, however, student affairs practitioners rarely work in isolation. Writing was not her strength, but being a thoughtful, creative, ethical, and well-rounded student affairs practitioner was. Limiting her assessment in the program to a written document would have been unfair, not holistic, applying a colonial academic and narrow standard of competence.

Waterman's story of using an oral examination instead of a written examination to assess practitioner competence as opposed to assessing writing strength at the expense of practitioner competence is a wonderful example of using a nondominant knowledge system to inform assessment methods. By adapting the assessment method to respect the student's strengths, she could truly assess the student's grasp of the literature rather than assessing the students' ability to write, which was not an outcome being assessed. Placing students at the center and considering how to center equity in assessment practice changes how assessment is implemented. A number of institutions have done just this.

Following are additional examples of practice submitted by institutional representatives. Please read them with our introduction in mind. These examples showcase how assessment for equity is carried out within classrooms, academic programs, student affairs units, cocurricular activities, and across an institution. They represent a variety of equitable assessment processes and practices at different levels throughout higher education.

Equity-Centered Assessment in the Classroom

Following are examples of equity-centered assessment being implemented in college classrooms.

University of Forest Haven—Course Reform

Professor Beatrice Gonzalez-Pruitt teaches educational philosophy in the doctor of education program at Palmetto Palms University. Through the course, students learn various educational philosophies and ways of knowing. The course consists primarily of reading and seminar-style discussion but includes a culminating assignment at the end of the course. Typically, this assignment has been a paper in which students compare and contrast four philosophies and/or ways of knowing and then articulate which philosophy will guide their dissertation work. This year, employing the principles of universal design for learning (UDL), Gonzalez-Pruitt allowed students a choice in the format of the final project. They could draft a paper, produce a professional quality video, or complete a project. Students could also propose a different format for the final assignment. Regardless of format, students had to address the same assignment prompt and rubric. Through negotiation, students were able to choose the method that best allowed them to demonstrate their learning.

Equity-Centered Assessment in an Academic Program

Following are examples of equity-centered assessment being implemented in academic programs.

Midwestern State College—Curricular Reform

Each summer, the faculty in the Department of Sociology at Midwestern State College review assessment data from the past year and discuss curricular changes for the upcoming year. Given protests on campus supporting Black Lives Matter, the faculty wanted to explore how to integrate equity into the sociology curriculum. Employing a transformative paradigm, the faculty decided to involve students in that process. During the fall, faculty teaching the qualitative methods and quantitative methods courses included a new group project to investigate how students in the program thought equity could and should be included in the curriculum.

Students in each methods course developed a research proposal that included an overview of why integrating equity into the curriculum was important, a literature review, and an outline for methods to be used to answer the research question. Students in the quantitative methods course implemented a survey to gather data while students in the qualitative methods course implemented talking circles. Students in each respective course analyzed the data and drafted reports. The instructors brought the two courses together for a special 3-hour extended class period to review the other course's report and discuss the findings. Working collaboratively, the students developed a set of recommendations based on both sets of data.

Students recommended that there be a required course on structural and institutional racism and its impact on social institutions. In addition, the students suggested that faculty integrate the issue of equity into all courses. Finally, they recommended a revision in both the program learning outcomes as well as the structure of those outcomes. Rather than simply having a list of program outcomes, students recommended organizing them into "pillars." These pillars included theory, theory application, research methods, and equity. Inclusion of equity as a pillar, rather than a singular outcome, emphasized the importance of the issue in the curriculum. Outcome areas within the equity pillar consisted of perspective-taking, communication, collaboration, social and self-awareness, and addressing inequities.

The benefits of this project expanded beyond the integration of equity in the curriculum. Students were able to apply what they were learning in their research methods courses to a project with immediate implications. Faculty were able to view the curriculum and the issue of equity from students' perspectives, which increased their understanding of each. Students became more invested in their learning as they cocreated the learning goals that applied to all courses. Finally, faculty and students united in equity as a learning goal.

Equity-Centered Assessment in the Cocurriculum

Following are examples of equity-centered assessment being implemented in the cocurriculum.

Big City Community College—Equity Audit/Program Review

The president of Big City Community College (BCCC) established an Equity and Inclusion Taskforce to explore and address issues of equity and inclusion on campus. In order to understand issues across the institution, the taskforce requested that each campus department perform a diversity audit during the current academic year. Departments were given flexibility in the approach they used, but the audit needed to include a summary analysis of strengths and weaknesses of the department along with an action plan for implementing recommendations.

Using the standards and process outlined by the Council for the Advancement of Standards in Higher Education (CAS), the BCCC division of student affairs decided to implement a modified version of program review for departments across the division. However, rather than implementing a comprehensive program review that covered all 12 sections of the set of CAS Standards for each department, the vice president for student affairs asked directors to focus only on Part 5: Access, Equity, Diversity, and Inclusion. For those not familiar, the CAS Standards are sets of standards for 47 functional areas in higher education that are developed, reviewed, and revised by the Council for the Advancement of Standards in Higher Education, (CAS, n.d.).

Each department in the division was given the fall semester to review existing data, collect additional data, complete section 5 of the Self-Assessment Guide (SAG) that pertained to the appropriate set of standards for that functional area, and draft a summary report. Evidence and reports were uploaded to a shared drive for all staff in the division to review prior to the division-wide retreat in mid-January. During the retreat, staff working in small groups identified key themes of strengths and weaknesses across the division in regard to access, equity, diversity, and inclusion. After the retreat, these themes were aggregated by a team of volunteers and presented to the division leadership team who drafted recommendations for action.

Western Michigan University—Disaggregating Cocurricular
Student Data and Using It for Change
The Office of Student Engagement at Western Michigan University (WMU) tracks event attendance and leadership and membership in registered student organizations (RSOs) as well as a wide variety of cocurricular campus events. Their goal is to ensure the engagement of every student. In 2018, they reported that over 75% of WMU students are engaged each year in some out-of-class activities. In the fall of 2018, only 750 new students (out of 3,000) had not swiped their student ID card to gain entry to any event on campus in the first 3 weeks of the academic year. In January 2019, a review of disaggregated event attendance and student organization data revealed that there were disparities between populations for event attendance and student organization involvement and leadership. For example, the data revealed that the Native American student population was significantly less engaged than other race groups on campus (82.5% not in an RSO in fall 2018 compared to the student body average of 75.9%, 55.3% not attending an event in fall 2018 compared to the student body average of 47.9%).

In response, the director of Western Michigan University's Signature Program (a student engagement program for students to reflect on their out-of-class learning experiences and explore and identify a passion that will be reflected on their WMU diploma) and the director of the Office of Student Engagement collaborated to restart the Native American Student Organization (NASO), a club that had been inactive for several years. All students who identified as Native American or Alaskan Native were invited to an initial meeting with a graduate assistant and the director of the WMU Signature Program. After this meeting, the students in attendance took control of the effort to restart (NASO) and held their first on-campus meeting in April 2019. Since this date, NASO has remained active again on WMU's campus. This is an example of why disaggregation of data, even with small Ns is important. Frequently Native American students are not included in analyses as their numbers are. If data disaggregation had not included Native American students, the Native American Student Organization would not have been restarted.

Illinois Skyway Collegiate Conference—Cocurricular Competitions
The Illinois Skyway Collegiate Conference (ISSC), established in 1969, consists of eight Illinois community colleges—College of Lake County, Elgin Community College, McHenry County College, Moraine Valley Community College, Morton College, Oakton Community College, Prairie State College, and Waubonsee Community College—all actively working to provide student-athletes with additional ways to connect to their institutions. Each year, one of the member institutions hosts a cocurricular competition, in addition to its regular athletic competitions, among its member institutions for all student-athletes. The general student population is also able to compete in such competitions. While the theme of the cocurricular competition varies each year (for example, Writing Festival, Art Competition, STEM competition, Jazz Festival, etc.), data are collected to assess the effectiveness of the events. The findings gathered highlighted the following data points of those Skyway student-athletes who participate in the designated cocurricular activity: higher credit and degree/certificate completion, higher overall GPA, higher rates of transfer to 4-year institutions, and higher retention rates. These outcomes are significant, especially for student athletes of color. Ensuring that student athletes of color, often overrepresented in certain sports, have access to inclusive, high-quality experiences, such as cocurricular competitions that could be considered high-impact practices (i.e., writing intensive, collaborative assignments, etc.) provides an additional outlet for such students to access such opportunities. Early research points to student-athletes who participate in these cocurricular competitions not only being more engaged within the institution but also with the faculty mentors associated with the program. Data

specific to various student athlete populations, and general student populations as a whole, are currently being collected to better understand student
results of participating in such cocurricular competitions.

Equity-Centered Assessment in Administrative Units

Following are examples of equity-centered assessment being implemented in
administrative offices and departments.

City College of San Francisco—Reserved Textbook Usage

The City College of San Francisco Library and Learning Resources Division
examined reserve textbook usage data that support its 32 foundation courses;
the data indicated that the cost of the textbook correlated with circulation;
expensive textbooks are checked out the most often, and least expensive
textbooks are checked out less often. Collected data confirmed that providing increased access to expensive, high demand, high-quality textbook collections to students from specific equity population groups helps such students
achieve stated equity goals, such as transfer degree completion, certificate
completion, and developing employment skills. Further, the library used this
data to request additional monies to add new reserve books to the collection by prioritizing textbook purchasing for courses/programs focused on the
defined equity groups.

Sinclair College—Using Data to Improve Administrative Departments

Sinclair College used mapping to assess its campus' administrative departments in an effort to more cohesively integrate student services. Using
feedback from students on how they experience departments such as advising, financial aid, bursar, and so forth, staff uncovered a variety of issues
during the orientation of students. By talking through and documenting
the actual orientation processes to different administrative departments,
which were found to be disjointed, students and staff used this information to improve processes integral to student success by enabling an
environment for learning. Using a variety of methods to gather student
and staff feedback ensures that these processes are seamless for a wide
variety of student populations. More importantly, this focused attention
on where administrative processes are not connected and addressing such
issues enables students to focus on learning, rather than worry about how
and when to pay. Using the Chutes and Ladders game to assist in developing its infographic, students and staff found a way to communicate, or
even unhide, what they learned about the student orientation process to
connect and align administrative process—a process often hidden from

first-generation students trying to navigate and make sense of while learning. By unmasking administrative processes, student and staff feedback can truly serve to improve student orientation as well as other support services important to student retention, especially for historically underserved and marginalized students.

Equity-Centered Assessment Across the Institution

Following are examples of equity-centered assessment being implemented across individual colleges and universities.

South Dakota State University—Learning Outcomes

The South Dakota Board of Regents requires the selection of cross-cultural skills for each university program. The goal of including cross-curricular skills is to enable each state institution to integrate and extend general education learning into academic programs in a way that is consistent with each institution's mission, vision, and values. Each institution must select at least five of the 11 cross-curricular skill requirements as programmatic student learning outcomes. South Dakota State University took this directive a step further by requiring all academic programs to include diversity, inclusion, and equity as one of their 11 institutional outcomes. Requiring diversity, inclusion, and equity as an outcome across all academic programs demonstrates the institution's commitment by centering this knowledge and skill set within academic disciplines.

San Diego State University—Redesigning Learning and Development to Close Equity Gaps

As one approach to closing equity gaps, San Diego State University (SDSU) has been iteratively redesigning their one-unit first-semester seminar to integrate the development of malleable intrapersonal competencies (e.g., resilience, academic self-efficacy, task and stress management, etc.), metacognitive concepts (e.g., cultural wealth, future self), and traditional 1st-year seminar content (e.g., advising, engagement opportunities). A keystone assessment component has been the semester-start and semester-end deployment of a Likert-based student survey comprising validated inventories such as sense of belonging, personal well-being, and metacognitive awareness, which has served as a keystone data source to inform, assess, and refine the curriculum. For example, inferential statistics are being used to ascertain which identities and their intersections need more or different learning opportunities to close equity gaps as measured by GPA and persistence of underrepresented minority, Pell-eligible, and first-generation populations. This approach is equitable in itself as it embodies the notion that no one size fits all and centers the student's lived experience and voice as the primary informant of what needs to change within the student's experience. These efforts have resulted in decreased academic probation and increased GPA and persistence for varying identity groups and their intersections. This teacher-scholar approach to evidence-based, equity-driven student success has also built a strong community among an expanding and diverse cross-divisional team of faculty, staff, graduate students, and administrators. Future endeavors include creating opportunities for students to actively reflect upon their early-semester survey results and select specific curriculum components for "deeper dives."

St. Edward's University—Equitable Outcome Collection and Analysis

St. Edward's University devised an equitable data collection and analysis process to assess outcomes in a new general education curriculum (DeSantis, 2020). The Office of Institutional Effectiveness and Planning (IEP) coordinated with faculty liaisons to identify course artifacts housed in the institution's learning management system to assess. Course faculty then identified which dimensions of the appropriate outcome rubric were addressed by the course assignment. After a systematic random sample of artifacts were extracted through the learning management system, IEP staff connected the artifacts to record-level data within the student information system. Through the process, IEP staff were able to align key variables such as gender, race, and Pell status to the appropriate artifact before anonymizing both to ensure results could not be traced back to an individual student. After a norming process, faculty volunteers scored the artifacts using the rubric for the appropriate general education outcome. Once scores were entered, IEP staff connected the scores with the anonymized data and built visualizations that showed rubric scores by different student populations. The dashboards were shared with key stakeholders before being shared with the broader campus community.

Benefits of this approach included faculty being more receptive to assessment because it was equity-based. Faculty also took a more holistic approach to assessment. Rather than focusing on performance of students in their own courses, analyses focused on why different populations over- or underperformed. Within-course assessment design was also improved as it was learned that student performance in writing programs declined for intermediate courses because assessed assignments in the entry and advanced writing courses allowed revision of those assignments, whereas the respective assignment in intermediate level courses did not allow for revision.

Themes and Reflection Questions

The examples provided here vary in approach, purpose, and institutional context, among other things. But even with such variability, there are some common themes that emerge as people integrate equity and assessment practices.

- *Respect for place/context.* Each example was unique to institutional context. Context drove data collection, findings, and institutional/divisional change.
- *A clear focus on equitable outcomes.* Each practice centered equity as the driving reason for the program, learning opportunity, or service being assessed as well as the approach to the assessment.
- *Faculty and staff are crucial to equity-minded efforts.* In nearly all of the curricular examples, faculty were mentioned as the "doers" of the work. For others, students, staff, and administrators were involved.
- *Collaboration across stakeholder groups.* No one person or department entered into this work alone. While the data might have been gathered from one department/unit, it was clear that others were sought to help with analysis and attempted improvement solutions. Collaboration increases a sense of relationship and responsibility.
- *Outcome driven/guided, comprehensive data collection and analysis process.* Data collection and analyses were guided by intentionally developed outcomes at either department or institutional level.
- *Respect of student voice.* Ensuring that student voice is included in the decision-making is a key aspect of equity-centered assessment. Throughout the cases presented, inclusion of student voice is evident for those wanting to make intentional improvements within an institution.
- *Evidence-informed changes.* In each of the examples presented, there was mention of data collection and disaggregation in order to better understand and respect an aspect of student experience at the institution as well as various student populations. After analysis, improvements were put into place making the assessment relevant to those involved.

Through these examples, possibilities are seen for expanding traditional assessment. Stakeholders were considered valuable knowledge holders and were actively sought to inform the work. Diverse forms of data were considered, data were disaggregated, and assessment was made relevant to the stakeholders. In these examples, assessment became more relational.

Conclusion

We began this chapter with a short introduction to Indigenous knowledge systems and the 4Rs of respect, relevance, reciprocity, and responsibility to help the reader approach assessment beyond methods that have been assumed to be bias-free or value-free. Our goal was to complicate assessment in ways that are respectful, responsible, relevant to stakeholders, and contextual. We then shared examples of how this might be done. The case studies presented in this chapter vary greatly, demonstrating that there are many ways to approach assessment with an equity lens, there is no one right way, especially when serving the unique needs of the students served by an institution. Some efforts have an institutional directive as well as buy-in and a variety of campus areas are aligning their efforts with those equity goals. Other examples are very specific to the unit, demonstrating that faculty, staff, and administrators can start where they are with the programs and services in their portfolio and begin to make substantive change. In all cases, it was apparent that faculty, staff, and administrators are reflecting on the unquestioned assumptions of higher education as a whole and the assumed associated practices. This reflection leads to new approaches to assessment that demonstrate the many faces of equitable assessment happening at colleges and universities today.

References

Archibald, J., Lee-Morgan, J. B. J., & De Santolo, J. (Eds.). (2019). *Decolonizing research: Indigenous storywork as methodology*. Zed Books.

Arola, A. (2011). Native American philosophy. In E. Edelglass & J. Garfield (Eds.), *The Oxford handbook of world philosophy*. Oxford University Press. https://doi .org/10.1093/oxfordhb/9780195328998.003.0048

Basso, K. H. (1996). *Wisdom sits in places: Landscape and language among the Western Apache*. University of New Mexico Press.

Bennett, R. (1997). Why didn't you teach me? In A. Garrod & C. Larimore (Eds.), *First person first people: Native American college graduates tell their life stories* (pp. 136–153). Cornell University Press.

CAS. (n.d.). *About*. https://www.cas.edu

Chavolla, R. (2019). *Guts* [Film]. https://filmmakermagazine.com/107677-watch-guts-noah-hutton-and-taylor-hesss-short-doc-on-the-feminist-anti-colonial-environmental-lab-clear/#.XSVNY3t7l0I

Chilisa, B. (2012). *Indigenous research methodologies*. SAGE.

Coulthard, G. S. (2014). *Red skin, white masks: Rejecting the colonial politics of recognition*. University of Minnesota Press.

Cuttler, C. (2017). Methods of knowing. In P. C. Price, R. Jhangiani, i.-C. A. Chiang, D. C. Leighton, & C. Cuttler (Eds.), *Research methods in psychology*. Washington State University. https://opentext.wsu.edu/carriecuttler/chapter/methods-of-knowing/

DeSantis, M. (2020, September). *St. Edward's University: Rethinking general education to support social justice*. University of Illinois and Indiana University, National Institute for Learning Outcomes Assessment, Council for the Advancement of Standards in Higher Education, and Campus Labs. https://www.learningoutcomesassessment.org/wp-content/uploads/2020/09/EquityCase_St_Edwards.pdf

Fryberg, S. A., & Townsend, S. S. M. (2008). The psychology of invisibility. In G. Adams, M. Biernat, N. R. Branscombe, C. S. Crandall, & L. S. Wrightsman (Eds.), *Commemorating Brown: The social psychology of racism and discrimination* (pp. 173–193). American Psychological Association.

Garland, J. L. (2007). [Untitled review of the book *Serving Native American students*, by M. J. Tippeconnic Fox, S. C. Lowe, & G. S. McClellan]. *Journal of College Student Development*, *48*(5), 612–614. http://doi.org/10.1353/csd.2007.0053

IB Better. (n.d.). 8 ways of knowing in TOK. https://ibbetter.com/ways-of-knowing/

Kaomea J. (2016). Qualitative analysis as hooku'iku'i or bricolage: Teaching emancipatory Indigenous research in postcolonial Hawaii'i. *Qualitative Inquiry*, *22*(2), 99–106. https://doi.org/10.1177%2F1077800415620222

Kirkness, V. J., & Barnhardt, R. (1991). First Nations and higher education: The 4Rs—respect, relevance, reciprocity, responsibility. *Journal of American Indian Education*, *30*(3), 1–15. https://www.jstor.org/stable/24397980

Kovach, M. (2009). *Indigenous methodologies: Characteristics, conversations, and contexts*. University of Toronto Press.

Lowe, S. C. (2005). This is who I am: Experience of Native American students. In M. J. Tippeconnic Fox, S. C. Lowe, & G. S. McClellan (Eds.), *Serving Native American students* (New Direction for Student Services, no. 109, pp. 33–40). Jossey-Bass. https://doi.org/10.1002/ss.151

Lunduist, A., & Henning, G. W. (2020). From avoiding bias to social justice: A continuum of assessment practices to advance diversity, equity, and inclusion. In T. Simpson & A. Spicer-Runnels (Eds.), *Developing an intercultural responsiveness leadership style for faculty and administrators*. IGI Global.

McFarland, J., Hussar, B., De Brey, C., Snyder, T., Wang, X., Wilkinson-Flicker, S., Gebrekristos, S., Zhang, J., Rathbun, A., Barmer, A., Bullock Mann, F., & Hinz, S. (2017). *The condition of education 2017. NCES 2017–144*. National Center for Education Statistics. https://files.eric.ed.gov/fulltext/ED574257.pdf

Minthorn, R. Z., & Shotton, H. J. (Eds.). (2018). *Reclaiming Indigenous research in higher education*. Rutgers University Press.

Pewewardy, C. (2013). 100 defensive tactics and attributions: Dodging the dialogue on cultural diversity. *Multicultural Education*, *20*(3/4), 9.

Pidgeon, M. (2016). More than a checklist: Meaningful Indigenous inclusion in higher education. *Social Inclusion*, *4*(1), 77–91. http://dx.doi.org/10.17645/si.v4i1.436

Pidgeon, M., Archibald, J., & Hawkey, C. (2014). Relationships matter: Supporting Aboriginal graduate students in British Columbia, Canada. *Canadian Journal of Higher Education*, *44*(1), 1–12. https://doi.org/10.47678/cjhe.v44i1.2311

Pidgeon, M., & Hardy Cox, D. G. (2002). Researching with Aboriginal peoples: Practices and principles. *Canadian Journal of Native Education*, *26*(2), 96–201.

Reyes, N. A. S. (2019). "What am I doing to be a good ancestor?": An Indigenized phenomenology of giving back among Native college graduates. *American Educational Research Journal*, *56*(3), 603–637. https://doi.org/10.3102%2F0002831218807180

Shotton, H. J., Lowe, S. C., & Waterman, S. J. (2013). *Beyond the asterisk: Understanding Native American students in higher education*. Stylus.

Smith, L. T. (1999). *Decolonizing methodologies: Research and Indigenous peoples*. Zed Books.

Smith, L. T., Tuck, E., & Yang, W. K. (Eds.). (2019). *Indigenous and decolonizing studies in education: Mapping the long view*. Routledge.

Walter, M., & Anderson, C. (2013). *Indigenous statistics: Quantitative research methodology*. Left Coast Press.

Wilson, S. (2008). *Research is ceremony: Indigenous research methodologies*. Fernwood.

PART THREE

HOW?

8

ASSESSMENT IN CLASS MEETINGS

Transparency Reduces Systemic Inequities

Mary-Ann Winkelmes

This chapter focuses on assessment practices that college and university teachers can use intentionally in their class meetings to combat systemic inequities and to complement equity-minded policies and practices that their institutions pursue. It considers assessment measures and practical, proactive pre-assessment tools from the Transparency in Learning and Teaching in Higher Education project (TILT Higher Ed) that already have demonstrated equitable benefits for students' learning, and it suggests how instructors can implement these tools immediately to predict and reduce systemic inequities in students' learning experiences.

In-Class Assessment

For millions of faculty and administrators in higher education in the winter and spring of 2020, a rapid shift to online teaching and learning, necessitated by the COVID-19 pandemic, highlighted stark systemic inequities in how students accessed, were included, and participated in online college class meetings and activities. Widespread recognition and concern around inequalities contributed to changes in how most institutions of higher education conducted assessment. Ninety-seven percent of respondents to a NILOA survey that included 624 institutions reported changes that mainly included: "modifying assignments and assessments, flexibility in assignment deadlines, shifting to pass/fail" (Jankowski, 2020, p. 3). Ninety percent of respondents indicated the changes were made specifically to address student needs, while 85% indicated that students' unequal access to technology prompted the modifications (Jankowski, 2020). While institutional changes to assessment practices in higher education often can be slow, these adaptations were prompt and decisive.

What made such promising change in the pursuit of equity possible? In a word, assessment. In-class assessment by faculty and instructors in colleges and universities across the globe identified inequities that required change. The vigilance with which teachers observed their students' learning during the winter and spring of 2020 responded to rapidly shifting educational conditions during the COVID-19 pandemic, as well as heightened global antiracism, and especially anti-Black racism awareness that resulted from protests around the nation and world over the death of George Floyd. Teachers could no longer rely upon expectations about how students would respond, based on their past experience with past students under similar conditions, as there were no similar conditions. College and university instructors across the world looked to their students' experiences, responses, and feedback to see how students were doing and what they were learning. Real-time, in-class assessment by teachers confirmed the greater equity gaps that have been documented in online education (Xu & Jaggars, 2014) and gathered incontrovertible evidence that prompted both individual teaching adjustments and institutional changes to assessment practices. This evidence-based approach to assessment illustrated the beneficial and responsive use of assessment to create change that improves students' learning experiences.

In-class assessment in the winter and spring of 2020 served formative purposes by following an assess-to-improve model that classroom assessment techniques (CATs) were designed to serve (Armstrong, 2020; McFadden, 2020; "Teaching in the Time of Corona," 2020). This model was visible in forums where teaching strategies were shared that responded to students' learning experiences, including publications like *The Chronicle of Higher Education*, *Inside Higher Education*, and social media platforms (Armstrong, 2020; McFadden, 2020; "Teaching in the Time of Corona," 2020). CATs offer insights about students' understanding of course content and mastery of disciplinary skills, and they inform teaching adjustments to enhance students' learning from one class meeting to the next, or even within a class meeting. Examples include: end-of-class minute-papers where students describe the main points they learned, their remaining questions, and what's the most confusing, muddiest point (Mosteller, 1989), frequent short quizzes (Light, 1990; Smith & Karpicke, 2014), and punctuated lectures where instructors teach a concept and then involve students in an activity that tests and reinforces their understanding (such as consulting with peers to share understanding and write a question or generate an example [Babb et al., 2018; Chickering & Gamson, 1987; Freeman et al., 2014; Middendorf & Kalish, 1996]). Eric Mazur's (1997) peer instruction variation on the punctuated lecture efficiently maximizes students' capacity in a large lecture course to improve each other's understanding during a 2–3-minute classroom assessment check in the middle of a class meeting. Over 50 CATs are explicated in a foundational book by Tom Angelo and K. Patricia Cross (1993), and still more in Elizabeth Barkley and Clair Major's handbook (2016) and their materials shared through the K. Patricia Cross Academy website (Barkley & Major, 2020).

Regular assessment in class meetings can offer more than a measure of students' learning. It can also shed light on students' unequal readiness to learn. For teachers who approach in-class assessment with the concern and vigilance that was common under pandemic conditions in the spring of 2020, in-class assessment highlights systemic inequities in higher education (Czerniewicz, 2020). Through the lenses of computers, cell phones, and other devices across the internet, teachers witnessed devastating inequities differently than they had in on-campus classrooms: students' unequal access to internet service, computer hardware and software, safe and quiet physical spaces for studying and participating in classes, as well as students' unequal exposure to risk from violence, contagion, homelessness, hunger, and associated traumas, and their unequal access to physical and mental health support (Anderson, 2020; Casey, 2020). The process of in-class assessment lent greater visibility to the systemic inequities that disproportionately disadvantage ethnically underrepresented students, especially Black and Indigenous students, as well as other students of color, low-income students, and students who are first-generation in their family to attend college (Czerniewicz, 2020). Students did not begin class meetings with equal readiness to learn in the spring and fall of 2020 (Czerniewicz, 2020). Teachers and other institutional leaders recognized that students neither created nor chose these invidious barriers to their success, nor did students possess the resources to combat them (Czerniewicz, 2020). Institutions addressed some of these inequalities by loaning out equipment to facilitate connecting to class meetings; awarding more financial aid; changing academic schedules, deadlines, workloads, and grading policies; and by offering additional mental health consultation services online (Jaschik, 2020a, 2020b; Lederman, 2020; St. Amour, 2020). These supports aimed to provide students with more equal access to the necessary preconditions for learning, yet they followed rather than preceded that learning and the assessment activities.

CATs aim to gather information while there is still time to identify students' misunderstandings, to explain a concept more effectively, and to adjust teaching and learning activities in order to improve students' learning outcomes as measured by future graded assessments in the course. Yet even when the CAT takes place during a class meeting, following immediately after a lesson or learning activity, the assessment is by necessity a posthoc activity. In this regard, CATs are similar to most forms of assessment of students' understanding of content and of their mastery of skills. An assessment of students' work completed on an in-class activity or quiz, an assignment, project, experiment, or exam always follows after that work is completed.

The posthoc nature of assessment prompts a question: What sort of assessment activity could precede a lesson, to better and more equitably prepare students to fully comprehend it? What assessment tools might bring students closer to the same starting line of preparation and understanding before a lesson begins? Figure 8.1 explicates when and why various in-class assessment tools might be used.

Figure 8.1. In-class assessment tools: When and why to use them.

Assessment Tool	When it is used	Evaluative Purpose
Transparent equitable learning readiness assessment for teachers	(Pre-) Before a class meeting	• Preclass planning for an in-class preassessment
Transparent equitable learning framework for students and teachers	(Pre-) At the beginning of a class meeting	• Prepares students for self-assessment and learning • Unites teachers with students to address inequities before learning begins
Transparent equitable learning framework for students and teachers	(Pre-) During class, before a learning activity	• Prepares students for self-assessment and learning • Unites teachers with students to address inequities before starting the activity
In-class learning activity	(Post-) During class, after a product (report, insight, solution) is completed	• Posthoc formative guidance for teacher and students

Assessment Tool	When it is used	Evaluative Purpose
Exam or quiz in class	(Post-) During class, after completion	• Summative measure of mastery • Some formative guidance for student and teacher
Assignment in class		
Minute paper or muddiest point or other CAT	(Post-) End of class or after class	• Posthoc formative guidance for teacher and student

Transparency Project Measures for Proactive Pre-Assessment in Class

TILT Higher Ed offers measures and tools to support a proactive approach to in-class assessment. Teachers can use these tools to enhance their effectiveness in reducing systemic inequities in students' learning experiences by engaging students in metacognitive reflection about how they can expect to learn and how they can monitor their learning before the lesson or activity or assignment begins. QR 8.1 is a link to the TILT higher education pre- and postterm survey for students.

TILT Higher Ed aims to advance equitable teaching and learning practices that reduce systemic inequities in higher education through two main activities: (a) promoting students' conscious understanding of how they learn, and (b) enabling faculty to gather, share, and promptly benefit from current data about students' learning (Winkelmes, 2014–2020). Transparent instruction focuses in-class attention both on what students learn and on how they learn it. It engages teachers and students in real-time collaborative reflection on why teachers choose specific teaching approaches and learning activities, and how students respond to them (Winkelmes et al., 2019). A 2016 national study indicated that transparent teaching and learning offer statistically significant learning benefits for students, with even greater gains for underserved students (ethnically underrepresented, low-income, first-generation in their family to attend college; Winkelmes et al., 2016). A later study suggested that transparent teaching and learning correlate with students' increased persistence in college (Winkelmes et al., 2019).

For teachers, approaching proactive pre-assessment for the benefit of students' learning in class requires consideration of how students will learn the necessary material in a forthcoming lesson or activity. What do they want students to be doing during the class meeting that will maximize their opportunities to learn? The TILT Higher Ed pre- and postterm surveys for students

QR 8.1. Link to TILT Higher Ed pre- and postterm surveys for students.

identify some metacognitive behaviors that teachers may want their students to apply consciously during a class meeting:

- separate and examine the pieces of an idea, experience, or theory
- connect information from a variety of sources
- apply concepts to practical problems or in new situations
- consider the ethical implications of your actions
- improve your ability to learn effectively on your own
- analyze and interpret data
- choose methods appropriate to solving a problem
- consider opinions or points of view different from your own
- evaluate the strengths and weaknesses of ideas
- judge the reliability of information from various sources
- recognize when you need help with your academic work
- collaborate effectively with others
- ask instructors about how coursework and course activities benefit your learning

Merely identifying these desired student behaviors that encourage students' metacognitive awareness of their learning does not guarantee that students will engage in these behaviors. A forthcoming study indicates that these desired metacognitive student learning behaviors are correlated with the following teaching behaviors:

- identify a specific learning goal for each activity, lesson, or assignment
- provide detailed directions for each learning activity
- provide tools students can use to assess the quality of their work while that work is underway (Weisz et al., n.d.)

Further, when students recognize that teachers are taking these three actions, they report their own metacognitive awareness of the following aspects of their learning:

- In this course, I knew the purpose of each assignment.
- In this course, I knew the steps required to complete my assignments.
- In this course, I knew how my work would be evaluated (Weisz et al., n.d.).

Note that these three outcomes indicate students' awareness before they undertook a learning activity or assignment. Before they began working on the assigned learning activity, students were aware of the purpose of each learning activity, how they should expect to learn and what tasks would be involved, and how to monitor their own progress using an established set of criteria.

Transparent Tools for In-Class Assessment That Combat Systemic Inequities

The main goal of the TILT project's transparency frameworks is to unite teachers and students in addressing systemic inequities that create barriers to learning, by examining together the purposes, tasks, and criteria for academic work. Bringing students to the same starting line with equal understanding and resources before the work of learning begins can reduce systemic inequities in education (Winkelmes et al., 2016). Two tools from the TILT project can support this work. Both the *Transparent Equitable Learning Readiness Assessment for Teachers* (Winkelmes, 2020a) and the *Transparent Equitable Learning Framework for Students* (Winkelmes, 2020b) promote equitable assessment, which is characterized by: a direct alignment of students' learning with course knowledge and skills, students' awareness of the knowledge and skills they will gain from assigned work, a focus on the applicability of the desired knowledge and skills, and clear processes and criteria for evaluating work (Singer-Freeman et al., 2019). In addition, both of these tools overcome an important challenge of in-class assessment: the after-the-fact nature of the evidence.

The *Transparent Equitable Learning Readiness Assessment for Teachers* (Figure 8.2) can serve as a checklist for teachers before a class meeting starts by posing questions about how to prepare students for equitable and effective

Figure 8.2. Transparent equitable learning readiness assessment for teachers.

This framework can help you prepare your learning expectations and how you'll communicate them to students at the beginning of an upcoming class meeting. It may help you identify and address inequitable conditions for learning, so that all students can have the same readiness for learning before the lesson begins.

PURPOSE:

Knowledge:

- How will you define the specific pieces of content knowledge that students will gain from the upcoming class meeting?
- How will you link this portion of course content knowledge to the larger context of:
  - recent topics of class sessions?
  - this unit of the course?
  - the whole course?
  - the major? the discipline?
  - your institution's main learning outcomes?
- How will you demonstrate the relevance and/or usefulness of the knowledge from this class meeting to the students' lives:
  - beyond the course? beyond the major? beyond college?

Skills:

- If students will practice a specific skill during the upcoming class meeting, how will you define that skill?
- How will you choose the way(s) that students will practice the skill in class? (For suggestions, see Weiman & Gilbert, 2014; Tanner, 2012; Tate, 2012.)
- How will you link that particular skill to examples/contexts where this skill is important in the context of:
  - recent class sessions?
  - this part of the course?
  - the whole course?
  - the major? the discipline?
  - your institution's main learning outcomes?
- How will you demonstrate the relevance and/or usefulness of this skill to the students' lives:
  - beyond the course? beyond the major? beyond college?
- Will the knowledge that students gain and the skills students practice in the upcoming class meeting benefit from segmentation into several in-class lessons and activities, each one focused on a discrete piece that should be mastered to ensure students' successful acquisition and mastery of the next piece in the sequence? (See Anderson & Krathwohl, 2000 for a suggested sequence.)

TASKS:
- How will you describe the actions and behaviors you expect students to engage in during the upcoming class meeting?
  - Does your description identify a sequence of action?
  - Does your description help students to avoid wasting their time on unnecessary or unhelpful behaviors?
  - Does your description help students to focus their in-class time efficiently on understanding and applying what they are learning?
  - Can you suggest ways for students to indicate during class when they first notice any confusion, to help you clarify and explain in real time so that students can learn effectively during class?
  - If you plan for students to develop their own approach without your guidance, tell them that confusion and creative thinking are intended parts of the exercise.

CRITERIA:
- Can you offer students some useful criteria for their in-class understanding and in-class learning behaviors so they can know during class whether they are learning effectively? (See Nilson, 2013 and Singer-Freeman et al., 2019 for suggestions.)
- Can you provide opportunities and guidelines for students to check their understanding with each other during class?
- What is your own standard for students' achievement during class? How well must all students understand and apply the lesson in the class meeting for you to succeed in teaching them the content and skills in this class meeting?

learning in the upcoming class meeting. Modeled on the *Checklist for Designing a Transparent Assignment* (Winkelmes, 2016), this variation of the transparency framework may be a helpful tool for teachers who are planning how they will prepare students at the beginning of a class meeting to recognize the relevance of what they will learn in the class meeting, how they can expect to learn it, and how they can monitor their achievement while they are learning.

While the framework for teachers can help with planning, it is not adequate to guarantee that students are at the same starting line together with the same readiness to learn at the beginning of the class meeting. This is because no teacher can fully understand each student's readiness and resources for learning. Even after a teacher has considered what they want students to learn in a given class meeting and how they want students to acquire learning, and they have developed satisfying answers to the questions on the *Transparent Equitable Learning Readiness Assessment for Teachers*, teachers still lack full knowledge of their specific students' lived experiences with respect to systemic inequities that interfere with their learning. As research catches up to the experiences of Black students in online courses, for example (Du et al., 2016), students can educate their teachers in real time about their learning experiences, promptly enough for teachers to make any possible improvements.

A live, in-class conversation with students about the purpose, tasks, and criteria for their learning is needed to draw on the students' expertise about where gaps in their understanding or preparation or resources exist, and how the teacher can address those to ensure that all students begin a class meeting with a fair opportunity to benefit from that class meeting. This is where the *Transparent Equitable Learning Framework for Students* (Figure 8.3) can be helpful.

Modeled on the *Transparent Framework for Students* (Winkelmes, 2015), this tool serves two important purposes. First, it helps teachers gather students' insights about how they will approach the upcoming in-class

Figure 8.3. Transparent equitable learning framework for students.

At the beginning of the class meeting, review your learning expectations with the instructor. This helps to identify and address inequitable conditions for learning so that all students may begin the class meeting with the same readiness for learning in this class meeting. (Bring this document to help frame the conversation with your instructor.)

Purpose

- What specific content knowledge will you gain from this class meeting?
- What skills will you practice during class?
- How you can use this knowledge and these skills in your life beyond the context of this class meeting, this course, and beyond college?

Tasks

- What learning behaviors or actions will you use during class?
- Is there a sequence for these? (Are there recommended steps?)
- What roadblocks/mistakes can you avoid?
- What guidelines will you follow during class to check on your understanding and/or on your classmates' understanding?
- How will you notify the teacher as soon as their assistance is needed to ensure that all students have a fair opportunity to learn effectively during class?

Criteria

- Checklist (How will you know you're doing what's expected?)
- What is your own standard for your achievement during class? How well must you be able to understand the lesson and apply the learning activities for you to succeed in this class meeting?

---

learning experience. Teachers can then adjust to address any unexpected barriers to learning that their students identify, before the lesson begins. Second, it heightens students' awareness of how they will approach the upcoming lesson, and how to watch for indicators of any barriers that arise in real time, when they can alert the teacher and ask for guidance. Strengthening students' self-awareness about their learning and offering a structure for them to monitor their understanding are as important as teaching them about the course content (Nilson, 2013).

These transparent framework tools support two of the most effective visible learning techniques: (a) informing students early about what success looks like, and (b) aligning claims about success, learning, and teaching (Hattie, 2015). Heightening students' awareness of the learning goals by discussing them and outlining a process for achieving them with the teacher may increase students' desire to meet those goals for at least two reasons: (a) transparently examining and coaching students' learning processes adopts an evidence-based growth mindset in which their learning capacity is accepted as malleable and not fixed; and (b) when instructors explicate learning goals, a Pygmalion effect occurs in both face-to-face and online classrooms (Dweck, 2006; Niari, 2016; Rosenthal & Jacobson, 1968).

The *Transparent Equitable Learning Framework for Students* can be used by teachers and students collaboratively to share the essential work of identifying and removing barriers to learning that can be resolved during a class meeting. Both the students' expertise about their lived learning experiences and the teacher's wisdom about the course content and skills are necessary for this work to succeed. When students are consciously aware of the expectations and goals for their learning in a course, they can more specifically provide feedback about how in-class teaching and learning activities will help them to acquire these skills. That feedback can help to guide a teacher's in-class assessment decisions, including when and how often to use a posthoc in-class assessment to check on students' understanding during the class meeting and at its conclusion.

In-class assessment techniques help teachers to recognize how well students are learning, promptly enough to inform teaching adjustments to enhance students' mastery of course content and skills, but by necessity after a lesson has been delivered. The posthoc nature of CATs is a limitation that tools from the TILT project can address. When the *Transparent Equitable Learning Readiness Assessment for Teachers* and the *Transparent Equitable Learning Framework for Students* are used proactively to guide pre-assessments at the beginning of a class meeting, they can help to identify inequitable learning conditions when teachers and students can still intervene to address and perhaps even rectify that inequity, at least in the context of that single class session. Both tools are freely available from the TILT Higher Ed project on its website (TILTHigherEd.org), where students and teachers may borrow and adapt them and even share their adaptations. This use of assessment and pre-assessment tools contributes to the essential work of rooting out systemic inequities in students' readiness for in-class learning, and it requires the expertise of students and teachers in collaboration to succeed.

References

Anderson, L., & Krathwohl, D. (2001). *A taxonomy for learning, teaching, and assessing: A revision of Bloom's taxonomy of educational objectives*. Longman.

Angelo, T. A., and Cross, K. P. (1993). *Classroom assessment techniques: A handbook for college teachers* (2nd ed.). Jossey-Bass.

Armstrong, B. (2020, November 18). To spark discussion in a Zoom class, try a 'silent meeting.' *Chronicle of Higher Education*. https://www.chronicle.com/article/to-spark-discussion-in-a-zoom-class-try-a-silent-meeting

Babb, S., Stewart, C., & Johnson, R. (2018). Applying the seven principles for good practice in undergraduate education to blended learning environments. In *Online course management: Concepts, methodologies, tools, and applications* (Vol. 7, pp. 1102–1124). IGI Global. http://doi.org/10.4018/978-1-5225-5472-1

Barkley, E. F., & Major, C. H. (2016). *Learning assessment techniques: A handbook for faculty*. Wiley.

Barkley, E. F., & Major, C. H. (2020). *About*. The K. Patricia Cross Academy. https://kpcrossacademy.org/about/

Casey, N. (2020, May 5). College made them feel equal. The virus exposed how unequal their lives are. *New York Times*. https://www.nytimes.com/2020/04/04/us/politics/coronavirus-zoom-college-classes.html

Chickering, A. W., & Gamson, Z. F. (1987, March). Seven principles for good practice in undergraduate education. *AAHE Journal*, 3–7. https://files.eric.ed.gov/fulltext/ED282491.pdf

Czerniewicz, L. (2020, September 23). A Wake-up call: Equity, inequality and Covid-19 emergency remote teaching and learning. *Postdigital Science and Education*, 1–22. https://www.ncbi.nlm.nih.gov/pmc/articles/PMC7509221/

Du, J., Zhao, M., Xu, J., & Lei, S. S. (2016). African American female students in online collaborative learning activities: The role of identity, emotion, and peer support. *Computers in Human Behavior*, *63*, 948–958. https://doi.org/10.1016/j.chb.2016.06.021

Dweck, C. (2006). *Mindset: The new psychology of success*. Random House.

Freeman, S., Eddy, S. L., McDonough, M., Smith, M. K., Okoroafor, N., Jordt, H., & Wenderoth, M. P. (2014). Active learning increases student performance in science, engineering, and mathematics. *Proceedings of the National Academy of Sciences*, *111*(23), 8410–8415. https://doi.org/10.1073/pnas.1319030111

Hattie, J. (2015). The applicability of visible learning to higher education. *Scholarship of Teaching and Learning in Psychology, 1*(1), 79–91. https://psycnet.apa.org/doi/10.1037/stl0000021

Jankowski, N. A. (2020, August). *Assessment during a crisis: Responding to a global pandemic.* University of Illinois and Indiana University, National Institute for Learning Outcomes Assessment.

Jaschik, S. (2020a, October 27). U of Vermont freezes tuition, room and board for all students. *Inside Higher Ed.* https://www.insidehighered.com/news/2020/12/01/live-updates-latest-news-coronavirus-and-higher-education

Jaschik, S. (2020b, November 3). Grinnell eliminates loans, citing coronavirus. *Inside Higher Ed.* https://www.insidehighered.com/admissions/article/2020/11/23/grinnell-eliminates-loans-citing-coronavirus

Lave, J. (2019). The long life of learning in practice. In *Learning and Everyday Life: Access, Participation, and Changing Practice* (pp. 1–9). Cambridge University Press.

Lederman, D. (2020, September 9). Tennessee evacuates residence hall so more students can isolate. *Inside Higher Ed.* https://www.insidehighered.com/news/2020/12/01/live-updates-latest-news-coronavirus-and-higher-education

Light, R. (1990). *The Harvard assessment seminars: Explorations with students and faculty about teaching, learning, and student life.* Harvard University Graduate School of Education.

Mazur, E. (1997). *Peer instruction: A user's manual.* Prentice-Hall.

McFadden, J. M. (2020, November 25). 3 more tips for teaching in a virtual classroom. *Inside Higher Ed.* https://www.insidehighered.com/advice/2020/11/25/three-ideas-more-effective-online-teaching-opinion

Middendorf, J., & Kalish, A. (1996). The "change–up" in lectures. *TRC Newsletter, 8*(1). https://sphweb.bumc.bu.edu/otlt/teachingLibrary/Lecturing/change-up_lecture.pdf

Mosteller, F. (1989). The muddiest point in the lecture as a feedback device. *On Teaching and Learning: The Journal of the Harvard-Danforth Center, 3,* 10–20.

Niari, M. (2016). The Pygmalion effect in distance learning. *European Journal of Open, Distance and E-Learning, 19*(1), 36–53. https://files.eric.ed.gov/fulltext/EJ1118299.pdf

Nilson, L. B. (2013). *Creating self-regulated learners: Strategies to strengthen students' self-awareness and learning skills.* Stylus.

Rosenthal, R., & Jacobson, L. (1968). Pygmalion in the classroom. *Urban Review, 3,* 16–20. https://doi.org/10.1007/BF02322211

Singer-Freeman, K., Hobbs, H., & Robinson, C. (2019). Theoretical matrix of culturally relevant assessment. *Assessment Update: Progress, Trends, and Practices in Higher Education, 31*(4), 1–3. https://doi.org/10.1002/au.30176

Smith, M. A., & Karpicke, J. D. (2014). Retrieval practice with short-answer, multiple-choice, and hybrid tests. *Memory, 22*(7), 784–802. http://dx.doi.org/10.1080/09658211.2013.831454

St. Amour, M. (2020, December 1). Mental health, for-profits and aid concerns for student veterans. *Inside Higher Ed.* https://www.insidehighered.com/news/2020/12/01/mental-health-profits-and-aid-concerns-student-veterans

Tanner, K. (2012). Promoting student metacognition. *CBE Life Science Education, 11*(2), 113–120. https://doi.org/10.1187/cbe.12-03-0033

Tate, M. L. (2012). *Sit and get won't grow dendrites: 20 professional learning strategies that engage the adult brain* (2nd ed.). Corwin Press.

Teaching in the Time of Corona: Resources. (2020). Facebook. https://www.facebook.com/groups/647445119134164

Verschelden, C. (2017). *Bandwidth recovery: Helping students reclaim cognitive resources lost to poverty, racism, and social marginalization.* Stylus.

Weiman, C., & Gilbert, S. (2014). The teaching practices inventory: A new tool for characterizing college and university teaching in mathematics and science. *CBE Life Sciences Education, 13*, 552–56. https://doi.org/10.1187/cbe.14-02-0023

Weisz, C., Richard, D., Oleson, K., Winkelmes, M. A., Powley, C., Sadiq, A., & Stone, B. *Confidence, belonging and metacognition with transparent instruction* [Manuscript in preparation].

Winkelmes, M. A. (2014–2022). *Transparency in learning and teaching.* TILT Higher Ed. https://www.tilthighered.com

Winkelmes, M. A. et al. (2014–2022). *Transparency in Learning and Teaching in Higher Education Project presurvey and end of term survey questions.* https://tilthighered.com/assets/pdffiles/TILTHigherEd%20Survey%20Questions%20.pdf

Winkelmes, M. A. (2015). *Transparent assignment template for students: Unwritten rules.* TILT Higher Ed. https://tilthighered.com/assets/pdffiles/Transparent%20Assignment%20Template%20for%20Students_v2.pdf

Winkelmes, M. A. (2016). *Checklist for designing a transparent assignment.* TILT Higher Ed. https://tilthighered.com/assets/pdffiles/Checklist%20for%20Designing%20a%20Transparent%20Assignment%20copy.pdf

Winkelmes, M. A. (2020a). *Transparent equitable learning framework for students and teachers.* TILT Higher Ed. https://www.tilthighered.com/assets/pdffiles/Transparent%20Equitable%20Learning%20Framework%20for%20Students.pdf

Winkelmes, M. A. (2020b). *Transparent equitable learning readiness assessment for teachers.* TILT Higher Ed. https://www.tilthighered.com/assets/pdffiles/Transparent%20Equitable%20Learning%20Readiness%20Assessment.pdf

Winkelmes, M. A., Bernacki, M., Butler, J., Zochowski, M., Golanics, J., & Harriss Weavil, K. (2016). A teaching intervention that increases underserved college students' success. *Peer Review, 18*(1/2), 31–36. https://cte.ku.edu/sites/cte.ku.edu/files/docs/Branding/Winkelmes%20et%20al%202016%20Transparency%20and%20Underserved%20Students.pdf

Winkelmes, M. A., Boye, A., & Tapp, S. (Eds.). (2019). *Transparent design in higher education teaching and learning: A guide to implementing the transparency framework institution-wide to improve learning and retention.* Stylus.

Xu, D., & Jaggars, S. (2014). Performance gaps between online and face-to-face courses: Differences across types of students and academic subject areas. *The Journal of Higher Education, 85*(5), 633–659. https://doi.org/10.1080/00221546.2014.11777343

9

CULTURALLY RELEVANT ASSESSMENT

Examining Equity Gaps in Assignment Types

Harriet Hobbs and Christine Robinson

Despite the number of years that higher education has spent focusing on student access and success initiatives, demographic disparities continue in retention and completion rates, and in the learning that is being assessed. National Student Clearinghouse data reveal that 72% of White and 77% of Asian students complete 4-year degrees within 6 years of matriculation, but only 48% of Black and 57% of Hispanic students complete degrees within this time frame (Shapiro et al., 2017, 2018). The disparity for Black and Hispanic students is not simply due to economics. Of the 111,000 Blacks and Hispanics who graduated in the top half of their class but did not graduate from a 2- or 4-year college, 44% of these students came from the top half of the family income distribution (Carnevale & Strohl, 2013). Completion gaps between White and Asian undergraduate students and Black and Hispanic undergraduate students are even larger for transfer students, those who earn credit at one institution and then move to another institution (Shapiro et al., 2018). One study found that transfer students were four times less likely to be retained after 1 year than nontransfer students (Fauria & Slate, 2014). If the assessment field is to address issues of equity, we must pay attention to the students who transfer to our institutions (Bahr et al., 2013; Blekic et al., 2020; Crisp & Nuñez, 2014).

Closing the educational equity gap will require educators to examine the systemic practices, processes, policies, and strategies that created the disparities.

> What is needed is not to help learners assimilate to the norms of higher education which reinforces inequities and expectations based on ideologies that students must ascribe to, but to empower students for success through intentional efforts that address inequalities within our structures, create clear transparent pathways, and ensure that credits and credentials are awarded by the demonstration of learning, in whatever form that may take. (Montenegro & Jankowski, 2017b, p. 16)

To close the educational equity gap, assessment practitioners in collaboration with influential organizations in higher education are searching for ways to improve performance by drawing on equity and social justice schemas (Association of American Colleges and Universities, n.d.; Association for Assessment of Learning in Higher Education, 2020; Brennan & Naidoo, 2008; Dover, 2013; Henning & Lundquist, 2018; Hurtado & DeAngelo, 2012; IUPUI Assessment Institute, 2020; Montenegro & Jankowski, 2017a; National Institute for Learning Outcomes Assessment, 2020). Socially just assessment is defined as justice of assessment practices and processes within higher education that nurture forms of learning that will promote greater social justice in society (Henning & Lundquist, 2018; McArthur, 2016). Scholars argue that a faculty member's bias and culture should be considered in a socially just assessment process (Henning & Lundquist, 2018).

We and others have found that developing a single term and definition that encompasses equity in assessment is complicated (Montenegro & Jankowski, 2017a). In the literature, equity in assessment is also referred to as culturally responsive assessment, culturally relevant assessment, inclusive assessment, and equitable assessment (Bevitt, 2015; Kaur et al., 2017; Montenegro & Jankowski, 2017a; Singer-Freeman et al., 2019; Slee, 2010; Suskie, 2000). We have adopted the term culturally relevant assessment and will build upon this concept. We posit that closing educational equity gaps in assignment types, which contribute to class grades, is an important element in closing gaps in college completion for all students.

Culturally relevant assessment requires a thoughtful selection of assessment methods and procedures targeted for different student groups (Jonson et al., 2014; Suskie, 2000). The literature addresses inappropriate assessments that negatively impact nondominant students' performance because they disadvantage and fail students for being culturally different from the dominant group (Johnston & Wananga, 2010). While it has been suggested by some that standardized tests are neutral, Gopaul-McNichol and Armour-Thomas (2002) indicated that the majority of standardized assessment practices reflect and prefer Western, Anglo, and European epistemologies. These types of assessments rely upon the dominant groups' norms of language, test strategies, and context (Craven, 2003; Johnston & Wananga, 2010; Philpott, 2007). Another example of a type of assessment that disadvantages students is norm-referenced grading or "curving of grades'" where students are assigned a grade based on their performance relative to the class as a whole, which can disadvantage certain students (Hurtado & Sork, 2015). A 2015 UCLA study found that students from the nondominant group performed worse in classes with norm-referenced grading where students were evaluated in relationship to one another than they did in classes with criterion-referenced grading where students achieve grades based on their mastery of course learning objectives (Hurtado & Sork, 2015).

Culturally relevant assessment also requires critically examining the assessment cycle. Jonson et al. (2014) argued that many higher education institutions do not monitor their use of assessment, which is essential for the improvement of academic programs. Therefore, Malcom-Piqueux and Bensimon (2017) and Heiser et al. (2017) posited that for assessment to be critical, practitioners must adopt an equity orientation when approaching each phase of the assessment cycle by considering positionality and agency. It is highly important to acknowledge students' differences in performance on assessments, as well as the tools that are used to assess the learning of students from various backgrounds (Jonson et al., 2014). Assessment practitioners and researchers conclude that a critical examination of the assessment methods and the differences that we see in learning across student groups are important in the equity and assessment of student learning (Arbuthnot, 2017; Henning & Lundquist, 2018; Montenegro & Jankowski, 2020; Stowell, 2004; Suskie, 2000).

Background

Students from diverse populations come to higher education institutions with different learning preferences, cultures, ways of thinking, and academic preparation. Therefore, it is highly important to administer assignments and assessments that are fitting for all students regardless of their backgrounds. One practice is to ensure that students, by virtue of gender, socioeconomic, cultural, or linguistic backgrounds, are not advantaged or disadvantaged when presenting their knowledge and skills (Cumming & Dickson, 2007). Another important practice is the need to be intentional in using assessment results to improve learning for all students (Montenegro & Jankowski, 2017a; Slee, 2010). Therefore, to reduce educational equity gaps, a semester-by-semester examination of disaggregated student grades, assignment types, and demographics must occur to identify when and where the underperformance occurs (Maki, 2017).

Students should be assessed using methods and procedures that are fair and most appropriate for them (Suskie, 2000). An equitable assessment takes into consideration "the core value of respect for the dignity and well-being of all students being assessed" (Scott et al., 2014, p. 55). We and others have begun to explore whether specific features of assignments increase or reduce equity gaps (Harackiewicz et al., 2016; Quinn & Spencer, 2001; Singer-Freeman et al., 2019; Steele & Aronson, 1995; Stiggins & Chappuis, 2005). One assignment feature that may reduce equity gaps is inclusive content (Singer-Freeman et al., 2019). Course materials that are equally accessible and familiar to all students have inclusive content (Gay, 2010). Proper alignment, clarity, and scaffolding of assignments all contribute to inclusive content. Multiple-choice test questions are often poorly aligned with content because they often have complex sentence structures (Butler, 2018; Singer-Freeman et al., 2019), thereby creating false achievement gaps. We define false achievement gaps as differences in grades based on student performance on ill-aligned assessments, not student competence. For example, standardized test results may reflect false achievement gaps if differences in scores measure differences in cultural and linguistic preparation rather than current mastery. When instructions for an assignment are unclear, students with previous, strong academic preparation are at an advantage because they may infer the correct approach and feel more comfortable asking for clarification (Ladson-Billings, 1998; Singer-Freeman & Bastone, 2016).

Courses that incorporate the scaffolding of assignments can help close the educational equity gap by reducing students' lack of prior preparation. Scaffolding is an assignment feature which provides students the opportunity to build on competencies that are practiced in early assignments and demonstrated in later assignments (Gay, 2010). Students from less advantaged backgrounds must be supported in mastering each step. A second assignment feature that may reduce educational equity gaps is utility value. Assignments have high utility value if students perceive coursework to have value beyond a grade (Eccles et al., 1983). Student achievement gaps can be reduced if the utility value of assignments is increased (Harackiewicz et al., 2016). Reflective writing and applied learning projects in comparison to tests, homework, and formal papers are more likely to have high utility value because students believe the assignments to have personal or professional value (Singer-Freeman & Bastone, 2018). Making adjustments to assignments so that they are high in utility value and high in inclusive content will improve equitability and ensure academic success for all students.

Our chapter addresses the ways in which assignment types (e.g., writing in the discipline, reflective writing, inclusive projects, quizzes, tests, and exams) may privilege certain groups of students over others, thereby impacting students' academic mindset, sense of belonging, and academic success (Farruggia et al., 2016; Han et al., 2017; Shen et al., 2016; Strayhorn et al., 2015). Using two assignment features, utility value and inclusive content, we describe the methodology that was used to examine whether educational equity gaps were present between student populations. We then discuss the challenges faced during and after preparing the results. Last, we identify lessons learned from our journey related to examining equitable assessment.

Findings From Examining Assignment Types

Selecting different and fair assignments provides students with an equitable opportunity to demonstrate their learning (Ibrahim & Ali, 2015). While our methodology has evolved over the past 3 years, our research question has remained the same: Is there a relationship between the assignment type, grades, and student demographics? We engaged in a three-step process to address this question. First, after reviewing the literature on culturally responsive assessment, inclusive assessment, and equitable assessment, we developed a theoretical matrix of culturally relevant assessment (Singer-Freeman et al., 2019) and tested features of the matrix using classroom data from multiple institutions and classes. Second, we tested these features using data from multiple courses at a different institution. Courses were selected based on large enrollments and high D, F, or withdrawal (DFW) rates. Third, we collaborated with a faculty member who wanted to examine the relationships between assignment types from her class with student performance on those assignments. To be included in the analyses, courses had to include graded assignments other than quizzes, exams, or completion-based grades (assignments in which students receive full credit for completion without any differentiation in grade based on the quality of the work). The types of differentiated assignments spanned those with low or high utility value and inclusive content. We describe each of the three stages in more detail as follows.

Stage #1

We analyzed features of classroom assignment types to understand if they reflected differences in performance. Classroom assignment types were drawn from a public urban community college and a public 4-year liberal arts college. Using research on two features of assignment types, inclusive content, and utility value, we made predictions and tested our hypothesis.

Utility value includes assignments that help individuals better understand themselves, have personal value to students, improve student understanding of a subject, and provide students with an experience that will be useful in a future career. Assignments with inclusive content are aligned with teaching and learning; provide clear and explicit instructions; build upon earlier readings, lectures, and assignments; and provide examples that are equally familiar to the students.

Data were drawn from two undergraduate classes (Child Development and Experimental Psychology) at a public 4-year liberal arts college and one course (Theater Appreciation) from a public urban community college. We conducted analysis of variance (ANOVA) tests on grades from the same students using different assignments disaggregated by underrepresented ethnic minority (URM) and Non-URM students. URM includes students who identify as African American, Hispanic, and Native American, and Non-URM includes students who identify as White and Asian.

Our data provided empirical evidence for the importance of assignment features (i.e., utility value and inclusive content) in the equitable assessment of student learning (see Figure 9.1). In Theater Appreciation, there was no evidence of an equity gap in the inclusive project grades between URM and Non-URM students. However, Non-URM students received higher grades than URM students on the multiple-choice exam. In the Child Development course, there was no evidence of equity gaps for the reflective writing assignment between URM and Non-URM students. The only evidence of a difference was that URM students received significantly lower quiz grades than Non-URM students. In Experimental Psychology, there was a marginal difference such that URM students' received higher grades on writing in the discipline assignments than on open-ended questions on tests but Non-URM students grades did not differ by assignment type. The inclusive project (high inclusive content and low utility value), tests (low inclusive content and low utility value), reflective writing assignment (high inclusive content and high utility value), and writing in the discipline (low inclusive content and high utility value) provide evidence for examining assignment features.

The data provided in the first stage was the foundation for the theoretical matrix of culturally relevant assessment (see Figure 9.1). We identified no equity gaps for reflective writing assignments, writing assignments in the discipline, and inclusive projects. In contrast, tests assessing similar material as the aforementioned assignments revealed educational equity gaps. We believe exam scores to be a false predictor of an URM student's knowledge and skills (Singer-Freeman et al., 2019).

Figure 9.1. An adapted version of the theoretical matrix of culturally relevant assessment.

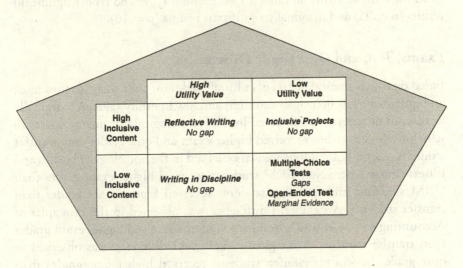

	High Utility Value	Low Utility Value
High Inclusive Content	*Reflective Writing* No gap	*Inclusive Projects* No gap
Low Inclusive Content	*Writing in Discipline* No gap	**Multiple-Choice Tests** *Gaps* **Open-Ended Test** *Marginal Evidence*

Note. Reprinted and adapted from "Theoretical Matrix of Culturally Relevant Assessment," K. Singer-Freeman, H. Hobbs, & C. Robinson, 2019, *Assessment Update*, *31*(4), 1–2; 15–16. Copyright 2019 by Wiley Periodicals Inc., Jossey-Bass. Reprinted [or adapted] with permission.

Stage #2

We expanded our research on assignment type, grades, and student demographics to other courses and other student statuses. At a public urban research-intensive university, we examined assignments in classes with 50 or more students. Classes were selected not only on enrollment but also on a large number of unsatisfactory final grades of D, F, or withdrawal (DFW). This resulted in 88 courses with high enrollments and high DFW final grades. We excluded 80 classes that did not offer differentiated forms of assignments. The courses included in the analyses were Principles of Accounting, Pre-Calculus, Introduction to Communication Theory, Network Theory II, Organic Chemistry Lab, Design & Implementation – Object Oriented Systems, Sociology of Health and Illness, and Physiological Psychology.

Across eight classes, we had a total sample of 745 students. We were interested in examining if educational equity gaps existed across different assignment types for URM students as compared to Non-URM students and for transfer students (those who transferred from a community college or another university) versus continuing students (those who began their studies at the university). We (Hobbs et al., 2021) conducted a *t*-test on scores from the same students on different assignment types and report significant results (p < .05) and marginally significant results (p < .10).

Exams, Test, and Quiz Grade Differences

Based on the theoretical matrix of culturally relevant assessment, exams, tests, and quizzes are low in inclusive content and low in utility value. A marginally significant difference was observed in the Physiological Psychology course in which freshmen students received higher exam and quiz grades than transfer students. A significant difference was observed in the Sociology of Health and Illness course where Non-URM students received higher exam grades than URM students, and freshmen students received higher exam grades than transfer students. A significant difference was observed in the Principles of Accounting course in which freshmen students received higher exam grades than transfer students. A marginally significant difference was observed in quiz grades in which freshmen students received higher quiz grades than transfer students. A marginally significant difference was observed in the Organic Chemistry Lab course, in which Non-URM students received higher quiz grades than URM students (Hobbs et al., 2021). The results in stage 2 demonstrate that certain assignment types (e.g., exams, tests, and quizzes) that lack inclusive content and utility value produce educational equity gaps.

Writing Grade Differences

Based on the results from stage 2, formal essays or papers that are low in inclusive content and utility value exhibit educational equity gaps. Three of the eight courses included writing assignments. A significant difference was observed in the Sociology of Health and Illness course in which Non-URM students received higher essay grades than URM students, and freshmen students received higher essay grades than transfer students. A significant difference was observed in the Introduction to Communication Theory course in which Non-URM students received higher in-class writing grades than URM students. There was no evidence of significance between freshmen and transfer students on the lab reports in the Organic Chemistry Lab course, and the in-class writing assignments for the Introduction to Communication Theory course (Hobbs et al., 2021). The results support that writing in the discipline which is low in inclusive content yet high in utility value reduces equity gaps, and formal essays or papers that are low in inclusive content and low in utility value exhibit equity gaps.

The data found from stage 2 provided some support for the adapted version of the theoretical matrix of culturally relevant assessment from stage 1. The results suggested that formal essays and papers should be further investigated to determine where the equity gaps exist within the assignment type.

Stage #3

In 2020, we collaborated with a faculty member who taught an online course on African- American Literature and Culture. This course is a requirement for both the major and minor in Africana Studies. The faculty member's research question was: How do the assessment instruments in the course contribute to positive student outcomes for diverse learners in a 100% asynchronous online environment? As part of the class, students must complete three multiple-choice section exams, one final essay exam, 10 discussion forums (written responses to a prompt and two other peers' comments), and eight reading guides (written short answer or essay responses). Based on our model, exams are low in inclusive content and low in utility value. Discussion forums and reading guides, which are based upon reflective writings, are high in inclusive content and high in utility value. We had a total sample of 277 students from spring 2017 and 2018 and fall 2018 and 2019. We conducted a t-test on scores from the same students on different assignment types and report significant results ($p < .05$) and marginally significant results ($p < .10$).

URM and Non-URM Students

There was a marginally significant difference where URM students received higher grades on the reading guides and discussion forums than Non-URM students. There was no significant difference between URM and Non-URM students on multiple-choice exams and the final essay exam. Since this was the first instance of URM students performing better than Non-URM students, we interviewed the faculty member and asked what she thought contributed to narrow equity gaps in the course. She indicated that she believed her assignments were both high in utility value and inclusive content because the course content "speaks to the personhood" of URM students. Furthermore, the faculty member indicated that URM students said, "Finally, a course that I can relate to and see my identity."

Continuing and Transfer Students

The results indicated that transfer students received significantly higher grades than continuing on reading guide assignments. Transfer students also received marginally higher grades on the discussion forums than continuing students. There were no significant differences between freshmen and transfer students on the multiple-choice exams and the final essay exam. In the interview with the faculty member, she stated, "Transfer students connect to the course content and it is of importance to them."

Whether drawing information from different types of institutions or courses with different assignment types, the findings support the practice of disaggregating and examining data at the assignment level. Simply examining final grade differences does not inform the faculty as to where the inequities exist. Hence, individual or cumulative scores may be a false predictor of URM and transfer student's knowledge and skills. Additionally, lower scores may contribute to students doubting their ability to succeed, feeling less than, and experiencing a lack of belonging in the class (Strayhorn et al., 2015). Although a great deal of work remains to be done in closing the educational equity gaps, our *Theoretical Matrix of Culturally Relevant Assessment* adds to the conceptual understanding of closing those gaps in assignment types. In particular, our findings suggest that assignment types that are high in utility value and inclusive content contribute to closing educational equity gaps in student learning.

Data Access and Decision-Making

In stage 1, data were gathered from faculty who were part of the research team. This data was easily accessible, and the courses included differentiated assignments. The goal in stage 1 was to understand if the data supported our hypothesis. In stage 2, the goal was to understand if we incorporated data from a different type of institution in the analysis would the results still support the model; courses with different assignment types, 50 or more students, and high DFW rates provided evidence to support the use of the theoretical matrix of culturally relevant assessment as a model for other institutions. In stage 3, the goal was to support a faculty member to examine if equity gaps existed in the assignment types in her course.

We were granted access to the public urban research-intensive university's learning management system which houses course information and student grades. To determine if courses included differentiated assignments, we reviewed course syllabi and assignment descriptions. We sent a request to the institutional research office for a list of all courses that had enrollments of over 50 students with DFW rates of 30% or more during the last three semesters. We selected these parameters because in gateway courses a passing grade is required for entry into a major. DFW rates have consistently been at

30% or higher, and success or failure in these courses impact the university's retention rate. Upon identifying the courses that we wanted to examine, a second request was sent to Institutional Research to provide student demographic data mapped to student assignment grades.

We made several decisions on what data to include in the analyses. First, to have a sizable population on whom to conduct analyses, we merged data from course sections that had low numbers of student enrollments and combined data from multiple semesters that had the same graded assignment types. Second, we determined what population of students to examine and compare. Given the demographics of the public urban research-intensive university, assignment type grades for URM and transfer students were considered important to investigate. Third, we discussed what assignment types to examine and how performance would be determined. We excluded completion-based assignments because it was not clear how this factored into grades since it was simply a checkmark. Fourth, we decided to include missing or incomplete assignments that had points attached to them and converted them to zeros because we thought zeros were important indicators of student performance. Fifth, we decided to report data as percentages. For consistency, we converted points earned for each assignment into percentages. Lastly, we aggregated similar assignments in a class, such as multiple homework assignments, into one grade for each student.

Challenges We Encountered

Most of the courses assessed learning using exams or tests; therefore, many of the classes that enrolled 50 or more students and had DFW rates of 30% or more (where a larger impact might be made) were not included in the analyses because assignment types were not differentiated. Many of these classes were STEM-related and included multiple-choice exams that were graded electronically. Although a best practice for faculty is to offer differentiated assignments, faculty with large classes find it challenging to adopt this method, especially if this involves written work. It becomes impractical to effectively and efficiently grade written assignments in large classes since it is time-consuming and makes uniform grading difficult.

The number of faculty willing to volunteer to have their classes examined was small. It is possible that faculty were sensitive about engaging in discussions around disaggregating and examining data from their courses. Some may have felt that certain types of assignments such as multiple-choice exams and quizzes were designed to be objective assessment measures and they may not be aware that objective assessments can be value laden. For example, an exam preparer from a dominant culture brings his/her experiences and perceptions to the design process which may not be appropriate for students of nondominant cultures. Critical to closing the educational equity gap is asking critical questions about whether assignment types assess knowledge and skills on an equitable basis; advantage certain groups over another; use biased, microaggressive, or unfamiliar language; and are aligned with teaching and learning.

Faculty may have initiative fatigue and be unable to add one more thing to their plates. Examining assignment types will compete with other initiatives such as developing adaptive, accelerated, or online courses, and increasing graduation retention, and enrollment rates. The challenge for assessment professionals is to get faculty to recognize that examining assignment types to increase educational equity is also an important initiative and best practice. Offering to pay faculty to participate in professional development to implement equitable assessment in their teaching and learning may contribute to their promotion and/or tenure process and may garner interest.

Addressing the Challenges

In stage 3, the faculty member with whom we collaborated was a scholarship of assessment (SOA) award recipient. SOA funds are for individuals or teams who examine student learning in the context of a program or course at the undergraduate or graduate level. To raise awareness that examining educational equity in assessment is an important initiative and a best practice, one of the SOA's topics was equity in assessment. The research could include an examination of differentiated assignment types in a course or courses where data were disaggregated by way of grades on individual assignments and student demographics to determine if equity gaps existed. Results from a funded study were described previously in stage 3.

To gain traction about the importance of educational equity in assessment, we are collaborating with others to conduct research at additional institutions. The more experience we gain and skills we develop, the more stories we can tell around this work, and the more faculty may be open to examining equity in assessment. To expand our work, we collaborated with a psychology faculty member from a public community college, and a biology faculty member from a different public community college. We are investigating the features of utility value and inclusive content within these assignment types. A future collaborative plan includes working with a small cadre of faculty from a private 4-year liberal arts college to examine if educational equity gaps exist in their courses.

Recently, our colleague, Karen Singer-Freeman, developed a survey for students to share their perceptions about whether or not certain assignment types had utility value and/or inclusive content. Preliminary results from a small group of students indicated that the theoretical matrix of culturally relevant assessment might be adjusted to move writing in the discipline to high in utility value and inclusive content. More student feedback is needed to determine what the assignment type features are for formal essays and oral presentations.

Tools or Tips for Others

In the following we offer tools and tips for assessment practitioners who are interested in this work.

- Tip #1 (Context Cultures) will address how one's cultural background impacts the way students approach and complete assignments.
- Tip #2 (Student Voice) will address how to give student voice to assignment type features.
- Tip #3 (Professional Development) will address providing professional development for faculty to reflect on behaviors that may maintain or exacerbate inequities and align objective test questions with student learning.
- Tip #4 (Institutional and Departmental Cultures) will identify strategies that are compatible with the cultures at the institution.

Context Cultures

First is understanding the different ways that students think and learn (Arbuthnot, 2017; Cohen & Ibarra, 2005). In Arbuthnot's assessment fairness framework, she examines how cultural contexts contribute to how students respond to assessments. She discusses high and low context cultures and asserts that individuals from high-context cultures usually prefer to work in groups for shared learning and problem-solving, while those from low-context cultures prefer to approach tasks and learning individually. In high-context cultures, knowledge is socially based, and facts are embedded in situations and integrated in structures that are not easily separated for analysis. In contrast, for low-context cultures, knowledge is less socially based and more rational, and facts are derived by objective analysis. Arbuthnot identifies low-context culture groups as males of European descent, and high-context culture groups as minority students and female students in the United States.

She argues that cultural background has an impact on how students complete assignments. We cannot assess what students know without attempting to understand how low and high contexts impact student learning and how we assess their learning (Arbuthnot, 2017; Cohen & Ibarra, 2005; Fisler, 2017; Montenegro & Jankowski, 2017a). Reviewing Arbuthnot's assessment fairness framework can be useful in understanding the different ways that students respond to assignments.

Student Voice

Second is to involve students in the assessment process by understanding the value they place on different assignment types (Aitken, 2011). Developing and administering student surveys and focus groups to gather students' perceptions of various assignment types can add value to this work. Faculty should consider evaluating the outcomes of their assessments by asking students why they did not do well on particular assignments. Sometimes assignment questions and prompts are not always clear and asking students for their feedback can reveal that the content was not well understood. Revising assessment tools, pedagogy, or both, has the potential to lead to better outcomes in student performance.

Professional Development

The third tip is based upon our thoughts about the knowledge faculty need while participating in the educational equity and assessment process. Providing professional development to faculty about the elements of culturally relevant assessment can promote success for all students and examining assignment features such as utility value and inclusive content can provide faculty with a heightened awareness of issues with course content and assessment design. Opportunities for professional development can be impactful for faculty who are engaging in assessment design. Educational opportunities should encompass course assignment/assessment design or redesign workshops that put assessment directly in the hands of faculty, who are uniquely qualified to make judgments about the quality of student work (Graham, 2017; Hutchings et al., 2014; Kuh, 2008). Assessment professionals can collaborate with centers for teaching and learning to offer the following trainings:

- Implicit/unconscious racial bias training examines the thoughts that pop into our minds and the quick random gut reactions when we think about a particular group that can foster negative attitudes and lead to damaging stereotypical behaviors (Brownicity.com, n.d.; Jackson et al., 2014). "Failure to consider our own biases, perspectives, and subjectivities in the interest of fairness perpetuates unfairness" (Rudnick, 2019, p. 1), and training people to suppress their stereotypical thinking increases the activation of stereotypes (Jackson et al., 2014).

- Utilize test blueprint training in large classes where faculty exclusively use multiple-choice tests for efficiency purposes and find it challenging to incorporate different assignment types because they are more time-consuming to grade. A test blueprint is a tool that faculty can use when developing exams, tests, and quizzes to conduct an item analysis of the content being assessed (Moberg, n.d.). Reviewing Moberg's test blueprint explanation, guidelines, and samples can be useful in aligning student learning outcomes with the course content and exams.

Institutional and Departmental Culture

A final tip is that part of change involves understanding institutional, departmental, and unit cultures before adopting new strategies. Practitioners must be aware of the values, assumptions, beliefs, and ideologies that faculty members hold (Peterson & Spencer, 1991). We recognized faculty members on our campus valued research results in multiple contexts about the benefits of culturally relevant assessment and needed us to share best practices that could be incorporated into different contexts. Identifying adoptable practices are methods we use to encourage faculty to incorporate culturally relevant assessment into their classrooms.

Conclusion

This chapter builds on and extends the research on equity in assessment. The three stages in this chapter support the assertion that assignment types that are high in utility value and inclusive content contribute to closing the educational equity gap in student learning. Although this chapter did not address gender, we found that in stage three, males did significantly worse than females on every assignment except exams. Future research should address gender educational equity gaps in higher education. As Montenegro and Jankowski (2020) posit, we have a responsibility to develop theories and practices that help students demonstrate their learning. Therefore, we urge campuses to have in place mechanisms for sharing data, have open dialogue and opportunities for deep reflections, and design action steps for reducing equity gaps. As assessment practitioners, we must be willing to look beyond the traditional ways that higher education has valued and addressed the assessment of student learning. We must design campuses and classrooms that are equity-minded and produce assessments that are appropriate for all students and are done in ways that do not privilege certain students over others (Montenegro & Jankowski, 2020). Overall, we hope this research will affect change in assignment design for the benefit of student learning.

Acknowledgments

We would like to acknowledge Andrea Marie Pope for offering significant scholarly feedback for our book chapter.

References

Aitken, N. (2011). *Student voice in fair assessment practice: In leading student assessment.* Springer Netherlands. https://doi.org/10.1007/978-94-007-1727-5_9

Arbuthnot, K. (2017). The Arbuthnot assessment fairness framework, global perspectives on educational testing: Examining fairness, high-stakes and policy reform. *Advances in Education in Diverse Communities, 13,* 23–35. https://doi.org/10.1108/S1479-358X20160000013009

Association of America Colleges and Universities. (n.d.). *Diversity, equity, and student Success.* https://www.aacu.org/diversity-equity-and-student-success

Association for Assessment of Learning in Higher Education. (2020). *President's committee on diversity, equity and inclusion.* https://www.aalhe.org/index.php?option=com_content&view=article&id=206:president-s-committee-on-diversity--equity-and-inclusion&catid=20:site-content

Bahr, P. R., Toth, C., Thirolf, K., & Massé, J. C. (2013). A review and critique of the literature on community college student's transition processes and outcomes in four-year institutions. In M. B. Paulsen (Ed.), *Higher education: Handbook of theory and research* (pp. 459–511). Springer.

Bevitt, S. (2015). Assessment innovation and student experience: A new assessment challenge and call for a multi-perspective approach to assessment research. *Assessment & Evaluation in Higher Education, 40*(1), 103–119. https://doi.org/10.1080/02602938.2014.890170

Blekic, M., Carpenter, R., & Cao, Y. (2020). Continuing and transfer students: Exploring retention and second-year success. *Journal of College Student Retention: Research, Theory & Practice, 22*(1), 71–98. https://doi.org/10.1177/1521025117726048

Brennan, J., & Naidoo, R. (2008). Higher education and the achievement (and/or prevention) of equity and social justice. *The International Journal of Higher Education and Educational Planning, 56,* 287–302. https://doi.org/10.1007/s10734-008-9127-3

Brownicity.com. (n.d.). *What LIES between us: Fostering first steps toward racial healing.* https://brownicity.com/resources/

Butler, A. (2018). Multiple-choice testing in education: Are the best practices for assessment also good for learning? *Journal of Applied Research in Memory and Cognition, 7*(3), 323–331. https://doi.org/10.1016/j.jarmac.2018.07.002

Carnevale, A. P., & Strohl, J. (2013). *Separate & unequal: How higher education reinforces the intergenerational reproduction of White racial privilege.* https://1gyhoq479ufd3yna29x7ubjn-wpengine.netdna-ssl.com/wp-content/uploads/SeparateUnequal.FR_.pdf

Cohen, S. A., & Ibarra, A. R. (2005). Examining gender-related differential item functioning using insights from psychometric and multicontext theory. In A. M. Gallagher & J. C. Kaufman (Eds.), *Gender differences in mathematics: An integrative psychological approach.* Cambridge University Press.

Craven, R. (2003, September 14–16). *Trekking beyond: Re-imagining a future role of evaluation for making a difference for indigenous students* [Paper presentation]. Australasian Evaluation Society International Conference, Auckland, New Zealand.

Crisp, G., & Nuñez, A. (2014). Understanding the racial transfer gap: Modeling underrepresented minority and nonminority students' pathways from two-to-four-year institutions. *Review of Higher Education, 37*(3), 291–320. https://doi.org/10.1353/rhe.2014.0017

Cumming, J. J., & Dickson, E. A. (2007). Equity in assessment: Discrimination and disability. *Education and the Law, 19*(3–4), 201–220. https://doi.org/10.1080/09539960701762854

Dover, A. G. (2013). Teaching for social justice: From conceptual frameworks to classroom practices. *Multicultural perspectives, 15*(1), 3–11. https://doi.org/10.1080/15210960.2013.754285

Eccles, J. S., Adler, T. F., Futterman, R., Goff, S. B., Kaczala, C. M., Meece, J. L., & Midgley, C. (1983). Expectancies, values, and academic behaviors. In J. T. Spence (Ed.), *Achievement and achievement motivation* (pp. 75–146). W. H. Freeman.

Farruggia, S. P., Han. C., Watson, L., Moss, T. M., & Bottoms, B. L. (2016). Noncognitive factors and college student success. *Journal of College Student Retention: Research, Theory & Practice,* 1–20. https://doi.org/10.1177/1521025116666539

Fauria, R. M., & Slate, J. R. (2014). Persistence rate differences of university students by race: A within groups comparison. *International Journal of University Teaching and Faculty Development, 4*(1), 1–10. https://doi.org/10.25082/AERE.2020.01.004

Fisler, J. (2017). *Questions & thoughts to continue the conversation on culturally responsive assessment* (Equity Response). University of Illinois and Indiana University, National Institute for Learning Outcomes Assessment (NILOA).

Gay, G. (2010). *Culturally responsive teaching: Theory, research, and practice.* Teachers College Press.

Gopaul-McNichol, S., & Armour-Thomas, E. (2002) *Assessment and culture: Psychological tests with minority populations.* Academic Press.

Graham, R. D. (2017). Professional development for student success. *Peer Review, 19*(3), 26–30. https://www.aacu.org/peerreview/2017/Summer/Dolinsky%20Graham

Han, C., Farruggia, S. P., & Moss, T. P. (2017). Effects of academic mindsets on college students' achievement and retention. *Journal of College Student Development, 58*(8), 1119–1134. https://doi.org/10.1353/csd.2017.0089

Harackiewicz, J. M., Canning, E. A., Tibbetts, Y., Priniski, S. J., & Hyde, J. S. (2016). Closing achievement gaps with a utility-value intervention: Disentangling race and social class. *Journal of Personality and Social Psychology, 111*(5), 745–765. https://doi.org/ 10.1037/pspp0000075

Heiser, C. A., Prince, K., & Levy, J. D. (2017). Examining critical theory as a framework to advance equity through student affairs assessment. *The Journal of Student Affairs Inquiry, 3*(1). https://drive.google.com/file/d/1ksQstiXwP51EdipgdylU7nvdenVpIJA-/view

Henning, G. W., & Lundquist, A. E. (2018). *Moving towards socially just assessment* (Equity Response). University of Illinois and Indiana University, National Institute for Learning Outcomes Assessment (NILOA).

Hobbs, H., Singer-Freeman, K., & Robinson, C. (2021). Considering the effects of assignment choices on equity gaps. *Research and Practice in Assessment, 16*(1), 49–62. https://www.rpajournal.com/dev/wp-content/uploads/2021/05/Considering-the-Effects-of-Assignment-Choices-on-Equity-Gaps.pdf

Hurtado, S., & DeAngelo, L. (2012). Linking diversity and civic-minded practice with student outcomes: New evidence from national surveys. *Liberal Education, 98*(2), 14–23. https://www.aacu.org/publications-research/periodicals/linking-diversity-and-civic-minded-practices-student-outcomes-new

Hurtado, S., & Sork, L. V. (2015). *Enhancing student success and building inclusive classrooms at UCLA.* https://ceils.ucla.edu/wp-content/uploads/sites/2/2016/11/Enhancing-Student-Success-Building-Inclusive-Classrooms-at-UCLA-Report_December-2015-Hurdado-Sork-Report.pdf?x30619

Hutchings, P., Jankowski, N. A., & Ewell, P. T. (2014). *Catalyzing assignment design activity on your campus: Lessons from NILOA's assignment library initiative.* National Institute for Learning Outcomes Assessment. https://files.eric.ed.gov/fulltext/ED550511.pdf

Ibrahim, H., & Ali, H. (2015). Toward differentiated assessment in a public college in Oman. *English Language Teaching, 8*(12), 27–36. https://doi.org/10.5539/elt.v8n12p27 IUPUI Assessment Institute. (2020). *What you'll learn at the Institute.* https://assessmentinstitute.iupui.edu/overview/about-institute.html

Jackson, S., Hillard, A., & Schneider, T. (2014). Using implicit bias training to improve attitudes toward women in STEM. *Social Psychology of Education, 17*(3), 419–438. https://doi.org/10.1007/s11218-014-9259-5

Johnston, G. M. P., & Wananga, O. T. W. (2010). Towards culturally appropriate assessment? A contribution to the debates. *Higher Education Quarterly, 64*(3), 231–245. https://doi.org/10.1111/j.1468-2273.2010.00463.x

Jonson, J. L., Guetterman, T., & Thompson, R. J. (2014). An integrated model of influence: Use of assessment data in higher education. *Research & Practice in Assessment, 9*, 18–30. https://www.rpajournal.com/dev/wp-content/uploads/2014/06/A1.pdf

Kaur, A., Noman, M., & Nordin, H. (2017). Inclusive assessment for linguistically diverse learners in higher education. *Assessment & Evaluation in Higher Education, 42*(5), 756–771. https://doi.org/10.1080/02602938.2016.1187250

Kuh, G. (2008). *High-impact educational practices: What they are, who has access to them, and why they matter.* Association of American Colleges and Universities.

Ladson-Billings, G. (1998). Just what is critical race theory and what's it doing in a nice field like education? *International Journal of Qualitative Studies in Education, 11*(1), 7–24. https://doi.org/10.1080/095183998236863

Maki, P. (2017). *Real-time student assessment: Meeting the imperative for improved time to degree, closing the opportunity gap, and assuring student competencies for 21st century needs.* Stylus.

Malcom-Piqueux, L., & Bensimon, E. M. (2017). Taking equity-minded action to close equity gaps. Peer Review, 19(2), 5–8. https://www.aacu.org/peerreview/2017/Spring/Malcom-Piqueux

McArthur, J. (2016). Assessment for social justice: The role of assessment in achieving social justice. *Assessment & Evaluation in Higher Education, 41*(7), 967–981. https://doi.org/10.1080/02602938.2015.1053429

Moberg, P. (n.d.). *Test blueprint for professor Moberg: Explanation, guidelines, and samples.* https://imoberg.com/files/Test_Blueprint_explanation_guidelines_and_samples.pdf

Montenegro, E., & Jankowski, N. A. (2017a). *Equity and assessment: Moving towards culturally responsive assessment* (Occasional Paper No. 29). University of Illinois and Indiana University, NILOA.

Montenegro, E., & Jankowski, N. A. (2017b). Bringing equity into the heart of assessment. *Assessment Update, 29*, 10–11. https://doi.org/10.1002/au.30117

Montenegro, E., & Jankowski, N. A. (2020). *A new decade for assessment: Embedding equity into assessment praxis* (Occasional Paper No. 42). University of Illinois and Indiana University, NILOA.

National Institute for Learning Outcomes Assessment. (2020, October). *Equity in assessment.* https://www.learningoutcomesassessment.org/equity/#equityconvo

Peterson, M., & Spencer, M. (1991). Understanding academic culture and climate. In M. Peterson (Ed.), *ASHE reader on organization and governance* (pp. 140–155). Simon & Schuster.

Philpott, D. F. (2007). Assessing without labels: Culturally defined inclusive education. *Exceptionality Education Canada, 17*(3), 3–34. https://ojs.lib.uwo.ca/index.php/eei/article/download/7608/6225

Quinn, D., & Spencer, S. (2001). The interference of stereotype threat with women's generation of mathematical problem-solving strategies. *Journal of Social Issues, 57*(1), 55–71. http://dx.doi.org/10.1111/0022-4537.00201

Rudnick, D. L. (2019). *Culturally responsive assessment is just good assessment* (Equity Response). University of Illinois and Indiana University, National Institute for Learning Outcomes Assessment (NILOA).

Scott, S., Webber, C. F., Lupart, J. L., Aitken, N., & Scott, E. (2014). Fair and equitable assessment practice for all students. *Assessment in Education: Principles, Policy, & Practice, 21*(1), 52–70. https://doi.org/10.1080/0969594X.2013.776943

Shapiro, D., Dundar, A., Huie, F., Wakhungu, P. K., Bhimdiwala, A., & Wilson, S. E. (2018, December). *Completing college: A national view of student completion rates—Fall 2012 cohort* (Signature Report No. 16). National Student Clearinghouse Research Center.

Shapiro, D., Dundar, A., Huie, F., Wakhungu, P., Yuan, X., Nathan, A., & Hwang, Y. A. (2017, April). *Completing college: A national view of student attainment rates by race and ethnicity—Fall 2010 cohort* (Signature Report No. 12b). National Student Clearinghouse Research Center.

Shen, C., Miele, D. B., & Vasilyeva, M. (2016). The relation between college students' academic mindsets and their persistence during math problem solving. *Psychology in Russia: State of the Art, 9*(3), 38–56. https://doi.org/10.11621/pir.2016.0303

Singer-Freeman, K. E., & Bastone, L. (2016). *Pedagogical choices make large classes feel small* (NILOA Occasional Paper No. 27). University of Illinois and Indiana University, National Institute for Learning Outcomes (NILOA).

Singer-Freeman, K. E., & Bastone, L. (2018). Catalyst in action: Case studies of high-impact ePortfolio practice. In B. Eynon & L. Gambino (Eds.), *ePortfolio and declarations of academic self: A tale of two contexts* (pp. 84–97). Stylus.

Singer-Freeman, K. E., Hobbs, H., & Robinson, C. (2019). Theoretical matrix of culturally relevant assessment. *Assessment Update, 31*(4), 1–2. https://doi.org/10.1002/au.30176

Slee, J. (2010). A systemic approach to culturally responsive assessment practices and evaluation. *Higher Education Quarterly, 64*(3), 246–260. https://doi.org/10.1111/j.1468-2273.2010.00464.x

Steele, C. M., & Aronson, J. (1995). Stereotype threat and the intellectual test performance of African Americans. *Journal of Personality and Social Psychology, 69*(5), 797–811. http://dx.doi.org/10.1037/0022-3514.69.5.797

Stiggins, R., & Chappuis, J. (2005). Using student-involved classroom assessment to close achievement gaps. *Theory Into Practice, 44*(1), 11–18. http://www.jstor.org/stable/3496986

Stowell, M. (2004). Equity, justice, and standards: Assessment decision making in higher education. *Assessment & Evaluation in Higher Education, 29*(4), 495–510. https://doi.org/10.1080/0260293030001689055

Strayhorn, T., Lo, M. T., Travers, C., & Tillman-Kelly, D. L. (2015). Assessing the relationship between well-being, sense of belonging, and confidence in the transition to college for Black male collegians. *Spectrum: A Journal on Black Men*, 4(1), 127–138. https://doi.org/10.2979/spectrum.4.1.07

Suskie, L. (2000). *Fair assessment practices: Giving students equitable opportunities to demonstrate learning*. American Association for Higher Education Bulletin.

10

CENTERING ʻĀINA IN ASSESSMENT

Striving for Equity and Social Justice

Monica Stitt-Bergh, Charmaine Mangram, Eunice Leung Brekke,
Kara Plamann Wagoner, Monique Chyba, Kaiwipunikauikawēkiu Lipe,
and Siobhán Ní Dhonacha

Ask yourself, what do you know about the place that you are standing in, and on, while reading this chapter? Who are the people that came before you 10 generations ago? How does the place impact education and learning assessment? How do education and people impact place? These are questions we ponder together when contemplating our relationship to place. We are a diverse group. Some of us grew up in Hawaiʻi; some moved from elsewhere; some have lived here for decades, and some for a handful of years. Some of us are Native Hawaiians (by genealogy and ancestral connection to place) and some of us are non-Hawaiian, settlers/residents of Hawaiʻi. The connection that we share is place: We live on the island of Oʻahu in Hawaiʻi and have realized we must learn about this place from Native Hawaiians, whose ancestors *are* this place. Through the kind generosity of Native Hawaiian *kumu* (teachers and sources), we are students who learn from Hawaiian cultural matter experts. We have realized a *kuleana* (a Native Hawaiian term that roughly translates to honor, privilege, and responsibility) to give back to and care for this *ʻāina*—the land, sea, and skies and people—that nourish us physically, intellectually, emotionally, and spiritually every day no matter who we are and where we have come from (Lipe et al., 2020). This is inherently a decolonial act: A statement that we want a Hawaiʻi that respects the ways Native Hawaiians live(d) using Indigenous knowledge (Nakaoka et al., 2020).

We have each been taught that Native Hawaiians, fewer than 200 years ago, maintained systems to live in harmony and balance with the ʻāina and practiced aloha ʻāina, a value system that Lipe et al. (2020) describe as a "relationship of love, caring, and sustainable reciprocity with the land and other natural resources" (p. 34). Native Hawaiians had honed and maintained well-designed, sustainable resource management (see Winter & Lucas, 2017) and a practical place-based education model (Thomas et al., 2012). Today, the negative effects of the illegal annexation of the Hawaiian Kingdom in 1898 (Darrah-Okike, 2020) and the dispossession of Kanaka Maoli (Native Hawaiians) persist. Settler colonialism and racism have disconnected most of us, Native Hawaiians and non-Native Hawaiians, from our kuleana to aloha ʻāina (see Lipe et al., 2020). One result is that the negative and dangerous effects of climate change in the place we live and love are now manifesting.

How does this all connect to equity in assessment? We contend that education and assessment have likewise been disconnected from place. Learning outcomes and class assignments that serve as the heart of an embedded, authentic assessment design (Wiggins, 1989) became generic, representing a White, continental U.S. viewpoint. Outcomes and assignments sourced from one (dominant) culture hinder learning and social justice by perpetuating belief in a hierarchy of cultures, with some ranked as "comparatively unworthy of respect or esteem" (Fraser, 2000, p. 114). Privileging one worldview and knowledge system essentially erases the others.

Through cultural recognition and "nourishing awareness of our own identities and our connection with others" (Ayers et al., 2009, p. xiv), we all move toward redressing and repairing historical injustices (Ayers et al., 2009). We have a responsibility to connect to the place we live via the people of the place (this is our kuleana) and to be allies to those who suffer the pernicious effects of racism and settler colonialism. Centering the ʻāina (a relative to Native Hawaiians) and/or aloha ʻāina (a value system of Native Hawaiians) in learning outcomes, learning evidence, and/or activities aligned to the outcomes/evidence promote equity in assessment. In Hawaiʻi, and arguably anywhere, recognizing and incorporating Indigenous knowledge systems, people, and the land upon which we teach and learn are beneficial, equity-minded practices. First, directly countering the erasure that privileges only one worldview and knowledge system is essential. Second, research shows that centering on ʻāina and/or aloha ʻāina leads to improved outcomes for Native Hawaiians (Kanaʻiaupuni et al., 2010; Semken et al., 2017). Third, preliminary research indicates that Native Hawaiian *and* non-Native Hawaiian students, personnel, and faculty benefit. For example, humans form emotional and cultural attachments to places—to where they live, to sacred or culturally significant sites—that result in positive effects on well-being and a willingness to care for that place, and disrupting that attachment can be devastating (Lewicka, 2011; Preston & Gelman, 2020; Scannell & Gifford, 2017).

In learning assessment processes, a reconnection to place, valuing Indigenous worldview, and allowing for multiple worldviews can occur via intentionally designed learning outcomes (see Montenegro & Jankowski, 2017), assignments/learning evidence aligned with outcomes, and evaluation instruments. We offer four examples from University of Hawai'i campuses that illustrate different approaches to these written by four of this chapter's authors.

Monique: I am non-Hawaiian and not raised in Hawai'i. By engaging in local community projects and working with Hawaiian language immersion charter schools, I was transformed by a connection to 'āina and wanted to give that opportunity to others. In my example, I use aloha 'āina activities in high-enrollment math classes to help students achieve quantitative reasoning learning outcomes and to connect mathematics to sustainable reciprocity with the land.

Eunice: I am Chinese American from Chicago and I saw the need for educators to value every person's identity, culture, and ancestry and current place because not doing so continued student suffering and marginalization. In my example, I describe activities that value students' cultural identities and are aligned to my class's sociological learning outcomes. These activities center on food, which is connective tissue between humans and 'āina.

Charmaine: I am a Black woman who came to Hawai'i seeking refuge from the state-sanctioned violence on Black lives in the continental United States. I was raised with the understanding to have kuleana to the place I live. My example highlights how a degree program's signature assignment and its alignment with program outcomes related to social justice and understanding and appreciating place leads to transformative experiences.

Kara: I am a non-Hawaiian who was raised in Wisconsin. I embrace the Quaker testimony of harmony with creation, which means treating people and places with care while learning from Indigenous peoples about the effects of my ancestors' migration. In my example, I describe the collaborative development of a rubric to evaluate student outcomes related to 'āina-based learning in classes across the curriculum.

The remaining three authors support 'āina-based and aloha 'āina efforts on the UH-Mānoa campus.

Monica: I am a White woman, not raised in Hawai'i. My understanding of why UH-Mānoa's goal of being a Hawaiian Place of Learning is important and how I can support it continues to grow as I learn more about Native Hawaiians and settler colonialism.

Siobhán: I am an Irish National who is a student of kuleana, a Hawaiian-based caring commitment to the 'āina, and I was first introduced to Hawaiian worldview and cultural practices in 2004.

Kaiwipuni: I am Native Hawaiian and raised in Hawai'i. I believe that if not before—then definitely now—is the time to think with an "all hands on deck" mentality to find the best pathways to taking care of one another and island earth. With that sentiment in mind, I am active in teaching others, mostly non-Hawaiians, not only about, but also how, to become active in aloha 'a ¯ina.

Finally, we want to be clear: We, this chapter's authors, carefully walk the path of recognizing and valuing 'āina from a Native Hawaiian perspective. We take seriously being helpful allies and accurately conveying what we learn from our Native Hawaiian teachers. We are mindful how our 'āina-based work may be valued by both peers and supervisors who do not yet fully understand the approach. We carefully consider student course evaluations and new teaching methods, especially how such evaluations may be used in high stakes contract renewal, tenure, and promotion. We recognize and commit to continually learning how to most effectively and authentically engage in kuleana and aloha 'āina.

Aloha 'Āina Mathematics (Monique)

It is easy to disconnect mathematics from cultural knowledge and land: It can be taught abstractly, without connection to the real world because mathematics is a universal language whose principles and foundations are shared everywhere. Despite this universality, mathematics in the United States is an elitist world dominated by White males. In addition, privileged students have access to resources that minority students do not (Carter & Welner, 2013; Riegle-Crumb et al., 2019). The field is working on equity issues, but there is a long way to go.

While a generic, decontextualized mathematics instruction/vision suits a small fraction of the population, I found that students respond better to mathematics curriculum interlaced with the practical world. Galileo Galilei (1623) stated, "the book [of nature] . . . is written in the language of mathematics" (p. 4), highlighting the profound connection between the land and mathematics. The state of Hawai'i motto, "Ua Mau ke Ea o ka āina i ka Pono," can be translated as "The life of the land is perpetuated in righteousness." The notion of eternality, core to mathematics, demonstrates connection to the land. Unfortunately, these connections are often lost in modern math curriculum, prompting the need for realignment with its origin.

The UH-Mānoa Department of Mathematics offers Math 100: Survey in Mathematics as a terminal course that satisfies the university's general education quantitative reasoning requirement. To be brutally honest, this is a course no professor wants to teach and most students do not want to take. Three hundred and fifty to 500 primarily non-STEM majors enroll each semester. Finding a textbook has been literally mission impossible! The available textbooks fell into two categories: (a) ones with great add-ons—online homework and quiz and test-making capabilities—but generic and not relevant to Hawai'i; and (b) ones that our students have an extremely hard time navigating, suited for small classroom environments. I therefore decided to write my own, which was a long journey.

Math 100 initially was offered as large lecture classes with little opportunities for active learning and for practicing the skills in real life applications. In fact, it was once taught at the Varsity Twin Cinema movie theater near the campus, with 700 students who enjoyed everything that a movie can offer, including popcorn! That was the issue, it was a "movie" and not an engaging educational experience. In fall 2018, the UH-Mānoa began a quantitative reasoning general education requirement with new learning outcomes, for example, select a mathematical approach for a practical application. The course structure had to change, and I and colleagues transformed one (of three) big weekly lecture into a recitation with groups of 50 students. This was possible through hiring teaching assistants (TAs) and learning assistants (LAs). LAs are undergraduate students who, through the guidance of weekly preparation sessions and a pedagogy course, facilitate discussions among groups of students that encourage active engagement (Learning Assistant Alliance, n.d.). This added an active learning component; however, the curriculum was still disconnected from the land and from Hawai'i.

In spring 2019, I joined a cohort of faculty to travel to the island of Kaho'olawe[1] and spent 4 days visiting the island, learning its history and the restoration efforts, and discussing venues to incorporate this new knowledge into my classrooms. The experience was transformative for me. I realized I knew nothing about the place where I lived, which was unacceptable given the devastating effects on the people and the land due to years of U.S. military bombing. In fall 2019, I incorporated a practical, 'āina-based assignment about Kaho'olawe restoration. My ideas about transforming the curriculum were still burgeoning in my head, a bit unstructured. But I was excited to have a few Math 100 students travel to the island of Molokai[2] alongside mathematics majors and a math faculty to work with Molokai High School students on Kaho'olawe restoration challenges. The skills learned in Math 100 were no longer abstract: They were connected to the island's restoration efforts. The curriculum finally incorporated the land.

In another effort to include practical, 'āina-based math assignments, I partnered with geography professor Camilo Mora's (n.d.) project, the Carbon Neutrality Challenge. Math 100 students calculated how much CO_2 they generate and estimated how many trees needed to be planted to offset their CO_2. In December 2019, they planted the trees. Students highlighted it as one of their best experiences of the semester (see also University of Hawaiʻi, 2019a; University of Hawaiʻi, 2019b). I want these and similar practical ʻāina-based activities to help students achieve the quantitative reasoning learning outcomes in all Math 100 classes and to be embedded in the curriculum.

In summer 2020, my department received an open educational resources (OER) award to write a textbook for Math 100 and the next chapter of our journey started. The textbook's units have students practice and demonstrate learning outcomes achievement using ʻāina-based assignments. The first unit focuses on Kahoʻolawe: The students explore topics such as clearing unexploded ordnance, quantifying the extent of the island's February 2020 wildfire, analyzing seabird restoration project barriers, and discovering the power of volunteers to carry on these challenges. In a unit on disaster and disease, students analyze mathematically some of Hawaiʻi's past hurricanes and quantify the real and predicted spread of COVID-19 in Hawaiʻi through travel. The textbook includes the carbon neutrality challenge, which allows students to make a direct impact by applying aloha ʻāina through tree planting. In another unit, students dive into the microbial world and Oʻahu's Waimea watershed, exploring Hawaiʻi's biodiversity. The land can be felt, understood, and experienced in many ways. Mathematics is one of them.

I do not believe that the term exists yet, but we hope to raise a new generation of ʻāina mathematicians. My ʻāina-based efforts bolster the typically underrepresented or silenced groups in math courses through Native Hawaiian Indigenous knowledge. As I said earlier, mathematics is a universal language; thus, the quantitative reasoning learning outcomes at UH-Mānoa are likely similar to many campus's outcomes. However, I realized my kuleana to develop content centered on Hawaiʻi, its history, and its peoples. It was daunting to step a foot out of the mathematical world and learn about how Native Hawaiians and others aloha ʻāina, but it turned out to be one of the most rewarding experiences of my career. I keep telling my students, "Mathematics loves you": It does not depend on who you are or where you are from. Mathematics does not discriminate; it is us human beings who do so and we can change that!

Growing Food, Growing Youth: Honoring Culture and Place (Eunice)

In Hawaiʻi, locals typically ask, "Where are you from?" More than just being inquisitive, we are locating relationships, relationships between people and place.

I started teaching after spending years in program evaluation reporting on the educational status of Native Hawaiians and Pacific Islander youth. When I was a PhD student, I took a full-time position teaching sociology at Leeward Community College (LCC), a campus that serves the central and west sides of Oʻahu. I visited a social problems class and noticed a group of students wearing shirts that said, "No Panic, Go Organic – MAʻO Farms." Compared to the other students, they engaged in a substantial way. Who are they? From Waiʻanae (an ahupuaʻa[3] on Oʻahu)? Wait, I thought that Waiʻanae kids did not go to college. That's what the statistics and negative stereotypes said.

Intrigued, I contacted MAʻO Farms. I wanted this grassroots program that merged food and education to be the subject of my dissertation research. Meeting with Summer, their educational coordinator, I realized I was one of many who approached them. While she was supportive, she was hesitant. Far too many researchers have entered the community, collected data, and then disappeared. I realized that I was living the realities of a form of colonization, one from academia and research. To reciprocate, I offered my services in program evaluation. Doesn't everyone want a logic model? Turns out, not really.

However, when one of the MAʻO program's key instructors left, I was then able to partner with the MAʻO Farms program to create the Sociology of Food course (SOC 151) as a requirement for their program. The course had no prefabricated textbook published for the generic mass, no text written by and from someone else's perspective or worldview. The freedom was awesome. Together, a group of the MAʻO Farms program students and I created a recipe to decolonize their education by finding their roots and using ancestral knowledge about food, farming, and place, along with their values to analyze the present and guide the future. I highlight salient course elements as follows.

In SOC 151, students use their ancestral knowledge and their values to demonstrate mastery of course learning outcomes such as the following:

1. Describe the social processes that have created our current food system and their impact on individuals, their communities, and the environment.
2. Identify the sociocultural values and attitudes that facilitate sustainable living.
3. Describe how traditional and Indigenous perspectives inform sustainable practices.

The course follows a genealogical sequence of past, present, and future. Students look to the past (their culture[s], their families) to identify how food was gathered, its purpose, and the intricacies of how food has symbolic meaning. To look to the past, students interview family members. This demonstrates to students firsthand that their families', their culture's, and their ancestors' knowledge is real and applicable today. They learn that history and culture cannot and should not be ignored, indeed, it is a central source of knowledge and a way to understand the present, so that we can do something about it (e.g., the sociological imagination, a central concept in sociology). For the present, students take what they learned about their family and their community and explore the current context. For the future, they consider their generation's purpose, place, and intent for a future including food, place, and their own (grand)children.

Specifically, the interview assignment, which is based on a Native Hawaiian worldview, tells students: I ka wā ma mua, i ka wā ma hope (the future is found in the past; see explanation in Kameʻeleihiwa, 1992, p. 22) and, "Tell me what you eat, and I shall tell you what you are" (Brillat-Savarin, 1825/1949, p. 15). Students determine the interview questions and interview someone who represents

- the past—the oldest person they can find (a grandparent or community member);
- the present—someone who represents the next generation (mom and/or dad); and
- the future—a younger sibling, cousin, niece, or nephew.

They organize the interview findings by past, present, and future and highlight generational changes and similarities. In the conclusion, students synthesize their discoveries and describe a future they would like to see. Here are excerpts from a student's interviews:

Q: What were your favorite foods growing up? What are your favorite ingredients to cook with?
A: (Grandpa/Past): Taro, breadfruit, fish, pandidense, and chicken
A: (Aunty/Present): Chicken, cake
A: (Cousin/Future): Hot pocket

The following excerpt presents typical lessons learned (e.g., food insecurity due to colonization and subsequent struggle, symbolic meanings of food for love of family, identity, place) and a vision for the future.

[My] grandmother's generation mostly grew and cooked their own food. Doing this they were able to stay connected with their culture and be more sustainable. . . . Hearing some stories from my grandma about how it was hard work growing your own food and not having to rely on fast food places was really interesting. For the present it really showed me how crazy it is that most people hardly cook and would rather go out and spend money to eat. . . . Giving our future generations the knowledge about our food culture will help keep us connected to our culture, land, and food.

Although this assignment is designed using Native Hawaiian worldview (i.e., the future is found in the past and aloha ʻāina), students who are not Native Hawaiian or not from Hawaiʻi demonstrate similar lessons learned.

I was born in rural North Carolina at the foothills of the Appalachian Mountains. . . . My grandmother had to miss school for 2 months of the school year and skip 2 days of class a week just to keep the cows milked and chickens fed. The hard life that my ancestors endured was not a figment, however, it brought with it colorful food choices and unique recipes that carried on for generations. . . . Today . . . [m]y family has adopted a fast food mentality, they don't grow their crops or even see the food before it's processed and ready to eat. In my family's future, I hope my family members can learn to teach their children the importance of growing a meal from scratch. . . . I want my kids to have the beautiful joy of pulling a carrot out of the ground on the cusp of fall.

There are many ways to teach a sociology of food course that will result in students meeting the learning outcomes. My desire to help students decolonize their education and value their ancestral knowledge, my ongoing relationship with MAʻO Farms, and my commitment to learn about and incorporate Native Hawaiian worldview, have led me to this curricular approach. It is grounded in the students' roots and creates authentic relationships with the community and the students. I want higher education to do more than impart extant academic knowledge. I provide opportunities for students to know and place value on their histories, their culture, their knowledge as the means to achieve learning outcomes such as analyzing society and solving societal problems. The result is that the learning outcomes have impact beyond the classroom: They have great meaning to students, their families, and their communities.

Exploring ʻĀina: Social Justice in Mathematics Teacher Education (Charmaine)

I am a faculty member in the UH-Mānoa Kahalewaihoʻonaʻauao Institute for Teacher Education (ITE) Secondary program, which is a three-term program for prospective teachers (i.e., teacher candidates). The program-level learning outcomes explicitly include place and social justice. For example, two of our outcomes state that the teacher candidates (our students) will have (a) an understanding of lineage and place and a connection to past, present, and future; and (b) a sense of Hawaiʻi through an appreciation for its rich history, diversity, and Indigenous language and culture. The program faculty also adopted Learning for Justice's *Social Justice Standards*, which contain 20 outcome statements in four domains: identity, diversity, justice, and action (Learning for Justice, 2016). The faculty carefully aligned the three-term curriculum and signature assignments with these outcomes.

For example, during the first term, teacher candidates write, implement, and reflect on a lesson plan that connects one social justice standard/outcome to the academic standards/outcomes in their discipline. During terms two and three, teacher candidates engage in the three-part informed action and social justice project (IASJP), a signature assignment designed with input from all current program faculty. These assignments support teacher candidates in developing an understanding of equity through the larger lens of social justice and through our program's explicit focus on developing educational change agents.

In term two, the teacher candidates complete part I of the IASJP: *Who Am I?*—a narrative essay in which they interrogate their own cultural frame and identity as it relates to issues of equity, diversity, access, and power by reflecting on questions such as the following, that are aligned with the social justice identity domain outcome 5:

- In what ways have you had to negotiate your identity in multiple spaces?
- How will you negotiate your own cultural frame and identity as you work with diverse people to address issues of equity, diversity, access, and power in schools and/or communities?

In my 2018–2019 classes, the mathematics teacher candidates had difficulties identifying and interrogating areas in which they hold both privilege and power. They seemed more easily able to identify areas in which they are oppressed or marginalized and less easily able to see areas in which they are the most powerful. I believe that recognizing both spaces and the spaces in the middle will ultimately guide us to our kuleana as mathematics educators. Kuleana (our privilege and responsibility) involves a multifaceted understanding of our own identities, as described in the identity domain outcomes, in order to know our relationships with others and communities. To help the mathematics teacher candidates understand how one can simultaneously be a member of an oppressed group and a privileged group,

I call attention to my intersecting identities. I share that my dark brown skin color and "dis"ability status place me as one of the most vulnerable in many environments; however, as one who also identifies with mathematics, I often experience unearned reverence and assumed competence in all things mathematics and finance (go figure) related.

Also in term two, teacher candidates complete part II of the IASJP, the *Community Asset Mapping and Inventory*, to help them better understand the social context of the school in which they will be student teaching and its community, as well as their strengths, needs, and wants. This supports student progress toward the program learning outcomes on (a) understanding lineage and place and (b) a sense of Hawaiʻi. In part II, candidates are asked to: (A) draw or download an asset map for their (1) classroom, (2) school, (3) community (neighborhood) the school serves, and (4) ahupuaʻa; (B) select three of the assets and reflect on how they might leverage each asset in their design of secondary mathematics learning experiences. A common "aha" moment is when students are struck by the genealogy of their school or community/neighborhood names—genealogy and names are important in the Hawaiian worldview. For example, one student learned that their school was named for pearls that were once plentiful in the nearby harbor. These realizations allow us to discuss the historical, economic, and political structures that have led to the changes in the community.

Part III, completed in term three, *Becoming Informed: Understanding the Needs of Our Community*, asks teacher candidates to interview community members to identify an issue of injustice related to the school community context that they would like to independently explore and then develop an action plan including "creative insubordination" strategies (Gutierrez, 2016). I assign Gutierrez's "Strategies for Creative Insubordination in Mathematics Teaching" (2016), which lists six strategies mathematics teachers might use to enact change at their schools (e.g., seek allies, turn a rational issue into a moral one). In class, students discuss their identified inequality with classmates to collaboratively identify possible strategies for addressing the identified inequality. At the end of their student teaching semester, the mathematics teacher candidates report on their questions and findings at the program's Secondary annual conference. Some areas of injustice explored during the 2018–2019 school year included a school's process for placing students into Algebra I courses, inconsistent school–parent communication related to Algebra workshop courses, and whether inequalities were inherent in a mathematics department's homework policies.

I share (as follows) the experience of Tania, one of the math teacher candidates I worked with, as an example of the transformative potential of these assignments on the desired learning outcomes. I had interviewed Tania as part of the program's application process and when asked about the biggest problem in education she mentioned parents' lack of involvement in their children's education. Later, during her classroom observations, she realized a problem with student placement into the ninth-grade Algebra Workshop (a companion course for those who might struggle with algebraic concepts). By listening closely to her mentor teacher and interviewing one student's parent, she learned that not all parents knew about the Algebra Workshop. As a part of her action plan, Tania decided to collaborate with ninth grade math teachers (i.e., she sought allies) to create an information flyer to send to parents of incoming ninth graders. She also had a serendipitous opportunity to shift her thinking about parents and to enact real change. Here is her story (edited slightly for brevity):

> When I first presented to [my mentor] my idea that Jeremy could be placed in one of our Algebra 1 workshops, she didn't think it would happen. Then, Jeremy's parents requested for an eligibility meeting and asked for all his teachers to be present. . . . Jeremy's dad asked, "I know Math is a very important subject Ms. Tania, I want him to really learn it." I said, "I believe Jeremy has really good Math skills. If only he could be placed in Algebra 1 workshop to hone these skills and have a better understanding of the concepts, then I think he would be successful." Jeremy's mom looked confused, "Workshop? What is that?" It started a long conversation. The next day, my mentor told me, "You did it, Jeremy will be in one of our workshop classes." She was the first one I talked to about the injustice I identified regarding the math workshops and she thought teachers have no power on this matter but what happened to Jeremy proved that teachers can do something.

Tania concludes her IASJP with the reflection that the assignment allowed her to transform into a courageous educator and "somehow" motivate her mentor to also see her own potential as a change agent. Our program models kuleana to 'āina and community through assignments in which students learn explicit strategies to fulfill their kuleana as educators to be change agents and then, through an exploration of a local community, employ these strategies aimed at addressing the injustices they uncovered.

Cultivation of an Institution-Wide Rubric (Kara)

Nestled in the slopes of Lē'ahi (Diamond Head) in urban Honolulu, Kapi'olani Community College (KCC) honors its namesake, Queen

Julia Napelakapuokaka'e Kapi'olani by living and adapting her motto of "Kū lia i ka Nu'u," to strive for the highest (Kapi'olani Community College, n.d., para. 3), which extends to its andragogy. After attending a local conference focused on Indigenous evaluation and assessment methods, a KCC Title III[4] project director set forth to create a comprehensive rubric on 'āina-based learning that could be meaningfully used across disciplines, so she assembled a team with a wide range of insight, abilities, and experiences.

Gathering the People to Make It Happen

This team of cultivators included the interim Hawai'i Pacific librarian who brought a wealth of resources and understanding to language and cultural aspects through her own studies and involvement with Nā Hawai'i 'Imi Loa (n.d.), a group devoted to advancing Hawaiian knowledge systems, services, and research in the library and information science profession. An analyst joined the team to provide expertise in evaluation and measurement. Finally, and most importantly, two instructors—a professor of economics and a professor of second language teaching and English as a second language—who have used 'āina-based teaching and assessment methods in their classroom for years—contributed both theory and practicum.

Clarifying the Cycle of Learning

Before developing the rubric framework, the team of cultivators emphasized that learning was a cycle of the continuous development of both intellect and life skills rather than a series of steps with a definitive end. They first focused on the content, context, and students, which formed a triad essential to the educational journey. In addition, they clarified that learners' understanding of key skills and concepts flowed from emerging to developing to implementing in a reiterative process.

Learning From Others

The seeds for an 'āina-based rubric had been planted many years ago as *kumu* (teachers) at KCC witnessed the transformative power of weaving topics around land and culture throughout their lessons. Kalāhū, an immersive faculty professional development experience dedicated to 'āina-based learning across the curriculum and campus wide, allowed for further growth through its 'āina-based learning course designation (like a general education overlay/ enhanced course designation), explaining that in such classes, "faculty create culturally responsive curriculum where course content is taught through a cultural context; the cultural context is Indigenous Native Hawaiian knowledge as it relates to wahi or place" (Gonzales et al., 2019, p. 3). The faculty who were already integrating Native Hawaiian traditional knowledge into an aspect(s) of a class did so through one of four core contexts of ʻāina-based learning:

- Mālama[5] ʻāina (geography, geology, ecology);
- ʻŌlelo Hawaiʻi (Hawaiian language);
- Moʻolelo (history, literature, stories, tradition); and/or
- Moʻomeheu (culture, cultural practices/values).

To see how instructors were using ʻāina-based methods in their learning outcomes, assessment tools, and active learning strategies, the cultivators asked for feedback via a simple survey, which guided the direction of the rubric. With these in mind, the cultivators framed learning through three existing hallmarks developed by Kalāhū: (a) Wahi Noho Like o Ka Poʻe (community engagement), (b) Ola Pono (life values), and (c) I Ka Wā Ma Mua, Ka Wā Ma Hope (the bridging of past, present, and future; Gonzales et al., 2019). A sample rubric element from the Community Engagement overview (Figure 10.1) reflects how everything was woven together.

Moving Forward

Throughout the process of the initial rubric creation, curriculum committee members from ʻAha Kalāualani, the campus Native Hawaiian Council, contributed feedback; they were a life force who helped grow ideas and support the cultivators' efforts. The dean of arts and sciences, a former Hawaiian language professor, helped illuminate how to tie pieces together through the holistic metaphor of planting the kukui tree, a symbol of enlightenment. Although the rubric has been created, it will not remain static. A living document provides a dynamic space for practitioner feedback, additional suggestions for classroom activities and assessments, and more.

Together, and after many years of attending to and supporting through professional development, an institution-wide ʻāina-based learning designation has come to fruition. The institution-wide ʻāina-based learning rubric is available to students, faculty, and the campus and is used to evaluate, as well as to inspire action. These efforts strengthen the campus's commitment as a Native Hawaiian Indigenous-serving institution, benefiting all students. After all, the knowledge of the place we live is incomplete without the Native Hawaiian worldview.

Figure 10.1. Rubric element from the Wahi Noho Like o Ka Poʻe (community engagement) section.

	Wahi Noho Like o Ka Poʻe *Community Engagement*		
Hallmark:			
Description:	Relying on community viewed as a Hawaiian sense of place and as an environment for learning, a class must include at least one major topic that connects ways Native Hawaiian traditional knowledge impacts and contributes to community engagement and a community's ʻāina/wahi (place).		
Student Learning Outcome:	Identify ways Native Hawaiian traditional knowledge may impact community engagement and a community's ʻāina/wahi.		
	Muʻo (Emerging)	**Liko (Developing)**	**Kumu (Implementing)**
General Assessment:	**Identify** Ways that Native Hawaiian traditional knowledge may impact a community's ʻāina/wahi.	**Connect** Ways that Native Hawaiian traditional knowledge impacts an individual's sense of place and engagement in the community.	**Transform** Native Hawaiian traditional knowledge to engage with the community or to impact community engagement and a community's ʻāina/wahi.
Core Contexts:	Mālama ʻĀina. ʻŌlelo Hawaiʻi. Moʻolelo. Moʻomeheu.		

Parting Words

We invite you and the students to consider where you and they are: the places you/they live, work, play, visit. These places and spaces shape and nurture in different ways. The multiple genealogies of a place can teach about the positive and negative shaping of the place in the past and can guide on how to take care of that place for present and future generations. The overarching question is, how to give back? As you work to promote equity and social justice via an embedded assessment, 'āina-based approach, we offer the following questions to consider:

1. Why would a program/campus want its students to know about the land/place they live, work, play, visit?
2. Who holds knowledge about those places? Knowledge about where the campus is located (if a physical campus exists)?
3. What learning outcomes related to land/place might be developed?
4. How can faculty, students, and others listen to the voices of land/place (it can be people's voices, beliefs, traditions)?
5. How might students demonstrate their knowledge of land/place? What culturally appropriate ways exist?
6. What are ways that faculty, staff, and students interact with the places they live? How do the genealogies of place shape current interactions?
7. How might assignments be simultaneously aligned with place and learning outcomes?
8. Who shares thought-provoking stories around data and evaluation? Who speaks from a place of classroom wisdom?
9. What existing frameworks can be enhanced to develop 'āina-based learning outcomes, aligned assignments, student demonstrations of achievement, evaluation tools? What professional development networks, department initiatives, and/or strategic planning can be leveraged?

Acknowledgments

Our understanding and desire to continue deep learning, to practice cultural humility, and to refine pedagogy and assessment tools are a direct result of many generous teachers, both Native Hawaiians and non-Native Hawaiians. We thank the students, faculty, and personnel in our specific departments and units within the University of Hawai'i. The seven of us are grateful to one another for sharing curriculum, learning from lived praxis, and engaging in rich scholarly and personal reflection. This intentional and open engagement has led us to a deeper understanding and active commitment to place equity and social justice at the forefront in Hawai'i and for Native Hawaiians.

Thank you to the youth whose soul and spirits inspired me and to the wisdom of their ancestors and commitment of our community partners. You have challenged me to rethink paradigms and to instill in all of us the challenge and love of learning for a purpose: thriving communities and homes. A special thank you to Kukui Maunakea-Forth, Gary Maunakea-Forth, Kamuela Enos, Cheryse Kauikeolani Sana, and Derrik Parker. [Eunice]

The Kapi'olani Community College 'āina-based rubric would not exist without the thinkers and doers who shared their knowledge and shaped perspectives across the institution. A special thank you to Kelli Goya (Title II project coordinator), Jaclyn Lindo (assistant professor, economics), Caroline Torres (assistant professor second language teaching and English as a second language), Erica Dias (interim Hawai'i Pacific librarian), Annie Thomas (acting head librarian), Lisa Kanae (chair, languages, linguistics, and literature), Nāwa'a Napoleon (dean, arts and sciences), and Kalāhū Hui. [Kara]

I would like to extend a special thanks to my fellow faculty of the UH-Ma¯noa Kahalewaiho'ona'auao Institute for Teacher Education (ITE) Secondary program who conceptualized, designed, and implemented numerous iterations of the Informed Action and Social Justice Project. Specifically, I would like to acknowledge: Charlotte Frambaugh-Kritzer, Amber Makaiau, Kirsten Mawyer, Chad Miller, 'Alohilani Okamura, and Cheryl Treiber-Kawaoka. [Charmaine]

Thank you to planet Earth for providing us with so many resources and a sense of identity, and to the Native Hawaiians for sharing their culture and wisdom to teach us how to understand, protect and respect those resources. Davianna McGregor and Noa Emmett Aluli, there are no words to describe how much an inspiration you have been throughout this journey. And last but not least: students, you are truly fabulous! Thank you. [Monique]

We extend our gratitude to the readers of our chapter and hope they find this work helpful and applicable in terms of concrete examples, cultural framing, and pedagogical approaches to long-standing issues of assessment inequity in the academy.

Notes

1. Kaho'olawe is a small island in the Hawaiian archipelago, about seven miles from the island of Maui, that the U.S. military used for bombing practice between World War II and 1993.

2. Molokai is a small, rural island in the Hawaiian archipelago about six miles from the island of Maui.

3. Ahupua'a is a Native Hawaiian land division usually extending from mountain to sea. These divisions were created to maximize and sustain natural resource management.

4. To learn more about Title III, visit: https://www.hawaii.edu/hawaiipapaokeao/titleiii/

5. *Mālama* translates as to take care of, tend, attend, care for, preserve, protect.

References

Ayers, W., Quinn, T. M., & Stovall, D. (2009). Preface. In W. Ayers, T. M. Quinn, and D. Stovall (Eds.), *Handbook of social justice in education* (pp. xiii–xv). Routledge.

Brillat-Savarin, J. A. (1949). *The physiology of taste, or, meditations on transcendental gastronomy* (M. F. K. Fisher, Trans.). The Heritage Press. (Original work published 1825)

Carter, P. L., & Welner, K. G. (Eds.). (2013). *Closing the opportunity gap: What America must do to give every child an even chance.* Oxford University Press.

Darrah-Okike, J. (2020). Theorizing race in Hawai'i: Centering place, indigeneity, and settler colonialism. *Sociology Compass, 14*(7), e12791. https://doi.org/10.1111/soc4.12791

Fraser, N. (2000). Rethinking recognition. *New Left Review, 3*, 107–120. https://newleftreview.org/issues/ii3/articles/nancy-fraser-rethinking-recognition

Galilei, G. (1623). *The assayer* (Abridged. S. Drake, Trans.). https://web.stanford.edu/~jsabol/certainty/readings/Galileo-Assayer.pdf

Gonzales, A., Anderson, A., Ewan, B., Polley, C., Torres, C., Primavera, C., Melim, C., Evans, D., Malm, E., Acoba, F., Harada, G., Lindo, J., Ogata, K., Nakamura, K., Burke, L., Scanlan, L., Bright, L. A., Kobuke, L., Minahal, M., . . . Kanaoka, Y. (2019). *Proposal for an 'āina-based learning designation at Kapi'olani Community College.* http://facultysenate.kapiolani.hawaii.edu/wp-content/uploads/2019/11/%E2%80%98A%CC%84ina-Based-Learning-Designation-Statement-of-Purpose-4.pdf

Gutierrez, R. (2016). Strategies for creative insubordination in mathematics teaching. *Teaching for Excellence and Equity in Mathematics, 7*(1), 52–60. https://www.todos-math.org/assets/documents/TEEM/teem7_final1.pdf#page52

Kame'eleihiwa, L. (1992). *Native land and foreign desires: Ko Hawai'i 'āina a me nā koi pu'umake a ka po'e haole: A history of land tenure change in Hawai'i from traditional times until the 1848 Māhele, including an analysis of Hawaiian ali'i nui and American Calvinists.* Bishop Museum Press.

Kana'iaupuni, S., Ledward, B., & Jensen, U. (2010). *Culture-based education and its relationship to student outcomes.* Kamehameha Schools Research and Evaluation. https://www.ksbe.edu/assets/research/collection/10_0117_kanaiaupuni.pdf

Kapiʻolani Community College. (n.d.). *In the name of a queen*. https://www
.kapiolani.hawaii.edu/about-kcc/in-the-name-of-a-queen/

Learning Assistant Alliance. (n.d.). *What are learning assistants?* https://www.learn-
ingassistantalliance.org/

Learning for Justice. (2016). *Social justice standards*. https://www.learningforjustice
.org/frameworks/social-justice-standards

Lewicka. M. (2011). Place attachment: How far have we come in the last 40 years?
Journal of Environmental Psychology, *31*(3), 207–230. https://doi.org/10.1016/
j.jenvp.2010.10.001

Lipe, K., Darrah-Okike, J., Lynch, M. K., Reilly, M., Zabala, S., Stitt-Bergh, M.,
Litton, C., Mangram, C., & Ní Dhonacha, S. (2020). Our Hawaiʻi-grown truth,
racial healing, and transformation: Recommitting to Mother Earth. In T. B.
McNair (Ed.), *We hold these truths: Dismantling racial hierarchies, building equitable communities* (pp. 34–37). Association of American Colleges and Universities.
https://www.aacu.org/we-hold-these-truths

Montenegro, E., & Jankowski, N. A. (2017, January). *Equity and assessment: Moving
towards culturally responsive assessment* (Occasional Paper No. 29). University
of Illinois and Indiana University, National Institute for Learning Outcomes
Assessment (NILOA). https://www.learningoutcomesassessment.org/wp-content/
uploads/2019/02/OccasionalPaper29.pdf

Mora, C. (n.d.). *The carbon neutrality challenge*. MoraLab. http://www.soc.hawaii.
edu/mora/Carbon%20Neutrality%20Project

Nā Hawaiʻi ʻImi Loa. (n.d.) *About us*. https://www.nahawaiiimiloa.com/about-us.
html

Nakaoka, S., Wilhelm, D., Wilhelm, M., Morelli, P., & Mahi, D. (2020, October
12–16). *Application of kūkulu kumuhana and the Aloha framework for evaluation* [Paper presentation]. Hawaiʻi-Pacific Evaluation Association 2020 Annual
Conference, Honolulu, Hawaiʻi, United States.

Preston, S. D., & Gelman, S. A. (2020). This land is my land: Psychological
ownership increases willingness to protect the natural world more than legal
ownership. *Journal of Environmental Psychology*, *70*. https://doi.org/10.1016/
j.jenvp.2020.101443

Riegle-Crumb, C., King, B., & Irizarry, Y. (2019). Does STEM stand out? Examining racial/ethnic gaps in persistence across postsecondary fields. *Educational
Researcher*, *48*(3), 133–144. https://doi.org/10.3102/0013189X19831006

Scannell, L., & Gifford, R. (2017). The experienced psychological benefits of
place attachment. *Journal of Environmental Psychology*, *51*, 256–269. https://doi
.org/10.1016/j.jenvp.2017.04.001

Semken, S., Ward, E. G., Moosavi, S., & Chinn, P. (2017). Place-based education
in geoscience: Theory, research, practice, and assessment. *Journal of Geoscience
Education*, *65*(4), 542–562. https://doi.org/10.5408/17-276.1

Thomas, S., Kanaʻiaupuni, S., Balutski, B. J. N., & Freitas, A. K. (2012). Access and success for students from indigenous populations. In J. Smart & M. Paulsen, *Higher education: Handbook of theory and research* (Vol. 27, pp. 335–367). Springer. https://doi.org/10.1007/978-94-007-2950-6_7

University of Hawaiʻi. (2019a, December 12). *Helping Hawaiʻi become carbon neutral one tree at a time.* UH News. https://www.hawaii.edu/news/2019/12/12/uh-manoa-carbon-neutrality-challenge/

University of Hawaiʻi. (2019b, September 3). *Project aims to make Hawaiʻi the first carbon-neutral state.* UH News. https://www.hawaii.edu/news/2019/09/03/carbon-neutrality-challenge/

Wiggins, G. (1989). A true test: Toward more authentic and equitable assessment. *The Phi Delta Kappan, 70*(9), 703–713. https://grantwiggins.files.wordpress.com/2014/01/wiggins-atruetest-kappan89.pdf

Winter, K. B., & Lucas, M. (2017). Spatial modeling of social-ecological management zones of the aliʻi era on the island of Kauaʻi with implications for large-scale biocultural conservation and forest restoration efforts in Hawaiʻi. *Pacific Science, 71*(4), 457–477. https://doi.org/10.2984/71.4.5

11

CULTURALLY RESPONSIVE ASSESSMENT 2.0 THROUGH FACULTY AND STUDENTS' VOICES

Chiara Logli

This chapter examines how assessment can be a vital ally with equity in the field of higher education. For decades, graduation rates, achievement gaps, and other numerical benchmarks have been the uncontested indicators of success. Recently, attention has started to shift toward inclusive initiatives that support learning of all students. Through a case study approach, this chapter illustrates how assessment can evaluate and increase the extent to which faculty integrate diverse practices to improve student achievement. Ultimately, the study demonstrates the relevance of diversity theories and diversified methodologies for assessment.

The conceptual framework builds on two paradigms—culturally responsive assessment and assessment 2.0. Culturally responsive assessment concerns matters of equity, such as shaping evaluation tools through diversity-based strategies and using results to enrich learning of all students (Montenegro & Jankowski, 2017). Assessment 2.0 refers to flexible and yet robust practices, including bottom-up processes and collective meaning-making (Metzler & Kurz, 2018). I combine the two paradigms because assessment in the 21st century requires culture-based considerations, which can only exist within adaptable approaches as assessment 2.0. Equity goes hand-in-hand with flexibility.

The grounded theory methodology expands from a previous pilot study around faculty experiences by adding student's perspectives (Logli, 2020). It maps faculty and students' surveys, activities, and focus groups to the universal design for learning model (UDL; Hehir, 2009; Rao, 2019; Rose & Gravel, 2009). It represents a further attempt to bring existing data sources about student learning in conversation with one another with a close look on diversity.

This study confirms that assessment data bloom naturally across campus, can be gathered in numerous manners, and can be examined through an equity lens in order to support student variability. Results show that faculty members are implementing inclusive strategies in their instruction and assessment, and closely collaborate with support services to engage all learners. Students also value diverse pedagogy but tend to focus on the logistical facets of their educational experience, such as facilities and finances, rather than on learning preferences.

Conceptual Framework: Assessment as Quality and Diversity Assurance

Quality assurance refers to embedding quality in all aspects of higher education, from student learning to administrative processes, rather than inspecting systems that have already been established (Ryan, 2015). Quality has historically been one of the most difficult specifications to measure and globalization has complicated it even further (Neubauer, 2018, 2019). Reductionist approaches have established quantitative tactics, such as the ranking phenomenon. Yet, the Fourth Industrial Revolution is revealing more complex progressions due to students' mobility, interdisciplinary demands, and need for learning that is autonomous, immersive, and interactive (Neubauer, 2018, 2019).

Student variability is possibly the most complex feature in the 21st-century classroom. Globalization is not only an "intensifier of interdependence," but also a multiplier and magnifier of differences" (Hershock, 2010, p. 30). Each individual identity holds both cosmopolitan (i.e., humanist and global) and grounded (i.e., local and national) affiliations (Kahn, 2004; Nilan & Feixa, 2006). Within education, variety tends to relate to gender, ethnicity, religion, and social class as well as learning preferences (Hershock, 2010). Concerns of access, survival, output, and outcome that relate to minority students are widespread (Farrell, 2007). Underrepresented students' probability of getting into college, completing a degree, learning the same knowledge, and experiencing similar post-graduation lives is slimmer compared to "traditional" learners.

Hershock (2010) makes a key distinction between variety and diversity. Variety is "a quantitative index of simple multiplicity that connotes things simply being-different" (Hershock, 2010, p. 35). Campuses can be like zoos, where variety is externally imposed—varied populations and programs merely coexist. By contrast, diversity is "a qualitative index of self-sustaining and difference-enriching patterns of mutual contribution to shared welfare" (Hershock, 2010, p. 35). Universities can be like ecosystems, where diversity rises from within—diverse populations and programs focus on how they "best differ-for one another," rather than how they "differ-from each other" (Hershock, 2010, p. 38).

This theory of diversity can find two entryways into the assessment domain. Assessment 2.0 is designed to "supplement the assessment work already being done" and to be "organic"—growing naturally from faculty and staff's expertise, rather than from over-imposed, linear, and standardized structures (Metzler & Kurz, 2018, p. 4). It infuses assessment with bottom-up processes, collective meaning-making within departments, and flexible opportunities to provide data, whether via formative, summative, quantitative, or qualitative approaches. Its premise is that assessment must lead to action—assessment should not be done unless there is readiness for instructional and institutional change in the students' best interest. Campuses are filled with data, but data without rigorous analysis and usage are useless (Baker et al., 2012; Kuh et al., 2014).

However, "culturally responsive assessment" involves students throughout the entire assessment process, develops evaluation tools that are appropriate for different learners, uses results to improve the academic experience of all students, and disaggregates the data to understand the student population (Montenegro & Jankowski, 2017). Where one assessment approach is dominant, it will sacrifice many individual learning preferences (O'Neill & Maguire, 2017). Equity-based strategies do not benefit underrepresented students only, but all students (Finley & McNair, 2013).

For example, some campuses frame assessment within social justice principles such as inclusion and collaboration (Zerquera et al., 2018). Other universities develop local assessment instruments and give students options to choose among presentation, poster, debate, or exam (Montenegro & Jankowski, 2017). Allowing students to select how they are evaluated improves their engagement, achievement, and the quality of the learning experience while addressing student variability (Gosselin & Gagné, 2014).

The UDL approach provides a useful application of culturally responsive assessment. It is based on the premise that variability among learners is the norm and individuals can become expert learners in varied ways—there is no one path to mastery (Hehir, 2009; Rao, 2019; Rose & Gravel, 2009). To design for variability, instructors can begin by identifying common barriers to students' learning, preferences, and needs for supports. The UDL model comprises three main principles—representation, action and expression, and engagement. Each principle has three guidelines (nine in total) and each guideline has a series of checkpoints (31 in total) that proactively build in flexibility, choice, and scaffolds as well as other pedagogical tools to facilitate the learning experience for all.

Several assessment scholars suggest similar methods, such as incorporating (a) global learning, collaborative assignments, research opportunities, and service-learning (Kuh et al., 2013); (b) group work, application of knowledge, interaction with peers, and real-life connection (Ewell, 2009); (c) information in alternative formats, including theory and practice (Halpern & Hakel, 2003); and (d) scaffoldings, such as sequenced lesson plans, rubrics, students' self-reflection, and assignments that culminate in a final demonstration (Hutchings et al., 2014).

Methodology: Grounded Theory Meets Universal Design for Learning

In this chapter, I illustrate how assessment can evaluate and amplify the extent to which faculty incorporate diverse practices to enhance student performance. This case study took place at the Honolulu Community College in Hawaii (HonCC). Around 100 faculty members offer both vocational and liberal arts programs to approximately 3,000 students, comprising 43% Asian, 28% Hawaiian, and 12% mixed ethnicities (Arbuckle, 2020). The five pillars of the university are student-focus, Hawaiian values, diversity, sustainability, and community partnerships. I encompassed a variety of methods, because a robust assessment program draws on multiple sources of evidence at multiple levels within the institution (Metzler & Kurz, 2018).

I analyzed three sets of faculty data that address gains and gaps in student learning:

- assessment reports from 654 course learning outcomes, across 210 classes, between 2014 and 2018, including narratives about strategies that support student mastery of the outcome
- 233 index cards from a campus-wide activity that was held at commencement in 2018, when 145 faculty and staff members wrote down how they purposefully engaged students
- field notes that I took at approximately 20 campus-wide meetings, such as assessment workshops and faculty development series, where faculty discussed barriers and supports to learning; these dialogues also became a space to validate the findings from the previous two methods—the results looked like "a typical day in the classroom," according to the participants

I also analyzed campus-wide documents on student experience:

- three surveys—2017 Campus-Wide Student Survey (233 respondents), 2018 Community College Survey of Student Engagement (CCSSE; 322 respondents), 2020 Purposeful Engagement Survey (312 respondents)
- 2018 "I wish my teacher knew" activity, where 154 students completed the sentence on a Post-it at different stations across campus (Abeshima & Cassandra, 2018)
- 2015 focus group on student success with approximately 20 students

With the exception of the course-level assessment reports, all other methods emerged organically outside preconceived assessment plans.

The methodology follows grounded theory principles, including two cycles of coding and saturation point (Charmaz, 2010). Through the first coding cycle, the emerging patterns resonated with the UDL model (Rao, 2019). Therefore, the second coding cycle mapped the six sets of data to UDL checkpoints. My student assistant also coded the data, providing a learner's perspective in the study (O'Neill & Maguire, 2017; Zerquera et al., 2018). We stopped adding sets of data when we reached a saturation point—no more new information surfaced.

With regard to qualitative data, I coded all sets of data, with the exception of the CCSSE, which contains numerical values only. With regard to quantitative data, I coded all available descriptive statistics, namely across the student's CCSSE, and faculty's assessment reports and index cards. Within the CCSSE analysis, I pointed out any differences between HonCC and the other 536 institutions in the 2018 cohort, regardless of their statistical significance.

Culturally Responsive Assessment 2.0: A Case Study

HonCC uses a variety of approaches to get a holistic picture of student learning, including quantitative and qualitative tools as recommended by Metzler and Kurz (2018). These sets of data indicate that faculty members are mindful of culture-based considerations and use assessment results to further the learning of all students (Finley & McNair, 2013; Montenegro & Jankowski, 2017). This case study adds the students' voice to a previous study (Logli, 2020), and helped confirm most of the patterns that had surfaced from the faculty experience.

The additional three sets of data from students are a testimony of student variability. Students juggle college, work, and family, often with no help. They may suffer from anxiety, depression, and a range of medical conditions. They sometimes struggle with new foster families, homeless shelters, language barriers, or just being a learner—"this is my first class in a very long time." In some cases, they catch multiple buses from the other side of the island, which takes hours and often involves delays. Compared to the 2018 CCSSE cohort, students at HonCC are more likely to withdraw from college due to lack of finances (75% vs. 67%) and work full-time (68% vs. 60%). Students also validate HonCC's commitment to diversity. They agree that HonCC is a student-centered campus (82%), maintains an equitable multicultural environment (85%), promotes appreciation of diversity (93%), and has faculty and staff who are accessible, caring, and helpful (93%).

Yet, students' voices also generated new evidence around learning that can steer future assessment endeavors. Students value inclusive teaching strategies, but mainly focus on the logistical supporters and barriers of their educational experience. Although they touch upon their learning preferences, their comments generally target facilities (e.g., parking), communication (e.g., resource finder), food (e.g., healthy and reasonably priced options), customer service (e.g., extended hours during night classes), and finances (e.g., scholarships).

In the following sections, this chapter presents the findings according to emerging themes by summarizing the faculty's contributions that were featured in Logli's (2020) previous study and complementing them with students' feedback. For easier readability, results are reported in an aggregate manner without specifying the exact data source. All direct quotes are from the participants' voices.

Diversified Assessment Methods

Students' comments demonstrate the variability of learning preferences as well as assessment methods on campus (Hehir, 2009; Rao, 2019; Rose & Gravel, 2009). Some learners find the homework difficult while others struggle with final exams, class presentations, or speaking up. Faculty respond to different cognitive styles by integrating a multiplicity of embedded assessments:

- exams (29%)
- embedded questions (21%)
- lab tasks (18%)
- activities (9%)
- presentations (8%)
- projects (7%)
- papers (4%)
- practica (3%)

These formative and summative approaches supplement the assignments already being done and draw from faculty's expertise, rather than over-imposed standardized assessment requirements (Metzler & Kurz, 2018). Faculty members diversify and contextualize their assessment methods by integrating mainstream measures with locally developed instruments that are better suited to gauge learning (Gosselin & Gagné, 2014; Montenegro & Jankowski, 2017; O'Neill & Maguire, 2017).

For instance, a faculty member developed the "About You Questionnaire," which allows her to better identify her students' barriers to learning and to design assessment from the outset for a broader range of learners (Hartline, 2018). As a result, she accepts handwritten, digital, or audio submissions to accommodate students who do not have a computer, a printer, or have dyslexia. She also replaces class presentations with group work to support students with anxiety and chooses the timing of her assessments carefully in consideration of students' cognitive and logistical needs (e.g., bus schedule).

Another department approaches assessment from two angles. A student self-assessment focuses on content areas, while embedded assessments target students' analytical skills, such as inclusion of primary sources, supporting examples, and vocabulary taught (Patterson, 2018). The faculty found that knowledge surveys provide a valid overview of what students are learning, because in the cultural context of Hawaii students appear to be modest in their self-reporting.

However, only a few faculty members across campus give students a choice on how to be assessed. During the discussions, faculty expressed interest in exploring new assessment approaches that honor student diversity and maintain rigor. The main challenge is how to expand student autonomy while also complying with standardized job certifications and ensuring that students demonstrate learning through various modalities.

Teaching for Student Variability

With regard to UDL and any other diverse and inclusive models, the expectation for a campus is to employ all three principles over time and across courses. Each faculty member should employ a couple of checkpoints per class; addressing all 31 checkpoints all the time would be impracticable (Hehir, 2009; Rao, 2019; Rose & Gravel, 2009). As a result, a UDL map looks different in each university, with different weights across the nine guidelines based on learners' characteristics, content matters, and pedagogical priorities of the moment.

On our campus, both faculty and students value inclusive practices to enhance learning, especially in support of content understanding (UDL guideline 3), instructional and noninstructional ties (UDL guideline 6), student persistence (UDL guideline 8), and optimizing students' motivation and coping skills (UDL guideline 9). These findings emerge from the combined numerical data of faculty's assessment reports and index cards and are further validated by all other sets of data. They also echo the campus's recent emphasis on student retention and completion, mainly by highlighting subject matters, a caring environment, and collaboration between academic and student affairs.

Principle I: Multiple Means of Representation

First, providing options for comprehension (UDL guideline 3) is at the forefront of faculty and students' concerns. Faculty members mention it 25% of the time across the assessment reports and index cards. They explain "stories behind place names," "replace textbook examples with local examples," and use familiar images like a rainbow to familiarize learners to salient scientific characteristics. They include hands-on activities to "help students make connections with class content" and to "show that what they are learning is practical, important, and related to both local and global perspectives" (e.g., Mālama ʻĀina or Take Care of the Land days).

Students value hands-on experiences and readings with faculty also highlighting the salient points. Compared to the 2018 CCSSE cohort, more HonCC students indicate that they learned to (a) form a new understanding from various pieces of information (97% vs. 95%); (b) make judgments about the soundness of information, arguments, or methods (93% vs. 89%); and (c) think critically and analytically (99% vs. 94%).

Principle II: Multiple Means of Action and Expression

Second, providing options for executive functions (UDL guideline 6) is important for both faculty and students. Faculty members mention it 19% of the time across the assessment reports and index cards. They guide appropriate goal setting by organizing the syllabus thoroughly, emailing e-newsletters to students before the start of the semester, and adjusting the course pace—they either "set quick turnaround time" or "allow more time" depending on the circumstances. In addition, they support planning and strategy development by connecting students to campus resources "that can help in overcoming their challenge." They invite guest speakers from support services in their classrooms, send students on scavenger hunts to key offices, and refer students to a variety of available aids.

They also facilitate managing information by "putting great thought" into structuring mind mapping, practice sheets, and transition projects. Furthermore, they enhance the capacity for monitoring progress by "having an assignment where students plot a course outline to reach their end goal," "keeping students accurately updated," and "correcting each deficiency before moving on to the next project" through outside-of-class optional review sessions, in-class practice exams with samples, and graded pre-quizzes.

Students appreciate when a teacher breaks down information, slows down, answers all their questions, ensures they understand the material before proceeding, and spaces assignments apart. For example, 78% of the CCSSE respondents mention that they prepared two or more drafts of a paper or assignment before turning it in. Among the support services in the CCSSE, students primarily use Academic Advising (79%), Library (76%), and Computer Lab (55%), which are also their favorite units (on average 95% of the respondents are satisfied with them). The Children's Center is also praised across the other student-based datasets. Compared to the 2018 CCSSE cohort, more students indicate that HonCC (a) contacts them if they are struggling with their studies to assist them (58% vs. 50%); (b) provides the support they need to succeed in college (99% vs. 96%) and thrive socially (82% vs. 75%); and (c) helps them cope with nonacademic responsibilities, such as work and family (73% vs. 64%).

Across all sets of data, students consistently advocate for removal of barriers in the curriculum map. For example, they recommend that courses are properly aligned, career-relevant, scheduled across semesters, and actually offered to ensure timely degree completion. They suggest departments be careful in combining courses at an accelerated pace, reclassifying classes at a more advanced level, and obliging students to wait a semester to retake a course. They call for simplified prerequisites and transfer processes across universities, especially within a state system.

Principle III: Multiple Means of Engagement

Third, providing options for persistence (UDL guideline 8) is another priority for faculty and students. Faculty members mention it 20% of the time across the assessment reports and index cards. They heighten the salience of objectives by engaging students in activities that are relevant for their lives (e.g., field studies, guest speakers, analyses of current events). In addition, they vary demands and resources to optimize challenges—"I diversify my teaching strategies, I switch mode every 10 minutes to support each learning preference." They also foster collaboration by engaging families when appropriate and integrating group activities (e.g., icebreakers, partnering in problem-solving) so students "get to know one another—who they are and what their interests are—and make discoveries, so they are happy to return to class because their friends are there."

Faculty encourage student participation in campus life (e.g., student clubs, social projects, leadership opportunities) so "they experience values like community and compassion and can be the positive change that ripples around." Moreover, they increase mastery-oriented feedback by using comments like "the essay would be better with punctuation," rather than "you need to work on punctuation," through lab follow-up, discussions on assignments, well-defined rubrics, peer mentorships, and learning communities where students "share their mistakes, discoveries, and learn from each other."

Students value being part of unique programs that are not offered in other system campuses and that are relevant in the job market. They praise the opportunity to practice certification tests, rather than generic exams, and to be "ready, prepared for the field." Compared to the 2018 CCSSE cohort, more HonCC students (a) acquire job-related knowledge and skills (85% vs. 79%); (b) receive prompt feedback from instructors (96% vs. 93%); (c) apply theories to practical problems (95% vs. 91%); and (d) use information to perform a new skill (94% vs. 92%).

Students also express appreciation for the "Ohana style" (family style), which makes HonCC as a "second home." They enjoy the small classes, which "allow faculty to get a close bond with the students." They also find that "a strong relationship among students is beneficial," and recommend more student mentorship and peer tutoring. Compared to the 2018 CCSSE cohort, more HonCC students (a) learn to work effectively with others (94% vs. 90%); (b) participate in a community-based project as part of a regular course (34% vs. 27%); and (c) work with instructors on activities other than coursework (47% vs. 35%).

Fourth, providing options for self-regulation (UDL guideline 9) was an important concern among faculty and students. Faculty members mention it 12% of the time across the assessment reports and index cards. They promote expectations that optimize motivation, by assisting students to solve issues instead of passing them along, taking the time to understand their needs, and "teaching them how to be students" (e.g., how to take notes, tackle quizzes, manage time). In addition, faculty facilitate personal coping skills by providing personal stories and professional mentorship around their passions and goals. For instance, faculty make an effort to learn students' stories (e.g., show up early to class, create talk story time) and provide professional guidance (e.g., write letters of recommendation, share networking, revise job applications, organize mock interviews, encourage students to think about "goals within the industry"). They also develop self-assessment through 1-minute surveys (e.g., What did you learn today? What did you have more questions about?), end-of-the-semester meetings, course evaluations, and involving them in rubric development.

Students appreciate that faculty have experience in the field, share personal testimonies, connect with students, "understand the hardship we [students] go through," and are helpful, organized, and prepared. Compared to the 2018 CCSSE cohort, more HonCC students are encouraged by faculty to (a) develop clearer career goals (90% vs. 85%); (b) spend significant amounts of time studying (98% vs. 96%); (c) gain information about career opportunities (88% vs. 81%); and (d) work harder than students thought they could to meet an instructor's expectations (95% vs. 90%). They also encourage faculty to offer a survey on why students drop a class, so the reasons can help faculty improve the course in the future.

Conclusion

Considerations of equity are leading forces in shaping the future of assessment. Accrediting agencies also encourage attention to diversity and leave room for flexibility in assessment schemes. Universities must make decisions that are equitable for students, otherwise they cannot gather meaningful evidence of their learning.

Despite its limited scale, this case study finds that as students learn in various ways, they also need to be assessed through assorted and contextualized approaches. Diverse teaching and assessment strategies are key, including collaborations between academic affairs and support services. The main challenge for faculty is to provide students a choice on how to be assessed. While they support student autonomy, faculty must also comply with state certification and third-party guidelines that remain quite standardized.

Any sets of data in higher education have the potential to be used as potent assessment instruments. Drawing from data sources that already exist minimizes the risk of social desirability biases, meaning providing information that is likely to be viewed favorably by assessment specialists. Data can be viewed as catalysts that move the institution forward, not sticks employed against constituents. Data should be approached safely and proactively, rather than left unexamined and unused. They should be explored from an equity angle so that their analyses can advance the learning and development of all students.

However, assessment studies about students' perspectives require more careful design and overt intent compared to faculty's feedback. Faculty tend to spontaneously frame broad educational queries within pedagogical insights. By contrast, students usually answer generic questions on their educational experience by focusing on logistical concerns, such as infrastructures and financial aid, rather than reflections on learning. Therefore, when including students' voices, assessment plans need explicit items around teaching strategies and reflections on learning. Learners can be a partner in finding solutions and enhancing learning; faculty and staff need to involve them, ask them direct questions, and use their responses as springboards toward effective change.

Establishing flexible and inclusive approaches to assessment is even more vital in the scenario of a crisis, such as natural disasters and pandemics, when all preexisting issues of inequity exacerbate. Tackling unexpected challenges is more realistic with robust foundations already in place. For example, substantial experience and creativity is required when moving learning experiences around experiential learning activities, community-based projects, and overall campus life to online platforms. The threads of flexible culturally responsive assessments need to weave through the university fabric so it can always endure any adversities in the best interest of our students.

References

Abeshima, A., & Cassandra, K. (2018). *What I wish my teacher knew*. Honolulu Community College.

Arbuckle, J. (2020). *Honolulu Community College: Enrollment report (Spring)*. Honolulu Community College.

Baker, G. R., Jankowski, N. A., Provezis, S., & Kinzie, J. (2012). *Using assessment results: Promising practices of institutions that do it well*. University of Illinois and Indiana University, National Institute for Learning Outcomes Assessment. https://www.learningoutcomesassessment.org/wp-content/uploads/2019/02/UsingAssessmentResults.pdf

Charmaz, K. (2010). *Constructing grounded theory: A practical guide through qualitative analysis*. SAGE.

Ewell, P. (2009). *Assessment, accountability, and improvement: Revisiting the tension* (Occasional Paper No. 1). University of Illinois and Indiana University, National Institute for Learning Outcomes Assessment. https://www.learningoutcomesassessment.org/wp-content/uploads/2019/02/OccasionalPaper1.pdf

Farrell, J. (2007). Equality of education: A half-century of comparative evidence seen from a new millennium. In R. Arnove & C. A. Torres (Eds.), *Comparative education: The dialectic of the global and the local* (pp. 129–150). Rowman & Littlefield.

Finley, A., & McNair, T. (2013). *Assessing underserved students' engagement in high-impact practices*. Association of American Colleges and Universities. https://www.aacu.org/sites/default/files/files/assessinghips/AssessingHIPS_TGGrantReport.pdf

Gosselin, J., & Gagné, A. (2014). *Differentiated evaluation: An inclusive evaluation strategy aimed at promoting student engagement and student learning in undergraduate classrooms*. Higher Education Quality Council of Ontario. https://heqco.ca/pub/

differentiated-evaluation-an-inclusive-evaluation-strategy-aimed-at-promoting-student-engagement-and-student-learning-in-undergraduate-classrooms/

Halpern, D., & Hakel, M. (2003). Applying the science of learning to the university and beyond: Teaching for long-term retention and transfer. *Change: The Magazine of Higher Learning, 35*(4), 36–41. https://doi.org/10.1080/00091380309604109

Hartline, E. (2018). *Creating an assessment plan: Understanding students as the foundation of assessment*. Honolulu Community College.

Hehir, T. (2009). Policy foundations of universal design for learning. In D. Gordon, J. Gravel, & L. Schifter (Eds.), *A policy reader in universal design for learning* (pp. 35–45). Harvard Education Press.

Hershock, P. (2010). Higher education, globalization, and the critical emergence of diversity. *Paideusis, 19*(1), 29–42. https://doi.org/10.7202/1072321ar

Hutchings, P., Jankowski, N., & Ewell, P. (2014). *Catalyzing assignment design activity on your campus: Lessons from NILOA's assignment library initiative*. University of Illinois and Indiana University, National Institute for Learning Outcomes Assessment.

Kahn, J. (2004, April 29). *Introduction: Identities, nations, and cosmopolitan practice* [Paper presentation]. Identities, Nations, and Cosmopolitan Practice: Interrogating the Work of Pnina and Richard Werbner Conference, Singapore.

Kuh, G., Ikenberry, S., Jankowski, N., Cain, T., Hutchings, P., & Kinzie, J. (2014). *Using evidence of student learning to improve higher education*. Wiley.

Kuh, G., O'Donnell, K., & Reed, S. (2013). *Ensuring quality and taking high-impact practices to scale*. Association of American Colleges and Universities.

Logli, C. (2020). Culturally responsive assessment 2.0: Repositioning equity and quality assurance. *Research and Practice in Assessment, 14*(Winter), 19–31. https://www.rpajournal.com/dev/wp-content/uploads/2020/02/A2.pdf

Metzler, E. T., & Kurz, L. (2018). *Assessment 2.0: An organic supplement to standard assessment procedure* (Occasional Paper No. 36). University of Illinois and Indiana University, National Institute for Learning Outcomes Assessment (NILOA). https://www.learningoutcomesassessment.org/wp-content/uploads/2019/02/OccasionalPaper36.pdf

Montenegro, E., & Jankowski, N. (2017). *Equity and assessment: Moving towards culturally responsive assessment* (Occasional Paper No. 29). University of Illinois and Indiana University, National Institute for Learning Outcomes Assessment. https://www.learningoutcomesassessment.org/wp-content/uploads/2019/02/OccasionalPaper29.pdf

Neubauer, D. (2018). *Reassessing the nature and dynamics of student mobility within Asia Pacific higher education* [Paper presentation]. UMAP International Forum, Osaka, Japan.

Neubauer, D. (2019). *Recalculating higher education in the Asia Pacific region within the emerging Fourth Industrial Revolution* [Paper presentation]. CHER Conference: Reassessing Higher Education in the Asia Region, Hong Kong.

Nilan, P., & Feixa, C. (2006). *Global youth? Hybrid identities, plural worlds*. Routledge.

O'Neill, G., & Maguire, T. (2017). *Developing assessment and feedback approaches to empower and engage students: A sectoral approach in Ireland.* National Forum for the Enhancement of Teaching and Learning in Higher Education.

Patterson, P. (2018). *Utilizing assessment data: A two-track approach.* Honolulu Community College.

Rao, K. (2019). Instructional design with UDL: Addressing learner variability in college courses. In S. Bracken & K. Novak (Eds.), *Transforming higher education through universal design for learning: An international perspective.* Routledge.

Rose, D., & Gravel, J. (2009). Getting from here to there: UDL, global positioning systems, and lessons for improving education. In D. Gordon, J. Gravel, & L. Schifter (Eds.), *A policy reader in universal design for learning* (pp. 5–18). Harvard Education Press.

Ryan, T. (2015). Quality assurance in higher education: A review of literature. *Higher Learning Research Communications, 5*(4). https://files.eric.ed.gov/fulltext/EJ1132941.pdf

Zerquera, D., Hernández, I., & Berumen, J. (2018). *Assessment and Social Justice: Pushing Through Paradox* (New Directions for Institutional Research, no. 177, pp. 1–144). Jossey-Bass. https://doi.org/10.1002/ir.20254

12

NEED FOR EQUITY-MINDED ASSESSMENT AND EVALUATION OUTSIDE OF THE CLASSROOM

Juan G. Berumen

The call to hold universities accountable with equity-focused assessment and evaluation should not be confined only to the classroom. These efforts also need to take place in cocurricular spaces, such as those in student affairs (Schuh, 2015). In addition to academics, these experiences outside the classroom also factor as an integral part of the college experience for students and cultivating their full potential. As a field, student affairs is devoted to those experiences and serving students, whether with their academics, accessing campus resources, preparing for a career, developing their multiple identities, or exploring other passions outside the classroom (Evans & Reason, 2001; Schwartz & Stewart, 2017). With this centering of student interests and development, it is only fitting that research methods should also be student-centered with students playing a greater role when assessing and evaluating services intended to support them. This role should go beyond that of a research subject and more toward research collaborator. An equity-minded approach to program assessment and evaluation can accomplish such positionality for students within the research process.

Being equity-minded in higher education is a paradigmatic shift where students have just as much of a say in their success as other campus stakeholders or institutions (Lundquist & Henning, 2020; USC Center for Urban Education, n.d.). This inclusivity of student voices becomes even more dire when assessing and evaluating services for marginalized students considering that assessment and evaluation can also perpetuate equity gaps (Montenegro & Jankowski, 2017a, 2017b, 2020; Singer-Freeman & Bastone, 2019; Singer-Freeman et al., 2019). Therefore, if addressing the equity gap and centering student voices is a priority, an equity-minded approach to assessment and evaluation is crucial, embodying socially just research methods while enacting transformational and systemic change (Lundquist & Henning, 2020). This section will examine one such approach to equity-minded assessment, applying a participatory action research methodology at a predominantly White institution in the Midwest during a highly xenophobic, anti-immigrant, and anti-Latinx climate.

Youth Participatory Action Research as an Approach to Equity-Minded Assessment in Student Affairs

Considering the centering of students in student affairs, youth participatory action research (YPAR) is an ideal model for conducting equity-minded assessment in student affairs and positioning students to confront institutional inequities in higher education (Buttimer, 2018; Cammarota, 2017; Cammarota & Romero, 2009; Delgado, 2006; Delgado & Staples, 2007). YPAR is a socially just approach to conducting research, positioning research participants (i.e., youth) as coproducers of knowledge with the exclusive intent to better their lives, those of their communities, and the institutions intended to serve them (Buttimer, 2018; Cammarota, 2017; Cammarota & Romero, 2009; Delgado, 2006; Delgado & Staples, 2007).

YPAR stems from an evolution of participatory research methods responding to the ethical abuses from academic and corporate researchers who prioritized their needs above those of the research subject(s) and their communities (Sabo Flores, 2008). YPAR continues this response by intentionally centering youth (typically ages 15 to 24), considering their needs and support needed to conduct research might be different than other populations (Cammarota, 2017). This positioning of youth in the center of the research process is a major reason YPAR is used by youth allies in education with students (Bland & Atweh, 2007; Buttimer, 2018; Cammarota & Romero, 2009; Stillwell, 2016; Zerquera et al., 2016).

The inclusionary and collaborative nature of YPAR acts as checks and balances, holding the researcher accountable to meet the needs of research participants. As a cyclical process of learning and action, research becomes more than an academic exercise, but an advocacy tool that identifies solutions to issues at the utmost interest of young people (Fetterman, 2003; Gillen, 2019). YPAR can therefore become instrumental for youth, including students who want to be changemakers, even more so those from marginalized communities (Bland & Atweh, 2007). Just as importantly, in YPAR, the research process is also an equitable one. Students are involved throughout the research process: in research design, data collection, its analysis, and presentation of the findings. As students partner with the researcher, the decision-making to conduct research is nonhierarchical with students and adults considered equals as researchers.

Some of the challenge to participatory research methods such as YPAR is the laborious and stressful nature of involving research participants in such a highly inclusive manner (Buttimer, 2018; London, 2007; Stillwell, 2016). A researcher needs to coordinate efforts and negotiate with research participants more so than in traditional research. According to Buttimer (2018), the positioning of research participants as research collaborators can lead to research taking longer to complete because of these extra efforts that do not exist in traditional research or assessment and evaluation. London (2007) and Stillwell (2016) explain how the fluctuating interest and commitment from research collaborators can also prolong a research project, if not threaten its completion.

Even so, YPAR in the end is one approach to conducting equity-minded assessment and evaluation in student affairs. For this research methodology, the process advocates for social justice as much as the eventual research findings. Just as importantly, YPAR empowers youth and students by providing the skill set and opportunity to address issues that affect them, their peers, and community. Such lofty goals make managing all of the moving parts worthwhile and rewarding. Unfortunately, despite these strengths, I have noticed that too often YPAR is overlooked by student affairs professionals as an assessment methodology, excluding student participation and their voices when assessing cocurricular activities.

The Alma Leadership Program as a Case Study

At Midwestern University or MU (pseudonym), this lack of YPAR in student affairs or any equity-minded assessment for that matter led me to launch a student-led assessment program using YPAR. Applying YPAR for assessment became an ideal methodology to assess cocurricular activities in higher education within a field such as student affairs that also centers students. The Alma Leadership Program (also known as ALMA) empowered Latinx undergraduates to pursue research interests that most impacted them and their communities. The program had two specific goals in mind: (a) inform the university about and develop policy addressing issues pertinent to Latinx students and (b) assess campus support services to better serve Latinx students, such as those at the Latinx Student Center (pseudonym) or LSC. Similar to cultural centers on college campuses, the LSC supports the academic success and personal growth of Latinx students by offering a variety of services, such as coordinating events on Latinx-related topics, information sessions on graduate school, and meeting space for many Latinx student organizations. Just as important, as a counterhegemonic public sphere (Fraser, 1990), the center provided a brave and safe space (Delgado & Staples, 2007) for Latinx students to bring their authentic selves and explore many facets of their identity.

Addressing Multiple Needs

I developed ALMA to address multiple gaps at MU pertaining to Latinx students using YPAR for equity-minded assessments and evaluations. After careful observations, I noticed that the university needed to fully comprehend the experience of Latinx students and their communities. Institutional decisions to support the success of Latinx students often lacked their voice, let alone a critical one that would challenge deep-rooted institutional inequities and advocate for social justice—not surface level band-aids. Latinx students' voices were crucial at that moment considering the political climate throughout the state. A vast majority of state residents were harboring anti-Latinx sentiments due to the increase in the state's Latinx population. As a result, hate crimes and race-specific harassment was on the rise, including the proposal of anti-immigrant and xenophobic policies by the state assembly. The university was also considering classifying undocumented students as international students, increasing their tuition almost threefold. Although this increase in tuition would impact only a fraction of Latinx students, many Latinx students saw it as an affront to their entire community and a continuation of hate targeted toward the Latinx and immigrant communities and the possible scaling up of similar, if not harsher, punitive policies. Acknowledging that research did not always lead to a critical analysis of power hierarchies, systems of oppression, and resulting inequities, YPAR became even more fundamental to ALMA for conducting equity-minded assessments considering this climate.

ALMA also fulfilled a need at the LSC. The center did not have the organizational norms nor the capacity to assess its efforts to support Latinx students. Similar to many student affairs programs, the center did not follow the rigorous evidence-based, decision-making process as outlined by student affairs research (Levy & Kozoll, 1998; Vaccaro et al., 2013). Instead, organizational decision-making heavily relied on institutional memory entirely based on the executive director's own memory or the personal interests of a handful of students and its student staff. This evidence-free practice led to the center becoming a contradiction of sorts. While many Latinx students felt welcomed and considered the center a second home, the LSC was also a source of contention for some. Several charged the center with favoritism, where some students held more influence than others in the decision-making. Such perceptions caused friction between different Latinx students and student organizations. In one extreme case, a student organization boycotted the center. Other Latinx students who did not belong to a student organization or belonged to an underrepresented pan-ethnic Latinx group felt alienated and excluded, avoiding the center altogether. Through YPAR, ALMA intended to research all of these organizational challenges (e.g., tense climate at the LRC, favoritism, negative perceptions of the LRC, toxicity between students) and potentially identify other blind spots to better support all Latinx students by creating a more transparent, evidence-based decision-making process at the LRC than what existed at the time.

Further, because students were developing valuable research and assessment skills practicing YPAR for equity-based assessment and evaluation, ALMA would prepare Latinx students to pursue a graduate degree. At MU, not enough Latinx undergraduate students were acquiring the research skill sets and experience necessary to prepare them to be competitive for places in graduate programs at top-tier research institutions. The few research opportunities that existed, such as the prestigious Chancellor's Undergraduate Research Program, were highly selective and competitive, excluding a vast majority of Latinx undergraduate students. ALMA filled this gap by training Latinx students in research rigor and providing Latinx students with the much-needed experience coveted by graduate programs.

Launching ALMA (Walking the Walk)

I launched ALMA as a pilot program at the start of the fall 2010 semester with an overwhelming response for participation from students. More than 30 students applied for a limited number of slots, speaking to the interest for such opportunities. As a nonpaid internship with a substantial workload, I thought we would get fewer applicants. Work-study positions have fewer responsibilities and would get about 20 applications. After an inclusive and thorough selection process, ALMA started with eight interns with a wide range of experiences and qualifications. I did not want to fall into the trap of other programs and only select high achievers (those who were highly qualified and could compete for the most prestigious opportunities on campus). Instead, we also selected those who could benefit the most from the internship (often those who would not be considered for other student programs). It was extremely difficult choosing these interns. While we wished we could have accepted more interns, we just did not have the capacity to support a larger staff. As a social justice advocate who understands the value of student development programs specifically designed to support students of color, I had to resist the urge to ignore our organizational limitations and accept them all.

The internship was developed into two major parts. In the first semester, I paid a lot of attention to team building and creating a safe and brave space that "encourages all youth to act on and explore their own truths" (Delgado & Staples, 2007, p. 138). In following participatory democracy values as outlined in many youth organizing models (Brodkin, 2009; Delgado, 2006; Delgado & Staples, 2007; Gillen, 2019; Gordon, 2009; Youth Speak Out Coalition & Zimmerman, 2007), I held a discussion at our first meeting with ALMA interns to identify assessment topics of interest and their role in such efforts. In designing this program, I was very intentional in acknowledging, validating, and building on the unique skill sets and interests of each intern, crucial for engaging youth in equity work (Delgado & Staples, 2007; Youth Speak Out Coalition & Zimmerman, 2007). I accomplished this objective through small group discussions and engagement exercises. The application process was also a useful artifact to gauge each student's skill sets and interests, acting as a reference throughout the program. Lastly, I introduced assessment and evaluation toward the end of the semester, dedicating one of the last workshops to the topic. By having them assess their experiences in ALMA for the fall semester, I was able to model and provide an example, which they would use as a reference in the spring when we would begin their formal training in assessment and evaluation.

The second semester would also continue the team building from the fall semester and begin training interns to conduct research using YPAR. Interns would identify campus topics to research through a series of interactive exercises. In addition, they would implement the assessment and evaluation of the center by refining the tools developed in the fall. Our target was to evaluate every event using short surveys and hold focus groups to assess the climate at the center. It was our plan to have student interns develop a report for the center and a policy brief to present to the university.

Lessons Learned

At the end of the pilot year, I experienced many of the highlights and challenges found in other YPAR case studies (Buttimer, 2018; London, 2007; Stillwell, 2016) with several lessons emerging after launching the ALMA

Leadership Program in the fall. In understanding these lessons, I will examine several contextual factors that impact social justice work (the norms, values, and capacity of an organization) and how they also impacted the implementation of YPAR as an equity-minded assessment and evaluation tool for ALMA at the Latino Student Center.

The Significance of Value Alignment

In conducting equity-minded work, I have realized the importance of having common ground toward certain analytical lenses critical of systemic inequities and the understandings of processes to achieve social justice. I have also noticed that conducting such work comes with a discourse and a value system that is not common and therefore unevenly learned by students, depending on a myriad of factors from contextual to experiential based on a range of lived realities and exposure to such concepts.

Having this understanding, I decided to lead a workshop at the beginning of the internship to make sure we shared many of the same equity-minded values. We discussed systemic inequities, using a conceptual framework consisting of critical race theory, structural functionalism, and postcolonial theory. We applied these lenses to discuss our positionality as people of color, specifically as Latinx within United States history, focusing on formal schooling. Given that students were engaging with complex and heavily conceptual content, I wanted to avoid lecture as much as possible. Instead, I used small group discussion where ALMA interns centered their experiences with oppression, which they could then reference to better digest the curriculum. I broke the interns into three groups to discuss two prompts, moments where they felt empowered and disempowered in K–12 and in higher education, focusing on place, key actors, and the impact of such events. Interns were then to describe these moments on poster paper and place them throughout the room. Once everyone was done, interns walked around the room, drawing symbols of affirmation (e.g., a happy face, check mark, a plus sign) next to common experiences. We then had a whole group discussion, comparing experiences and applying the conceptual framework to better understand these experiences. Afterward, I had interns reflect on the exercise and assess it as well. Their response gave me the impression that we were all on the same page and shared a common understanding.

While I had assumed all interns held common knowledge after the training, that was not the case as they still had different interpretations of social justice and related topics. I had a general understanding of patriarchy, for example, however, interns had their own with variances in causes, outcomes, and resolutions. Patriarchy and other related concepts then became what Lévi-Strauss (1987) referred to as a floating signifier, a referent that is understood but has no agreed upon meaning and hence has multiple interpretations.

I did not fully understand the extent that this misalignment hindered practicing YPAR for equity-based assessment and evaluation within ALMA. I overlooked microaggressions in the form of jokes or sly remarks and side comments whenever sharing space. Consequently, the brave space that I hoped to build did not fully realize as ALMA interns who did not grasp certain concepts or who practiced social justice differently started to feel alienated and persecuted. Based on an exit survey for the ALMA internship, this sentiment was expressed mostly by 1st- and 2nd-year students. In hindsight, I could have spent more time throughout the internship furthering their growth, using this initial workshop as a baseline for future discussions and avoiding confusion and frustration among the ALMA interns and work-study staff.

Throughout the internship, it also became apparent that many of the interns also had different understandings of the importance of the work that we were doing. Some applied to the internship to transform the university while others saw it as only a résumé builder. This misalignment of values for equity-minded assessment and evaluation further hindered practicing YPAR as the commitment level varied among the interns. For example, after discussing and identifying research topics as a group, I assigned interns into research groups, with a set of responsibilities and benchmarks to complete for their assessment or evaluation project. Because of the different levels of interest, many of the groups struggled meeting their benchmarks. Some interns mentioned the challenges of getting certain group members to return emails or complete their share of the work on time or at all. I tried to address this in several ways, including having individual meetings and reinforcing the value of our work. However, I had limited options for holding interns accountable considering the director's unwillingness to dismiss staff members in the past. Knowing this, certain interns took advantage of this long-standing practice, inhibiting the YPAR from progressing accordingly.

Capacity as Inhibiting

The laborious nature of YPAR was another challenge for conducting equity-minded assessment and evaluation considering my own and the organization's capacity limitations (bandwidth and resources). As mentioned, YPAR involves additional steps and processes not practiced in traditional research, assessment, and evaluation. Because of the large workload for the director, she would frequently joke about how much she wanted to be cloned so there would be another person to assist. She was extremely involved not just on campus, but locally, statewide, and regionally. Throughout the pilot year of the ALMA Leadership Program, I began to understand her sentiment and felt the same. The program staff consisted of myself as part-time assistant director for the center, a doctoral student volunteer, and four work-study students (10 hours per week each). The staff and I also had other obligations at the center in addition to the ALMA internship. Halfway through the academic year I realized how overcommitted we all were, with fatigue affecting our decision-making, commitment, and disposition toward the program. For me, it was an extremely difficult and exhausting year considering the amount of groundwork needed to just launch the program. I had spent the 4 months prior to the fall semester planning the program, including developing a curriculum to apply YPAR as a research method to equity-minded assessment and evaluation. At our last staff meeting for the academic year, we admitted to purposely avoiding raising certain issues that would require additional time and energy for fear of having to address them and adding to our already heavy workload.

For many of the ALMA interns, bandwidth capacity was also an issue as the internship started to conflict with other responsibilities, such as work and courses. Interest and commitment fluctuated for the interns, even more so during midterms and finals. As the academic year progressed, I noticed dominating many of the discussions, even more so in those toward the end of the academic year focused on analyzing findings and exploring recommendations, a common practice in YPAR. Instead of challenging the interns to push through the fatigue, I sensed the exhaustion in the room and decided to move forward, bringing closure to the assessment rather than revisiting it later and challenging groups to go beyond superficial recommendations that lacked creativity and would not sufficiently address systemic inequities, let alone lead to transformational change. I needed to move on and focus on the other research projects.

With time, it became obvious that the lack of funding to hire professional staff to adequately launch and manage new initiatives such as the ALMA program or to conduct YPAR for equity-minded assessment and evaluation severely compromised our work. We simply did not have that capacity to always make adjustments to address challenges within the program and to attend to the needs of the interns. This fatigue stunted innovation and the growth of the program and practice of YPAR, an issue compounded considering it was a pilot program and had no organizational infrastructure or memory to reference. All structures had to be created anew as we built the plane as we flew it, an issue further discussed as follows.

Norms as References to Decision-Making and Informing Practice

The lack of already established policies and practices for the ALMA Leadership Program and YPAR made it difficult to always know what to expect, leading to other issues as well. Without previous experience and considering the limited capacity issues, it was easy for me to default to less democratic ways when facilitating decision-making, often decentering the interns and undermining the collaborative and inclusive nature of YPAR. For example, at the start of the spring semester, ALMA interns in teams needed to identify a campus service or policy to assess or evaluate based on their interests. I unilaterally rejected some proposals as they did not seem realistic to complete within the time frame of a semester. But what was the basis of this decision other than my own intuition? Without prior experiences or organizational memory conducting YPAR for equity-minded assessment and evaluation, I really had no way of knowing what was possible within a semester.

At the same time, we relied too heavily on the ALMA interns to represent the student experience and bear the burden of being the student voice. How did they know what were the major issues facing all Latinx students and their experiences on campus, with the LRC or other support services? There were numerous assumptions based on the individual experiences and perceptions of the ALMA interns, which made it difficult to accept different realities from other Latinx students and have a healthy discussion regarding differences. For example, when discussing the findings of a survey assessing the campus climate for Latinx students, ALMA interns who had not experienced the hostilities to the extent of several participants minimized those responses, citing the low frequency of such responses. Ironically, I have witnessed this practice on an institutional level and in nonequity spaces, where student groups are made invisible by data. Consequentially, this incident caused friction within the group as several interns who could identify with traumatic campus experiences felt minimized as well.

Instead of launching the program as a pilot, we should have scaled down the scope and timeline of the program and spent that year establishing the organizational infrastructure. A first and essential step could have been to create an advisory group of Latinx students, staff, faculty, allies, and, just as importantly, someone experienced in YPAR for equity-based assessment and evaluation in higher education. Acting as a sounding board, they could have helped to develop the program, including expectations and curriculum, and with the decision-making throughout the year. Their involvement could have also extended to address many of the aforementioned issues, such as facilitating workshops to inject new perspectives and reinvigorate discussions or gauging the feasibility of assessment projects. The advisory board could have participated in the selection process of ALMA interns and facilitating some of the workshops. This involvement would have helped in staving off fatigue and redirecting my attention to supporting interns conducting YPAR and equity-minded assessment. Instead, all of it fell on me as I balanced my other responsibilities at the center.

Conclusion

Conducting YPAR for equity-minded assessment and evaluation is complex, with lots of moving pieces. After this experience, it was obvious to me how traditional methods are a lot more favorable and how student affairs professionals would rather use those approaches than add more work to an already stacked workload. Nonetheless, this experience was worthwhile as ALMA interns appreciated the opportunity to gain research experience and conduct equity-minded assessments and evaluations. As a result, they have an experience which they can highlight on their cover letter as they launch their careers or discuss on their personal statement as they apply for graduate school. In either case, they gained a valuable understanding of the complexities in advocating for equity, one that they can build on as well.

References

Bland, D., & Atweh, B. (2007). Students as researchers: Engaging students' voices in PAR. *Educational Action Research, 15*(3), 337–349. https://doi .org/10.1080/09650790701514259

Brodkin, K. (2009). *Power politics: Environmental activism in south Los Angeles.* Rutgers University Press.

Buttimer, C. J. (2018). The challenges and possibilities of youth participatory action research for teachers and students in public school classrooms. *Berkeley Review of Education, 8*(1), 39–81. https://doi.org/10.5070/B88133830

Cammarota, J. (2017). Youth participatory action research: A pedagogy of transformational resistance for critical youth studies. *Journal for Critical Education Policy Studies, 15*(2), 188–213. http://www.jceps.com/wp-content/ uploads/2017/10/15-2-7.pdf

Cammarota, J., & Romero, A. F. (2009). A social justice epistemology and pedagogy for Latina/o students: Transforming public education with participatory action research. In T. M. Brown & L. F. Rodríguez (Eds.), *Youth in Participatory Action Research* (New Directions in Student Services, no. 123, pp. 53–65). Jossey-Bass. https://doi.org/10.1002/yd.314

Delgado, M. (2006). *Designs and methods for youth-led research.* SAGE.

Delgado, M., & Staples, L. (2007). *Youth-led community organizing: Theory and action.* Oxford University Press.

Evans, N. J., & Reason, R. D. (2001). Guiding principles: A review and analysis of student affairs philosophical statements. *Education Publications, 42*(4), 359–377. https://dr.lib.iastate.edu/handle/20.500.12876/22872

Fetterman, D. (2003). Youth and evaluation: Empowered social-change agents. In K. Sabo (Ed.), *Youth Participatory Evaluation: A Field in the Making* (New Directions for Evaluation, no. 98, pp. 87–92). Jossey-Bass. https://doi.org/10.1002/ev.87

Fraser, N. (1990). Rethinking the public sphere: A contribution to the critique of actually existing democracy. *Social Text, 25/26,* 56–80. https://doi.org/10.2307/466240

Gillen, J. (2019). *The power in the room: Radical education through youth organizing and employment.* Beacon Press.

Gordon, H. R. (2009). *We fight to win: Inequality and the politics of youth activism.* Rutgers University Press.

Lévi-Strauss, C. (1987). *Introduction to Marcel Mauss.* Routledge.

Levy, S. R., & Kozoll, C. E. (1998). *A guide to decision making in student affairs: A case study approach.* Charles C Thomas Pub.

London, J. K. (2007). Power and pitfalls of youth participation in community-based action research. *Children, Youth, and Environments, 17*(2), 406–432. https://www.jstor.org/stable/10.7721/chilyoutenvi.17.2.0406

Lundquist, A. E., & Henning, G. (2020). From avoiding bias to social justice: A continuum of assessment practices to advance diversity, equity, and inclusion. In A. D. Spicer-Runnels & T. E. Simpson (Eds.), *Developing an intercultural responsive leadership style for faculty and administrators* (pp. 47–61). IGI Global.

Montenegro, E., & Jankowski, N. A. (2017a). *Equity and assessment: Moving towards culturally responsive assessment* (Occasional Paper No. 29). University of Illinois and Indiana University, NILOA.

Montenegro, E., & Jankowski, N. A. (2017b). Bringing equity into the heart of assessment. *Assessment Update, 29*(6), 10–11. https://doi.org/10.1002/au.30117

Montenegro, E., & Jankowski, N. A. (2020). A new decade for assessment: Embedding equity into assessment praxis (Occasional Paper No. 42). University of Illinois and Indiana University, NILOA.

Sabo Flores, K. (2008). *Youth participatory evaluation: Strategies for engaging young people.* Jossey-Bass.

Schuh, J. H. (2015). Assessment in student affairs: How did we get here? *Journal of Student Affairs Inquiry, 1*(1). https://drive.google.com/file/d/13Qc_uXm-bLbc5La2rQmyHmqbYIztS-KFX/view

Schwartz, R., & Stewart, D-L. (2017). The history of student affairs. In J. H. Schuh, S. R. Jones, & V. Torres (Eds.), *Student services handbook: A handbook for the profession* (6th ed.; pp. 20–38). Jossey-Bass.

Singer-Freeman, K. E., & Bastone, L. (2019). Developmental science concepts guide effective support of underrepresented STEM students. *Journal of Biochemistry and Molecular Biology Education, 47*(5), 506–512. https://doi.org/10.1002/bmb.21292

Singer-Freeman, K. E., Hobbs, H., & Robinson, C. (2019). Theoretical matrix of culturally relevant assessment. *Assessment Update, 31*(4), 1–16. https://doi.org/10.1002/au.30176

Stillwell, C. (2016). Challenges to the implementation of youth PAR in a university-middle school Partnership. *i.e.: inquiry in education: 8*(1). https://digitalcommons.nl.edu/ie/vol8/iss1/2

USC Center for Urban Education. (n.d.). *Equity mindedness.* https://cue.usc.edu/about/equity/equity-mindedness/

Vaccaro, A., McCoy, B., Champagne, D., & Siegel, M. (2013). *Decisions matter: Using a decision-making framework with contemporary student affairs case studies.* NASPA-Student Affairs Administrators in Higher Education.

Youth Speak Out Coalition, & Zimmerman, K. (2007). Making space, making change: Models for youth-led social change organizations. *Children, Youth, and Environments, 17*(2), 298–314. https://www.jstor.org/stable/10.7721/chilyoutenvi.17.2.0298

Zerquera, D., Berumen, J. G., & Pender, J. (2017). Assessment for social justice: Employing participatory action research (PAR) as a framework for assessment and evaluation. *The Journal of College and University Student Housing, 43*(3), 14–27. https://www.nxtbook.com/nxtbooks/acuho/journal_vol43no3/index.php#/p/14

13

ADVANCING EQUITY IN STUDENT AFFAIRS THROUGH ASSESSMENT PRACTICE

Ciji A. Heiser and Joseph D. Levy

This chapter focuses on using assessment to advance equity in higher education with specific application to student affairs work. Assessment will be contextualized historically and in relation to growing inequities in higher education. Building on prior work in assessment and evaluation, the authors present core tenets of equity-centered assessment practice. These tenets are applied as a critical lens to guide traditionally established approaches to assessment. This chapter seeks to expand upon applications and opportunities throughout the assessment cycle to advance equity and provide content through four themes central to assessment work: asking the right questions, competency frameworks, data collection and analysis, and data interpretation and sharing. The purpose of this chapter is to articulate the value of leveraging assessment to advance equity, describe existing opportunities in student affairs to utilize assessment to foster equity, and encourage the reflection and planning of integration of the recommended strategies to assessment work.

Historically, assessment work has focused on responding to demands for accountability (Ewell, 2009; Levy et al., 2018). More recently, this has shifted to include measures of student learning, engagement, and outcome attainment (Kuh et al., 2015; Levy et al., 2018). With calls for accountability increasing and the ongoing change in student demographics, there is an emerging need in higher education and student affairs for assessment strategies which are inclusive of and attend to historically underrepresented student experiences (McFarland et al., 2018; Montenegro & Jankowski, 2017, 2020). Student-facing services are uniquely positioned to center student experiences and voices in shaping processes often used to evaluate and tell the story of student learning and continuous improvement. Student affairs assessment is also uniquely positioned to amplify student voices to foster systemic and social change. This chapter integrates elements of critical assessment (power, positionality, collaboration, and multiple methods) into the American Association of Higher Education's ([AAHE], 1992) principles of good practice for assessing student learning to position assessment work as transformational work and provides core examples of how to embed this integration into key areas of assessment practice in student affairs.

Assessment Within a Context

Designed during the colonial era, the founders of American higher education institutions adopted the English, Oxford, and Cambridge model of education and the students served in that model were affluent, White males (Thelin, 2019). Initial attempts at expanding student diversity started with the enrollment of Native American men in an effort to expand Christianity, often with disastrous consequences (Thelin, 2019). In the 1860s, the educational experience had broadened to include Black and African Americans and women, as well as expanding to include meaningful cocurricular engagement activities such as clubs, sports teams, and debate teams (Thelin, 2019). The year 1900 marked the onset of the development of criteria from which to determine the quality of institutions with differentiation between "great American universities" and "standard American universities" (Thelin, 2019, p. 111). Fourteen university presidents met and formed the Association of American Universities to respond to concerns about education standards, which they did by forming the College Entrance Examination Board, credited with establishing criteria for "ratings, rankings, and reputations" (Thelin, 2019, p. 147). Currently, quality in higher education is driven by national rankings, calls for accountability, and student outcomes (Jankowski et al., 2018; Schuh, 2015; Schuh & Associates, 2009).

Calls for accountability are related to calls for quality and often focus on retention, graduation, and attainment outcomes. The release of the Spellings Commission Report (Commission Appointed by Secretary of Education Margaret Spellings, 2006) marked a significant call for accountability in higher education and challenged institutions to demonstrate accountability, stating, "colleges and universities must become more transparent about cost, price, and student success outcomes, and must willingly share this information with students and families" (p. 4). Bresciani et al. (2009) reflected on demands for accountability, writing that institutions of higher education "currently face a mix of accountability demands, accreditation standards, and outcomes-based assessment of student learning. State and federal governments continue to question whether institutions of higher education actually produce the learning that has for centuries been assumed" (p. 12). Assessment became a mechanism for responding to calls for accountability and a measure of quality student learning and engagement independent of rankings. Despite having educational evaluation roots in the early 1900s, with the mid-20th century beginning to frame evaluation in relation to goals for student achievement (Schuh, 2015), it was not until the 1980s that assessment of student learning was emphasized and encouraged in practice across institutions in the United States (Ewell, 2009; Schuh, 2015). Assessment specific to student affairs was mentioned in the 1990s in literature and cemented as practice in the 2010s as regional accreditors included cocurricular assessment in standards and criteria (Levy et al., 2018). Recent trends in student affairs assessment practice continue to evolve by adopting good practices, encouraging use of results, and, more recently, positioning assessment with social justice considerations for equitable student learning outcomes (AAHE, 1992; Heiser et al., 2017; Kuh et al., 2015; Montenegro & Jankowski, 2017, 2020). This chapter responds to calls for advancing equity in assessment by integrating good assessment principles with core principles of assessment for equity practice.

Core Principles of Assessment for Equity Practice

The racial and socioeconomic profile of students advancing from K–12 education to higher education has changed substantially over time (McFarland et al., 2018). Higher education has become more accessible to students historically underrepresented in this context; however, persistent disparities in educational outcomes suggests that the ways in which underrepresented students experience higher education institutions are fundamentally different than their majority peers (McFarland et al., 2018). In response to an increasingly diverse population and the continued emphasis on outcome measurement, calls for assessment approaches which are culturally responsive, leverage data to address inequities, and improve outcomes for historically marginalized populations have emerged (Heiser et al., 2017; Montenegro & Jankowski, 2017; Zerquera et al., 2018).

Individuals develop in contexts shaped by culture, which shapes how learning occurs and the rules for demonstrating learning (Hughes et al., 1993). Culturally responsive and equity-centered approaches prioritize the thoughtful inclusion of contextual and demographic variables, address the influences of power and institutional racism, center minoritized ways of knowing and meaning-making, and work to reduce marginalization and inequities (Bledsoe & Donaldson, 2015; Mertens, 2010; SenGupta et al., 2004). As different cultures value different ways of sharing their experiences, implications extending to ways in which students learn and demonstrate achievement need to be reconsidered (Maki, 2010; Mertens & Hopson, 2006). Montenegro and Jankowski (2017) published a white paper in 2017 on the topic of culturally responsive assessment in higher education. The authors describe cultural responsiveness as "mindful of the student populations the institution serves in ways that bring students into the assessment process including the development and use of tools appropriate for measuring student outcomes" (Montenegro & Jankowski, 2017, p. 10). They call for the alignment of assessment practices with practices that better capture the experiences of marginalized populations in higher education. Montenegro and Jankowski (2017) write that, "by being mindful of how culture affects students' meaning-making process, cognition, and demonstrations of learning, we can better understand and appreciate the learning gains that students make" (p. 13).

The authors of this chapter argue that mindfulness should extend to include an active centering of the lived experiences of students in the assessment and evaluation mechanisms used to measure and tell the story of their learning to instigate social and transformative change. Professionals who are student facing, in student service units, are uniquely positioned to move beyond mindfulness and toward the active integration, engagement, and centering of historically marginalized student experiences in processes related to strategic planning, program review, and assessment. Integrating student perspectives and lived experiences into assessment processes increases validity and credibility of such evidence for students and student-facing practitioners (Kirkhart, 1995, 2013). Through the integration of core principles of assessment for equity into good principles of assessment practices, student affairs practitioners are positioned to operationalize institutional and departmental mission statements and strategic plans beyond performative statements into action-oriented and data-driven social change with students as stakeholders at the center of the work. To this end, the core principles are articulated as follows:

- **Power:** Power and politics shape the context in which assessment work is performed, and are embedded in strategic planning, program review, and assessment processes. Assessment practitioners as content experts bring a level of power in their instrument choice, data analysis, and interpretation of findings which can lead to resource allocation and programmatic changes.

- **Positionality:** Practitioner positionality is shaped by intersecting identities and lived experiences. This positionality comes with bias. Bias may manifest as deficit-based explanations for data. An added element of assessment practitioner positionality is their role in upholding or dismantling oppressive structures through assessment work.

- **Agency:** Agency is the ability for one to speak to their experiences. Equity-centered practitioners create spaces which address power and practitioner positionality for students to operationalize their agency. Creating spaces to collaborate and engage students in the evaluation of their lived and learning experiences elevates and centers student voice in assessment processes.

- **Collaboration and stakeholder involvement:** Organizational and individual culture influence assessment practices. The inclusion and centering of students at the center of assessment processes fosters agency, amplifies the voices of students, and mitigates bias.

- **Methodological diversity:** The approaches assessment practitioners employ to collect, analyze, interpret, and report data foster one way of knowing and sharing while inhibiting others. The use of multiple methods best captures students' diverse ways of knowing and knowledge demonstration. Student involvement in shaping methodological selection, designing items, and providing feedback on rubrics or program review templates is critical and keeps their experience at the center of assessment work. In analysis and reporting, determinations of credible evidence should not be made solely by those with power and privileged positionalities. Knowledge of methods is necessary, but so is ability to gauge appropriateness to best represent student voice and experience.

The aforementioned core principles of assessment for equity are drawn from culturally responsive evaluation, critical theory, and culturally responsive assessment literature and are aligned to principles of good practice for assessing student learning, as articulated by the AAHE and outlined in Table 13.1. Despite being 30 years old, AAHE's (1992) nine principles of good assessment practice remain relevant to the current landscape of higher education, as well as to key considerations in leveraging assessment for equity.

TABLE 13.1

**Principles of Good Practice for Assessment and
Core Principles of Assessment for Equity**

Principles of Good Practice for Assessing Student Learning	Core Principles of Assessment for Equity
1. The assessment of student learning begins with educational values.	Agency, Positionality, Power
2. Assessment is most effective when it reflects an understanding of learning as multidimensional, integrated, and revealed in performance over time.	Collaboration and Stakeholder Involvement, Methodological Diversity, Power
3. Assessment works best when the programs it seeks to improve have clear, explicitly stated purposes.	Agency, Positionality
4. Assessment requires attention to outcomes but also and equally to the experiences that lead to those outcomes.	Agency, Collaboration and Stakeholder Involvement, Positionality
5. Assessment works best when it is ongoing, not episodic.	Collaboration and Stakeholder Involvement, Methodological Diversity, Power
6. Assessment fosters wider improvement when representatives from across the educational community are involved.	Agency, Collaboration and Stakeholder Involvement, Positionality, Power
7. Assessment makes a difference when it begins with issues of use and illuminates questions that people really care about.	Agency, Methodological Diversity, Positionality, Power
8. Assessment is most likely to lead to improvement when it is part of a larger set of conditions that promote change.	Agency, Positionality, Power
9. Through assessment, educators meet responsibilities to students and to the public.	Agency, Collaboration and Stakeholder Involvement, Power

Assessment in Student Affairs to Advance Equity

To exemplify the integration of good assessment practice and core principles of equity in assessment, the remainder of this chapter focuses on how practitioners can embed the integration of equity into four core areas of assessment work or assessment processes in student affairs. In relation to the eighth principle of good practice for assessing student learning, larger conditions are necessary to situate assessment to best promote change for educational inequities. The authors posit the following four themes can be valuable conditions or context to promote equitable advancement: asking the right questions, competency frameworks, data collection and analysis, and data interpretation and sharing.

Asking the Right Questions

A foundational aspect of assessment practice is asking the right questions. On a broad scale, questions related to assessment are shaped by institutional missions and values, focus on clear and concise shared goals, and carry the most impact when attending to mission critical concerns with relevant and credible data (AAHE, 1992). Questions are embedded in student affairs strategic planning, assessment planning, and program review processes. Results of such efforts and responses to these questions are powerful in that they shape resource allocation, program structures, and power dynamics in the academy, as well as determine future action planning. Centering context, voice, power, and stakeholder experiences in best practices for program review, strategic planning, and assessment planning prompts practitioners to reevaluate what the right questions may be, and for whom.

On a global level, work grounded in the social sciences is reflective of a history rooted in power and colonization (Stanfield, 1999). Comparisons of us and other across cultures stem from roots in European expansion and colonialism, and often center and validate White ways of knowing (Hall, 1992). One of the lasting effects of this history is that majority, dominant perspectives continue to shape which questions are prioritized and how they are measured, creating an ethnocentric approach to research, maintaining existing power structures, and perpetuating inequalities and injustices (Gordon et al., 1990; Hughes et al., 1993; Stanfield, 1999). On a local and individual level, assessment practice is embedded and shaped by practitioner positionality such that,

> as individual leaders, we practice within norms, assumptions, values, beliefs, and behaviors originating in our multiple identities . . . In addition, identity influences experiences and perceptions of power or lack thereof and affects how we think about and practice within power structures of colleges and university. (Chávez & Sanlo, 2013, p. 9).

The individuals asking the questions may do so from a place which centers their own lived experiences, and their positionality, power, and voice may be informed by implicit bias. The history of higher education and assessment in education is important to expose because it has lasting implications on which students succeed in higher education and how success is measured (Heiser et al., 2017). To advance equity in student affairs, assessment practitioners and divisional leaders should:

- **Foster collaboration:** Collaborate with students in determining critical questions and openly examine and critique the perspectives and lived experiences shaping the questions asked in program review, strategic planning, and assessment planning. How are the most critical stakeholders in student affairs—students—shaping the future goals of the organization, how those goals are measured, and how data around achievements or fallbacks are communicated?

- **Address and balance power:** Determining guidelines for priority setting and the inclusion of student voices in these priorities serves as a way to create space to balance power dynamics and engage students in planning and program review processes. This centers questions most important to students, engages in good assessment practices, balances power, and elevates student voices. In aligning questions with the goals, mission, and values, use data and metrics to transparently exemplify how the mission and values (especially those with mention of diversity, equity, and inclusion) are embeddded in practice and shape student experiences for their success.

- **Make data-informed decisions:** Educational leadership often operates on a spectrum of decisions made based on gut instincts, professional opinion, or dictated by past practice while also having folks experience analysis paralysis or drowning in data. Making data-informed decisions, which include data on historically marginalized students, allows leaders to attend to diverse experiences and make choices which serve all students, rather than focusing solely on the majority. Dedicate space in assessment plans and reports to identify specific populations for which data will be analyzed and interpreted for change. Use existing data to establish benchmarks, targets for advancing benchmarks, individuals responsible for reaching the targets, and check-in dates at regular intervals for accountability.

In an effort to advance equity in student affairs assessment and integrate equity-centered assessment practices into program review, strategic planning, and assessment planning, assessment practitioners should consider adding two questions to their daily practice:

1. How are White, heteronormative, cisgender, and other Western perspectives shaping the process? How can we work to decenter these perspectives?
2. Who is at the table? Who should be at the table? What voices and perspectives are missing that should shape the assessment process?

Competency Frameworks

Student learning outcome frameworks are a foundational aspect of student affairs assessment practice. Regardless of the framework used—Bloom's taxonomy (Anderson et al., 2001), learning and development outcomes from the Council for the Advancement of Standards in Higher Education (2019), the medicine wheel (LaFever, 2016), and others—the ways in which students learn and demonstrate that learning are as complex and unique as students themselves (Maki, 2010). Good assessment practices attend to engaging students and the broader community in continuous improvement and attend to student learning experiences, student learning outcomes, and student learning outcome demonstration as nuanced and multifaceted (AAHE, 1992). Student learning outcome frameworks articulate the knowledge, attitudes, competencies, and skills valuable for students to progress through their experience, grow, develop, and effectively take their next steps. Centering student voices and experiences in the development, implementation, and assessment of developmental experiences, outcome attainment, and outcome mapping positions practitioners to reevaluate which learning is valuable to students and how learning is determined to be credible and valid, and evaluate which students attain outcomes that serve them in progressing successfully toward degree completion.

While the student population enrolled across higher education institutions is increasingly diverse, clear differences across groups in the attainment of outcomes related to persistence, educational progress prior to completion, and graduation persists. Data collected by the National Center for Education Statistics (2016) showed graduation rates for White students entering 4-year public institutions as 38.5%, while Black students graduated after 4 years at 18.1%. In 2006, 33% of first-generation college students left their institutions without returning, compared to 14% of their peers whose parents had a bachelor's degree (Cataldi et al., 2018). Although graduation in 4 years is the definitive student success outcome in higher education, a number of other indicators demonstrate student success toward completion, including academic outcomes (e.g., faculty interactions, study skills) and engagement outcomes (e.g., campus engagement, discussions with diverse peers). Evidence suggests that students from historically underrepresented backgrounds in higher education demonstrate differences in both academic outcomes (National Center for Education Statistics, 2016) and engagement outcomes (Kuh et al., 2008). Competencies provide a blueprint for engaging in meaningful experiences and skill development for student growth. They can also serve as a reference point for training and hiring student employees, developing interactions, and allocating resources to promote student development and success. However, competency frameworks are also reflective of the lived experiences, values, and beliefs of the individuals who contributed to the framework development. Competency frameworks signal institutional priorities for student learning and, if not inclusive of the diverse student body, can work to affirm dominant ideologies and delegitimize diverse ways of knowing.

A tension exists between responsive assessment approaches and standardized assessment approaches. Responsive approaches to assessment can honor and elevate diverse learning experiences, while more standardized reporting contributes to a larger institutional picture, beyond individual programs. The following strategies can help navigate individual and collective needs:

- **Centering student voice:** Prioritizing student voices and lived experiences in the development of learning outcomes and outcome maps provides an opportunity for students to validate what and how they learn. Students shape the outcomes using their own language and lived experiences. Students provide insight into the student learning journey and bring to the forefront that there are multiple ways of knowing and learning.

- **Collaborate with students:** Engaging diverse student populations in the outcome development process integrates multiple ways of knowing and values and belief systems into a learning framework for all students. This can be accomplished by intentionally seeking out diverse perspectives when designing learning outcomes and mapping outcomes to student experiences through focus groups, open town halls, talking to student employees, or attending student organization meetings.

- **Use multiple methods:** Student input on the measurement of such outcomes is also critical. Incorporating student perspectives creates space for multiple realizations of how students make meaning out of their experiences and adds validity and credibility to the evidence collected. Ask students how they would describe their learning, which opportunities helped them grow and develop, and partner them in mapping curricular and cocurricular experiences. Often, substantial amounts of time are invested in the development of outcomes and mapping outcomes and practitioners could collaborate with students to help them connect the dots between their own learning through language that reflects authentic student experiences. Directly involving students in the development and mapping of outcomes is critical, as is incorporating students into the data interpretation. Involving student stakeholders in data interpretation contextualizes student experiences and learning.

All students should see their learning and experiences reflected back to them as important aspects to the institution. To foster dynamic and inclusive outcome frameworks, reflect on the following questions:

1. What are the motivating factors behind each of the learning outcomes or competencies?
2. What types of learning, knowledge, and knowledge demonstrations are valued or privileged?
3. How have student voices and experiences shaped the outcome framework?
4. How do the competencies reflect multiple ways of knowing and meaning-making?
5. In what ways have student perspectives shaped the language used to define the outcomes?
6. How have students been engaged in the design of outcome measures?

Data Collection and Analysis

Methodology and methods of data collection can be rooted in power, with critical consequences for representing students' voices and lived experiences (Heiser et al., 2017; Hood et al., 2015). Prioritizing power and positionality over student learning in method selection can create boundaries and parameters for crafting the story of student learning (AAHE, 1992; Hood et al., 2015; Kuh et al., 2015; Montenegro & Jankwoski, 2017). Student voice should be a priority in method selection given the diverse ways of knowing demonstrated by students in their ongoing endeavor for learning, as well as the role methodology and data collection can have in knowledge construction during analysis and interpretation (AAHE, 1992; Heiser et al., 2017; Maki, 2010; Montenegro & Jankowski, 2017; Steinberg & Cannella, 2012).

Data collection and analysis can depend on practitioner knowledge and strategy. While surveying is the most common assessment method in student affairs, practitioners may not be aware of survey limitations or when surveying is most appropriate for a situation or population being assessed (Angelo & Cross, 1993; Kuh et al., 2014; Montenegro & Jankowski, 2017, 2020). Appropriate method selection can enable student learning to be recorded in ways that create space for student storytelling and benefit practitioners in meaning-making from rich data sets (Heiser et al., 2017; Kuh et al., 2015; Montenegro & Jankowski, 2017, 2020; Steinberg & Cannella, 2012). Intentionality and thoughtfulness is necessary, as foundational literature in culturally responsive evaluation positions all approaches to data collection and analysis as value-laden, shaped by context and culture, influencing validity and credibility of data, requiring decisions shaped by positionality, and carrying implications for equity and justice (American Evaluation Association, 2011; Frierson et al., 2002; Hood et al., 2015; Hughes et al., 1993; Mertens, 2007; SenGupta et al., 2004).

Power and positionality are important to examine in data collection and analysis (Heiser et al., 2017; Hood et al., 2015; Montenegro & Jankowski, 2020). There is a real tension in assessment with respect to bias and subjectivity; practitioners strive to reduce bias and be objective in measurement but attempting to do so can invalidate underrepresented student perspectives or reinforce dominant structures shaped and maintained by privileged, majoritized populations (Bensimon, 2005; DeLuca Fernández, 2015; Heiser et al., 2017; Montenegro & Jankowski, 2020). Positionality should be accounted for by including multiple perspectives to challenge bias and interrogate methods which might construct deficit-based or dominant narratives (Heiser et al., 2017; Hood et al., 2015; Levy & Heiser, 2018; Montenegro & Jankowski, 2020). Specifically, considering student culture in the selection of methodologies and analysis is critical as these choices shape who is heard and how knowledge is shaped; dominant perspectives are reinforced or disrupted through methodological choices. Practitioners should respond to cultural context to examine underlying assumptions present in the selection, construction, implementation, and analysis of methods (Hood et al., 2015; Hughes et al., 1993).

Considering the core themes of agency, collaboration, methodological diversity, power, and positionality, the following strategies can apply equity considerations in data collection and analysis:

- **Use data collection methods other than surveys:** Engage students in the selection, review, and implementation of methods to best capture the complexity of learning across diverse students, as well as ensure assessment is meaningful and provides useful evidence to inspire equity improvement. Instead of defaulting to surveys, consider the following methods:

o Rubrics, coconstructed with students to clearly articulate learning expectations for evaluating student employees, reviewing résumés and cover letters, or documenting progress meetings with advisors and counselors.

o Reflection papers and other forms of narrative writing, which can facilitate storytelling, foster counternarratives and capture learning from leadership positions, sanctions, community service, or goal setting.

o Interviews, focus groups, or talking circles, where students can collaborate as cofacilitators to measure sense of belonging, equity and diversity issues, or student success behaviors.

o Portfolios, where students can compile multiple artifacts across different mediums to best portray demonstrated competency.

- **Focus on specific outcomes:** When only measuring a few outcomes, a department can be encouraged to employ methodological diversity with each outcome, enabling practitioners to best capture learning from students and triangulate data for a more comprehensive view of the student experience. Reporting on select outcomes versus many may provide practitioners more capacity to disaggregate data to evaluate equivalent learning across student populations.

- **Peer review assessment plans:** Assessment planning creates a natural opportunity for collaboration and stakeholder involvement to draw data-informed conclusions. While content may be unique per area, practitioners can use peer review to check positionality and power dynamics, helping distribute accountability for quality or completeness of work, and simultaneously building capacity around approaches. Peer review can promote critical self-reflection and better development of methods for valid results.

Data collection and analysis straddle planning and active phases of an assessment cycle, which can have plenty of moving pieces to manage. To help diagnose opportunities for improvement or areas for application, consider the following reflection questions to approach data collection and analysis from an equity lens:

1. What or who impacts your selection of method or data collection approach?
2. How diverse in type are your assessment methods?

3. What student voices or experiences are not included in the data collected?
4. Thinking practically and strategically, who could be collaborative partners to offer feedback on your assessment approaches?
5. How could you best engage students as partners in the assessment planning process?

Data Interpretation and Sharing

Power, positionality, and agency are all relevant for data interpretation and sharing to impact equity. As higher education professionals have a responsibility to their institutional community, care must be taken to reflect assessment purposes and illuminate issues relevant to the needs of stakeholders with respect to continuous improvement (AAHE, 1992; Blaich & Wise, 2011; Kuh et al., 2011; Kuh et al., 2015; Ryan & Deci, 2000; Stupnisky et al., 2018; Suskie, 2014; West, 2017). This section argues practitioners should do so in ways that are mindful of positionality and motivational for audience engagement (AAHE, 1992; DeLuca Fernández, 2015; Heiser et al., 2017; Hood et al., 2015; Montenegro & Jankowski, 2020). In both data interpretation and sharing, practitioners should be intentional about perspectives examined and included in reporting—specifically, whether students are invited to participate (AAHE, 1992; Heiser et al., 2017; Levy & Heiser, 2018; Montenegro & Jankowski, 2017, 2020).

For effectiveness, assessment practitioners should share meaningful content relevant to audience needs (AAHE, 1992; Ewell, 2009; Kuh et al., 2015; Levy, 2013; Yousey-Elsener et al., 2015). Aiming to effectively share meaningful and relevant content, there is plenty of insight and context to share by employing an investigative approach: considering intended and unintended outcomes emergent in the data (Hood et al., 2015), disaggregating the data (Frierson et al., 2010; Hood et al., 2015), and conducting within and between group analysis (Frierson et al., 2010; Gordon et al., 1990; Hood et al., 2015; Hughes et al., 1993). Audiences are most likely to have positive impressions or be motivated to discuss or use assessment results when they have a relational connection to assessment activity (Metzler & Kurz, 2018; Ryan & Deci, 2000; Slavit et al., 2013; Svinicki, 2016). Consequently, likelihood of assessment-related action taking place exponentially increases when impacted populations are included as collaborators in the assessment process (Ewell, 2009; Kuh et al., 2015; Ryan & Deci, 2000; Svinicki, 2016). To advance equity, practitioners should be robust and transparent with information, promote action with context, and be inclusive of relevant populations as collaborators in reporting (AAHE, 1992; Heiser et al., 2017; Montenegro & Jankowski, 2017, 2020).

Knowing use of assessment results is one of the top-reported issues to effective assessment practices (Jankowski et al., 2018), motivation for behavior with interpreting and using assessment results may be worth examining (Fuller et al., 2016). A sense of relatedness or belonging to assessment work or people involved—coupled with a sense of autonomy—can influence individual agency and action in relation to assessment interpretation and use of results (Ryan & Deci, 2000; Stupnisky et al., 2018; Svinicki, 2016). Individuals with majoritized identities are likely to have more personal and professional confidence (and opportunity) to invite and empower others in collaborative involvement around common data goals or interests toward improvement. Keeping motivation in mind for authentically and meaningfully engaging in assessment work, practitioners can leverage data interpretation and sharing in ways which appeal to and meet the needs of stakeholder audiences (including colleagues and students), as well as catering messages to operationalize agency to challenge inequitable structures.

Going from theory to practice, the following are applicable suggestions to embed equitable considerations into data interpretation and sharing practices:

- **Allow transparency to signal intent:** Determine when data interpretation will take place and invite individuals in advance so they can plan for collaboration. Engaging audiences prior to reporting enables agency for these populations to clarify needs, as well as opt in as active contributors to the process. Transparency also has implications for power and agency. Openly communicating motivations and priorities for data decisions and actions across areas can call for accountability with respect to equitable outcomes and using results to inform action.

- **Role model desired behavior:** With data interpretation and sharing, practitioners can make it a point to avoid any deficit-based language, as well as avoid comparisons of all groups to Whiteness, which can affirm privileged or majoritized populations as the standard. Institutional leadership can motivate and create space for the agency of individuals to use assessment results for improvement, instilling accountability mechanisms (e.g., performance expectations, awards, recognition) related to staff use of assessment results for improvement.

- **Leverage foundations for motivation:** Look to institutional values and priorities to impact motivation acting on results and ground practitioner approach to data interpretation through common goals. If access is an institutional value and a student experience assessment is reviewed, results could be interpreted with considerations such as whether student affairs events or programs were held at a time and place equally accessible to all students or whether data collection was dependent on access to smartphones (precluding some student responses). Orienting an assessment sharing and action plan around institutional foundations promotes collaboration and stakeholder involvement through common goals, where multiple perspectives can balance positionality when interpreting or using data for improvement.

Data interpretation and sharing can be one of the most powerful elements of assessment practice considering the potential for influence and engagement to use results among audience stakeholders. As such, practitioners should be intentional in their process in order to be effective to appeal to and motivate collaborators for change. The following reflection questions can help you consider how to leverage data reporting and sharing for equity:

1. What foundational values or principles give purpose and ground your data interpretation efforts?
2. What influences (political considerations, extrinsic motivations) might you need to navigate at your institution when interpreting and reporting data?
3. How appropriate is the amount and type of perspectives you include in your data interpretation efforts?
4. Which individuals deserve to learn of the results of your assessment efforts?
5. How can you most effectively share the results of your assessment efforts to respective audiences?

Conclusion

This chapter presented necessary context for student affairs and assessment practice, as well as the need to advance equity in education. The demonstrated alignment of core principles of assessment for equity with the principles of good practice for assessing student learning underscores the relevance and opportunity to use assessment to advance equity by way of the four themes and strategies presented in this chapter: asking the right questions, competency frameworks, data collection and analysis, and data interpretation and sharing. Practical recommendations and reflection questions were presented for practitioner application of content in their everyday assessment practice.

Assessment practitioners in student affairs are uniquely positioned to prioritize the student experience and elevate those experiences for data-informed change. Student affairs assessment practitioners are surrounded by colleagues who are student-facing and -serving, while collecting data on student experiences related to learning, housing, conduct, engagement, and employment. Equity-centered practitioners center student voices, collaborate, create space for agency, acknowledge and disrupt power, and use multiple methods for robust analysis and reporting to elevate good assessment practices to become transformative and equity-focused assessment practices. Some view advocacy and justice work as a choice. For those professionals, engaging in equity-centered assessment will also be a choice. Equity-centered assessment draws on the practices of assessment, centers principles of equity, and leverages the integration of these practices to best serve those students from the global majority historically marginalized by the privileged in higher education.

References

American Association for Higher Education. (1992). *9 Principles of good practice for assessing student learning.* https://www.ncat.edu/_files/pdfs/campus-life/nine-principles.pdf

American Evaluation Association. (2011). *Public statement on cultural competence evaluation.* https://www.eval.org/About/Competencies-Standards/Cutural-Competence-Statement

Anderson, L. W., Krathwohl, D. R., & Bloom, B. S. (2001). *A taxonomy for learning, teaching, and assessing: A revision of Bloom's taxonomy of educational objectives* (Complete ed.). Longman.

Angelo, T. A., & Cross, K. P. (1993). *Classroom assessment techniques: A handbook for college teachers* (2nd ed.). Jossey-Bass.

Bensimon, E. M. (2005). Closing the achievement gap in higher education: An organizational learning perspective. In A. Kezar (Ed.), *Organizational Learning in Higher Education* (New Directions for Higher Education, no. 131, pp. 99–111). Jossey-Bass. https://doi.org/10.1002/he.190

Blaich, C. F., & Wise, K. S. (2011, January). *From gathering to using assessment results: Lessons from the Wabash National Study* (Occasional Paper No. 8). University of Illinois and Indiana University, National Institute for Learning Outcomes Assessment (NILOA). https://www.learningoutcomesassessment.org/wp-content/uploads/2019/02/OccasionalPaper8.pdf

Bledsoe, K., & Donaldson, S. I. (2015). Culturally responsive theory-driven evaluation. In S. Hood, R. Hopson, & H. Frierson (Eds.), *Continuing the journey to reposition culture and cultural context in evaluation theory and practice* (pp. 3–28). Information Age.

Bresciani, M. J., Gardner, M. M., & Hickmott, J. (2009). *Demonstrating student success: A practical guide to outcomes-based assessment of learning and development in student affairs*. Stylus.

Cataldi, E. F., Bennett, C. T., & Chen, X. (2018). First-generation students: College access, persistence, and postbachelor's outcomes. *Stats in brief* (NCES 2018-421). National Center for Education Statistics. https://nces.ed.gov/pubs2018/2018421.pdf

Chávez, A. F., & Sanlo, R. (2013). *Identity and leadership: Informing our lives, informing our practice*. National Association for Student Personnel Administrators.

Commission Appointed by Secretary of Education Margaret Spellings. (2006). *A test of leadership: Charting the future of U.S. higher education*. U.S. Department of Education. https://www2.ed.gov/about/bdscomm/list/hiedfuture/reports/pre-pub-report.pdf

Council for the Advancement of Standards in Higher Education. (2019). *CAS professional standards for higher education* (10th ed.). Author.

DeLuca Fernández, S. (2015). *Critical assessment* [PowerPoint slides]. http://studentaffairsassessment.org/structured-conversations

Ewell, P. T. (2009, November). *Assessment, accountability, and improvement: Revisiting the tension* (Occasional Paper No. 1). University of Illinois and Indiana University, National Institute for Learning Outcomes Assessment (NILOA). https://www.learningoutcomesassessment.org/wp-content/uploads/2019/02/OccasionalPaper1.pdf

Frierson, H. T., Hood, S., & Hughes, G. (2002). Strategies that address culturally responsive evaluations. In J. Frechtling (Ed.), *The 2002 user-friendly handbook for project evaluation* (pp. 63–72). National Science Foundation.

Fuller, M. B., Skidmore, S. T., Bustamante, R. M., & Holzweiss, P. C. (2016). Empirically exploring higher education cultures of assessment. *The Review of Higher Education, 39*(3), 395–429. http://doi.org/10.1353/rhe.2016.0022

Gordon, E. W., Miller, F., & Rollock, D. (1990). Coping with communicentric bias in knowledge production in the social sciences. *Educational Researcher, 19*(3), 14–19. https://doi.org/10.3102/0013189X019003014

Hall, S. (1992). The west and the rest: Discourse and power. In S. Hall & B. Gieben (Eds.), *Formations of modernity* (pp. 275–331). Polity Press.

Heiser, C. A., Prince, K., & Levy, J. D. (2017). Examining critical theory as a framework to advance equity through student affairs assessment. *The Journal of Student Affairs Inquiry, 3*(1). https://drive.google.com/file/d/1ksQstiXwP51EdipgdylU7nvdenVpIJA-/view

Hood, S., Hopson, R., & Kirkhart, K. E. (2015). Culturally responsive evaluation. In S. Newcomer, H. Hatry, & J. Wholey (Eds.), *Handbook of practical program evaluation* (4th ed., pp. 281–317). https://doi.org/10.1002/9781119171386.ch12

Hughes, D., Seidman, E., & Williams, N. (1993). Cultural phenomena and the research enterprise: Toward a culturally anchored methodology. *American Journal of Community Psychology, 21*(6), 687–703. https://doi.org/10.1007/BF00942243

Jankowski, N. A., Timmer, J. D., Kinzie, J., & Kuh, G. D. (2018). *Assessment that matters: Trending toward practices that document authentic student learning*.

University of Illinois and Indiana University, National Institute for Learning Outcomes Assessment (NILOA). https://www.learningoutcomesassessment.org/wp-content/uploads/2019/02/2018SurveyReport.pdf

Kirkhart, K. (1995). Seeking multicultural validity: A postcard from the road. *Evaluation Practice, 16*(1), 1–12. https://doi.org/10.1016/0886-1633(95)90002-0

Kirkhart, K. (2013, April 21–23). Repositioning validity. In *Plenary on Perspectives on Repositioning Culture in Evaluation and Assessment* [Paper presentation]. Repositioning Culture in Evaluation and Assessment, CREA Inaugural Conference, Chicago, IL, United States.

Kuh, G. D., Cruce, T. M., Shoup, R., Kinzie, J., & Gonyea, R. M. (2008). Unmasking the effects of student engagement on first-year college grades and persistence. *The Journal of Higher Education, 79*(5), 540–563. https://doi.org/10.1353/jhe.0.0019

Kuh, G. D., Ikenberry, S. O., Jankowski, N. A., Cain, T. R., Hutchings, P., & Kinzie, J. (2015). *Using evidence of student learning to improve higher education.* Jossey-Bass.

Kuh, G. D., Jankowski, N., Ikenberry, S. O., & Kinzie, J. (2014). *Knowing what students know and can do: The current state of student learning outcomes assessment in US colleges and universities.* University of Illinois and Indiana University, National Institute for Learning Outcomes Assessment (NILOA). https://www.learningoutcomesassessment.org/wp-content/uploads/2019/02/2013SurveyReport.pdf

Kuh, G. D., Kinzie, J., Schuh, J. H., & Whitt, E. J. (2011). Fostering student success in hard times. *Change: The Magazine of Higher Learning, 43*(4), 13–19. https://doi.org/10.1080/00091383.2011.585311

LaFever, M. (2016). Switching from Bloom to the Medicine Wheel: Creating learning outcomes that support Indigenous ways of knowing in post-secondary education. *Intercultural Education, 27*(5), 409–424. https://doi.org/10.1080/14675986.2016.1240496

Levy, J. D. (2013). ABCs of ineffective assessment cultures: Spelling out the wrongs to make right. *Journal of Student Affairs*, 22, 35–40. https://issuu.com/dsawebmaster/docs/journal_of_student_affairs_2013/3

Levy, J. D., & Heiser, C. A. (2018). Inclusive assessment practice. *NILOA guest paper response.* https://www.learningoutcomesassessment.org/wp-content/uploads/2019/08/EquityResponse_LevyHeiser.pdf

Levy, J. D., Hess, R. M., & Thomas, A. S. (2018). Student affairs assessment & accreditation: History, expectations, and implications. *The Journal of Student Affairs Inquiry, 4*(1). https://drive.google.com/file/d/1uJ2f6DTswtx27RhLn42LK7DKVamH4o9G/view

Maki, P. L. (2010). *Assessing for learning: Building a sustainable commitment across the institution* (2nd ed.). Stylus.

McFarland, J., Hussar, B., Wang, X., Zhang, J., Wang, K., Rathbun, A., Barmer, A., Cataldi, E. F., Mann, F. B., Nachazel, T., Smith, W., & Ossolinski, M. (2018). *The condition of education 2018* (NCES 2018-144). National Center for Education Statistics. https://files.eric.ed.gov/fulltext/ED583502.pdf

Mertens, D. M. (2007). Transformative paradigm: Mixed methods and social justice. *Journal of Mixed Methods Research*, *1*(3), 212–225. https://doi.org/10.1177/1558689807302811

Mertens, D. M. (2010). Transformative mixed methods research. *Qualitative Inquiry*, *16*(6), 469–474. https://doi.org/10.1177/1077800410364612

Mertens, D. M., & Hopson, R. K. (2006). Advancing evaluation of STEM efforts through attention to diversity and culture. In D. Huffman & F. Lawrenz (Eds.), *Critical Issues in STEM Evaluation* (New Directions for Evaluation, no. 109, pp. 35–51). Jossey-Bass. https://doi.org/10.1002/ev.177

Metzler, E. T., & Kurz, L. (2018, November). *Assessment 2.0: An organic supplement to standard assessment procedure* (Occasional Paper No. 36). University of Illinois and Indiana University, National Institute for Learning Outcomes Assessment (NILOA). https://www.learningoutcomesassessment.org/wp-content/uploads/2019/02/OccasionalPaper36.pdf

Montenegro, E., & Jankowski, N. A. (2017, January). *Equity and assessment: Moving towards culturally responsive assessment* (Occasional Paper No. 29). University of Illinois and Indiana University, National Institute for Learning Outcomes Assessment (NILOA). https://www.learningoutcomesassessment.org/wp-content/uploads/2019/02/OccasionalPaper29.pdf

Montenegro, E., & Jankowski, N. A. (2020, January). *A new decade for assessment: Embedding equity into assessment praxis* (Occasional Paper No. 42). University of Illinois and Indiana University, National Institute for Learning Outcomes Assessment (NILOA). https://www.learningoutcomesassessment.org/wp-content/uploads/2020/01/A-New-Decade-for-Assessment.pdf

National Center for Education Statistics. (2016). *Graduation rate from first institution attended for first-time, full-time bachelor's degree- seeking students at 4-year postsecondary institutions, by race/ethnicity, time to completion, sex, control of institution, and acceptance rate: Selected cohort entry years, 1996 through 2009*. https://nces.ed.gov/programs/digest/d16/tables/dt16_326.10.asp

Ryan, R. M., & Deci, E. L. (2000). Self-determination theory and the facilitation of intrinsic motivation. *American Psychologist*, *55*(1), 68–78. https://selfdeterminationtheory.org/SDT/documents/2000_RyanDeci_SDT.pdf

Schuh, J. H. (2015). Assessment in student affairs: How did we get here? *The Journal of Student Affairs Inquiry*, *1*(1), 1–10. https://jsai.scholasticahq.com/article/366

Schuh, J. H., & Associates. (2009). *Assessment methods for student affairs*. Jossey-Bass.

SenGupta, S., Hopson, R., & Thompson-Robinson, M. (2004). Cultural competence in evaluation: An overview. In M. Thompson-Robinson, R. Hopson, & S. SenGupta (Eds.), *In Search of Cultural Competence in Evaluation: Toward Principles and Practices* (New Directions for Evaluation, no. 102, pp. 5–19). Jossey-Bass. https://doi.org/10.1002/ev.112

Slavit, D., Nelson, T. H., & Deuel, A. (2013). Teacher groups' conceptions and uses of student-learning data. *Journal of Teacher Education*, *64*(1), 8–21. https://doi.org/10.1177%2F0022487112445517

Stanfield, J. H., Jr. (1999). Slipping through the front door: Relevant social scientific evaluation in the people of color century. *American Journal of Evaluation, 20*(3), 415–431. https://doi.org/10.1177%2F109821409902000301

Steinberg, S. R., & Cannella, G. S. (2012). *Critical qualitative research reader*. Peter Lang.

Stupnisky, R. H., BrckaLorenz, A., Yuhas, B., & Guay, F. (2018). Faculty members' motivation for teaching and best practices: Testing a model based on self-determination theory across institution types. *Contemporary Educational Psychology, 53*, 15–26. https://doi.org/10.1016/j.cedpsych.2018.01.004

Suskie, L. (2014). *Five dimensions of quality: A common sense guide to accreditation and accountability*. Jossey-Bass.

Svinicki, M. (2016). Motivation: An updated analysis. *IDEA Paper, 59*(May), 1–8. https://ideacontent.blob.core.windows.net/content/sites/2/2020/01/PaperIDEA_59.pdf

Thelin, J. R. (2019). *A history of American higher education* (3rd ed.). Johns Hopkins University Press.

West, J. (2017). Data, democracy, and school accountability: Controversy over school evaluation in the case of DeVasco High School. *Big Data & Society, 4*(1), 1–16. https://doi.org/10.1177%2F2053951717702408

Yousey-Elsener, K., Bentrim, E. M., & Henning, G. W. (2015). *Coordinating student affairs divisional assessment: A practical guide*. Stylus.

Zerquera, D., Reyes, K. A., Pender, J. T., & Abbady, R. (2018). Understanding practitioner-driven assessment and evaluation efforts for social justice. In D. Zerquera, I. Hernández, & J. G. Berumen (Eds.), *Assessment and Social Justice: Pushing Through Paradox* (New Directions for Institutional Research, no. 177, pp. 15–40). Jossey-Bass. https://doi.org/10.1002/ir.20254

14

ASSESSING EQUITABLE ACCESS TO STEM FIELDS OF STUDY

Alicia C. Dowd, Leticia Oseguera, and Royel M. Johnson

Among the many research methodologies utilized by scholars and practitioners of higher education, participatory critical action research (PCAR; Kemmis & McTaggart, 2005) and developmental evaluation (Patton, 2011) are particularly relevant to assess policies and practices that promote or inhibit equity (byrd, 2019; Dowd & Bensimon, 2015; Dowd et al., 2018; Stewart, 2019). PCAR and developmental evaluation—a form of evaluation tailored to supporting change and innovation as it is unfolding—are also appropriate methods to use when seeking to foster equitable change in organizations through "equity-minded assessment" (Montenegro & Jankowski, 2020, p. 4). These approaches actively involve people in professional development activities who have power and authority over the curriculum and student learning assessments, with the expectation that they will apply what they learn to make changes that will improve the status of equity in their classrooms, programs, and colleges.

When administrators adopt PCAR (specifically practitioner inquiry, or self-study) and developmental evaluation to self-assess program quality with an equity-minded stance concerned with social justice issues, it is referred to as "critical assessment" (Dowd, 2008, p. 411; Montenegro & Jankowski, 2020, p. 9). The word critical, derived from critical theory, signals a commitment to engaging issues of power, oppression, and injustice (Anderson, 2012; Bensimon & Bishop, 2012). To be critical and equity-minded during assessment processes involves "questioning processes, biases, assumptions, within ourselves, others, and the processes followed" (Montenegro & Jankowski, 2020, p. 13). This chapter illustrates how equity-minded assessment practice can be carried out collaboratively by a diverse group of assessment researchers and administrators who wish to involve faculty and administrative colleagues in critical assessment work with a focus on racial equity.

We draw on our own work collaborating with administrators in a science, technology, engineering, and mathematics (STEM) college,[1] illustrating the strategies we utilized to enact these standards. A STEM focus is much needed because these fields are marked by homogenizing cultures and unremitting professional socialization to an ideology that celebrates individualism, merit, and objectivity (despite evidence of bias; Dowd, 2012; Posselt, 2020). Racial inequities in STEM participation result from cultural, instructional, and organizational practices that disproportionately and negatively impact African American, Indigenous, and Latinx students. Racially minoritized students often experience racial microaggressions, bias, discrimination, or experience a sense of neglect during interactions with faculty and advising staff (Johnson et al., 2019; Museus, 2014; Strayhorn, 2012). To address deep-seated cultural challenges, organizational change strategies, such as equity-minded assessment, are needed.

The STEM-focused critical assessment work we report on here was part of a larger initiative underway at a historically and predominantly White research-intensive university (a PWI). The action research component included a focus on producing equitable access to undergraduate STEM bachelor's degree majors. As part of that component of the action research design, the authors collaborated with senior administrators in a STEM college who had responsibility for determining whether students who were seeking an exception from entry-to-major requirements at their college should receive an exception. The administrators viewed the existing policies that guided their current enrollment exceptions as lacking in transparency. Further, they were concerned that the lack of transparency was exacerbating known racial equity issues in access to competitive, high-status majors in the college, where enrollments disproportionately included White, Asian ancestry, and international students. Black men and women, students from Native American and Indigenous communities, and Latinx students were under-enrolled, especially in the college's most selective, high-demand majors.

In the next section, we summarize the elements of our multifocal equity-minded assessment model, which incorporates our respective areas of research and expertise. The core of the chapter unfolds in three sections detailing the assessment and evaluation steps we took, how the professional development was experienced by the participants, challenges we encountered, and the outcomes. The chapter concludes with reflections on future work and recommendations for STEM scholars and practitioners who wish to carry out similar initiatives.

Researchers' Positionality and Conceptual Framing

Figure 14.1 represents an equity-minded assessment model that incorporates essential elements of our scholarship. As indicated by our descriptions of researcher positionality (Milner, 2007) in this section, we drew on differences in our professional training and our racial, ethnic, and gendered social identities to bring a multifocal perspective to bear in this study.

The conceptions of horizontal and vertical equity represented on the cube in the figure reflect theories of justice developed in the tradition of White male European philosophy (Rawls, 1971) that we articulated to engage practitioners in reflection on their (often unexamined) ideological conceptions of fairness, equal opportunity, and meritocracy. Where horizontal equity sets a standard of equal access, treatment, and resource provision, vertical equity immediately introduces the tension of historical and contemporary racism, sexism, and other forms of oppression that must be countered through unequal allocation of resources. Applications of equity concepts in the economics of education and policy literature have tended to focus on the allocation of human, financial, and physical resources. Efficiencies of various types are also prioritized for consideration, including productive efficiency (i.e., producing desired quality of overall

Figure 14.1. Equity-minded assessment model.

Sense of Community and Belonging

Are we creating an engaging campus environment?

Crafting a Class for Holistic Student Success

Do we express program values to build community?

Do underrepresented students experience disparate negative impacts due to the quality of our pedagogy, advising, and academic support programs?

Vertical Equity

Are our procedures fair?
Do all students have equal access and receive equal treatment?

Does our program quality enable equal participation?

Are campus champions and cultural navigators ready to create networks of support for students from racially minoritized groups?

Horizontal Equity

Do we allocate resources (human, financial, physical, symbolic) to counter historical and contemporary racism, sexism, and other forms of oppression?

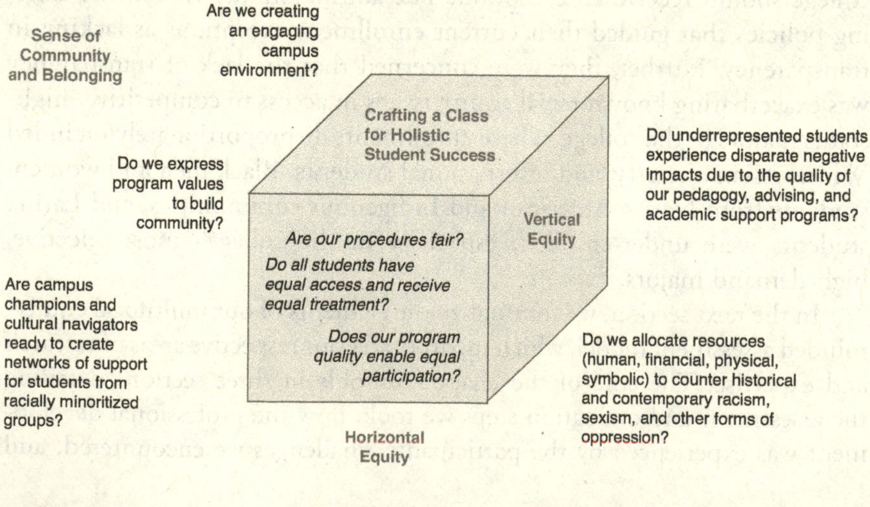

student outcomes with optimal resource allocation), economic efficiency (i.e., producing a diverse graduating class to meet workforce needs), and social efficiency (i.e., producing a diverse graduating class to meet societal and community needs).

While drawing on these foundational concepts, Dowd's scholarship has also emphasized the importance of countering symbolic and representational exclusion as well as cultural forms of taxation and violence (see e.g., Dowd & Bensimon, 2015; Dowd & Fernandez Castro, 2020). As a White woman initially trained by White professors in rational, rather than critically race conscious (Bensimon & Bishop, 2012) perspectives on equity, Dowd has sought to counter her socialization into majoritarian cultural narratives (Yosso et al., 2004) through collaboration with diverse colleagues to meaningfully engage critical perspectives on racial justice.

The research communities in which Leticia Oseguera and Royel Johnson were trained integrally center issues related to race, equity, and community uplift. As illustrated in Figure 14.1, their work brings badly needed understandings of the characteristics of academic programs that express and effectively uphold inclusive values; create opportunities for student engagement with campus champions and cultural navigators who affirm students' sense of community and belonging; and take a holistic view of student success.

Leticia Oseguera identifies as a Latina woman and has studied student perceptions of the benefits of diversity and academic program quality defined in terms of the behaviors of educational agents and champions who act vigorously to support students, affirm their racial and STEM identities, and help them create networks of support on and off campus. Her research reveals how important it is for educational program leaders to articulate program values through the inclusion of multidimensional representations of successful students (Oseguera et al., 2019; Oseguera et al., 2020). Oseguera's studies provide highly contextualized analyses of academic resources that interrogate the extent to which the cultural traditions of diverse groups of students are respected in academic offerings rather than subject to deficit-minded assumptions.

Royel Johnson identifies as a Black man. His race and gender identities significantly shape his scholarship, which unapologetically centers the voices and experiences of racially minoritized people. Specifically, his work aims to shed light on and offer recommendations for addressing how institutional policies, practices, and logics conspire in the educational failure of racially minoritized students and other underserved student populations (e.g., Johnson, 2015; Johnson et al., 2019). Thus, equity-minded assessment, which emphasizes race and power-conscious approaches to improving student learning and development, is congruent with Johnson's epistemological stance and scholarly commitments.

Equity-Minded Assessment in Action

As is the case in many STEM colleges, access to major fields of study in our focal college was competitive. To enter a major, a student had to complete six prerequisite courses and earn a minimum cumulative grade point average (GPA, thresholds varied). In addition, they had to earn those credits and meet the GPA threshold without taking too long. A time to qualify requirement established a window of time (called the "credit window") in which they had to meet these requirements. Some high-demand, high-status majors had more competitive admissions than others. These restrictive majors had enrollment limits that were routinely filled by the many applicants who had met all the entry-to-major requirements. Area coordinators in these enrollment-controlled majors provided very few waivers for admission to students who did not manage to initially meet the admission-to-major requirements. While a few exceptions were made for entry to the restrictive (enrollment controlled) majors, the criteria for gaining entry through the exceptions process was not publicized or transparent.

In contrast, area coordinators in majors without high enrollment demand had flexibility, under the existing entry-to-major policies, to admit students whose GPA was somewhat below the cut point, who had taken a little longer to complete prerequisites, or who were missing a required course. These lower enrollment demand majors routinely granted admission waivers.

The Action Research Goal

The existing entry-to-major policies at the STEM college created a context for arbitrary and potentially inequitable administration of waivers and for racially segregated patterns of enrollment in different fields of study to be further exacerbated. Research involving first-generation and racially minoritized students shows that, when navigating collegiate academic support systems, they do not feel as entitled to receive help in the same way as their more privileged peers (Alexitch, 2006; Rendón et al., 2000). Further, they may have fewer opportunities, due to working off campus or family responsibilities, to receive information through peer networks about how to work administrative procedures to their advantage (Goldrick-Rab, 2016; Sallee & Tierney, 2007). Given the strong association between race, socioeconomic status, and having a family member who had attended college, it stands to reason that racially minoritized students are disproportionately among those *least* likely to seek an exception.

The Equity-Minded Professional Development and Assessment Design

Through our conversations with the senior administrators who collaborated with us, we articulated four goals for the Equity in Access to STEM majors workshop series:

1. Develop a shared language and framing of concepts of equity, justice, and fairness.
2. Develop shared reference to and collaborative sensemaking concerning the application of equity principles to decision-making.
3. Develop an initial rubric to evaluate whether equity as a standard of practice was evident in entry-to-major criteria.
4. Identify strategies for the college to self-assess equity in the design of practices and policies that affect entry-to-major for students who are members of racially and ethnically minoritized groups.

Through a three-part series of 2-hour workshops conducted in spring 2020 via Zoom (after COVID-19 prohibited our original plan to meet in person), we articulated equity-minded assessment principles and guiding questions for our collaborators to consider when redesigning their exceptions policies. Montenegro and Jankowski (2020) advanced standards of practice for conducting equity-minded assessment that were reflected in our design. They emphasized, for example, that it is important for assessment practitioners to "increase transparency in assessment results and actions," to check their biases by asking questions about their own "positions of privilege," and to draw on "multiple sources of evidence" (p. 13). In this section, we illustrate how we applied these standards in the Equity in Access to STEM Majors workshops we designed, facilitated, and evaluated.

Fostering Transparency in Policy Implementation

With respect to the standard of transparency, it was the lack of transparency in the provision of exceptions for the entry-to-major process in the STEM college, and the threat it created to racial equity in admissions at an institution and college that prominently espoused a commitment to diversity, equity, and inclusion, that motivated our involvement from the outset. The action research goal was to design an equitable and transparent exception process for use in determining admission to high-demand, restrictive majors, which could also be implemented in those major fields of study with more flexibility in admissions.

Transparency and the need to address the too-often unquestioned assumptions of those with power and privilege were served by the participation of those who held power to make change. The workshop participants were recruited by a senior administrator in the collaborating college, who also participated along with a second senior administrator. Eight of the other participants were faculty members who played administrative roles called area coordinators, where they had responsibility for determining exceptions for entry to majors in their areas of study. Two professional staff who had responsibility for promoting diversity, equity, and inclusion (DEI) in the college also participated, for a total of 12. Due to their different roles, participants had different levels of exposure to previous DEI professional development opportunities, with some having attended many similar workshops and others participating for the first time.

Using Multiple Forms of Data to Promote Reflective Practice

Consistent with developmental evaluation principles (Patton, 2011), we incorporated pre- and post-workshop survey evaluation results by presenting them for discussion by participants in dialogue with the defining concepts of our multifocal assessment model. This approach supported the first of Montenegro and Jankowski's (2020) standards that emphasizes asking reflective questions in order to check biases. We also utilized multiple sources of evidence, such as numerical data from the institutional research office and qualitative data from open-ended survey questions. The numerical data represented student course grades disaggregated by race, Latinx ethnicity, and U.S. domestic or international status in a key prerequisite gateway course to majors. These data showed that the Black and Latinx students were not proportionally represented among those receiving the A and B grades that best position students for entry to major and success in subsequent classes. We interrogated these data in an equity-minded way that emphasized institutional responsibility to educate, dispelling go-to explanations based on deficit perspectives often imposed on students and communities of color. Throughout the workshops and breakout discussions, observation notes were taken by graduate student researchers. These informed our planning for each subsequent workshop and our recommendations.

We also wrote a case study vignette called "A Budding Engineer" that fictionalized the ways new college students sometimes struggle to address common barriers to success in STEM. The barriers we incorporated were taken from a list of common barriers to entry-to-major provided to us by one of the collaborating STEM administrators. Telling the story of a student who struggled in an early prerequisite course, the vignette was written to invite holistic considerations of students' challenges in meeting standardized entry-to-major criteria as well as their potential to succeed in their desired major if provided a chance to do so.

The vignette served as a reference point for reflection, called for questioning assumptions and privileges, and invited collective sensemaking using multiple dimensions of equity. Breakout discussions in smaller groups asked participants to consider how their decision process might differ if they knew more about the fictional student's unnamed racial and ethnic characteristics, thereby inviting reflection on how their perceptions of merit might shift due to racialized perceptions of a student's ability to benefit. The discussion of the case helped us to move beyond abstract concepts of equity. We added humanistic considerations (e.g., exceptions provided due to illness or death in the student's family) and broadened the conception of student success by incorporating the importance of sense of community, belonging, and mattering. We also urged participants to consider the various environments (including family, work, community) which students simultaneously navigate while in college and that also impact their success.

We then asked participants to use principles derived from the multifocal decision-making lens illustrated in Figure 14.1 to discuss the conditions under which they would provide an exception from standardized entry-to-major requirements. Participant views were collected by administering a survey prior to the third workshop and discussion of the results during it. Variations on the standardized qualification(s) that the interested student lacked included a cumulative GPA below the required threshold for the major, unsuccessful completion of all required prerequisites, or both. The options for administering the exception included to give additional time (a semester or more) to complete missing courses, to raise the cumulative GPA, or to accomplish both; or accepting the student with a GPA lower than the standardized threshold or with one or more courses substituting for those required. The elements students might be missing (prerequisite course, successful course completion during credit window, and cumulative GPA) intersected with the decision options to yield a variety of scenarios. These were summarized in a table provided to participants for discussion of how they would decide and what principles they would draw on in making their decision.

Evaluation Results

With respect to a pre-workshop survey question *"What does equity mean to you?"* participants' responses highlighted equity as fairness and equal treatment; increasing participation of members of groups that are underrepresented in

STEM to the point that enrollment of those groups is representative of state demographics; recognizing the whole student (moving beyond standardized scores); and addressing systemic barriers to access and success. These values, espoused by multiple members, are wide ranging. They reflect values of equal opportunity and compensatory justice. Replying to the question, *"In your view which of the decision principles described [during the workshops] should be applied when making entry-to-major exception decisions?"* all but one of 10 survey respondents agreed that humanistic concerns should be accorded consideration. Other responses were less uniform, but the principles of horizontal equity (providing equal resources to those with equal needs), vertical equity (providing greater resources to those with greater educational needs), and ability to benefit (an efficiency concern) were deemed relevant by the majority of respondents. Survey responses showed, too, that a few participants were concerned that the social efficiency standard would be implemented in the form of "quotas" and did not believe that social identities such as race, gender, or nationality should be considered relevant criteria for decision-making about entry-to-major.

It is important to note that while the ruling in the 1978 Supreme Court case of the *University of California Regents v. Bakke* did declare quotas unconstitutional, subsequent court cases have affirmed that colleges, universities, and U.S. society have a compelling interest in fostering diversity in higher education and employment (Yosso et al., 2004). Formal statements of vision and values issued by our partnering college also espoused the value of diversity. These results, combined with our observational data from small group discussions, revealed a tension among the ideals held by the participants. This is not atypical and represents an ongoing challenge to implementation of racial equity as a standard of practice (Dowd & Bensimon, 2015).

Prior to the final workshop, we administered an evaluation survey asking how participants would weigh consideration of three different entry-to-major appeal scenarios. The scenarios, which were written to capture typical and realistic cases of students seeking exceptions, were: (a) provide more time for the student to reach course completion; (b) allow an exception with a lower grade point average; and (c) deny the appeal altogether. Responses were mixed. Seventy percent prioritized admission for students who were only missing an entry-to-major course and 44% prioritized those only missing the GPA cutoff. Few were in favor of allowing exceptions to students who were below the GPA threshold and missing an entry-to-major course. Allowing extra time for students to complete the courses needed or to raise the GPA were favored by most, but only a few favored allowing a lower grade average at entry. Under any scenario regarding why a student might need an exception, allowing a course substitution was rarely the favored option.

As equity-minded assessment researchers, we asked if there was empirical evidence that the GPA was a strong predictor of success. College administrators had evidence available from institutional research that the current GPA threshold for restricted majors was arbitrary. It was set primarily as a form of enrollment control due to enrollment capacity issues. The ambiguous status of GPA as a predictor of the academic success of students receiving grades at the margins of the existing GPA thresholds provides a compelling rationale for consideration of alternative measures of student readiness.

Overall, workshop evaluation results indicated that participants were generally positive about their experience, though unsure about how best to move forward. Participant comments expressed the difficulty of applying equity principles in practice, with the observation it was hard work. We reminded participants throughout the workshop that learning to be equity-minded takes practice and self-reflection. Nearly all respondents agreed that the workshop series caused them to reflect in new ways on their own work and that the focus on designing an equitable entry-to-major policy was necessary and important. However, fewer than half felt the exceptions to entry-to-major *would* ultimately center equity. Further, half the participants noted uncertainty about their own capacity to play an active role or to make a difference in addressing issues of equity. Qualitative responses to open-ended survey items stressed the need to hold conversations about equity-minded decision-making with higher level leadership.

Outcomes of Equity-Minded Assessment

In collaboration with the STEM administrators who partnered with us in this work, we surmised that the best course of action for next steps—and one that would garner support to enhance successful implementation—would involve renaming and reframing the "exceptions" to entry to major policy process as a "request for holistic review" for entry to major. This equity-minded change in orientation moves away from stigmatizing students who needed more time to complete coursework or who did not earn high grades in one or more prerequisite courses. The strongest equity framing would allow appeal by students who are missing a course *and* who have a below-threshold GPA, as the two circumstances may have been produced by the same underlying social, institutional, or familial conditions. Political considerations, our evaluation results, and feasibility of management of the greater number of appeals (as the opportunity becomes more public and transparent) suggest that an initial implementation of the holistic review process that allows appeal only by students who are missing a course *or* below the required GPA would garner more support.

Holistic review moves away from standardized entry-to-major metrics. Reviewing the results of our assessment process with our collaborators and generating next steps in dialogue with them, we recommended that students seeking entry-to-major through holistic review be asked to explain in a narrative statement of application why they wished to enroll in the major. Such a statement would provide students with the opportunity to speak to their ability to benefit from education in the major and their ability to collaborate with and lead members of a team in a way that would create an inclusive environment conducive to achieving team tasks and goals. Specifically, students should *not* be required to write an essay about the reasons they did not meet the standardized GPA, credit window, and prerequisite course requirements (though of course they might touch on this in answering the prompt posed). The reason for this is to avoid retraumatizing students who experienced a family or personal illness or, for racially minoritized students, who experienced racism or racial microaggressions in classes that oppressed their chances of success.

The STEM college administrators were in the process of creating a questionnaire about different forms of student engagement on and off campus in order to administer a scholarship award designed to promote racial diversity in the college. We recommend that these engagement indicators utilize indicators of students' sense of belonging, their engagement in communities on and off campus, and their successful discharge of responsibilities to their families and chosen community of peers. To apply a vertical equity standard and support the engagement of racially minoritized students, the college will develop specific forms of engagement for Black, Indigenous, People of Color (BIPOC) students that will be accorded weight on the engagement questionnaire. To ensure this approach supports vertical equity, it will be important for the college to evaluate student experiences in those engagement opportunities. This raises a very focused opportunity for the college to collect and incorporate data capturing student "voice" into their decision-making.

Admissions decisions based on these materials will be aided by an assessment rubric with the following questions:

1. Does the student demonstrate ability to succeed in the major, through their narrative statement and/or through their responses to the engagement questionnaire?
2. Does the addition of this student to the major advance the diversity and equity goals of the college?

Recommendations for Ongoing Equity-Minded Assessment

We found it rewarding to combine our expertise and articulate a multifocal assessment model, through which workshop participants could explore their different perspectives and (sometimes conflicting) values. As Montenegro and Jankowski (2020) emphasized, we need to check our biases and assumptions, promote transparency in assessment policies and practices, and employ multiple sources of evidence during equity-minded assessment. Through this collaboration, we sought to incorporate these standards. In addition, we continually reminded the participants in our workshops of the college's espoused values and missions as well as the equity principles discussed.

Montenegro and Jankowski (2020) advanced six standards of practice for conducting equity-minded assessment, three of which we have illustrated in this chapter. In this slice of our work, other than through our involvement of three doctoral research assistants, we did not "include student perspectives and take action based on [student] perspectives," the fourth of Montenegro and Jankowski's standards (p. 13). However, we concur that this is an important standard of equity-minded assessment practice, and as reflected in conclusion of the preceding section, we view it as essential to support vertical equity as the STEM college administrators initially implement and evaluate the engagement assessment scale they design.

In the work conducted in spring 2020, we looked only briefly and at a minimal amount of data disaggregated by race and ethnicity. Through another project that the three authors are involved in, we will have additional opportunities to interrogate and design ongoing assessments informed by disaggregated data (Montenegro & Jankowski's standard 5), again using data on the distribution of course grades in key gateway and gatekeeper courses, which we have obtained for 1 year and will now update as the new academic year has begun. We view this as an essential step to keeping inquiry-based assessments of equity "close to practice" (Dowd et al., 2018) by using fine-grained data. Such data also support the standard of making "evidence-based changes that address issues of equity that are context-specific" (Montenegro & Jankowski, 2020, p. 13).

Despite our commitment to these principles, and experience in carrying out various forms of action research and evaluation, we also found it challenging in the short time frame of one semester to facilitate and unpack the ideological assumptions of the dozen or so participants in the workshops about the relationships between academic merit, race, and equitable admissions practices. Some participants found the ideas we presented to be confusing or they experienced frustration in that we did not reach a clearly specified set of standards. Our recommendations for those who would carry out a similar project are to recognize (a) the importance of "right-sizing" the focal problem of practice to gain leverage in reforming inequitable policies and practices and (b) the need to manage participant expectations about the relative simplicity or complexity of addressing racial inequities at PWI research universities. The entry-to-major policies that were the focus of our work were narrow relative to the systemic structural racism incorporated into the college and university's admissions practices. It was difficult to take a micro-focus when the macro issues were so apparent, but we understood that reflective practice at the micro level by higher education practitioners can have an impact on systemic issues embedded in the curriculum, pedagogy, advising, recruitment, admissions, and standards for degree completion.

Effectively implemented, race-conscious inquiry compels educators to use firsthand insights from interactions with colleagues and students in self-reflective ways by attentively pondering micro questions such as:

1. How do I contribute to the cyclical production of engagement disparities that disadvantage students from racially minoritized groups?
2. How can I more deliberately engage these students in my research and other value-added, enriching educational experiences on campus?
3. What have I done to help racially minoritized students who have taken my courses get into competitive graduate schools?
4. How do personal biases and stereotypes affect my engagement with racially minoritized students?

Reflection on these questions is the basis for developing culturally sustaining practices that foster a sense of belonging of academic and racial identity in educational settings (Strayhorn, 2012). Such validation is especially important for members of racial and ethnic groups that are underrepresented in STEM (National Academy of Sciences, 2011). We recommend that colleges create diverse groups who can intentionally work to develop multifocal knowledge and racism-conscious (Dowd & Elmore, 2020), culturally informed practices for application in STEM fields.

Conclusion

Through this chapter, we brought our experiences to the community of assessment researchers and practitioners to communicate the strategies we employed and the challenges we faced in doing so. We believe the work must be carried out with urgency paired with racial realism, which recognizes that those who benefit from racial inequities (predominantly White men) are not likely to interrogate dominant norms without professional incentives and contexts that insist on racial equity as a standard of practice for all educators.

Research on change in STEM fields indicates that direct faculty involvement in college initiatives is necessary to sustain cultural change because faculty reject what appears to them to be superficial "quick fixes" from outsiders (Henderson et al., 2011). By contrast, data-informed inquiry and experimentation yields insight and commitment to improved practice. Inquiry is a knowledge production process that, when occurring in a cyclical manner and informed by systematic use of data, generates the expertise practitioners need to bring about changes in institutional policies, practices, and organizational structures to address inequities in student experiences and outcomes. Through inquiry, practitioners attain a higher level of adaptive expertise, which is necessary in dynamic educational settings. Expert practitioners are those who can adapt to changing conditions and meet their students' needs effectively. Becoming conscious of the relationship between beliefs, behaviors, and organizational routines is critical to inquiry. It is clear, however, that this type of work requires sustained and multifaceted implementation (Dowd & Liera, 2018).

Acknowledgments

The authors thank Artemio Cardenas, Marlon Fernandez Castro, and Ali Watts, doctoral students in the higher education program and CSHE research assistants, for much valued research assistance in support of the project and data collection referenced in this chapter. We also acknowledge the anonymous senior administrators who collaborated with us in the design of the professional development workshops described in this chapter and whose expertise and ideas integrally shaped the process, outcomes, and recommendations presented here.

Notes

1. To protect the confidentiality of study participants, the specific college and university is not named.

References

Alexitch, L. R. (2006). Help seeking and the role of academic advising in higher education. In S. A. Karabenick & R. S. Newman (Eds.), *Help seeking in academic settings: Goals, groups, and contexts.* Erlbaum.

Anderson, G. M. (2012). Equity and critical policy analysis in higher education: A bridge still too far. *Review of Higher Education, 36*(1), 133–142. https://10.1353/rhe.2012.0051

Bensimon, E. M., & Bishop, R. (2012). Introduction: Why "critical"? The need for new ways of knowing. *Review of Higher Education, 36*(1), 1–7. https://10.1353/rhe.2012.0046

byrd, d. (2019). The diversity distraction: A critical comparative analysis of discourse in higher education scholarship. *The Review of Higher Education, 42,* 135–172. https://10.1353/rhe.2019.0048

Dowd, A. C. (2008). The community college as gateway and gatekeeper: Moving beyond the access "saga" to outcome equity. *Harvard Educational Review, 77*(4), 407–419. https://10.17763/haer.77.4.1233g31741157227

Dowd, A. C. (2012). Developing supportive STEM community college to four-year college and university transfer ecosystems. In S. Olson & J. B. Labov (Eds.), *Community colleges in the evolving STEM education landscape: Summary of a summit* (pp. 107–134). The National Academies Press.

Dowd, A. C., & Bensimon, E. M. (2015). *Engaging the "race question": Accountability and equity in higher education.* Teachers College Press.

Dowd, A. C., & Elmore, B. (2020). Leadership for equity-minded data use towards racial equity in higher education. In A. Kezar & J. R. Posselt (Eds.), *Administration for social justice and equity in higher education: Critical perspectives for leadership and decision making.* Routledge.

Dowd, A. C., & Fernandez Castro, M. (2020). Equity. In M. E. David & M. J. Amey (Eds.), *The SAGE encyclopedia of higher education* (pp. 467–470). SAGE.

Dowd, A. C., & Liera, R. (2018). Sustaining organizational change towards racial equity through cycles of inquiry. *Education Policy Analysis Archives, 26*(65), 1–46. https://doi.org/10.14507/epaa.26.3274

Dowd, A. C., Witham, K., Hanson, D., Ching, C., Liera, R., Drivalas, J., & Castro, M. F. (2018). *Bringing accountability to life: How savvy college leaders find the "actionable N" to improve equity and effectiveness in higher education.* American Council on Education. https://www.acenet.edu/news-room/Pages/Bringing-Accountability-to-Life.aspx

Goldrick-Rab, S. (2016). *Paying the price: College costs, financial aid, and the betrayal of the American dream.* University of Chicago Press.

Henderson, C., Beach, A., & Finkelstein, N. (2011). Facilitating change in undergraduate STEM instructional practices: An analytic review of the literature. *Journal of Research in Science Teaching, 48*(8), 952–984. https://doi.org/10.1002/tea.20439

Johnson, R. M. (2015). Measuring the influence of juvenile arrest on the odds of four-year college enrollment for Black males: An NLSY analysis. *Spectrum: A Journal on Black Men, 4*(1), 49–72. https://doi.org/10.2979/spectrum.4.1.04

Johnson, R. M., Strayhorn, T. L., & Travers, C. S. (2019, December 24). Examining the academic advising experiences of Black males at an urban university: An exploratory case study. *Urban Education.* https://doi.org/10.1177/0042085919894048

Kemmis, S., & McTaggart, R. (2005). Participatory action research: Communicative action and the public sphere. In N. K. Denzin & Y. S. Lincoln (Eds.), *Handbook of qualitative research* (3rd ed., pp. 559–603). SAGE.

Milner, H. R., IV. (2007). Race, culture, and researcher positionality: Working through dangers seen, unseen, and unforeseen. *Educational Researcher*, *36*(7), 388–400. https://doi.org/10.3102/0013189X07309471

Montenegro, E., & Jankowski, N. A. (2020). *A new decade for assessment: Embedding equity into assessment praxis*. University of Illinois and Indiana University, National Institute for Learning Outcomes Assessment (NILOA).

Museus, S. D. (2014). The culturally engaging campus environments (CECE) Model: A new theory of college success among racially diverse student populations. In M. B. Paulsen (Ed.), *Higher Education: Handbook of Theory and Research* (pp. 189–227). Springer.

National Academy of Sciences. (2011). *Expanding underrepresented minority participation: America's science and technology talent at the crossroads*. The National Academies Press.

Oseguera, L., de los Rios, M. J., Park, H. J., Aparicio, E. M., & Rao, S. (2019). *A framework for expanding STEM student success* [Paper presentation]. Association for the Study of Higher Education, Portland, OR, United States.

Oseguera, L., de Los Rios, M. J., Park, H. J., Aparicio, E. M., & Rao, S. (2020). Understanding who stays in a STEM scholar program for underrepresented students: High-achieving scholars and short-term program retention. *Journal of College Student Retention: Research, Theory, & Practice*, 1–37. https://doi.org/10.1177/1521025120950693

Patton, M. Q. (2011). *Developmental evaluation: Applying complexity concepts to enhance innovation and use*. The Guilford Press.

Posselt, J. R. (2020). *Equity in science: Representation, culture, and the dynamics of change in graduate education*. Stanford University Press.

Rawls, J. (1971). *A theory of justice*. Harvard University Press.

Rendón, L. I., Jalomo, R. E., & Nora, A. (2000). Theoretical considerations in the study of minority student retention in higher education. In J. M. Braxton (Ed.), *Reworking the student departure puzzle* (pp. 127–156). Vanderbilt University Press.

Sallee, M. W., & Tierney, W. G. (2007). The influence of peer groups on academic success. *College and University*, *82*(2), 7–14. https://aacrao-web.s3.amazonaws.com/files/X6Dm20GTToCUnvuGdovC_CUJ8202.pdf

Stewart, D.-L. (2019). Envisioning possibilities for innovations in higher education research on race and ethnicity. *Journal Committed to Social Change on Race and Ethnicity*, *5*(1), 7–32. https://doi.org/10.15763/issn.2642-2387.2019.5.1.6-32

Strayhorn, T. L. (2012). *College students' sense of belonging: A key to educational success for all students*. Routledge.

University of California Regents v. Bakke, 438 U.S. 265 (1978)

Yosso, T. J., Parker, L., Solórzano, D. G., & Lynn, M. (2004). From Jim Crow to affirmative action and back again: A critical race discussion of racialized rationales and access to higher education. *Review of Research in Education*, *28*, 1–25. http://10.3102/0091732X028001001

15

EQUITABLE ASSESSMENT IN COMMUNITY COLLEGES

A Call for Collaboration and Culturally Responsive Practices

Raina Dyer-Barr, Kaylan Baxter, and Eboni M. Zamani-Gallaher

It has been 120 years since the origination of one of the most unique inventions, the American community college. With the establishment of Joliet Junior College in 1901 in the state of Illinois, the junior college movement began. Junior colleges later referenced as community colleges, from their early beginnings to present day, offer an open door to postsecondary education (e.g., general education/transfer, workforce training, lifelong learning, etc.) that serves the needs of a diverse community of attendees. Broadening participation through the open-door concept has been a centerpiece of the vision and mission of community colleges. Chief in the institutional ethos of community colleges is a commitment to student success. Undergirding the purpose, role, operations, and functions of community colleges is fostering student self-actualization and prioritizing aiding students in achieving their educational and career goals (Kelsay & Zamani-Gallaher, 2014; Nevarez & Wood, 2010). Generally, institutions determine if there is evidence of student learning, determine the worth and impact of offerings, as well as whether outcomes have been achieved through institutional and program assessment practices.

Assessment is an integral part of higher education. Faculty and staff, as well as institutional research (IR) professionals, engage in routine assessment practices to improve instruction, programs and services, student learning (Banta & Palomba, 2015), and overall institutional effectiveness. The extensiveness of the higher education research literature on IR and assessment practices and approaches bears out the significance and relevance of postsecondary assessment. However, upon closer inspection, it is evident that the body of research literature, though expansive, (a) largely centers the 4-year institutional context, and (b) tends to be heavily focused on the assessment of students' in-class learning and learning outcomes (Schuh & Gansemer-Topf, 2010).

Higher education assessment experts have written about the necessity and importance of assessment in community colleges (Bresciani et al., 2014; Gardner et al., 2014; Nunley et al., 2011; Russell, 2016) and there is widespread consensus about the impact of high-quality student affairs programming and support services on student success (Astin, 1993; Pascarella & Terenzini, 2005; Schuh & Gansemer-Topf, 2010). In stark contrast to well developed, structured, and formalized assessments of academic programs in higher education, few postsecondary institutions establish and integrate institution-wide assessments of the out-of-class and cocurricular aspects of the collegiate experience; thus, few "engage in formal institutional measurement of student affairs and services effectiveness" (Lowry et al., 2018, p. 762). Unfortunately, research that explores the critical role of student affairs departments and practitioners at community colleges in the assessment of cocurricular or "out-of-class" student learning outcomes is still quite underdeveloped.

Explanations for this notable disparity are generally attributed to the unique and often complex challenges community colleges present for both IR professionals and academic and student affairs practitioners (Nunley et al., 2011). As previously noted, community colleges are largely open-access institutions that serve diverse student populations (e.g., racially/ethnically minoritized, low socioeconomic status, first-generation, adult learners, etc.) with a range of academic skill levels, educational backgrounds (Nunley et al., 2011), and goals and purposes for enrollment, and that provide postsecondary access and opportunities to "millions of Americans who otherwise would not have the opportunity to earn a degree" (Crisp et al., 2019, p. 1375). As institutions marked by multiple missions and the diverse student populations they have traditionally served, community colleges present both challenges and opportunities for learning outcomes assessments that are "distinctive to these institutions and the students they serve" (Nunley et al., 2011, p. 3).

Because of the multifaceted and complex community college milieu, we assert that it is imperative for community colleges to not only formalize and better integrate assessment practices and approaches institutionally; to advance equitable student outcomes and success, this assessment must be equity-minded and culturally responsive. Furthermore, we maintain that there is a prime opportunity for community colleges to make strides in the development and institutionalization of the assessment of students' out-of-class learning experiences and outcomes by encouraging and facilitating collaboration between IR professionals and student affairs practitioners that engages equity-minded and culturally responsive assessment methods to identify and address equity gaps in community college student affairs services and programs that impact students' learning outcomes and success.

Equitable Assessment in Community Colleges: IR + Assessment

The field of IR formally emerged in 1966 with the incorporation of the Association for Institutional Research (AIR), the largest professional organization for IR and assessment professionals (AIR, n.d.). AIR's mission is to "empower higher education professionals at all levels to utilize data, analytics, information, and evidence to make decisions and take actions that benefit students and institutions and improve higher education" (AIR, n.d., para. 7). In line with its mission, AIR designates five competencies core to the IR profession: (a) identification of information needs; (b) collection, analysis, interpretation, and reporting of data and information; (c) planning and evaluation; (d) service as stewards of data and information; and (e) education of information producers, users, and customers. Simply put, higher education IR and assessment professionals collect and analyze data to inform colleges and universities' decision-making and to promote institutional effectiveness and continuous improvement.

Since its inception, IR has become effectively integrated and institutionalized in most 4-year colleges and universities; today, IR is viewed as a primary aspect of higher education that serves an important and necessary institutional function. Despite the expansion and formalization of IR in higher education since the 1960s, it is only within the past 3 decades or so, and largely in response to increased federal and state calls for accountability, that community colleges have begun to institutionalize and utilize IR to a similar degree as 4-year institutions (Schulte, 2005, p. 2).

In fact, a study of 100 community colleges conducted in 2005 still found wide disparities in the presence and use of IR noting "impressive institutional-research offices and operations" at some community colleges but finding the "institutional-research capacity of community colleges" to be very "limited" in most cases (Morest & Bailey, 2005, para. 7–8). Moreover, the study found that nearly one-third of the community colleges that responded to the survey "had no position devoted to institutional research" and among those that did, many of the IR professionals often had additional responsibilities and "very few were heavily involved in assessment of teaching and learning" (para. 8) or had the time or resources to support or assist faculty or student affairs professionals to develop, conduct, or analyze their own assessments of student learning outcomes (Morest & Bailey, 2005). Though there has undoubtedly been some change over the past 15 years, it is still largely true that IR widely varies in the community college context based on differences in the size of the institution, availability of funding and other resources, and institutional priorities.

Higher education IR professionals typically conduct assessments designed to measure and meet broader institutional needs. These assessment professionals use data to conduct analysis for institutional benchmarking, to measure performance, and to meet the reporting requirements of governing bodies, accreditors, and state and federal governments. For example, annual enrollment projection is a function of many IR offices, and these projections inform budgetary planning for nearly every aspect of campus operations, including faculty and staff hiring, facilities management, and fundraising. Community college IR offices and professionals tend to focus on "enrollment management and related business functions of the college rather than measuring—much less analyzing—what determines student success" (Morest & Bailey, 2005, para. 9). Typically, community college IR offices are either not involved in the direct assessment of students' out-of-class learning outcomes or assessing students' out-of-class learning outcomes is a relatively low priority (Morest & Jenkins, 2007; Pickering & Sharpe, 2000).

Student Affairs Practitioners as Cocurricular Partners in Collegiate Learning

Student affairs, like IR, is also a critical component of higher education that serves an essential function. Student affairs departments administer and manage cocurricular activities and programs that support the academic and personal development of students. Whitt (2005) asserted that "the contribution of out-of-class experiences to student engagement cannot be overstated" (p. 1) and that institutions committed to prioritizing "student achievement, satisfaction, persistence, and learning . . . must have competent student affairs professionals whose contributions complement the academic mission of the institution in ways that help students and the institution realize their goals" (p. 1).

As higher education has evolved over the years, so has the student affairs profession. In the 1980s and 1990s, the profession was grounded in student development theories, many of which "were developed with a 'traditional' undergraduate student in mind—between the ages of eighteen and twenty-two years, usually white, and most frequently male" (Long, 2012, p. 5). However, as higher education institutions have become more diverse and largely responsible for educating more racial/ethnic students, women, LGBTQ, nontraditional/adult learners, and others, student affairs departments and professionals have had to adapt to address the specific needs and interests of multiple and various student populations. Nowhere in higher education is this adaptation and the need for culturally competent student affairs practitioners more apparent than in community colleges, which serve the most diverse postsecondary student bodies. Yamamura (2016) aptly highlighted a primary difference in student affairs in the 2- and 4-year context, noting that because of the diverse student populations community colleges serve most have "home-grown programs tailored to their unique student population and community. And if the community changes, the community college willingly adapts—unlike most 4-year institutions whose services and institutional structures remain the same no matter if their local community changes" (para. 5).

In contrast to assessments conducted by institutional researchers, the purpose of student affairs assessment is to measure students' out-of-class experiences (Lowry et al., 2018). Student affairs practitioners collect and analyze data to improve students' experiences and learning, as well as the programs and services they offer (Blimling, 2013). Student affairs personnel also use data to inform decision-making, but typically more to evaluate the student support services, programs, and interventions they offer and their impact on students' outcomes like retention and completion, and to identify and garner information about students' needs, experiences, insights, and attitudes—all in efforts to facilitate student success (Parnell et al., 2018; Pickering & Sharpe, 2000).

However, researchers (Blimling, 2013; Hoffman & Bresciani, 2010; Schuh & Gansemer-Topf, 2010; Schuh & Upcraft, 1998; Seagraves & Dean, 2010) have noted that often student affairs practitioners lack "adequate preparation or training in how to conduct meaningful assessment of student learning outside the classroom" (Russell, 2016, p. 3), yet are frequently expected by their institutions to develop and conduct assessments of student learning outcomes (Rodriguez & Frederick, 2014). While this is a conundrum for student affairs departments and personnel across higher education, it is especially challenging for community college student affairs departments and practitioners—who often not only need assessment training in general, but given their specific student populations and the types of supports they need, the importance, relevance, and necessity for equity-centered and culturally responsive assessment training in particular becomes even more critical for pursuing equitable student learning outcomes. Yamamura (2016) provided some insight into the existent training deficit among community college student affairs personnel, writing,

> Typically, many student affairs master's students are reluctant to take a course on community colleges . . . most students have had very little experience with this context . . . In addition, many students come in with deficit perspectives about community colleges since they have less knowledge or experience in this area. (para. 3)

A Call for Collaboration: Community College IR and Student Affairs in Partnership

While some IR departments do collaborate in formalized ways with student affairs departments and practitioners to assess the effectiveness of the various programming and services they offer, this type of collaboration does not typically occur at many community colleges where IR departments and personnel may be scant and/or students' out-of-class learning experiences and outcomes are not an assessment priority of the institution or within the purview of institutional researchers. Additionally, often higher education professionals fail to "recognize or seek out the expertise of other professionals on their campus" (Fuller, 2013, para. 2) and with respect to assessment specifically, "professional or disciplinary boundaries may prevent collaborations that would otherwise prove beneficial for autonomous units, the institution, and students" (Fuller, 2013, para. 2). Thus, we assert that community college IR professionals could and should fill this identified assessment knowledge and skills gap by collaborating with student affairs practitioners to coordinate and conduct equity-minded and culturally responsive assessments of student-centered programming and services, and students' out-of-class learning experiences and outcomes.

It is important and necessary that all assessments of student learning outcomes are equity-minded because if they fail to examine equity issues, they may also fail to accurately identify the very students who may stand to gain the most from assessment efforts (Montenegro & Jankowski, 2017). Therefore, it is imperative that equity is central to assessment efforts utilized by community college student affairs practitioners to identify gaps in students' participation and use of the services, programs, and interventions they develop, implement, and administer (Owens et al., 2017). Equity-centered assessments are not only critical for helping community college student affairs practitioners determine whether the support services and programs that they offer are effectively serving the students who need them most, but also their impact on reducing, or widening, equity gaps in student learning and outcomes. To best address equity gaps, entire institutions must "explore the combination of solutions and supports needed for students to be successful" (Montenegro & Jankowski, 2017, p. 5). Therefore, getting IR professionals more involved in supporting and assisting with community colleges' general assessment of learning outcomes could be especially beneficial for student affairs practitioners as they strive to develop and conduct effective equity-minded and culturally responsive assessments of students' out-of-class and cocurricular learning experiences and outcomes.

Equity-Minded Assessment

The term "equity-mindedness" (Bensimon & Malcolm, 2012; Dowd & Bensimon, 2015) is a very useful concept for imagining the role that IR professionals can play in broad institutional assessment efforts, as well as more specific unit level (e.g., student affairs) assessment efforts, especially those aimed at fostering racial equity through the identification and reduction of racialized equity gaps. Dowd and Bensimon (2015) defined equity-mindedness as being: (a) color-conscious in a positive sense; (b) aware that race-neutral knowledge, beliefs, and practices can disadvantage racially minoritized students, even without being overtly racist; (c) accountable for eliminating racial inequities through changes in practice; and (d) aware that the root of racial disparities may exist in institutional norms and practices that perpetuate unequal outcomes. Dowd and Bensimon (2015) also noted the potentially significant role of institutional researchers in facilitating the data-informed learning necessary for equity-minded practice. Therefore, we envision IR professionals as ideal facilitators of the equity-minded assessment likely to lead to organizational learning about the state of equity at community colleges broadly, and in student affairs departments and units specifically.

IR professionals are uniquely positioned to guide equity-minded assessment for several reasons, including their analytical acuity and proximity to institutional data as well as their ability to leverage IR-specific tools to assess racialized barriers to equitable student success. Also, as community college IR professionals work with their student affairs colleagues to conduct assessments, those who are equity-minded are well equipped to assist with incorporating measures of racial equity into assessment tools and metrics and provide guidance for equity-minded, unit-level assessments of student affairs programs and services.

As leaders capable of shaping assessment-related policy and practice, equity-minded institutional researchers can and should lead the much-needed institutionalization of equity-enhancing assessment practices in community colleges generally and student affairs departments specifically by facilitating opportunities for critical inquiry and collaborative, action-oriented assessment. These professionals have the unique ability to build broad awareness of racial inequities and can leverage their resources, skills, and positionalities to actualize the race-conscious approaches to assessment necessary to enhance equity in community colleges (Dowd et al., 2012).

Fostering Culturally Responsive Assessment

Culturally responsive assessment (CRA) also has a critical role to play in this endeavor as it is an inherently equity-minded assessment approach that instead of reinforcing "notions of neutrality, sameness and objectivity, which hinder potential for transforming inequitable policies, procedures, and outcomes" purposefully and intentionally attends to "the differences between groups and seeks to remedy underlying systemic inequities that produce differential outcomes" (Heiser et al., 2017, p. 4). More specifically, CRA is cognizant of the varied and diverse student populations that institutions serve and is not only mindful of these differences, but in fact uses them to inform the development of appropriate learning outcomes and assessment tools to effectively improve student learning outcomes (Montenegro & Jankowski, 2017). Because CRA is an inherently equity-centered approach with a keen focus on improving and achieving success for all students, while also being mindful of students' many differences—especially racial/ethnic and cultural differences—it is a particularly well-suited assessment approach to measure how community college student affairs programming and practices "affect change, benefit students, and promote completion" (Lowry et al., 2018, p. 763) among the diverse student populations they serve.

CRA is strongly data driven and necessitates using data, more specifically disaggregated data, to inform decision-making. Therefore, collaborations between IR professionals and student affairs practitioners to develop and conduct equity-minded assessments should prioritize the usage of CRA methods when collecting and analyzing data to measure various student populations' engagement with and use of support services and programs. Moreover, appropriately disaggregating data would allow student affairs practitioners to identify inequities and possibly any unintended consequences of the supports they offer that may have disproportionate impacts for specific student populations, especially those that are already marginalized.

However, failing to disaggregate data in culturally responsive ways can result in significant consequences not only for assessment findings and interpretations, but ultimately for student experiences and learning outcomes, especially for student populations with diverse and distinct needs and experiences (Dowd & Bensimon, 2015; Goldrick-Rab & Cook, 2011; Montenegro & Jankowski, 2017). More specifically, neglecting to appropriately disaggregate data can result in failing to identify disparities in outcomes or usage of cocurricular programs and experiences by certain groups like women, LGBTQ students, or first-generation students for whom a program may be specifically intended to benefit. Thus, it is important that community college student affairs practitioners are able to properly analyze and interpret data in equity-minded and culturally responsive ways in order to positively impact students' collegiate experiences and also to inform the development of solutions to address inequities in student learning outcomes. Collaborating with skilled equity-minded and culturally responsive IR professionals is critical to these efforts.

It is important to note, however, that equity-minded assessment is much more than just disaggregating data and equity-minded institutional researchers are more than mere data analysts. They can and should serve as outward-facing facilitators of discourse and action around college-specific issues of race and institutional racism (Dowd et al., 2012). To do this, they must possess certain competencies like being racially literate (Guinier, 2004), able to critically engage with their colleagues and senior administrators, and willing to be change agents. Having these competencies and utilizing them effectively positions equity-minded IR professionals to be excellent collaborators with community college student affairs practitioners who can serve as guides and provide knowledge-based assistance for conducting equitable and culturally responsive assessments of students' out-of-class learning experiences and outcomes.

Moreover, CRA requires transparency and thus when community college student affairs practitioners commit to using equity-minded and culturally responsive assessment methods, they are in effect committing to sharing the findings of their assessments in efforts to foster, promote, and contribute to institution-wide collaborative efforts to advance equitable student learning outcomes and student success. This type of collaboration with other campus departments, units, faculty, and staff, such as IR professionals, is important for connecting specific assessments to the institution's larger assessment strategy and helps get the larger campus community involved in identifying equity gaps in student learning outcomes across the institution, and subsequently more involved in devising solutions and supports for fostering and promoting student success. Being transparent about the findings that result from CRAs not only helps inform how to improve student supports but sharing those findings with others across the institution can also be instrumental for improving larger institutional policies and processes that impact achieving equitable student learning outcomes among diverse student groups.

The markers of CRA as overtly student-focused, data driven and data-informed, and transparent make it a particularly useful method for community college student affairs practitioners to engage to conduct assessments that measure and directly impact the needs and learning outcomes of their diverse student populations. Because CRA is student-focused and explicitly necessitates "keeping students at the center" (Montenegro & Jankowski, 2017, p. 9) it can be an especially valuable and effective assessment approach for community college student affairs practitioners in particular as they must always be aware and mindful of student differences in order to best accommodate and improve learning outcomes for the various student groups they serve, especially those on the margins of higher education. Engaging student-focused methods like interviews and focus groups to capture student perspectives about their out-of-class needs and experiences not only helps student affairs practitioners better determine whether support programs and services are working as intended, but also whether they are having an equitable impact on student learning outcomes, by benefiting the particular student groups for whom they were designed to serve and who need them most. Utilizing CRA offers community college student affairs practitioners the ability to conduct assessments that help ensure they are providing the specific and appropriate services to meet diverse students' various needs (whether they be cultural, linguistic, economic, etc.) and ultimately "to improve the cocurricular experiences for students who use the programs and services" (Wawrzynski et al., 2015, p. 122).

Ultimately, formalized and intentional collaboration between equity-minded student affairs practitioners and IR professionals who ground their assessment practices in the tenets, tools, and methods of CRA, thereby embedding equity directly into the assessments they utilize, not only helps institutions better measure and understand the impact of the various student support services offered, but also ensures that they are serving their diverse student populations as intended, as well as equitably. Collaboration between community college student affairs practitioners and IR professionals to conduct equity-minded, culturally responsive assessments to improve both institutional performance in service of students and students learning outcomes is not only ideal, but is much needed and should be strongly encouraged, if not required, at community colleges.

We call for an increased focus on assessment in community colleges that is equity-minded and encourages collaboration between IR offices and professionals and student affairs practitioners and personnel. It is not uncommon for practitioners to confuse equity-mindedness with producing equitable student learning experiences. While employing an equity lens is essential, it is through the intentional application of CRA practices and approaches to addressing equity gaps that can result in improved outcomes for diverse student populations served by community colleges. While there are examples of collaborative efforts to build student affairs assessment capacity in community colleges like those detailed in the work of Lowry et al. (2018), they do not specifically call for collaboration between IR professionals and student affairs practitioners, nor do they explicitly focus on conducting equity-minded and culturally responsive assessment to impact equitable student learning outcomes among community college students. Given the diverse array of educational and career goals of community college attendees, student affairs practitioners must be able to assess the student outcomes for participation in a variety of internships, apprenticeships, and workforce development programs and a host of other cocurricular and nonacademic programs and services that they offer. It is important that collaborative efforts between IR professionals and student affairs practitioners are equity-minded and culturally responsive not only to better understand whether and how the various types of support services that community college students engage and utilize actually impact students' educational and career or workforce goals, but also whether they are advancing equitable student learning outcomes and success.

References

Association for Institutional Research. (n.d.). *Vision and mission.* https://www.airweb.org

Astin, A. W. (1993). *Assessment for excellence: The philosophy and practice of assessment and evaluation in higher education.* Oryx Press.

Banta, T., & Palomba, C. (2015). *Assessment essentials: Planning, implementing, and improving assessment in higher education* (2nd ed.). Jossey-Bass.

Bensimon, E. M., & Malcom, L. E. (Eds.). (2012). *Confronting equity issues on campus: Implementing the equity scorecard in theory and practice.* Stylus.

Blimling, G. S. (2013). Challenges of assessment in student affairs. In J. H. Schuh (Ed.), *Selected Contemporary Assessment Issues* (New Directions for Student Services, no. 142, pp. 5–14). Jossey-Bass. https://doi.org/10.1002/ss.20044

Bresciani, M. J., Hoffman, J. L., Baker, J., & Barnes, J. (2014). Looking ahead: Moving toward a more holistic approach to assessment. In M. M. Gardner, K. A. Kline, & M. J. Bresciani (Eds.), *Assessing student learning in the community and two-year college: Successful strategies and tools developed by practitioners in student and academic affairs* (pp. 154–171). Stylus.

Crisp, G., Horn, C. L., Kuczynski, M., Zhou, Q., & Cook, E. (2019). Describing and differentiating four-year broad access institutions: An empirical typology.

The Review of Higher Education, 42(4), 1373–1400. https://doi.org/10.1352/rhe.2019.0069

Dowd, A. C., & Bensimon, E. M. (2015). *Engaging the "race question": Accountability and equity in U.S. higher education.* Teachers College at Columbia University.

Dowd, A. C., Malcom, L. E., Nakamoto, J., & Bensimon, E. M. (2012). Institutional researchers as teachers and equity advocates. In E. M. Bensimon & L. E. Malcom (Eds.), *Confronting equity issues on campus: Implementing the Equity Scorecard in theory and practice* (pp. 191–215). Stylus.

Fuller, M. B. (2013). *Student affairs staff support, resistance, or indifference to assessment.* American College Personnel Association (ACPA). https://www.myacpa.org/article/student-affairs-staff-support-resistance-or-indifference-assessment

Gardner, M. M., Kline, K. A., & Bresciani, M. J. (Eds.). (2014). *Assessing student learning in the community and two-year college: Successful strategies and tools developed by practitioners in student and academic affairs.* Stylus.

Goldrick-Rab, S., & Cook, M. A. E. (2011). College students in changing contexts. In P. G. Altbach, P. J. Gumport, & R. O. Berdahl (Eds.), *American higher education in the twenty-first century: Social, political, and economic challenges* (3rd ed., pp. 254–278). The Johns Hopkins University Press.

Guinier, L. (2004). From racial liberalism to racial literacy: *Brown v. Board of Education* and the interest-divergence dilemma. *Journal of American History, 91*(1), 92–118. https://doi.org/10.2307/3659616

Heiser, C. A., Prince, K., & Levy, J. D. (2017). Examining critical theory as a framework to advance equity through student affairs assessment. *Journal of Student Affairs Inquiry, 3*(1), 1–18. https://drive.google.com/file/d/1ksQstiXwP51Edipg dylU7nvdenVpIJA-/view

Hoffman, J. L., & Bresciani, M. J. (2010). Assessment work: Examining the prevalence and nature of assessment competencies and skills in student affairs job postings. *Journal of Student Affairs Research and Practice, 47*(4), 495–512. https://doi.org/10.2202/1949-6605.6082

Kelsay, L. S., & Zamani-Gallaher, E. M. (Eds.). (2014). *Working with students in community colleges: Contemporary strategies for bridging theory, research, and practice.* Stylus.

Long, D. (2012). The foundations of student affairs: A guide to the profession. In L. J. Hinchliffe & M. A. Wong (Eds.), *Environments for student growth and development: Librarians and student affairs in collaboration* (pp. 1–39). Association of College & Research Libraries.

Lowry, K., Horton, D. W., & Royster, K. S. (2018). Building student affairs assessment capacity: Lessons from two community colleges. *Community College Journal of Research and Practice, 42*(11), 762–769. https://doi.org/10.1080/10668926.2018.1444521

Montenegro, E., & Jankowski, N. (2017). *Equity and assessment: Moving towards culturally responsive assessment* (Occasional Paper No. 29). University of Illinois and Indiana University, National Institute for Learning Outcomes Assessment.

Morest, V. S., & Bailey, T. (2005, October 28). Institutional research: Both practical and vital. *The Chronicle of Higher Education.* https://www.chronicle.com/article/institutional-research-both-practical-and-vital/?cid2=gen_login_refresh

Morest, V. S., & Jenkins, D. (2007). *Institutional research and the culture of evidence at community colleges* (Report No. 1 in the Culture of Evidence Series). Center for Community College Research Center. https://ccrc.tc.columbia.edu/media/k2/attachments/insitutional-research-culture-evidence.pdf

Nevarez, C., & Wood, J. L. (2010). *Community college leadership and administration: Theory, practice, and change.* Peter Lang.

Nunley, C., Bers, T., & Manning, T. (2011). *Learning outcomes assessment in community colleges* (Occasional Paper No. 10). University of Illinois and Indiana University, National Institute for Learning Outcomes Assessment. https://www.learningoutcomesassessment.org/documents/CommunityCollege.pdf

Owens, D. R., Thrill, C. R., & Rockey, M. (2017). Equity and student services. *Office of Community College Research and Leadership Feature Brief, 3*(2), 1–8. https://occrl.illinois.edu/docs/librariesProvider4/student-services/equity-and-student-services.pdf

Parnell, A., Jones, D., Wesaw, A., & Brooks, D. C. (2018). *Institutions' use of data and analytics for student success: Results from a national landscape analysis.* NASPA–Student Affairs Administrators in Higher Education, the Association for Institutional Research, and EDUCAUSE. https://www.naspa.org/images/uploads/main/data2018_download.pdf

Pascarella, E. T., & Terenzini, P. T. (2005). *How college affects students: A third decade of research.* Wiley.

Pickering, J. W., & Sharpe, M. S. (2000). Slicing the pie: Institutional research, assessment, and student affairs research. In J. W. Pickering & G. R. Hanson (Eds.), *Collaboration between student affairs and institutional researchers to improve institutional effectiveness* (pp. 79–90). Jossey-Bass. https://doi.org/10.1002/ir.10806

Rodriguez, B. J., & Frederick, J. (2014). Developing shared learning outcomes and determining priorities for assessment. In M. M. Gardner, K. A. Kline, & M. J. Bresciani (Eds.), *Assessing student learning in the community and two-year college: Successful strategies and tools developed by practitioners in student and academic affairs* (pp. 39–51). Stylus.

Russell, T. L. (2016). *Advancing evaluation in community colleges: A mixed methods case study of outcomes-based assessment training in student affairs* [Doctoral dissertation, Western Michigan University]. ScholarWorks. https://scholarworks.wmich.edu/dissertations/2462

Schuh, J. H., & Gansemer-Topf, A. M. (2010). *The role of student affairs in student learning assessment* (NILOA Occasional Paper No. 7). University of Illinois and Indiana University, National Institute for Learning Outcomes Assessment. http://www.learningoutcomesassessment.org/documents/StudentAffairsRole.pdf

Schuh, J. H., & Upcraft, L. M. (1998). Facts and myths about assessment in student affairs. *About Campus, 3*(5), 2–8. https://doi.org/10.1177%2F108648229800300502

Schulte, R. C. (2005). *An investigation of institutional research in Tennessee community colleges: Functions, technology use, and impact on decision-making by college Presidents* [Doctoral dissertation, University of Tennessee]. TRACE. https://trace.tennessee.edu/utk_graddiss/2291

Seagraves, B., & Dean, L. A. (2010). Conditions supporting a culture of assessment in student affairs divisions at small colleges and universities. *Journal of Student Affairs Research and Practice, 47*(3), 307–324. https://doi.org/10.2202/1949-6605.6073

Wawrzynski, M. R., Brock, A., & Sweeney, A. (2015). Assessment in student affairs practice. In M. J. Amey & L. M. Reesor (Eds.), *Beginning your journey: A guide for new professionals in student affairs* (4th ed., pp. 121–141). NASPA.

Whitt, E. J. (2005). *Promoting student success: What student affairs can do* (Occasional Paper No. 5). Indiana University, Center for Postsecondary Research. https://files.eric.ed.gov/fulltext/ED506531.pdf

Yamamura, E. K. (2016, April 11). *Preparing professionals who advance educational equity: Exploring the importance of the community college student affairs context.* NASPA. https://www.naspa.org/blog/exploring-the-importance-of-the-community-college-student-affairs-context

16

CULTURAL AWARENESS AND PRAXIS

The Aesthetics of Teaching and Learning at HBCUs

Verna F. Orr

During a hearing of oral arguments for the case *Fisher v. University of Texas at Austin* (2016), to decide whether race-conscious admissions should be upheld at Texas's flagship university, U.S. Supreme Court Justice Antonin Scalia cited:

> There are those who contend that it does not benefit African Americans to get them into the University of Texas where they do not do well, as opposed to having them go to a less-advanced school—a slower track school where they do well . . . one of the briefs pointed out that most of the Black scientists in this country don't come from schools like the University of Texas . . . they come from lesser schools where they do not feel that they're being pushed ahead in classes that are too fast for them. (p. 67)

According to a report from the Council of Graduate Schools (Sowell et al., 2015), 17 of the 21 schools producing the largest numbers of Black students who go on to earn science doctorates are historically Black colleges and universities (HBCUs). These "less-advanced" and "slower track" schools, at one point in history, were the only higher education option available to the vast majority of Black Americans prior to *Brown v. Board of Education* of 1954 and the Civil Rights Act of 1964.

Historically, HBCUs have suffered the conundrum of Justice Scalia's (and many others') ill-informed conclusion about organizational cultural competence in teaching and learning opportunities at their campuses.

Unfortunately, the words of the late Justice Scalia resonate across the literature with the major contributions of HBCUs being limited to and measured by Western, European ideals (Nahal et al., 2015; Orr, 2018). This effect has shifted the conversation from HBCUs being producers of knowledge to consumers of the same. Notwithstanding these factors, HBCUs intentionally position student learning at the core of their educational values and missions (Favors, 2019; Nahal et al., 2015; Wooten, 2015). Additionally, HBCUs' strength, defining what makes them successful, is their culturally relevant assessment practices (Montenegro & Jankowski, 2017), but how have they communicated their success stories? More specifically, what can HBCUs teach the higher education community, specifically assessment scholars and practitioners, about creativity, innovation, transformation, and equitable assessment approaches, strategies, and competencies?

This chapter highlights organizational cultural competence and teaching and learning experiences at HBCUs. This chapter was not written to provide answers to questions such as what cultural competence is and how it is infused at HBCUs. Instead, it should be read more as an assignment to activate thinking on the future of diverse learning experiences and strategies for increasing organizational cultural competency in higher education. First, it is important to state that the author is a graduate of an HBCU and a predominantly White institution (PWI). Second, throughout this chapter, HBCUs will be centered. Moreover, a brief overview of the founding and historical significance of HBCUs will be highlighted. Third, assessment will be defined and an overview on the history of assessment operationalized with a focus on unique teaching and learning trends standard across HBCU campuses will provide context. Fourth, and finally, with equity being a crucial consideration in assessment work that is underemphasized in the research and data, examples are provided of equitable assessment operationalized at HBCUs via the HBCU Collaborative for Excellence in Educational Quality Assurance (HBCU-CEEQA), a professional learning collaborative of HBCU assessment and institutional effectiveness leaders.

Centering Historically Black Colleges and Universities

Increasing organizational cultural competency begins with reflection—who we are, why we do this work, and for whom we serve is vital. The following section centers HBCUs and provides reflections—the who and the why. Guided by a brief historical lens, I unpack assumptions about teaching and learning experiences at HBCUs and highlight cultural competencies that are synonymous with the HBCU experience (Anderson, 1988; Nahal et al.,

2015; Wooten, 2015). First, the Higher Education Act of 1965 describes an HBCU as any Black college that was established prior to 1964, whose mission is the education of Black Americans (Higher Education Act, 1965).

In addition to the constraints highlighted in the formal definition, over the years, and through many iterations of rigor and relevancy, HBCUs are considered among the nation's most storied and indispensable institutions having contributed significantly to the production of the world's Black professional, intellectual, artistic, and entrepreneurial leaders (Anderson, 1988; Favors, 2019; Nahal et al., 2015; Ricard & Brown, 2008). They address indicators of the educational, economic, political, housing, and health condition of the Black community and beyond. The Black place-making contributions of HBCUs have been the strategic response to the challenges and opportunities before the Black community.

Race, Racism, and the Establishment of HBCUs

Almost all HBCUs were founded by northern missionary organizations for the stated purpose of providing educational opportunity for Black people in the post-Civil War era (Anderson, 1988). At the close of the war, literacy rates among Black Americans were horribly low due to a ban against slaves learning to read: The south, having recently lost the Civil War, did not look favorably upon the prospect of free and educated Blacks. Furthermore, most Black people owned no property having been prohibited from ownership by the restrictions of slavery. Accordingly, philanthropic support for these organizations was crucial for the early institutions, and with few alternative sources of support for early HBCUs, White northern philanthropists and the federal government filled this need (Anderson, 1988).

Though philanthropy, as a factor in education for Blacks, dates to the very origins of virtually all HBCUs, this has not been without a degree of controversy (Anderson, 1988; Andrews et al., 2016; Bonner, 2001; Ricard & Brown, 2008). Historically, there have been two opposing perspectives regarding the role of philanthropy: On one hand, philanthropy has been touted as evidence of the nation's coming to terms with its legacy of slavery and an attempt to make amends with former slaves. On the other hand, there also exists the historical perspective that White philanthropists intended the donations as a subversive means of maintaining social control and subjugation of Blacks—some scholars have asserted that philanthropy has been used to perpetuate racial inequality and societal stratification (Anderson, 1988; Bonner, 2001; Ricard & Brown, 2008; Willie, 1981). With few alternatives, Blacks flocked to these schools during the late 1800s despite a deep-seated distrust of the motives of the institutions' funders.

Lincoln University, established in Pennsylvania in 1854, and Wilberforce University, established in Ohio in 1856, were the first private colleges established for the education of Blacks prior to the American Civil War (Anderson, 1988; Brown & Freeman, 2002; Willie, 1981). Modeled after the classical colonial postsecondary institutions, HBCUs such as Fisk, Howard, Lincoln, and Wilberforce were established to provide classics-related education for African Americans at the end of the 19th century (Willie, 1981). However, it also was during the years leading up to the Civil War that abolitionist agitation calling for the end of slavery originated from the few traditionally White, liberal institutions of higher education such as Oberlin (Ohio) and Bowdoin (Maine) universities, which allowed the enrollment of African American students (Anderson, 1988). Meanwhile, as the early HBCUs were growing in popularity in the mid-Atlantic states, access to education for African Americans in the south remained extremely limited due to the segregation laws instituted there (Anderson, 1988).

The Impact of the Morrill Land-Grant Acts on Blacks' Participation in Postsecondary Education

One of the first pieces of federal legislation designed to increase the opportunities and offerings of postsecondary institutions in the United States was the Morrill Land Grant of 1862. The legislation was passed by Congress to offer more practical educational opportunities for U.S. citizens in fields such as agriculture, mechanical arts, and home economics, which were perceived as advancing the nation's productivity. Conversely, the land "grant" was created to educate children of the industrial class as opposed to the focus on theoretical or religious studies of the earlier, more established colonial institutions. The 1862 Morrill Act granted each state a minimum of 30,000 acres of federal land with the stipulation that the income from the rent or sale of those lands must be used to establish land-grant colleges or universities (Anderson, 1988). A total six million acres of federal land was donated to the states. Rather than educating for the sake of educating, the original Morrill legislation shifted the focus of higher education from classical and theological studies to scientific and liberal arts-type studies. The resulting land-grant institutions became the multipurpose, publicly funded, state institutions of higher education that continue to enroll hundreds of thousands of students from all segments of society today.

Opposition to the education of Blacks grew even amid the political climate that fostered Congress's passage of the 1862 Morrill Act (Anderson, 1988; Willie, 1981). In 1890, Congress enacted a second Morrill Act, which increased the endowment of land to the original land-grant but forbade federal monies from being given to any state college or university with an admissions policy that discriminated against Blacks unless a separate facility for Blacks existed nearby (Anderson, 1988). The second Morrill Act was designed to address the former confederate states' refusal to admit Blacks to the institutions established under the first Morrill Act (Anderson, 1988). These states' "separate but equal" land-grant institutions for Blacks became known as the "1890s" schools. Unlike the original Morrill Act, the 1890 Act granted cash instead of land; however, colleges established under the second Morrill Act hold the same land-grant college designation as the 1862 Act's colleges. Among the 70 colleges and universities that eventually evolved from the original Morrill Act, 17 of today's modern HBCUs were established through the second Morrill Act.

The passing of the 1890 Morrill Act was an opportunity to elevate the standing of Blacks in U.S. society through participation in higher education, but there were many different views about the focus and purpose of an HBCU education (Anderson, 1988). Mirroring the earlier 19th century arguments surrounding classical or theological versus agricultural or applied education, early 20th century Black leaders debated the focus and mission of HBCUs. One notable and early leader in the education of Blacks, Booker T. Washington, argued that HBCUs should focus on teaching Blacks skilled trades and vocations (Anderson, 1988). Washington, born enslaved in rural southwestern Virginia, worked his way through Hampton Normal and Agricultural Institute (now Hampton University) and later founded Alabama's Tuskegee Normal School for Colored Teachers (later renamed the Tuskegee Institute, now Tuskegee University). His contemporary, W.E.B. DuBois, the first Black to earn a doctorate from Harvard University, advocated that HBCUs should emphasize education in the arts and classics to cultivate the African American leaders and teachers of the next generation to uplift the race (Anderson, 1988). Despite these conflicting ideologies, America's HBCUs continued to embrace the notion of service and the goal of training the future leaders of the Black community.

HBCUs played significant roles in both exposing and removing barriers based on race, gender, and class in U.S. higher education. Conversely, given that the number of HBCUs is less than 3% of the total number of higher education institutions in the United States and their average institutional endowment is a fraction of the average endowment nationally, HBCUs have provided service to society above and beyond their means (Gallup, 2015; Ricard & Brown, 2008). In fact, as the only higher education option available to the vast majority of African Americans prior to *Brown v. Board of Education* of 1954 and the Civil Rights Act of 1964, HBCUs have been credited with significantly increasing, if not creating, the Black middle class.

HBCU Alumni at Work and in the Community, a recent study by Gallup-USA Funds, revealed that Black graduates of HBCUs are more likely than Black graduates of other colleges to strongly agree that they had the support and experiential learning opportunities in college that Gallup finds are strongly related to a graduate's well-being later in life (Gallup, 2015). Researchers were interested in learning about the relationship between students' college experiences and life outcomes in areas such as employment and well-being, and if there is a relationship among graduates of different racial and ethnic backgrounds. Results identify areas in which graduates of HBCUs are thriving, and areas to which other higher education institutions need to pay extra attention. For instance, Black graduates of HBCUs are more than twice as likely as Black graduates of non-HBCUs to recall experiencing all three support measures that Gallup tracked: (a) they had at least one professor who made them excited about learning, (b) the professors cared about them as people, and (c) they had a mentor who encouraged them to pursue their goals and dreams. These practices which have often been labeled as "innovative" experiences at predominately White institutions (PWIs) and are presented in numerous outlets as providing new and groundbreaking advances—in access, retention, and preparation of underrepresented students, specifically, Black students—in the face of economic, political, and social changes and challenges have already been in progress at HBCUs.

And, despite historical and present challenges—resource inequities, funding disparities, student learning differences, and the relevancy question of 21st-century HBCUs—Black graduates of HBCUs are more likely to be thriving in purpose and financial well-being than Black graduates who did not receive their degrees from HBCUs (Gallup, 2015). HBCUs are vital in the American economy. They create more jobs, stronger families, and stronger communities (Cheek, 1972; Gallup, 2015). It is this economic strength stemming from said jobs which is credited with creating and maintaining the Black middle class (Brown & Freeman, 2004; Humphreys, 2017).

It is noteworthy to state that HBCUs have and continue to serve large populations of underrepresented, low-income, first-generation students as well as students of color (Nahal et al., 2015), while being severely underfunded (Anderson, 1988; Toldson, 2016; Wooten, 2015). It is important to note, too, that while HBCUs were founded to provide educational opportunities for Black Americans—a traditionally underrepresented population in higher education—they are not monolithic: HBCUs include 2- and 4-year, public and private, land-grant, and religious institutions whose endowments range from a high of approximately $700 million to a little under $1 million. Their student body populations range from approximately 300 to almost

12,000 (Williams et al., 2020). HBCUs are indeed culturally diverse institutions that share an unwavering commitment to their missions while providing unique learning experiences that have sustained and positively impacted the Black experience in America and beyond.

An Overview of Assessment

Assessment has a broad reach regarding understanding and definition. Ratcliff (1996) defines assessment as the process of defining, selecting, designing, collecting, analyzing, interpreting, and using information to increase students' learning and development (p. 5). Banta and Associates (2002) define assessment as a systematic collection, review, and use of information about educational programs undertaken for the purpose of improving student learning and development. The Higher Learning Commission (HLC)—an organization tasked with regional accreditation responsibilities for postsecondary education—previously defined assessment as

> a participatory, iterative process that provides data institutions need on their students' learning, engages the college and others in analyzing and using that information to confirm and improve teaching and learning, produces evidence that students are learning the outcomes the institution intended, guides colleges in making educational and institutional improvements, evaluates whether changes made improve or impact student learning, and documents the learning and institutional efforts. (NILOA, 2019, p. 1)

And, according to Ewell (2009):

> the most established definition [has its roots in the mastery-learning tradition], where assessment referred to the process used to determine an individual's mastery of complex abilities . . . adherents of this tradition emphasized development over time and continuous feedback on individual performance, symbolized by the etymological roots of the word assessment in the Latin ad + sedere, "to sit beside." (p. 9)

According to Ratcliff (1996), outstanding assessment practices are embedded in institutional culture, make good use of current technology in the methods and tools to track outcomes, include extensive use of faculty and strong faculty support, are supported by institutional leadership, and involve approaches to outcomes that can be replicated. Contextually, in

U.S. higher education institutions, assessment deals with courses, programs, policies, procedures, and operations. Assessment is an effective way to know what institutions are doing and includes the skills, knowledge, and dispositions a graduate should have. Assessment gives institutions a better understanding of what students are getting from their programs and experiences. But which students?

Early assessment-related studies and practices center on experiences and intellectual development of "traditional" college students—18–22-year-olds who enrolled directly after high school, attended full-time, lived on campus, and never had major work-life responsibilities (Ewell, 2002; Gilbert, 2015). This previous research virtually excludes "nontraditional" students (25-year-old+, women, African Americans, veterans, etc.) who now make up the student majority (Lumina Foundation, 2019). In haste to stay relevant and ready to meet the needs of this shift in student demographics, higher education leaders are beginning to consider questions like, how do we support all our students, and how will we strengthen and secure the long-term future of our campus? How are we enabling an environment in which all our students are learning as opposed to some students of a certain type? On the other end of the spectrum, HBCUs have a historic mission of educating Black Americans while being open to all students, no matter their differences, and were founded to contest the general practice of exclusion in higher education based on discriminatory policies that directly or indirectly kept many from having access to education.

Assessment Operationalized at HBCUs: Beyond the Reach of Outsiders

The culture of HBCUs can best be characterized as one of caring, one that builds confidence, and one that equips students with the requisite knowledge and skills needed to make an immediate contribution to the global environment. Culture reflects the way people give priorities to goals, how they behave in different situations, and how they cope with their world and with one another. According to Jackson-Hammond (2020), "students graduating from HBCUs develop the cultural identity of the institution, which includes personal resourcefulness; quality performance; continuously improving; and the characteristic attributes of determination and perseverance" (p. 2). Culture is transmitted from generation to generation. Likewise, culture and traditions at HBCUs are deeply rooted in the consciousness of their leaders, faculty, staff, and students.

Cultural competence is not a state at which one arrives; rather it is a process of learning, unlearning, and relearning. It is a sensibility cultivated throughout a lifetime. Cultural competence requires awareness of self, reflection on one's own cultural position, awareness of others' positions, and the ability to interact genuinely and respectfully with others. (American Evaluation Association, 2011, p. 3)

HBCUs are saturated with a community of culturally diverse scholars dedicated to building on rich histories and legacies in ways that speak to quality assurance and diverse student learning experiences. The historic and contemporary approaches practiced at HBCUs frame assessment activities on improving teaching and learning, supported by ongoing processes designed to engage and support student success. More than 80 years ago, W.E.B. DuBois (1935) wrote, *Does the Negro Need Separate Schools?* in which he asserted:

> The proper education of any people includes sympathetic touch between teacher and pupil; knowledge on the part of the teacher, not simply of the individual taught, but of his surroundings and background, and the history of his class and group; such contact between teacher and pupil, on the basis of perfect social equality, as will increase this sympathy and knowledge . . . and the promotion of such extracurricular activities as will tend to induct the child into life. (p. 328)

Similarly, in April 2017, Dillard University President Walter Kimbrough wrote, "while Black students have been admitted to some of these 'better' schools, they have not been accepted." He goes on to state: "on these campuses where they [Black students] pay to attend, they simply occupy space without fully accessing the resources that space provides" (para. 7). Both DuBois and Kimbrough assert that the manifestation of schools cannot take the place of an education with DuBois going on to say "to my mind it is clear . . . they [separate schools] are needed just so far as they are necessary for the proper education of the Negro race" (p. 328).

More recently, Jelani Favors (2019) in *Shelter in a Time of Storm* asserts:

> Beyond the written course of study, at Black colleges, an unwritten second curriculum thrived. This second curriculum defined the bond between teacher and student, inspiring youths to develop a "linked sense of fate" with the race. This second curriculum was a pedagogy of hope grounded in idealism, race consciousness, and cultural nationalism. More importantly, within the noncollapsible space of Black colleges, this instruction and mentoring was beyond the reach of outsiders. Emerging from the

teacher–student relationship, the second curriculum was shielded from the hostilities of whites who, despite their best efforts, remained unaware of how fruitful this association would eventually become. Thus, the second curriculum formed the heartbeat of the Black college communitas. (p. 10)

According to the American Evaluation Association (2011), "cultural competence is an ethical imperative" (p. 4). HBCUs have mastered and practiced cultural competency before it was even a term: They are committed to their mission of providing access and a quality higher education learning experience to underrepresented people, specifically Black people, and create institutional cultures for meaningful assessment and use innovative assessment practices that support student success. In doing so, expressions of student learning subsequently transpire in different ways. For example, HBCU faculty and staff members intentionally collaborate with professionals across disciplines to collect, analyze, and use data to improve. They also strive to strike a balance between accountability, transparency, and meaningful learning experiences.

Moreover, HBCU faculty and staff understand that there are reports to be composed and submitted to be utilized by stakeholders at the university, state, regional, national, and international levels, however, accountability to their students is priority, and does not necessarily supersede institutional compliance mandates. HBCUs move students beyond their comfort levels into real possibilities and do not solely focus on accountability because in doing so, they lose the opportunity to focus on meaningful learning opportunities. Student success tends to bolster, seemingly because of the teaching and learning experiences and various opportunities for students to explore and collaborate with faculty and staff on a deeper level.

Again, HBCUs have historically successfully matriculated and graduated culturally diverse student populations. For example, the First-Year Experience Program at Florida A&M University (FAMU) has seen a growth in the number of first-generation students who have a cumulative GPA of 2.5 and above (Reneau & Howse, 2019). They attribute this to the socialization and integration of students and their introduction into the community which help them understand what it means to be a student at FAMU, *atop the highest of Tallahassee's seven hills*. Additionally, FAMU implemented living learning communities and summer bridge programs that were designed to provide their culturally diverse and differently prepared students—who may not have the requisite knowledge and skills to come in and hit the ground running—an opportunity to flourish, together. These programs are an example of how HBCUs fill the gap and speak to their holistic assessment approaches that consider the needs of all their students (Williams et al., 2020).

Another demonstration of HBCU assessment approaches that takes various needs of different student populations into consideration is Morehouse School of Medicine's (MSM) student-centered learning assessments that include learning style and preference inventories, analysis, and training (Orr, 2018). Before entering any program at MSM, students are highly encouraged to take the Myers & Briggs Type Indicator, a personality inventory. This inventory helps faculty and staff understand better how they need to deliver information, how incoming students learn, and who (groups) they will learn best with. This speaks to the legacy of HBCUs. They build and sustain institutional cultures for meaningful assessment and continuously seek to identify promising practices that support student success and improve their assessment practices.

As HBCUs continue to evolve, they have made great strides in guiding improvements while leveraging accountability expectations (Jackson-Hammond, 2020; Williams et al., 2020). They understand the importance of accountability and compliance, but also create assessment activities with the goal of improving teaching and meaningful learning experiences. Jackson-Hammond (2020) asserts, "despite their everyday, yearly challenges and commitment to provide quality academic experiences, HBCUs have maintained an equal commitment to quality institutional assurances" (p. 1). For those who know and understand the history and mission of HBCUs, qualitative assessment begins when students enter and it does not end when they depart.

HBCU students' narratives guide assessment: From recognizing food and/or housing insecurities to asking sometimes intrusive questions, HBCUs mobilize resources without a script, plan, or incentives. Conversely, COVID-19 has positively propelled the HBCU community into the national dialogue with regard to meeting students' needs. For instance, Valbrun (2020) reported: "HBCUs tend to have stricter social rules . . . administrators refer to it as 'more hands-on guidance'" (para. 8). Valbrun goes on to note, "college leaders partly credit Black college culture—and student awareness of the toll of the pandemic on Black, Latinx and Indigenous communities" (para. 1). So, a lot of what the HBCU community does is in service to their students and doesn't necessarily fit a prescribed assessment plan.

The major initiative that helps HBCUs guide improvement is their commitment to their missions and the success of their students. Various assessment activities are part of the HBCU institutional design, where student success is in concert with meaningful learning experiences. For example, there is a powerful connection between meaningful learning and high impact practices (HIPs), a list of 11 teaching and learning practices that have been widely tested and accepted as effective (Kuh, 2008). HIPs allow students to engage at their home institutions and obtain global experiences that build connections and bridge their academic life to career paths. HIPs include 1st-year seminars and experiences, common intellectual experiences, learning communities, writing-intensive courses, collaborative assignments and projects, undergraduate research, diversity/global learning, eportfolios, service learning, community-based learning, internships, and capstone courses and projects.

Another institutional example of what has worked well on an HBCU campus to guide improvement while leveraging accountability expectations is the assessment approaches of North Carolina A&T State University (NCA&T), the largest HBCU in the country, which supports accountability measures and other program reviews while being responsive to the needs of their students first (Baker, 2012). Moreover, their students' needs, including protection from COVID-19 and racial aggression and hostility, are indicators that allow NCA&T to respond to their diverse students (rural and low-income, adult learners, international students, etc.) who are still gaining their confidence. For instance, NCA&T has experienced low positive COVID-19 cases, approximately 2.7% of voluntary testers. NCA&T SGA President Brenda Caldwell shared:

> Some of it [COVID-19 precautions] is the HBCU culture . . . we're just like a community and we want to keep our community safe. We know that Black and brown communities have been affected by COVID and some of us have had family sick from it. And we know we are going to go back to our vulnerable communities, and I think that motivates us. (Valbrun, 2020, para. 18)

Moreover, NCA&T assessment practices require them to review assessment data, including student enrollment projections during a global pandemic, among other factors, and seek improvements to ensure all students are learning, performing, safe, and service centered. This culture of assessment has worked well—it responds to accountability expectations while continuous improvement and a deep appreciation and understanding of the student body lead the way.

HBCU-CEEQA Telling the Story

Until the lion learns how to write, every story will glorify the hunter.

—J. Nozipo Maraire

Given the missions of HBCUs, their role in fighting for equity, and the need to highlight more of the many examples of good assessment practice happening in HBCUs like those covered in the prior section, HBCU-CEEQA was created. A little more than 3 years ago, the Office of Educational Outcomes and Assessment at Morehouse School of Medicine, the Office of University Assessment at Florida Agricultural and Mechanical University, along with the National Institute for Learning Outcomes Assessment (NILOA), teamed up to conceptualize the HBCU Collaborative for Excellence in Educational Quality Assurance (HBCU-CEEQA), a structured collaborative comprised of assessment and institutional effectiveness professionals dedicated to advancing student learning, institutional quality, and student success (Orr et al., 2020). HBCU-CEEQA has been in existence for almost 4 years with members sharing more than 100 years in higher education and an average of 15 years of service in assessment, research, and institutional effectiveness.

The vision of HBCU-CEEQA is to be a leader in building the capacity to demonstrate the impact and effectiveness of HBCUs within the postsecondary context. In alignment with the vision, the mission of the collaborative is to demonstrate the effectiveness of HBCUs through the use of best practices in assessment and evaluation by leveraging the collective expertise of assessment and institutional effectiveness professionals and other stakeholders. To realize its mission and vision, the work of the collaborative is focused around the following five goals:

Goal 1: Provide a collaborative space for sharing and promoting the use of best practices and resources in outcomes assessment and evidence-based decision-making at partner HBCU institutions.

Goal 2: Enhance the use of systematic, evidence-based practices for assessment and institutional effectiveness among partner institutions.

Goal 3: Provide a platform for showcasing the culturally relevant assessment and evaluation practices that are used to tell the story and demonstrate the impact of HBCUs through scholarly output in the form of joint research, publications, and conference presentations with partner institutions.

Goal 4: Communicate the impact and effectiveness of HBCUs to internal and external stakeholders through culturally relevant processes, measures, and metrics.

Goal 5: Cultivate strategic partnerships that advance the goals and mission of HBCU-CEEQA. (Orr et al., 2020, p. 8)

HBCU-CEEQA's inaugural partner, the National Institute for Learning Outcomes Assessment (NILOA), was established in 2008 and is "a research and resource-development organization dedicated to documenting, advocating, and facilitating the systematic use of learning outcomes assessment to improve student learning" (NILOA, n.d., para. 1). HBCU-CEEQA and NILOA's objectives align as both organizations strive "to discover and disseminate ways that academic programs and institutions can productively use assessment data internally to inform and strengthen undergraduate education, and externally to communicate with policy makers, families and other stakeholders" (Orr, 2018, p. 2). However, HBCU-CEEQA's objectives differ from NILOA in that HBCU-CEEQA aims to discover and disseminate various assessment approaches that consider various needs (i.e., culture and diversity) of the HBCU student populations.

Moreover, HBCU-CEEQA provides an opportunity for scholar practitioners to "leverage the collective expertise of assessment and institutional effectiveness professionals" (Orr et al., 2020, p. 8). Connected by a lineage of resilience, creativity, and innovation, HBCU-CEEQA members dig deeply into the work and communities that support teaching and learning success at HBCUs. HBCU-CEEQA pushes the present theories about HBCU assessment practices and student learning through its usage of theory that is not often applied to this phenomenon.

HBCU-CEEQA members write and present on topics ranging from innovative assessment practices on their respective campuses to the dearth of literature on the specifics as to how HBCUs provide a variety of options for gathering, documenting, using, and sharing meaningful actionable evidence of student learning (Orr, 2018). In that vein, HBCU-CEEQA leans on their collective expertise of practicing and retired professionals to tell the HBCU student learning outcomes success story. This approach, beyond the reach of outsiders, promotes a positive transformation of student learning and increases the effective transfer of innovations throughout HBCUs.

Are We Listening to the Lessons From Our HBCU Colleagues?

U.S. higher education institutions are currently experiencing an unprecedented pandemic. And while COVID-19 is calling out the inequities that must be considered to understand fully the impact of inequities plaguing the higher education system, HBCUs continue to successfully operate in a stratified system that embodies the inequities and discrimination of our nation. Considering this, HBCUs:

- are committed to their mission(s) of providing access and a quality higher education learning experience to underrepresented people, specifically Black people;
- create institutional cultures for meaningful assessment and use creative assessment practices that support student success; and

- are the hub for imagination and ideas to thrive: they guide improvement, leverage accountability expectations, and provide diverse techniques and interventions to ensure student success.

Finally, the hope is that this chapter will activate our thinking on the future of diverse learning experiences and strategies for increasing organizational cultural competency in higher education. Now, more than ever, the remarks of the late Supreme Court Justice Antonin Scalia must be called out for their racist undertones and obvious insensitivity to context and culture. I wonder if the struggles PWIs like the University of Texas at Austin are experiencing amid COVID-19 would be on Justice Scalia's list of "less-advanced" and "slower track" schools? HBCUs own a commitment to acknowledging, studying, and celebrating the diverse cultures that make up their student population. Humility, creativity, innovation, and equity are the heartbeat of HBCUs. And although learning and assessment on HBCU campuses can, on the surface, look different, their institutional strength lies within the traditions and culture of continuous improvement. At this transformational moment in history, the writing is on the wall—cultural awareness and equity must accompany policy and practice.

Acknowledgments

The great poet Nikky Finney asserted, "If my name is ever called out, I promised my girl poet self—so too would I call out theirs." My scholar sister friends, Ereka, Ebonierose, Ruth-Nicole, Nadia, Robyn, Chauntee, Lauren, JoJo, and Stephanie, proven tried and true, have provided love and laughs even in times of great confusion. Thank you, Natasha Jankowski, for your mentorship and more importantly, friendship. President Roslyn Clark Artis, your aplomb and candor are extraordinary—it is a privilege and honor to work for and learn from you. Finally, to the 100+ HBCUs across America, thank you for believing in me and countless others. The seriousness and beauty of the aesthetics of teaching and learning at HBCUs is not lost on me.

References

American Evaluation Association. (2011). *Public statement on cultural competence in evaluation.* www.eval.org/ccstatement

Anderson, J. (1988). *The education of Blacks in the South, 1860–1935.* The University of North Carolina Chapel Hill.

Andrews, D. R., No, S., Powell, K. K., Rey, M. P., & Yigletu, A. (2016). Historically Black colleges and universities' institutional survival and sustainability: A view from the HBCU business deans' perspective. *Journal of Black Studies, 47*(2), 150-168.

Baker, G. (2012). *North Carolina A&T State University: A culture of inquiry.* University of Illinois and Indiana University, National Institute for Learning Outcomes Assessment. https://www.learningoutcomeassessment.org/documents/NCAT2 .pdf

Banta, T., & Associates. (Eds.). (2002). *Building a scholarship of assessment.* Wiley.

Bonner, F. (2001). Addressing gender issues in the historically Black college and university community: A challenge and call to action. *Journal of Negro Education, 70*(3), 176–191. https://doi.org/10.2307/3211209

Brown, M.C., & Freeman, K. (Eds.). (2002). Research on historically Black colleges. *The Review of Higher Education, 25,* 237–368.

Brown, M. C., & Freeman, K. (Eds.). (2004). *Black colleges: New perspectives on policy and practice.* Praeger.

Cheek, J. (1972). *A Lingering legacy: The neglect and deprivation of the higher education of Black Americans.* Howard University.

Crenshaw, K. (1989). Demarginalizing the intersection of race and sex: A Black feminist critique of antidiscrimination doctrine, feminist theory, and antiracist politics. *University of Chicago Legal Forum, 1989*(1), pp. 139–167. http://chica-gounbound.uchicago.edu/uclf/vol1989/iss1/8

DuBois, W. E. B. (1935). A critique: The courts and the Negro separate school. *The Journal of Negro Education, 4*(3), 442. https://doi.org/10.2307/2291879

Ewell, P. T. (2002). An emerging scholarship: A brief history of assessment. In T. W. Banta & Associates (Eds.), *Building a scholarship of assessment* (pp. 3–25). Jossey-Bass.

Ewell, P. T. (2009). *Assessment, accountability, and improvement: Revisiting the tension* (Occasional Paper No. 1). University of Illinois and Indiana University, National Institute for Learning Outcomes Assessment. https://www.learningoutcomesass-essment.org/wp-content/uploads/2019/02/OccasionalPaper1.pdf

Favors, J. (2019). *Shelter in a time of storm: How Black colleges fostered generations of leadership and activism.* University of North Carolina Press.

Fisher v. the University of Texas at Austin, 570 U.S. 67 (2016). https://www.supre-mecourt.gov/oral_arguments/audio/2015/14-981

Gallup, I. (2015). *Gallup-USA funds minority college graduates report.* https://www .gallup.com/services/186359/gallup-usa-funds-minority-college-graduates-report-pdf.aspx

Gilbert, E. (2015, August 14). Does assessment make colleges better? Who knows? *The Chronicle of Higher Education,* 1–3. https://www.chronicle.com/article/does-assessment-make-colleges-better-who-knows/

Higher Education Act of 1965, Pub L. No. 89-329, 79 Stat. 1219 (1965). https:// www.govinfo.gov/content/pkg/STATUTE-79/pdf/STATUTE-79-Pg1219 .pdf#page=37

Humphreys, L. (2017). *HBCUs make America strong: The positive economic impact of historically Black colleges and universities.* UNCF (United Negro College Fund).

Jackson-Hammond, C. (2020). Accreditation, quality, and HBCUs: Match or mismatch? [Letter to the editor]. Council for Higher Education Accredita-

tion (CHEA). https://www.chea.org/sites/default/files/pdf/Hammond_
OpEd_1.16.2020_Final.pdf

Kimbrough, W. M. (2017, April 18). Why historically black colleges should be a
choice. *Education Week.* https://www.edweek.org/teaching-learning/opinion-
why-historically-black-colleges-should-be-a-choice/2017/04

Kuh, G. (2008). *High-impact educational practices: What they are, who has access to them,
and why they matter.* Association of American Colleges and Universities. https://
secure.aacu.org/imis/ItemDetail?iProductCode=E-HIGHIMP&Category=

Lumina Foundation. (2019). *Today's student.* https://www.luminafoundation.org/
resource/todays-student/

Montenegro, E., & Jankowski, N. A. (2017). *Equity and assessment: Moving towards
culturally responsive assessment* (Occasional Paper No. 29). University of Illinois
and Indiana University, National Institute for Learning Outcomes Assessment.
https://www.learningoutcomesassessment.org/wp-content/uploads/2019/02/
OccasionalPaper29.pdf

Morrill Act of 1862, Pub. L. 37-130, 12 Stat. 503 (1862)

Morrill Act of 1890, Pub. L. 51-841, 26 Stat. 417 (1890)

Nahal, A., Thompson, A., Rahman, M. A., & Orr, V. (2015). Ethnic and cultural
diversity at HBCUs and its impact on students, faculty, and staff. In T. Ingram,
D. Greenfield, J. Carter, & A. Hilton (Eds.), *Exploring issues of diversity within
HBCUs* (pp. 135–161). Information Age.

National Institute for Learning Outcomes Assessment. (n.d.). *Our mission.* https://
www.learningoutcomesassessment.org/about/niloa-mission/

National Institute for Learning Outcomes Assessment. (2019). *Assessment glossary.*
https://www.learningoutcomesassessment.org/wp-content/uploads/2019/05/
NILOA-Glossary.pdf

Orr, V. F. (2018). *Assessment, accountability, and student learning outcomes at Historically Black Colleges and Universities.* University of Illinois and Indiana University,
National Institute for Learning Outcomes Assessment. https://www.learningout-
comesassessment.org/wp-content/uploads/2019/02/CEEQA_Report.pdf

Orr, V. F., Reneau, F. H., Howse, M., & Stanford, S. (2020). HBCU collaborative
for excellence in educational quality assurance experiences significant growth in
two years. *Assessment Update, 32*(5), 8–11. https://doi.org/10.1002/au.30228

Ratcliff, J. L. (1996). Assessment, accreditation, and evaluation of higher
education in the US. *Quality in Higher Education, 2*(1), 5–19. https://doi
.org/10.1080/1353832960020102

Reneau, F. H., & Howse, M. (2019, October). *Trekking towards sustainable excellence through systematic outcomes assessment.* University of Illinois and Indiana
University, National Institute for Learning Outcomes Assessment (NILOA).
https://www.learningoutcomesassessment.org/wp-content/uploads/2019/10/
AiP-ReneauHowse.pdf

Ricard, R., & Brown, M. C. (2008). *Ebony towers in higher education: The evolution,
mission, and presidency of historically Black colleges and universities.* Stylus.

Sowell, R., Allum, J., & Okahana, H. (2015). *Doctoral initiative on minority attrition and completion.* Council of Graduate Schools. https://cgsnet.org/ckfinder/userfiles/files/Doctoral_Initiative_on_Minority_Attrition_and_Completion_2015.pdf

Toldson, I. (2016). The funding gap between historically Black colleges and universities and traditionally White institutions needs to be addressed* (Editor's Commentary). *The Journal of Negro Education, 85*(2), 97–100. https://doi.org/10.7709/jnegroeducation.85.2.0097

Valbrun, M. (2020, September). Hitting close to home. *Inside Higher Ed.* https://www.insidehighered.com/news/2020/09/24/hbcus-experiencing-better-student-compliance-pandemic-restrictions-other

Williams, E. R., Orr, V. F., & Barnett, N. G. (2020). Finding community in the assessment field: Holding space for our HBCU colleagues. *Assessment Update, 32*(5), 1–16. http://doi.org/10.1002/au.30224

Willie, C. (1981). *The ivory and ebony towers: Race relations and higher education.* Lexington Books.

Wooten, M. E. (2015). *In the face of inequality.* State University of New York Press.

PART FOUR

NOW WHAT?

17

LEVERAGING TECHNOLOGY-ENABLED ASSESSMENT CAPABILITIES TO PROMOTE EQUITABLE STUDENT OUTCOMES

Peggy L. Maki

> *We just need the tools to understand each person as an individual, not as a data point on a bell curve.*
>
> —Rose, 2015, p. 14

Closing graduation gaps across our historically underrepresented student demographics remains a persistent challenge for higher education, documented in longitudinal 6-year graduation rates reported by the National Center for Education Statistics. Compared with Asian and White students' graduation rates, those for students representing different races and ethnicities continue to remain lower (de Brey et al., 2019). Socioeconomic factors also contribute to lower graduation rates across racial and ethnic lines (Fain, 2019). Although institutions typically may not be able to address several factors that cause many of these students to withdraw or drop out, such as familial, financial, or work-related responsibilities, faculty and other education professionals now have the opportunity to narrow and even close achievement gaps across our diverse student demographics when they occur and as they persist along the progression of a course—even in large enrollment courses. Specifically, real-time longitudinal evidence of students' individual academic performance patterns generated along the trajectory of a course provides educators insight into the specific obstacle or obstacles that prevent any student from progressing toward achieving equitable learning outcomes. This real-time evidence, in turn, prompts faculty and other professionals to develop or identify timely, targeted, and tailored strategies, interventions, or resources that address specific individual student challenges, enabling students to immediately improve their underperformance patterns and continue to progress toward achieving an equitable course learning outcome. How is this possible? The answer: the seismic shift in current and emerging technology-enabled assessment capabilities integrated into learning management systems (LMSs), courseware, tutoring platforms, etextbooks, apps, and expanding digital teaching and learning options that position educators and students on the front line of students' learning in real time or near real time along the trajectory of a course. Educators who learn how to leverage these assessment capabilities gain timely, improved, and even new insights into the range of learning obstacles individual students confront as they learn new course material in real time and then apply what they have learned in real time in graded and ungraded tasks, exercises, or assignments. Timely assessment data reported on both faculty and student dashboards enable faculty, other educators, and, yes, students themselves to also develop timely strategies that lead to improving each student's underperformance patterns as those patterns emerge or persist along students' educational pathways, thus closing achievement gaps in real time to promote students' attainment of equitable learning outcomes.

Sequencing of the Chapter

To appreciate the contributions of current and emerging technology-enabled assessment capabilities to advancing students' achievement of equitable learning outcomes, this chapter begins by summarizing relevant current research on learning that heightens awareness of the individualized ways in which humans learn and, thus, the need to closely monitor and address the real-time learning needs of each student—key to achieving parity across our student demographics. The chapter then raises the related initial importance of designing equitable tasks or assignments (more comprehensively discussed in other chapters in this collection) and aligned criteria to assess students' performance patterns along the trajectory of a course. Focused primarily on assessment capabilities integrated into LMSs—given this system is the most common digital learning system used on campuses—this chapter identifies the kinds of data these capabilities generate, and ways faculty and other professional educators can use them in real time or near real time to gauge, monitor, and address the individualized needs of each student in a commitment to advancing all students to equitable attainment of learning outcomes. Additionally, the chapter also discusses the expanding integration of technology-enabled assessment capabilities into digital teaching and learning options, such as in courseware or intelligent tutoring platforms, that generate continuous real-time evidence of an individual student's patterns of performance while that student is engaged in learning material or applying new knowledge and skills or even behaviors. The chapter conclusion focuses on (a) major contributions of technology-enabled assessment capabilities to closing inequitable learning outcomes across our demographics as well as on (b) the critical importance of educators' judgment in analyzing and using technology-enabled assessment data and in selecting digital teaching and learning options with assessment capabilities that are designed based on research on learning.

Achieving Equity by Focusing on Individuality

Although big picture reports on progress colleges and universities are making in narrowing graduation gaps among historically underrepresented students are helpful gauges of collective institutional efforts, our ability to close those gaps requires diving down beneath broad group classifications and even more defining demographic variables, such as age, disability, socioeconomic status, and educational background, to (a) identify the specific set or sets of challenges an individual student faces while learning and demonstrating or representing that learning and then to (b) develop tailored interventions to assist a student to overcome those challenges as they occur or persist along that individual's educational pathway.

Sensitizing educators to the importance of addressing our students' individual learning needs are major findings from current research on learning that document the individualized ways each person learns, other factors that also influence an individual's learning process, and the complex ways in which all humans learn—more complex than many models represent. The National Research Council's publication of *How People Learn: Mind, Brain, Experience, and School: Expanded Edition* in 2000 represented groundbreaking research conducted over the previous 2 decades that expanded our understanding about the processes and functions of learning. Thereafter, research on learning continued, leading to the National Academies of Sciences, Engineering, and Medicine's 2018 consensus report, *How People Learn II: Learners, Contexts, and Culture.* Major findings from that research led contributors to now define learning as "a dynamic, ongoing process that is simultaneously biological and cultural" (p. 9). Although humans share basic brain structures and processes, contributors state: "Learning does not happen in the same way for all individuals" because they function within "complex developmental, cognitive, physical, social and cultural systems" (p. 2) that affect individual learning. To complicate matters even more, researchers describe the complex ways in which individuals learn, using the example of memorization—an important cognitive process in learning. Challenging models that represent memorizing as a storage and retrieval process that occurs in a single part of the brain, researchers have found that individuals scatter memories throughout their brains. The actual process of memorizing is "a complex process that interacts with other learning processes such as the abilities to categorize and reason" (p. 7). Furthermore, each "individual processes memories from subjective perspectives and constructs those perspectives by drawing on prior learning experiences, including cultural ones that affect cognitive processes" (p. 74). In some cases, "an individual's prior inaccurate or insufficient learning experiences can undermine that person's acquisition of new skills or knowledge" (p. 91). For example, in science a student's long-held misconception—often represented in an incorrect visual image—that the sun rotates around the earth rather than the earth rotates around the sun—may well inhibit that student's ability to understand other earth-sun relationships. Insufficient or inaccurate prior learning and related research findings from *How People Learn II: Learners, Contexts, and Cultures* that focus on the complex processes and factors involved in how an individual learns contribute to making the case for why it is now necessary for faculty and other educators to:

- gain increased insight into the specific real-time challenges or obstacles an individual student confronts while learning new material or demonstrating new knowledge or skills along the progression of each course or educational experience to assist any student overcome those challenges before those obstacles inhibit that student's progress toward achieving equitable learning outcomes; and
- provide each student timely, targeted, and tailored feedback in that "dynamic ongoing process" of learning or applying learning: (a) to help each student progress toward attaining equitable exit-level course-, program-, and institution-level outcomes, and (b) to enable each student to become a self-regulated learner responsible for identifying the causes of underperformance patterns, developing strategies to improve them, and assuming responsibility for continued improvement.

DESIGNING EQUITABLE ASSESSMENT TASKS AND ASSIGNMENTS

Preceding the process of assessing students' patterns of strength and weakness in the work they produce or tasks they perform is the process of designing equitable tasks and assignments. Winkelmes's focus on transparency in assignment design and the Center for Applied Special Technology's (CAST) principles of *Universal Design for Learning Guidelines* (2018) offer valuable guidance in the process of designing equitable tasks or assignments.

Focused on identifying assignment components that contribute to underserved college students' success Winkelmes (n.d.), founder and principal investigator of Transparency in Learning and Teaching (TILT), identified three essential components that instructors should discuss with students before they begin an assignment: (a) the purpose of the assignment: identification of the skills students will practice and the knowledge they will gain; (b) the tasks involved to fulfill the assignment: what steps students will need to take, how they should take them, and which ones to avoid; and (c) the criteria for assessing the assignment: presentation of rubrics or checklists to students before they begin the assignment along with some annotated successful examples. Based on Winkelmes et al.'s (2016) research using these assignment components—importantly, also used for teaching and learning—Winkelmes et al. concluded that these efforts level the playing field of opportunities, not just for underserved students, but for all students (para. 6). Writing about the importance of transparently designed assignments for online learners, Bose et al. (2020) from Boise State University reported that because many online learners may not have frequent or consistent communication with their instructor because of their work or family responsibilities, "transparently designed assignments can be especially useful when learners access assignments remotely" (para. 3).

Winkelmes's (2016) "Checklist for Designing a Transparent Assignment" addresses the importance of alignment between expectations of an assignment prompt and the specific rubric or checklist used to assess each student's work. Misalignment between the stated directives of an assignment or task that identify cognitive process, knowledge, skills, or behaviors a student should demonstrate and the specific criteria or checklist items that an instructor or facilitator uses to score students' work thwarts students' abilities to equitably demonstrate their learning (see also predictive or diagnostic and formative use of assessment data to identify subskills or processes certain students need to develop to achieve equitable outcomes, pp. 292–297, this chapter). That misalignment can occur—even with the best of faculty intentions—is documented in a recent research project conducted by Nicholas et al. (2019), involving 25 faculty from a large public university in the Northeast, representing the humanities, natural sciences, and social sciences. Analyzing verbs used in both faculty prompts for critical thinking assignments and the agreed upon criteria used to assess students' responses, researchers found types of misalignment. For example, in one case the level of clarity that appeared in a grading instrument "was noticeably different than the prompt" (p. 41). In another case researchers found "greater variety of verbs in a grading instrument than the prompt" (p. 41). And in some cases, they "found that the grading instrument required higher cognitive processes than were outlined in the assignment prompt" (p. 41). Misalignments such as these findings document raise questions about how, when, or if students were prepared to navigate those kinds of misalignments in order to equitably represent their learning.

Contributing to students' progress toward attaining equitable learning outcomes is designing assessment tasks that initially offer students alternative options or means of demonstrating or representing their knowledge, skills, or habits of mind, such as using media tools, or asking students to identify contexts within which to demonstrate their learning. For example, instead of asking all students to perform a standardized formative assessment task, asking students initially to identify a context within which they can perform that task or providing them with optional contexts grounds individual students in more familiar territory rather than unfamiliar territory that stymies them right off the bat. These options extend beyond a "one size fits all" assessment approach, effectively challenged by Todd Rose (2015), director of the Mind, Brain, and Education program at Harvard's Graduate School of Education. In *The End of Average: How We Succeed in A World That Values Sameness* Rose explores our nation's historic obsession with defining what an "average" student should be able to demonstrate in a standardized instrument when, in fact, there is no average student. Contributing to the development and presentation of assignments, course materials, and alternative assessments are CAST's *Universal Design for Learning Guidelines* (UDL; 2018), originally developed to address the needs of students with disabilities and now used to design for all learners to optimize individuals' opportunities to learn and represent their learning.

Integration of Technology-Enabled Assessment Capabilities in LMSs and Digital Teaching and Learning Options

Real-time assessment of each student's patterns of performance and underperformance in online tasks or assignments in a course or in an online component of a hybrid course, such as a discussion board, is now possible given a pivotal development in digital learning technologies. That development is the integration of technology-enabled assessment capabilities into LMSs and into the design of new digital teaching and learning options as well as the redesign of existing digital options. These capabilities generate real-time data about each student's performance and underperformance patterns as students learn and as they apply their new knowledge, skills, and related behaviors in course assignments and tasks. Faculty and other educators' real-time access to these kinds of assessment data now enables them to continuously gauge and monitor each student's patterns of performance and then nimbly identify or adapt teaching practices, interventions, or resources that assist students across the demographics of a course to improve their individual underperformance patterns in real time in order to achieve equitable course learning outcomes. Two major types of technology-enabled assessment capabilities that now position faculty and other educators to accommodate the learning needs of individual students in a course to advance each one toward attaining equitable learning outcomes are the following:

- Learning Analytics (LA) software bundled into an LMS and into redesigned or new digital teaching and learning options—algorithmic-based software that mines data sets, such as students' performance patterns on assigned tasks developed in an LMS, and then reports resulting patterns in real time or near real time on faculty and even student dashboards; and
- adaptive learning software integrated into digital teaching and learning options, such as courseware or intelligent tutorial platforms, that (a) mines individual students' performance patterns as they are learning or applying that new learning and then (b) based on an individual's underperformance patterns immediately personalizes instruction and aligns support to improve that student's underperformance patterns in real time.

Developed by applying tools and strategies used in subfields of artificial intelligence (AI), such as machine learning, and applying research on learning from the learning sciences, these technological capabilities are increasingly being integrated into the architecture and design of emerging digital teaching and learning options. The integration of LA and adaptive learning technology in these options instantiates research on how people learn, make decisions, and solve problems. Both LA and adaptive learning represent an evolution in digital teaching, learning, and assessment. This evolution in learning technologies now makes it possible to identify and address the learning needs of each student made visible through the connective role of technology-enabled real-time evidence of student learning along the trajectory of a course as discussed in the following sections.

Leveraging Technology-Enabled Assessment Capabilities in LMSs

The typical environment within which faculty and other educators have access to technological assessment capabilities is their institution's LMS—the design and delivery system for online courses, modules, online components of blended courses, or for hosting a digital component of a face-to-face delivered course, such as a discussion board. In 2020 as COVID-19 rapidly spread, many who had not taught online suddenly shifted to this system, but likely had little time or sufficient support (based on excessive demand for it) to learn about the kinds of technology-generated assessment evidence that are now available for each student in a course. Real-time access to assessment data is now possible in an LMS based on the system's data storage capabilities, together with the integration of data mining and data reporting software—learning analytics (LA). LA is an algorithmic-based software, designed based on new applications of algorithms used in subbranches of AI that are trained to mine specific kinds of data and report resulting patterns, such as students' performance patterns in their work or in their related learning behaviors. On a personal level, we experience the contributions of LA in our own lives on many levels. For example, analytics software integrated into a wearable device reports real-time data for specific health indicators, such as blood pressure or blood sugar levels.

LA integrated into LMSs mines the following kinds of evidence of individual student's learning: (a) patterns of student responses to questionnaires, surveys, or polls developed within an LMS; (b) patterns of student behaviors as students work with online course materials or engage in online course activities, exercises, or group discussions; and (c) patterns of student performance on tests, quizzes, short answer question sets, and results of scoring rubrics that faculty or other evaluators apply to authentic student work—all of which are developed within an LMS. These patterns provide sources of evidence of students' learning for predictive or diagnostic, formative, and summative assessment purposes.

Predictive or Diagnostic Assessment: Initial Doors to Equitable Assessment

LA bundled into an LMS has the capability to mine students' survey, poll, and questionnaire responses based on formats built into an LMS into which specific questions or items can be inserted. LMSs also may integrate externally developed information gathering software such as Poll Everywhere. Distributed preferably before a course or a learning experience begins or, at least, on the first day, a questionnaire serves an important initial purpose for faculty or other educators on campus to learn about each student's prior knowledge, preparation, experiences with, or even anxiety about the course or experience they have enrolled in. LA integrated into an LMS mines and reports patterns of student responses to the questions asked or perhaps to choices students select in a poll or survey and reports those results in real time on a faculty member's or other facilitator's dashboard, thus providing baseline information about each student for two purposes:

- predictive, to identify students who appear to be academically at risk (though that does not automatically mean those students cannot achieve) and, thus, alert an instructor or facilitator about the need to identify additional support, such as tutorials, other learning materials, or adaptations of current course materials to assist individual students to gain a firm footing and continue to progress; and
- diagnostic, to identify major misconceptions or misunderstandings or levels of anxiety across the student population that will require additional longitudinal focus.

Predictive or diagnostic assessments can continue to be used longitudinally in a course or educational experience to identify lingering questions or misunderstandings students have after a lecture, video, an experiment, or specific experience, for example, or to learn about students' readiness to tackle more complex material. They also are useful in gauging how well each student has developed underlying subtasks or subskills, knowledge or behaviors that are necessary to attain desired outcomes, alerting faculty to the need to identify strategies or resources to assist specific students in developing them. These kinds of assessment evidence inform proactive steps in the teaching and learning processes.

Formative Assessment: A Longitudinal Commitment to Students' Equitable Progress Toward Achieving Exit-Level Outcomes

An LMS environment also has the capacity to store and mine (a) patterns of individual student behaviors related to access, use, and engagement with course materials or engagement in required online activities and (b) patterns of individual student performance levels on graded and ungraded tasks and assignments along the trajectory of a course, prompting faculty to work with students in real time or near real time to assist them in improving patterns of underperformance as part of the "dynamic, ongoing process of learning" defined by contributors to *How People Learn II: Learners, Contexts, and Cultures* (National Academies of Sciences, Engineering, and Medicine, 2018, p. 9).

An LMS keeps logs of each student's learning behaviors: when or even if a student accesses course materials, exercises, or resources; how long a student spends with those materials; how long or even if a student engages in a required online discussion. These kinds of data—again, reported in real time on faculty or facilitator dashboards—provide longitudinal evidence of a students' engagement in course learning activities. Educators can take steps themselves to draw correlations between longitudinal evidence of a students' engagement in course learning activities and other real-time formative data such as a student's performance on a graded or ungraded quiz or a brief written response to a prompt. Low patterns of engagement in online course materials or resources or in interactive online activities do not signal that a specific student is unable to achieve; rather those patterns prompt faculty or other facilitators to work with specific students to identify the challenge or challenges each student faces before those challenges become entrenched. Time stamps indicating that a student or even several students spent a minimum amount of time reading a resource may mean that resource itself was too difficult for one or more students to read; thus, they gave up. But the reasons for giving up can vary across students: for one student it may be that individual has difficulty processing complex reading material; for another it may mean that individual did not have time to dedicate to the reading given family or work-related responsibilities. High patterns of low reading time dedicated to a specific document may trigger the instructor to take a different approach altogether: opening wider discussion about a document to identify specific issues most or all students are facing. Low participation in online discussion boards may signal an individual's fear of expressing views in such an open environment, cultural reluctance to participate, or even lack of understanding of the discussion prompt itself. In an experiment using frequent real-time student surveys in the process of revising an introductory chemistry course to learn more about the challenges students face while learning, Van Heuvelen et al. (2019) report that many students "found group work challenging, especially in the early part of the course. This is partly due to the social risks inherent in asking questions in front of their peers" (p. 18). Issues students encounter while reading online resources, responding to related online questions about those resources, or engaging with peers in a discussion group may necessitate different and often interdependent instructor approaches—from working with each student to uncover the root cause of an issue and identify strategies to move forward (also discussed on p. 300

of this chapter) to identifying alternative equitable approaches to learning difficult material—such as shifting from a text-based format to a speech-based format.

Automated or manual scoring of students' performance patterns are options available in an LMS to assess quizzes, multiple choice, fill-in-the-blank, or short answer tests developed within that system. Results of individual as well as group performance levels are reported in real time on an instructor's or facilitator's dashboard. In addition, the availability of an item analysis report for each assessment method provides educators with data about the level of difficulty of each item or each question asked in a task, about the number of attempts each student made to respond to an item, or about the number of students who were unable to answer a specific question, signaling the need to reach out to those students immediately to address the learning challenges they face that can prevent them from achieving equitable outcomes. These kinds of data also prompt faculty or facilitators to explore how much time they dedicated to teaching material related to answering the question students struggled to answer or how effectively they provided alternative ways for students to learn. Students also receive real-time assessment results on their individual dashboards so they remain informed of their patterns of performance.

LA can also report on faculty and student dashboards the results of scoring rubrics developed with a rubric builder tool built into an LMS and applied by scorers to student work. In keeping with the misalignment cautions raised by Nicholas et al. (2019), results of scoring rubrics developed with a rubric builder may turn out to be invalid if they are not carefully aligned with the specific assignment prompt or if students have not had equitable opportunities to develop the underlying knowledge, skills, or subskills necessary to demonstrate the desired level of performance. Using another tool, SpeedGrader, faculty can provide students real-time feedback on tests, quizzes, multiple choice, short answer questions, and scoring rubric results either through automated or personalized feedback options via text, audio, or video. Although automated feedback might be sufficient for students who have performed well, a personalized approach to feedback will be more effective in assisting students who need to improve specific patterns of underperformance. In their guide to digital options for providing feedback to students, Fiock and Garcia (2019) in *How to Give Your Students Better Feedback With Technology* discuss the efficacy of different approaches to feedback as well as identify other digital feedback options, many of which are free.

LMS reporting options can also translate patterns of student behaviors and patterns of student performance on graded and ungraded work into visual representations on faculty dashboards: charts, graphs, or tables.

For example, an instructor can turn on one or more reporting tools to longitudinally monitor each student's behaviors related to accessing, reading, and even responding to online materials, or engaging in group discussions. Figure 17.1, for example, illustrates one LMS visual report from Canvas that documents an individual student's weekly online activity represented in number 1. Number 2 summarizes that student's total page views and participations. Participations include actions such as posting comments, submitting assignments or quizzes, joining a web conference, or posting a new comment to a discussion. Numbers 3 and 4 chart her average page views and average participations. Number 5, the dotted line, shows the week is still in progress; number 6, the download button, enables the instructor to download that week's data. Why declining patterns occurred and how those patterns may have correlated with that student's performance on a graded assignment are avenues a faculty could then investigate with that student.

Figure 17.1. A student's weekly online activity reporting page views and participations. Reprinted with permission from Canvas.

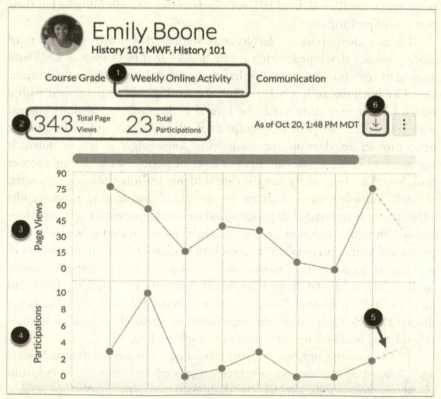

It is also possible to compare several types of performance patterns for each student over a period of time such as a student's patterns of behavior accessing and using course material, engaging in discussions or group work, submitting timely assigned work, and performing on formative assessments and major assignments.

Continuous access to assessment data means that faculty or other facilitators remain apprised of how well each student and the class as a whole are performing along the trajectory of a course and what kinds of emerging or persistent challenges need to be addressed to enable students to equitably progress from one unit or module of a course to the next. For example, to identify patterns of misunderstanding or misconceptions that students may have after a module has been presented, an instructor might ask students to respond to a set of online questions related to that module the night before the next course meeting—a practice used in flipped classrooms. LA's real-time reporting of students' patterns of misunderstanding or misconceptions that same evening helps faculty address the range of challenges students still face in the next course meeting. Left unaddressed, those patterns may well hinder one or more students' immediate or longer-term performance. Access to real-time assessment data provides educators nonstop actionable evidence.

Summative Assessment: A Means to Evaluate the Efficacy of Educational Practices, Course Materials, and Resources in Promoting Students' Equitable Attainment of Learning Outcomes

LA integrated into an LMS can also mine and report the results of students' culminating course work, perhaps results of a final test or rubric scores on their authentic work. Using these results, faculty or facilitators can learn more about the efficacy of their specific educational practices or approaches; required student activities, such as discussion boards or collaborative projects; course materials; and course resources in contributing to students' attainment of equitable learning outcomes in a course. Researchers Muljana et al. (2021) in "Applying A Learning Analytics Approach to Support Students' Achievement: Using Data Stored in Learning Management Systems" discuss the benefits of drawing correlations between (a) the efficacy of specific teaching and learning approaches, course materials, course resources, specific interventions to assist a student, and student behaviors and (b) students' exit-level performance patterns. For example, did targeted interventions or alternative ways of teaching used with specific students enable them to overcome their specific barriers to learning or did those options have little to no lasting effect as demonstrated in those students' final work? These correlations assist faculty to identify effective, less effective, or ineffective approaches or strategies to advancing students to achieve equitable outcomes, thus prompting them to revise or redesign the next iteration of that course to continue to optimize all students' learning. For example, what alternative ways of teaching or learning enabled one or more students in an introductory physics course to overcome their misunderstanding of a disciplinary concept: an interactive online simulation? A self-paced tutorial? A demonstration? An analogy? Also contributing to course revision or redesign aimed at fostering students' achievement of equitable outcomes are students' self-reports on the effectiveness of educational practices, activities, or specific interventions. Online polls or surveys administered near the end of a course that ask students to identify the resources, materials, strategies, or activities, for example, that contributed to their learning are firsthand sources of data that also verify the efficacy of educational practices and course components. Faculty and other educators' ability to evaluate the efficacy of their practices and activities directed toward students' attainment of equitable learning outcomes, together with student feedback about the efficacy of those practices, becomes a continuous means to identify as well as improve a repertoire of practices that effectively addresses our diverse students' learning needs to promote their success.

Leveraging Technology-Enabled Assessment Capabilities in Digital Teaching and Learning Options

Outside of the LMS environment are constantly expanding digital teaching and learning options that are increasingly integrating LA to report patterns of students' performance while they are learning or demonstrating that learning. For example, LA is integrated into the interactive video platform Echo 360 (echo360.com). In the process of teaching on that platform, faculty can ask students in real time to respond to questions related to their content and receive immediate results documenting students' patterns of understanding and misunderstanding or confusion that, heretofore, might have been difficult to uncover—especially in a large enrollment course. Yet, left unidentified, underperformance patterns could well account for a student's lower than expected performance in a follow-up quiz as well as for that student's long-term lower performance. Immediate access to students' misunderstandings prompts a teacher to address them in real time to avert the possibility that students will move forward holding onto incorrect understanding.

Based on research on large samples of individuals performing specific tasks such as solving representative professional or disciplinary problems, performing a process, calculating, or making decisions, increasingly course-ware platforms, apps, digital devices, etextbooks, and even interactive simulations integrate LA. Etextbooks integrate LA into student exercises, providing faculty and students data about the kinds of challenges individual students are facing as they learn new course material in real time. In these digital options, LA software has been trained to mine and report the specific kinds of performance and underperformance patterns specific to the task or tasks or exercises students perform. Thus, based on research on learning, LA built into some current and emerging digital teaching and learning options provides heretofore invisible and granular evidence of each students' patterns of performing a task or demonstrating skills or behaviors—evidence that faculty or facilitators do not have time to harvest or even see, such as discrete errors or missteps a student takes.

Gaining gradual visibility in higher education is adaptive learning software, used in the AI movement in the 1970s, built into some course-ware, interactive simulations, laboratory experiments or online scenarios, etextbooks, and into intelligent tutoring platforms. Adaptive learning technology integrated into any one of these options has the capacities not only to identify students' patterns of underperformance as students are learning or demonstrating their knowledge, skills, or related behaviors in real time but also to use those data in real time to develop personalized instruction to improve an individual's underperformance patterns. Intelligent tutoring platforms integrate adaptive learning technology to identify the specific learning needs of an individual in contrast with traditional online tutoring platforms that offer predesigned tutoring pathways. Pearson is now designing adaptive platforms upon which faculty can build their own courses, rather than purchasing predesigned adaptive courseware (Wan, 2020). Faculty or course facilitators remain continuously informed about each students' progress in adaptive learning courseware or in an adaptive learning component of a hybrid course so that they can address individual challenges as they emerge.

Recognizing the Contributions of Technology-Enabled Assessment Capabilities While Valuing Professional Judgment

Saving time traditionally spent on assessing student work and gaining real-time access to assessment results, instructors have the potential to become nimble evidence-informed teachers who flexibly adapt or redesign their educational practices, course materials, and support materials to address the range of student learning needs. Addressing underperformance patterns in real time, that is, closing time gaps between teaching and learning, technology-enabled assessment results position both faculty or facilitators and students on the front line of students' learning as it unfolds. Used in real time or near real time, formative assessment data available to faculty or other course or experience facilitators and to students have the potential to transform traditional teacher and student roles. Beyond monitoring and addressing the needs of specific learners in real time or near real time, faculty or facilitators have the opportunity to become evidence-informed teachers who learn in real time about the efficacy of their educational practices, materials, or resources in advancing all students' toward attaining high-quality exit-level outcomes. Timely evidence can prompt teachers or facilitators to identify or adapt educational practices or materials to improve currently enrolled students' learning as it unfolds. For some instructors or facilitators identifying other practices or resources to support students' learning may mean turning to research on learning to identify new and tested teaching and learning practices such as those identified in MIT's Open Learning Research (n.d.) findings or toward the plethora of resources available in open educational resources—ever expanding online searchable websites that house teaching, learning, and resource materials that faculty and even students can use or adapt.

Reducing traditional time gaps between teaching, learning, and assessment also has the potential to position faculty in the role of a mentor who develops students' agency for their learning. Rather than always expecting an authority to direct how students should improve their performance, students can develop their potential to become self-regulated learners, developed with faculty interventions. These interventions are directed toward assisting students to do the following: (a) self-reflect on the causes of their patterns of underperformance, (b) identify strategies or resources to improve those patterns, (c) demonstrate improvement in those patterns, and (d) monitor future performances to assure sustained improvement. Thus, real-time technology-generated assessment data position both faculty and students as learners: faculty as evidence-informed learners about the efficacy of their practices; students as self-regulated learners.

Professional judgment, however, must guide the sets of decisions educators make about when and how to use and analyze technology-enabled assessment evidence to advance all students to achieve equitable outcomes. That is, assessment data do not dictate faculty or even student actions; rather they inform their actions. For example, early assessment results in a course might identify a student who appears to be at risk for not succeeding in that course, leading to stereotyping that student. Yet in face-to-face discussion or interactive video conferencing with that student, an instructor can assist that student to surface the cause or causes of low performance patterns and offer resources to enable that student to overcome those patterns, such as strengthening skills or subskills or tasks.

Professional judgment must also guide an educator's selection of digital teaching and learning options that have integrated technology-enabled assessment capabilities. Some options on the higher education market may not have LA or adaptive learning capabilities developed based on research on learning or tested on large representative samples of our student populations. Learning as much as possible about product development and design is important in the process of selecting an option, including investigating the demographics used to develop and test these capabilities in relation to student demographics in a specific course an instructor intends to teach. To that end the following resource site has been designed to provide educators more in-depth information about the development and design of current and emerging digital disciplinary learning technologies: Courseware in Context Framework (CWiC, n.d.), available at https://cwic.learnplatform.com.

To reach higher education's larger purpose—to close equity gaps to achieve racial and social justice and to prepare individuals who reflect our national demographics—we are now able to learn far more about the individual challenges each of our students faces than ever before. With that deepened learning we are now also able to address the range of needs of our individual students as well as develop their agency for a continued life of personal and professional learning. Perhaps, as well, we are closer to realizing the definition of learning as a "dynamic, ongoing process," made possible through the generation of real-time assessment evidence.

References

Bose, D., Dalrymple, S., & Shadle, S. (2020, May 13). A renewed case for student success: Using transparency in assignment design when teaching remotely. *Faculty focus: Higher ed teaching strategies*. Magna Publications. https://www.facultyfocus.com/?s=transparency&submit

Canvas LMS. (2020). *Home page*. https://www.instructure.com/canvas/

Center for Applied Special Technologies. (2018). *Universal design for learning guidelines* (Version 2.2). http://udlguidelines.cast.org

Courseware in Context Framework. (n.d.). https://cwic.learnplatform.com

de Brey, C., Musu, L., McFarland, J., Wilkinson-Flicker, S., Diliberti, M., Zhang, A., Branstetter, C., & Wang, X. (2019). *Status and trends in the education of racial and ethnic groups 2018* (NCES 2019-038). U.S. Department of Education. https://nces.ed.gov/pubs2019/2019038.pdf

Echo 360. (2020). *Home page.* https://echo360.com

Fain, P. (2019, May 23). Wealth's influence on enrollment and completion. *Inside Higher Ed.* https://www.insidehighered.com/news/2019/05/23/feds-release-broader-data-socioeconomic-status-and-college-enrollment-and-completion

Fiock, H., & Garcia, H. (2019, November 11). How to give your students better feedback with technology: Advice guide. *The Chronicle of Higher Education.* https://www.chronicle.com/interactives/20191108-Advice-Feedback

MIT Open Learning Research. (n.d.). *Research.* https://openlearning.mit.edu/research

Muljana, P. S., Placencia, G. V., & Luo, T. (2021). Applying a learning-analytics approach to improve course achievement: Using data stored in learning management systems. In P. Maki & P. Shea (Eds.), *Transforming digital learning and assessment: A guide to available and emerging practices and building institutional consensus* (pp. 142–179). Stylus.

National Academies of Sciences, Engineering, and Medicine. (2018). *How people learn II: Learners, contexts, and cultures.* The National Academies Press. https://doi.org/10.17226/24783

National Research Council. (2000). *How people learn: Brain, mind, experience, and school* (Expanded ed.). The National Academies Press.

Nicholas, M. C., Storandt, B., & Atwood, E. K. (2019). Reexamining three held assumptions about creating classroom assignments that can be used for institutional assessment. *Journal of Assessment and Institutional Effectiveness, 9*(102), pp. 29–48. https://doi.org/10.5325/jasseinsteffe.9.1-2.0029

Rose, T. (2015). *The end of average: How we succeed in a world that values sameness.* HarperCollins.

Van Heuvelen, K. M., Blake, L. P., Daub, G. W., Hawkins, L. N., Johnson, A. R., Van Ryswyk, H., & Vosburg, D. A. (2019). Emphasizing learning: The impact of student surveys in the reform of an introductory chemistry course. *Journal of Assessment and Institutional Effectiveness, 9*(1–2), 1–28. https://doi.org/10.5325/jasseinsteffe.9.1-2.0001

Wan, T. (2020, January 20). Pearson bets on adaptive learning (again) with $25m acquisition of Smart Sparrow. *EdSurge.* https://www.edsurge.com/news/2020-01-22-pearson-bets-on-adaptive-learning-again-with-25m-acquisition-of-smart-sparrow

Winkelmes, M. A. (n.d.). *Designing transparent assignments for equitable learning opportunities* [Video]. YouTube. https://www.youtube.com/watch?v=xqUQhSKmD9U

Winkelmes, M. A. (2016). *Checklist for designing a transparent assignment.* TILT Higher Ed. https://tilthighered.com/assets/pdffiles/Checklist%20for%20Designing%20a%20Transparent%20Assignment%20copy.pdf

Winkelmes, M. A., Bernacki, M., Butler, J., Zochowski, M., Golanics, J., & Weavil, K. H. (2016, Winter/Spring). A teaching intervention that increases underserved college students' success. *Peer Review, 18*(1–2). https://www.aacu.org/peerreview/2016/winter-spring/Winkelmes

18

DEVELOPING INDIVIDUAL AWARENESS

The Role of the Assessor

Danielle Acheampong, Marilee Bresciani Ludvik,
and Anne E. Lundquist

Most assessors conduct their work with the goal of being *objective*. The concept of objectivity assumes that there is a truth or independent reality that exists outside of the investigation or observation and the assessor's role is to uncover this "truth" without interfering or distorting it in any way.

Gergen (2001) stated that:

> to be objective is to play by the rules within a given tradition of social practices . . . To do science is not to hold a mirror to nature but to participate actively in the interpretive conventions and practices of a particular culture. The major question that must be asked of scientific accounts, then, is not whether they are true to nature but what these accounts . . . offer to the culture more generally. . . . A postmodern empiricism would replace the "truth game" with a search for culturally useful theories and findings with significant cultural meaning. (pp. 806–808)

Throughout this text, authors offer examples of methods and practices that not only work to decrease bias from the assessment process, but actively seek to transform systems of power and oppression, expose policies that harm or impede already marginalized students, and use assessment as a transformative process on behalf of social justice and decolonization in the academy and the world. For these practices to be meaningful and effective, assessors must begin by examining themselves and the role they play in the assessment process (Magee, 2019). While most assessors espouse the principles of diversity, equity, access, and inclusion, many continue to unwittingly perpetuate positivist, Western, heteronormative, neoliberal assumptions regarding reality and knowledge in their assessment practices. These nonjustice-based paradigms and methods (Zerquera et al., 2018) value and prioritize objective quantitative approaches that separate the knower from the known and do not attend to the lived experiences, culture, and identities of students (Bresciani Ludvik, 2019; NAS, 2017, 2018).

In the assessment field, the identity of the assessor is often ignored or unexamined, yet it is obviously extremely relevant if assessors are to reframe what it means to be objective. Assessors' "identities influence how they see themselves, how they interact with others, the decisions they make, and how they live their lives" (Evans et al., 2010, p. 229). And a person's identity does not exist in a vacuum; those multilayered, interconnected, shifting identities are bound up with the constructs of systemic privilege and oppression. Culturally, some identities are more valued and come with power, unearned entitlements, and conferred dominance (McIntosh, 1989, 2003). Most privileged people in the U.S. society cannot see the power they hold, thus making their privilege invisible to them (DiAngelo, 2018; Kendi, 2019; Robinson & Howard-Hamilton, 2000). Those unaware of their privileges perpetuate structural advantages and continue to entitle White, upper-class, male, heterosexual, able-bodied, Christian identities and social norms. Simultaneously, other identities are devalued and result in individual and systemic inequity, exploitation, and marginalization, perpetuating oppression. Most assessors were educated and learned to view the world within the confines of these invisible mental models of systemic bias resulting in assumptions, stereotypes, prejudices, and isms (sexism, genderism, racism, classism, and more). "To recognize and eliminate oppression, the visible and invisible interaction of privilege and oppression must be inspected" (Evans et al., 2010, p. 236).

Assessors practice within the norms, assumptions, and beliefs of these dominant cultural paradigms and "identity influences experiences and perceptions of power or lack thereof and affects how we think about and practice within power structures of colleges and universities" (Chavez & Sanlo, 2013, p. 9). Structural and systemic privilege, oppression, and bias affect how university administrators administer, how faculty teach, and how higher education professionals assess. "Recognizing how privilege and oppression intersect our complex lives and those of others helps untangle the systems of injustice perpetrated by those with privilege and power in our diverse higher education institutions" (Evans et al., 2010, p. 250). Failing to be aware of our own biases as assessors leads to assessment decisions and results that are inaccurate, perpetuate negative stereotypes, and cause harm to already marginalized and oppressed students. Thus, to ensure equity in higher education, all educators—including assessors—must acknowledge their various identities and become aware of the associated privileges and oppression that accompany them.

Assessors must become aware of their own, and others, positionality in relation to the social, cultural, and campus-specific context of the assessment project. Positionality affects the entire assessment process, from the way the question or problem is initially constructed, designed, and conducted to how data is analyzed and reported (Coghlan & Brydon-Miller, 2014). Positionality influences how we approach knowledge and what we believe we know (Bettez, 2015).

It is important for assessors to examine their own power, positionality, and biases as part of their assessment practice. As a White, cis, third-generation-educated, upper-middle-class-raised, able-bodied, woman, I (Anne) am coming into deeper awareness of how I have benefited from the educational and economic privilege of my grandparents and parents. I'm working to increase my awareness of the subtle ways that doors open for me, or access is granted in ways that they are not for those with marginalized identities and try daily to be mindful of where I can use my privilege and power to benefit others rather than perpetuate and contribute to that systemic oppression. As a White, cis, first-generation, working-class, disabled woman, I (Marilee) acknowledge that I had fully bought into the colonized mindset of higher education to hide the sense that I didn't belong. Now, unpacking where I intentionally and unintentionally perpetuate that systemic, marginalizing system requires constant awareness of owning my many privileges and taking actions to counteract those privileges. As a cis, biracial woman in the field of higher education, I (Danielle) know well the ways that higher education (and the systems that underpin it) are hostile to those lacking privilege and academic social capital. Knowing that I have privilege in some areas and lack it in others, I actively work to build and promote an intersectional approach to assessment that does not dismiss the voices and experiences of any community.

Assessors cannot shed their identities, nor would they want to. And, in fact, assessors cannot be objective. What they can do is actively explore and articulate their identities, become aware of their own positionality, privilege, and power in the assessment process, and engage multiple stakeholders in the assessment process, including students, who can and should bring the view of the world from their identity and positionality to the assessment process, enriching and illuminating the decisions assessors all too often make on their own from their limited, and biased, point of view.

The Aware Assessor

What is awareness? Awareness is noticing what you are noticing. Awareness is the quality or state of being *aware* (having or showing realization, perception, or knowledge): knowledge and understanding that something is happening or exists" (Merriam-Webster, n.d.). In this definition, it is inferred that awareness is more than a cognitive act of acknowledging something exists; instead, awareness is an embodied state of knowing. In essence, awareness is the intertwining of a felt sense of knowing something with the analytical understanding of knowing something. Neuroscience research on awareness is helpful here. By studying brain maladies, researchers have discovered that awareness is not just a brain process. Rather it is more like a computational rhythm that follows the laws of quantum physics (Pereira, 2016). The act of being aware gives rise to a subjective experience within individuals who are aware (Pereira, 2016). Because this awareness of noticing what you are noticing involves more than just your academic analytical self, the way you are experiencing that awareness is very subjective. And embodied awareness may or may not be easy to convey to your academic colleagues.

Perhaps an example is helpful here. Have you ever noticed getting caught up in a movie or a video and identifying with a character even though in your life you have very little in common with that character on the screen? When that happened to you, were you aware of it? Or did you become so involved, you didn't notice you were involved until after the video ended? Neuroscientists have shown that emotions play a role in cognitive decision-making processes (Damasio, 2003). This can happen instantly and without a person's awareness (Panksepp, 1998). Damasio (1994) has argued that emotions will rule the decision-making brain if people don't integrate awareness of the emotions into the decision-making process.

Being able to be with what you are noticing in an inquisitive, gentle, nonattached to judgment kind of way is often called mindfulness (Kabat-Zinn, 2013). Mindfulness is a type of awareness that has some explicit qualities for how you are experiencing your state of awareness and mindfulness is something that the aware assessor can practice and develop and bring to the assessment process. *Awareness breeds wise action* is a common wisdom teaching. Awareness can create opportunities for decolonization and equity-minded practices to prevail without knowing the exact action that needs to take place immediately. And an embodied awareness even means breeding a pause in the action when dialogue needs to ensue or more inquiry needs to take place. We argue that we won't know how to create something different without it.

Awareness Around the Assessment Cycle

Aware assessors recognize that discomfort in approaching assessment with an equity lens is part of the process. And that's okay. Throughout the rest of this chapter, we'd like to engage you in a dialogue about what becoming an aware assessor might look like. Awareness allows assessors to work through discomfort to "shift thinking about assessment from a set of structured steps that if followed guarantees fair evaluation and treatment of students to a tool that has to be considered within the larger institutional and social context" (Dorimé-Williams, 2018, p. 54). As you cultivate awareness, you'll feel more comfortable learning how to use frameworks and methods unfamiliar to you and not covered in your past experiences. You'll take a more critical look at research ideas and theories of knowledge that might once have seemed set in stone. Being an equity minded assessor means that you spend some time interrogating the work you do. You'll notice how at each stage of the assessment cycle, there are opportunities where you can act to improve equity on your campus.

Rather than a list of "dos and do nots," which are prescriptive and rarely invite awareness cultivation, it can be helpful to have sets of questions to explore as you think about your assessor role generally and throughout specific stages of your assessment practice. Consider that while they are posited as cognitive questions, the invitation is to notice what you are noticing in the emotional centers of the body as you apply these questions to your assessment work. Even if there are no words to describe what you may be sensing, consider speaking to, drawing, or leveraging other forms of self-expression to bring that awareness forward. Sometimes, simply inviting a pause in the decision-making process so that more dialogue and discernment can ensue advances thoughtful equity decisions.

The key to being aware as an assessor is to avoid falling into "blind proceduralism" (McArthur, 2016) or habitual patterns of doing things as they always have been done. Assessment practices are constructions, as influenced by historical inequity as much as society. That's not to say you must throw out all the rules and training you might be familiar with, but it does mean actively choosing to view those foundations through a critical lens.

> The decision as to what does or does not get included in an assessment rule or procedure is itself a socially constructed one reflecting many values and assumptions. Similarly, there is a normative social element to what gets included in the "fairness" equation—and a more complex commitment to social justice requires bringing these assumptions to the surface for scrutiny and debate. (McArthur, 2016, p. 973)

Most assessors are familiar with some form of an assessment cycle to guide their planning and practices. The specifics of assessment cycles can vary from institution to institution (Keeling, 2008; Schuh et al., 2016; Suskie, 2009; Yousey-Elsener et al., 2015) contain the same essential parts. Without a doubt the assessment cycle is a foundational element of assessment work and provides structure in planning. However, it should not be viewed as an opportunity to go on autopilot, moving mindlessly though familiar patterns. When considering what awareness looks like in each step of the assessment cycle, it may look like something different for each one of you. We'll explore equity-minded practices and approaches using this cycle: Determining Outcomes, Considering Methods and Collecting Data, Analyzing Data, and Using and Sharing Results (see Figure 18.1).

During each stage of the cycle, no matter the size and scope of the project, you can make choices that promote equity in assessment and in the decisions made as a result of assessment. You can use a critical eye to examine

Figure 18.1. The assessment cycle.

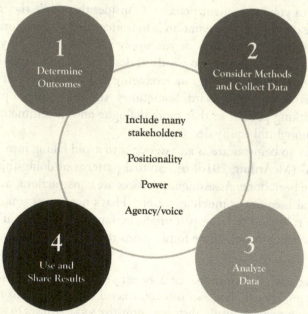

Note. The image was reproduced with permission from Lundquist, A. E. & Heiser, C. A. (2020). Practicing Equity-Centered Assessment. https://www.anthology.com/blog/practicing-equity-centered-assessment

and advocate to make better assessment choices in your work at every stage of the assessment process.

Reflective Questions for Embodying Awareness in All Stages of the Assessment Process

1. What promotes your acting from a place of awareness in the assessment process?
2. As you examine your assessment process, where are you forgetting to consider that this process and resulting data represent human beings that we are committed to serving and empowering their success?
3. Where in the process are you forgetting that outliers represent human beings too?
4. Who is around the table in dialogue and who is not?
5. Where are you assuming the application of shared values and where do values need to be clarified?
6. How is culture and context being considered in the process and data interpretation and usage?
7. Where are your community partners being leveraged to advance equity within all aspects of the assessment process?
8. How are you monitoring your own biases and emotions to advance equity?

Determining Outcomes

"Outcomes are critical components of any assessment program" (Henning & Roberts, 2016, p. 85) as they help determine what should be assessed, provide direction for planning and assessment, help students know what they are learning, and communicate to stakeholders the impact of programs, courses, and services (Henning & Roberts, 2016). It is critical that equity be addressed at the outcomes level; otherwise, the rest of the assessment process will be inequitable by default. There are three types of outcomes: operational (administrative or service), program, and learning and development (Henning & Roberts, 2016). Here, we'll focus on student learning outcomes specifically.

When developing learning outcomes, it is important to remember that there are many ways of knowing and being. As an aware assessor, the goal is not to develop and advocate for outcomes that evaluate all students as having the same identity and experiences. Our responsibility is to inquire into, understand, and account for the different ways students experience higher education. Neuroscience has shown that emotions are inextricably intertwined with student learning and development and cannot be separated (Damasio, 2003). This finding affirms the artificial separation of demonstrating evidence of "knowing" (Bresciani Ludvik, 2016, 2018, 2020; NAS, 2017, 2018). As such, it is ignorant and irresponsible to ask students to ignore or set aside any aspect of their identity, spiritual beliefs, ancestral ways, community culture, or any other aspect of their way of being to ask them to learn, develop, or assess their competence of what you expect them to know or do.

You will want to expand your toolbox to include unfamiliar frameworks or even develop new frameworks to understand the experiences of many different communities of students. You are probably already familiar or have done assessment work using frameworks such as Maslow's (1943, 1954) hierarchy of needs or Bloom's (1956) learning taxonomy. These are useful frameworks, but do not necessarily capture all student learning or experiences, and so should not always be the default choice when developing outcomes. It doesn't mean that they are *never* relevant, rather that each assessment and project should be given careful consideration when developing outcomes, without unconsciously privileging more familiar paradigms. In practice, this means that you, the assessor, remain open to learning and applying new knowledge and approaches to thinking about outcomes.

Many assessors inherit existing outcomes frameworks or have pressures from those who are not aware assessors. In these situations, it is imperative to advocate for expanding or using a variety of outcomes and outcomes frameworks to more equitably understand students. This could mean adapting existing models as well as including other ones that are more reflective of student populations. For example, LaFever (2016) in "Switching From Bloom's to the Medicine Wheel" outlined a four-domain framework that expands the three domains of learning set forth by Bloom to a four-domain framework based on the medicine wheel, expanding the cognitive, psychomotor, and affective domains to include the spiritual.

Being an aware assessor does not mean there's always an expectation of developing a new framework or reworking existing ones every time you do the work of assessment. But it does mean having an awareness of and willingness to explore new models, learning from your students, other ways of knowing that have meaning to them, and using new models that more equitably describe the student experience. It can also mean including students more directly in the drafting of the outcomes for the specific learning environment in which they will participate.

Aware assessors don't rush the outcome step or fall into autopilot. They take the time to consider the best way to articulate outcomes that are relevant to the student populations they want to assess. They consider and when possible, involve students in the development of the framework of outcomes to be assessed.

Reflective Questions for Determining Outcomes

1. Do you have a set of equity indicators that you monitor annually? Do you annually align your assessment outcomes and results to these indicators? (Bensimon & Malcolm, 2012; Dowd & Bensimon, 2015)
2. Do you collaborate with, lead, or invite your campus leaders to create assessment goals and achievement targets that are explicitly stated for identities and their intersections to improve retention, graduation, STEM participation, and [Insert name of other indicators that are important at your own institution]? And are your assessment outcomes and results aligned to these? (Bensimon & Malcolm, 2012; Dowd & Bensimon, 2015)
3. Have you evaluated your outcomes framework for dominant epistemologies and beliefs?
4. Does your outcomes framework include the experiences and values of all students and the communities to which they belong, especially marginalized populations?
5. Have you included students in the drafting of outcomes statements?
6. Do you revisit your outcomes regularly and make changes to reflect changing student populations?

Considering Methods and Collecting Data

The survey method for data collection is as ubiquitous as Bloom's taxonomy is to learning outcomes. Often, with little to no discussion or consideration as to whether a survey is the best method to answer the questions at hand or to reach the communities of focus, it is a default method for collecting data.

That is not to say this discussion is anti-survey or supportive of the removal of surveys from the higher education landscape. Far from it. There are many circumstances and questions where gathering data from a survey is completely appropriate. There is a preference for and higher value attributed to surveys because that information is considered more "valid" or "reliable" and often because they are more expeditious to implement. However, surveys can also hide the experiences of populations who experience inequity within the educational system. Too often, the voices of Black, Latinx, Asian, Indigenous, LGBTQ+, and first-generation students are lost in the mean or averages, viewed through deficit-minded lenses, or left to be mere "asterisk notes" (Shotten et al., 2012) in reports, thus remaining unheard. Particularly an issue for Native American student populations, similar knowledge deficits exist for other marginalized communities. Reliability and statistical significance matters, but the aware assessor advocates for methods that make visible the experiences of the invisible and raise the voices of the unheard as well. After all, how can institutions better serve students that surveys tell us little about?

The aware assessor considers multiple methods of data collection and selects the ones most appropriate to the context and assessment purpose. Mixed methods, focus groups, and interviews are equally valid assessment tools. The former takes more work and resources to implement well, which will likely result in pushback, but these methods can also be the best ways to gather information, both in terms of better understanding experiences and for building trust and relationships with specific populations. For developing relationships, focus groups and interviews can be great opportunities because they allow for students to share more narrative expressions of their experiences and assessors to ask follow-up questions, as opposed to the more structured format of a multiple-choice survey. The aware assessor should always consider what population's voices are absent or lost by choosing any method and make those limitations known in the instrument development and reporting.

Reflective Questions for Determining Assessment Questions and Selecting Methods

1. In selecting methods, have you considered how your students learn and develop?
2. Have you selected methods that balance the demand for rigor and generalizability with methods that inform cultural attentiveness and justice?
3. Have you solicited stakeholder input on the questions and prompts developed?
4. Have you examined the theory supporting standardized survey design and ascertained whether it is applicable across cultures?
5. Have you considered multiple and varied methods (e.g., storytelling circles, video blogs, rubrics, eportfolios, narratives, photos, document analysis, existing data analysis) that feature student voice?
6. Have you examined and evaluated language for bias, inclusion, signals of "normalcy" or homogeneity, and supportive identity orientation?

7. Have you provided opportunities to view all data through the lens of the student's lived experience (that first-person, direct-report student voice)?

Like the other parts of the assessment cycle, being present and conscious of the choices made during data collection is essential. Demographics and how people conceptualize their identities are ever evolving, so it's important that assessors stay up to date with how terminology around those groups of people changes over time. You might have colleagues pushing to continue to utilize the same demographics to maintain the same framing of existing longitudinal data and it may be tempting to do so, but that can "in turn lead to misguided notions of who the research applies to, who it might be generalizable to, or even result in communicating subtle but painful messages that perpetuate marginalization" (Hughes, 2016, p. 148).

Biased wording (such as out of date words used in the past to describe race or gender identity) in assessment questions can be harmful and could play a role in depression of the response rates of individuals in oppressed groups. Coding and communication can help you contextualize your data over time, even as the demographic and identity terminology change. Advocating for and updating terms is an action that an assessor can take that will not only help remove barriers that deter someone from a marginalized community from completing your assessment, but also will help the institution better understand how these groups conceptualize their identities. The aware assessor will also advocate for more accessibility in the tools used to gather evidence.

In some contexts, and for some campuses, accessibility in languages other than English also can help remove barriers to participation. Qualtrics and many survey vendors have tools for creating more accessible surveys and addressing these considerations. Campus partners can help ensure you can make equitable decisions on your campus when it comes to accessibility. Commitment to being an aware assessor means anticipating and planning for data collection in the most accessible ways. If no one is asking these questions or preparing to collect data with these considerations, speak up.

An aware assessor also takes into account the full context of how data collection impacts their campus. Most assessors are familiar with survey fatigue on their campuses, but the aware assessor also considers how data collection might impact certain populations more heavily. The aware assessor weighs the risks and benefits of how the data is collected. While it is not possible to entirely remove risk, it can be minimized when considered appropriately. For example, if much of the campus assessment focus at a given time is on particularly small populations on campus (such as Black men or undocumented students), it may be difficult for those from those populations to be bombarded with solicitations to share their lived experiences, particularly ones that touch on vulnerable topics. Students may be less likely to participate in assessment at all. An aware assessor will want to advocate for more coordinated data collection and requests that are not burdensome to that group.

Given the inequities in both societies and universities, marginalized populations already deal with the adverse impacts of systems not designed to foster their success. To improve circumstances, aware assessors balance the risks to those students by ensuring that the opportunity to benefit impacted students is always at the forefront of planning and execution. Will participants all receive benefits from the results of assessment?

Reflective Questions for Data Collection

1. Can people who are visually impaired take your surveys?
2. Do people who are deaf or hard of hearing have ways of participating in interviews or focus groups?
3. Are you choosing locations on your campus that people who use a wheelchair are comfortable reaching?
4. Are you using language that accurately reflects the identity of communities you want to reach?
5. Have you considered the risks and benefits that marginalized respondents might encounter as a result of the way the data was collected?

Analyzing Data

Biased analysis will lead to data being misused in ways that do not improve or expand the experiences of marginalized students, so it is important that the aware assessor actively reframes and questions how data is interpreted and utilized. When conducting analysis, it's important to remember that the outliers or small sizes represent human beings and tell just as much of the story as the aggregate, especially when small populations are involved (Bresciani Ludvik, 2020). It is imperative to maintain confidentiality and privacy for small sample sizes, however there are also ways to analyze and report on these data without revealing information that allows a respondent's identity to be inferred.

A focus on only the averages or most common responses should not be the only aspect of the results you highlight during analysis and reporting. For example, aggregate or average results from an assessment on "belonging" at a predominately White institution might reveal that most of your students feel comfortable at your institution. Using that data without digging deeper to examine targeted populations in context will not move the campus any closer to equitable education for all students because it will leave out the voices of those outside the dominant group. This means disaggregation of data and using qualitative data to understand the experiences of different student populations. Considering the context of your institution (Dorimé-Williams, 2018) is a key part of usefully interpreting assessment data and influences how you interpret student experiences. The experiences of students at Hispanic service institutions (HSIs) or historically Black colleges and universities (HBCUs) may be very different from those at predominantly White institutions (PWIs).

Often collaborative analysis, where you as a single assessor are not the only one interpreting the data, can help ensure that deeper campus context influences the analysis of the data. Similarly, a single assessor might utilize a checklist developed in collaboration to stay aware of key contextual issues. Triangulating multiple data sources, that is, bringing in multiple data sources and interpreting them in concert with each other, can also be an excellent way to understand the broader context of the experiences of populations that might not show up in an aggregate.

Reflective Questions for Analyzing Results

1. Have you triangulated your findings?
2. Have you engaged stakeholders in the interpretation and reporting process to ensure that the results are representative of the voices that matter, bias has been mitigated, and any deficit-orientated language can be readily identified, removed, and rewritten?
3. Have you disaggregated data by populations?
4. Have you engaged in multiple types of data analysis (e.g., within group and across group analysis; when comparing across groups, do not hold the White student experiences as the benchmark for comparison; consider equally the results for each group)?
5. When drawing comparisons across groups, have you contextualized the results in student experiences (e.g., not all students have the same resources, access, or experience)?
6. Have you had discussions around the "small N," remembering that they represent human beings so as not to silence historically marginalized students?
7. How much support do you provide your team members to examine the results of assessment data in a way that will lead to meaningful

improvements of the student experience, explicitly the advancement of equity and student success? (Bensimon & Malcolm, 2012; Dowd & Bensimon, 2015)

Using and Sharing Results

Ultimately, a major way to ensure that the results of an assessment benefit students and make for a more equitable campus experience is to use the data to make meaningful change. If you have data or know of data that is just sitting around or has not been reviewed or taken into consideration for decision-making (and it is still recent enough to be relevant), speak up. Ensure the data are analyzed and bring them to the attention of areas of your institution that influence change. How can an institution meet students' needs if there is no reported information on what those needs are? The campus will not be capable of understanding how to be more equitable without gaining some insight into student experiences. This is particularly important for students of color, given that higher education is a field where most with decision-making power do not resemble them.

Assessment can be used to build relationships among colleagues on campus as well as student populations. There are opportunities to do so throughout the assessment cycle and sharing the results of an assessment and changes made as a response is just one way of cultivating relationships using assessment. When assessment data is used to make changes or improvements, remember to follow up with the populations you are trying to better serve. Let them know that they and their fellow students' voices impacted a decision and maintain that relationship so that you can find out as time goes on whether the changes made improved their experiences.

Assessment professionals can have varying levels of power when it comes to influencing how data is used on campus. Administrators who sometimes lack assessment training or knowledge might ask for data to be presented in ways that do not promote progress or more socially just educational experiences. Aware assessors take every opportunity to present the information in such a way that equity and social justice are consistent in presenting the experiences of diverse student communities to policymakers and stakeholders. They might have specific topics in mind, but you get to choose how to present and what to emphasize. You get to contextualize and frame the information they receive. Adoption of a strategy that gives stakeholders the information they think they want, while also framing that data around issues of social justice, can educate and keep the experiences of marginalized students at the forefront, promoting that equity be the guiding star in making policy choices.

Reflection Questions for Using and Sharing Results

1. How will the data be used and by whom?
2. Who has the power to make change based on the results of the assessment?
3. What are the various ways that results will be shared with stakeholders, including students?
4. Do you collaborate with, lead, or invite your campus leaders to publish an annual report on the state of equity among various identities and their intersections and is that report informed by assessment outcomes and results? If it does not, who would need to make it happen? (Bensimon & Malcolm, 2012; Dowd & Bensimon, 2015)

The Role of Compassion and Self-Compassion in the Aware Assessor

As you read the examples of what awareness looks like within each step of the assessment cycle, you may have already experienced some moments of recalling times when you acted without awareness. Or you may be thinking about colleagues who are engaging in assessment without awareness. As such, you may be wondering what action looks like when awareness reveals choices that have been unjust. Given space limitations, we share only two specific types of actions that are grounded in awareness to promote justice. To frame this section, please consider that we are guided by Martin Luther King Jr.'s notion of justice illustrated into action by Rhonda Magee (2019), in that justice is "power correcting everything which stands against love. For example, racial justice, then, is about taking actions against racism in favor of liberation, inspired by love of all humanity, including actions at the personal, interpersonal, and collective levels" (p. 20). Magee contends that this notion of justice connected to awareness, like compassion, is just one form of an ethically grounded, mindful response to suffering in our lives. Moreover, "mindful racial justice seeks to alleviate not merely isolated incidents of racial suffering, but all suffering caused by racism—including suffering that is hard to see [or is missed because of a lack of awareness]" (Magee, 2019, p. 20).

Before we describe what compassion specifically means for restoring justice in unaware assessment practices, let's define what we mean by compassion. Compassion, like awareness, has a great deal of neuroscientific research to back up its existence. In short, compassion is defined into four parts:

- a feeling for another who is suffering,
- a genuine understanding of why another is in suffering even though you may not agree with what caused that suffering,

- a motivation or desire to have that suffering alleviated, and
- the action to collaboratively alleviate that suffering without harming self or other (Jazaeiri et al., 2012, 2013, 2014).

In this definition, awareness is woven through every aspect, not only with regard to the presence or absence of specific neural networks, but with regard to the necessity that a specific level of awareness must be present in order for each step of the compassion definition to be identifiable in human behavior.

For example, in the awareness cycle, a feeling for another's suffering is an action of expressed concern for those who may be inequitably impacted by unaware assessment practices. That is one vocally conveyed action but for compassion to truly be conveyed, the other three parts of the definition need to be identified. As such, the next component would be for the person to explain why that person may be inequitably impacted. Next, the person would express a genuine motivation to change the inequitable part of the process, and then finally act to make that change. With all four parts of the compassion definition identifiable in behavior, justice can be restored or acted upon in the first place. As you can see also in this definition, awareness of what is present in any step of the assessment process that is not equitable is a precursor for action.

Interestingly, there is additional mind training that needs to take place beyond that of awareness cultivation. While the awareness cultivation that we previously discussed serves as the foundation for action, awareness can exist without action ensuing. While we argue that awareness breeds wise action, awareness can also exist as simply awareness. As such, we recommend specific compassion cultivation training for that awareness to become realized into action that repairs harm or avoids harm caused by the assessment process.

Self-Compassion

It is important for the aware assessor to practice self-compassion and apply these four action steps toward oneself to continue to increase awareness and move toward equitable action. What is less obvious is just how to do that. Based on neuropsychology research (Germer & Neff, 2019; Neff, 2015; Neff & Germer, 2018), self-compassion is an action process that calms the inner critical voice that can take us out of the hard work of equitable assessment. The inner voice of the critic can look like the voice that beats you up when you made a mistake or missed the opportunity to act more equitably. It can also soften the inner voice that wants to criticize everyone else for their not being enough or not doing enough, which can more quickly lead to burnout and maladaptive stress behaviors.

While self-compassion also involves additional training, the steps to self-compassion will look familiar, particularly if you have studied student success research. The first two steps in the self-compassion action involve (a) acknowledging that you are in pain and suffering, and then (b) naming your suffering. This can, as we mentioned, be something as simple as acknowledging how you keep beating yourself up for making a mistake or not becoming more aware of something in the moment and naming it as regret, blame, or remorse. Or it can be feeling sadness or anger for witnessing another moment when you tried to get a colleague who still "doesn't get it" to understand why the process must change. Sometimes, the naming part is difficult and so sometimes, we just call our pain and suffering names that we can't reprint in this chapter. Neurologically, acknowledging and naming our pain and suffering—even with just one word—begins to soothe the overactive emotional center of the brain and allows the analytical reason portions of the brain to come online (Bresciani Ludvik, 2016). This can help us move back into compassionate action. However, sometimes we need more support and so additional self-compassion action steps offer that support.

Therefore, the third and fourth steps of the process involve (c) validating that you are in pain and suffering, such as saying to yourself silently, of course, I am angry with myself for messing up or I am angry I still can't get my colleague to understand why this is so important. And as you validate your own feelings, you (d) connect with others who have experienced what you have experienced, as in, who wouldn't be upset if they did what I did or said what I said or experienced what I experienced? Others have had this experience as well. I am not alone in this. Validating and connecting with others who have had your same experience, even silently, can again soothe the emotional pain and begin to move us back into compassionate action. And sometimes, we need more support, so there are more steps to self-compassion.

The fifth and sixth steps invite us into beginning to soothe our own pain and suffering by either (e) offering a soothing touch such as bringing your hands to your face, gently caressing your forearms, or bringing a hand to your heart. You can even give yourself a hug. And in offering that soothing touch which research has also shown to reduce physiological reactions to emotional pain and suffering, we can offer ourselves soothing words similar to words you would offer your best friend if they were in exactly the same position as you. Next, you can (f) silently ask yourself what you need to hear in this moment. And offer those words to yourself silently or speak them out loud if you feel safe to do so.

Finally, there is the seventh step of (g) asking yourself what you need to do in this moment to actively alleviate you from your pain and suffering and then give yourself permission to (h) act on that if that action does not harm you or another. This is our favorite step. Sometimes, we think eating an entire 16-ounce bag of peanut M&Ms will alleviate our pain and suffering, but that will cause us harm, so we have to ask again. And sometimes, it's journaling or reaching out to request a meeting with the person we need to talk to most in this moment. Regardless, you likely can see how awareness plays a foundational role in the act of self-compassion and compassion. Acting with compassion and self-compassion is one way that justice can be either restored or ensured in every step of the equitable assessment process.

The Role of Restorative Justice for the Aware Assessor

Though the field is now cultivating awareness and moving toward models of equitable assessment, the reality is that assessment work (like the rest of higher education) *has* caused hurt and harm to marginalized populations on our campuses. There is no way to erase it, but aware assessors who embed equity into their roles both acknowledge the existence of that harm while also working to use assessment as a path to restorative justice.

In *The Little Book of Restorative Justice* (2002), Howard Zehr describes restorative justice as "a process to involve to the extent possible, those who have a specific stake in a specific offense and to collectively identify and address harms, needs, and obligations, to heal and put things as right as possible" (p. 36). Restorative justice is a process by which communities work together to repair and remedy damage caused by harm. This offers validation and vindication to those who experienced the hurt and creates accountability and ideally growth for the parties or systems that perpetrated the damage.

Assessment differs from research in that its focus is on "gathering and analyzing data to convey information that can be used to make changes" (Yousey-Elsener et al., 2015, p. 9). Bias, harmful methods, deficit lensed analysis, unused or misused data, and more have happened and are happening in the field of assessment, causing harm to marginalized students and preventing universities from making socially just choices. Returning to focus with a slight reimagining of the idea of *conveying information to make changes* is where assessment and restorative justice should work hand-in-hand. A community cannot understand, identify, or account for harms, without the voices of the harmed.

Universities are all too often very siloed and paths to decision-making can be very unclear. Individuals doing assessment work and assessing programs might not feel fully empowered or as though you have the ability to make decisions that move the campus toward equity, let alone to use assessment for restorative justice. While you might not be able to use assessment to change the entire institution all at once, you do have the power to impact the aspects of your work that you control and through the collaborators you touch and seek out. Relationships are a major part of cultivating assessment culture on campus, and if you use your awareness of social justice to guide your work, being explicit that this is a driving motivation, others on campus will see or be impacted by the work you are doing.

Build connections with student groups who were potentially harmed by prior assessment practices and seek their feedback for developing new assessments. Educate other individuals on campus on how to develop their own awareness and to use that in the assessment work they might conduct for their programs. Partner with areas of the institution that have knowledge for driving equitable change and bring your assessment skills to support their efforts. As your network grows and the campus culture of assessment changes, the influence of many individuals will put pressure on the policymakers to adopt restorative justice practices.

The reality is, higher education, as a whole, is only just beginning to engage with practices of restorative justice. Academia, much like the history of the United States, has a deep history of oppression against many communities. Students are impacted by intersectional and overlapping hardships. Students who hold multiple oppressed identities deal with micro and macro aggressions in the world at large as well as in their educational experience. Few people with seats at the institutional decision-making level share those experiences, and the rest are not always aware of just how impactful these systems are or just how insidious of a role that universities play in perpetuating oppression. Once an assessor becomes aware, it is imperative to speak up, continue learning, and spread the awareness to colleagues. If you are in a position to make institutional-level decisions and changes, then assessment is so much more than just understanding and hearing the voices of marginalized students. You must also push for the university to move in a direction that seeks to remedy the ways in which higher education has caused harm. Always express context and share student voices, build connections and bring more people (maybe even the students themselves) to the table, and challenge your institution to use assessment to grow by taking accountability for changing harmful policies and frameworks.

Some impacts and harms can't be fully remedied until broader systemic changes happen in the world. However, universities have the ability to influence many transformative changes within their locus of control. By committing to restorative justice actions, colleges and universities have the opportunity to model how those systemic changes might work on larger scales, while also pressuring for those to occur in other parts of our society.

Students who benefit from a more equitable education and who experience policy changes they understand to come from a restorative motivation will go into post-collegiate life demanding (and creating) it everywhere.

Some Final Questions for the Aware Assessor

Your positionality, power, and privilege as an assessor may shift from assessment project to assessment project depending on the role you have at your institution, the other stakeholders involved, the stakes involved in the assessment project, among other factors. However, regardless of your identity, it is imperative to keep in mind that systemic racism is embedded in the very fabric of our institutions of higher education and that every assessment project provides an opportunity for assessors to examine their own biases and use assessment to expose practices that further marginalize students. We can begin with ourselves, approaching each new project with "beginner's mind," seeing the project with fresh eyes, as if you don't know what to expect and haven't already done it a thousand times, not taking anything for granted or clouding it with prejudgments.

And, finally, a simple list that you might tack to your wall as a gentle reminder to yourself:

1. Do you routinely examine your assessment practices to determine whether they meet criteria of equity-mindedness?
2. Have you conducted a study of assessment procedures to identify implicit bias and or outright discriminatory practices?
3. How does my identity influence the assessment project? How and where is that appropriate? Helpful? Harmful?
4. In what ways have I examined my own biases related to this assessment project?
5. What power do I have in this assessment project?
6. Given my identity, power, and privilege, what other stakeholders should I engage in this assessment project?
7. Are there ways for me to repair harm?
8. How am I practicing self-compassion?

As we close this chapter, we hope we have left you with several questions to ask in every step of your assessment process. Cultivating awareness is far from being a static process. It is a constant inquiry into self in the context of the lived experience so as to avoid causing harm to others. The greater your privilege, the more vigilant you must become with your inquiry.

References

Bensimon, E. M., & Malcom, L. E. (2012). *Confronting equity issues on campus: Implementing the equity scorecard in theory and practice*. Stylus.

Bettez, B. C. (2015). Navigating the complexity of qualitative research in postmodern contexts: Assemblage, critical reflexivity, and communion as guides. *International Journal of Qualitative Studies in Education*, *28*(8), 932–954. https://doi.org/10.1080/09518398.2014.948096

Bloom, B. S. (1956). *Taxonomy of educational objectives: The classification of educational goals*. Longmans, Green & Co.

Bresciani Ludvik, M. J. (Ed.). (2016). *The neuroscience of learning and development: Enhancing creativity, compassion, critical thinking, and peace in higher education*. Stylus.

Bresciani Ludvik, M. J. (2018). *Outcomes-based program review: Closing achievement gaps in and outside the classroom with alignment to predictive analytics and performance metrics* (2nd ed.). Stylus.

Bresciani Ludvik, M. J. (2019). How do we know what our students know they know? *US-China Education Review B*, *9*(5), 176–191. https://doi.org/10.17265/2161-6248/2019.05.002

Bresciani Ludvik, M. J. (2020). A new era of accountability: Resolving the clash of public good and economic stimulation performance indicators with evidence. In J. P. Freeman, C. Keller, & R. Cambiano (Eds.), *Higher education's response to exponential societal shifts*. IGI Global.

Chávez, A. F., & Sanlo, R. (Eds.). (2013). *Identity and leadership: Informing our lives, informing our practice*. NASPA.

Coghlan, D., & Brydon-Miller, M. (2014). *The SAGE encyclopedia of action research*. SAGE. https://dx.doi.org/10.4135/9781446294406.n277

Damasio, A. (1994). *Descartes' error: Emotion, reason, and the human brain*. Putnam.

Damasio, A. (2003). *Looking for Spinoza: Joy, sorrow, and the feeling brain*. Houghton Mifflin.

DiAngelo, R. (2018). *White fragility: Why it's so hard for white people to talk about racism*. Beacon Press.

Dorimé-Williams, M. (2018). Developing socially just practices and policies in assessment. In D. Zerquera, I. Hernández, & J. G. Berumen (Eds.), *Assessment and Social Justice: Pushing Through Paradox* (New Directions for Institutional Research, no. 177, pp. 41–56). Jossey-Bass. https://doi.org/10.1002/ir.20255

Dowd, A. C., & Bensimon, E. M. (2015). *Engaging the "race question": Accountability and equity in U.S. higher education*. Teachers College Press.

Evans, N. J., Forney, D. S., Guide, F. M., Patton, L. D., & Renn, K. A. (2010). *Student development in college: Theory, research, and practice*. Jossey-Bass.

Gergen, K. (2001). Psychological science in a postmodern context. *American Psychologist*, *56*(10), 803–813. https://psycnet.apa.org/doi/10.1037/0003-066X.56.10.803

Germer, C., & Neff, K. (2019). *Teaching the mindful self-compassion program: A guide for professionals*. Guilford Press.

Henning, G. W., & Roberts, D. (2016). *Student affairs assessment: Theory to practice.* Stylus.

Hughes, J. L. (2016). Rethinking and updating demographic questions: Guidance to improve descriptions of research samples. *Psi Chi Journal of Psychological Research, 21*(3), 138–151. https://cdn.ymaws.com/www.psichi.org/resource/resmgr/journal_2016/21_3Fall16JN-Hughes.pdf

Jazaieri, H., Jinpa, G. T., McGonigal, K., Rosenberg, E. L., Finkelstein, J., Simon-Thomas, E., Cullen, M., Doty, J. R., Gross, J. J., & Goldin, P. R. (2012). Enhancing compassion: A randomized controlled trial of a compassion cultivation training program. *Journal of Happiness Studies, 14*(4), 1113–1126. https://doi.org/10.1007/s10902-012-9373-z

Jazaieri, H., Jinpa, G., McGonigal, K., Rosenberg, E., & Finkelstein, J. (2013). Enhancing compassion: A randomized controlled trial of a compassion cultivation training program. *Journal of Happiness Studies, 14*(4), 1113–1126.

Jazaieri, H., McGonigal, K., Jinpa, T., Doty, J. R., Gross, J. J., & Goldin, P. R. (2014). A randomized controlled trial of compassion cultivation training: Effects on mindfulness, affect, and emotion regulation. *Motivation and Emotion, 38*(1), 23–35. https://doi.org/10.1007/s11031-013-9368-z

Kabat-Zinn, J. (2013). *Full catastrophe living: Using the wisdom of your body and mind to face stress, pain, and illness* (Rev. ed.). Bantam.

Keeling, R. P. (2008). *Assessment reconsidered: Institutional effectiveness for student success.* ICSSIA.

Kendi, I. X. (2019). *How to be an antiracist.* Penguin Random House.

LaFever. M. (2016) Switching from Bloom to the Medicine Wheel: Creating learning outcomes that support Indigenous ways of knowing in post-secondary education. *Intercultural Education, 27*(5), 409–424. https://doi.org/10.1080/14675986.2016.1240496

Lundquist, A. E., and Heiser, C. A. (2020, August 21). *Practicing equity-centered assessment.* Anthology. https://www.anthology.com/blog/practicing-equity-centered-assessment

Magee, R. V. (2019). *The inner work of racial justice: Healing ourselves and transforming our communities through mindfulness.* Tarcher Perigee.

Maslow, A. H. (1943). A theory of human motivation. *Psychological Review, 50*(4), 370–396.

Maslow, A. H. (1954). *Motivation and personality.* Harper and Row.

McArthur, J. (2016). Assessment for social justice: The role of assessment in achieving social justice. *Assessment & Evaluation in Higher Education, 41*(7), 967–981. https://doi.org/10.1080/02602938.2015.1053429

McIntosh, P. (1989, July/August). White privilege: Unpacking the invisible knapsack. *Peace and Freedom,* 10–12. Women's International League for Peace and Freedom. https://psychology.umbc.edu/files/2016/10/White-Privilege_McIntosh-1989.pdf

McIntosh, P. (2003). White privilege: Unpacking the invisible knapsack. In S. Plous (Ed.), *Understanding prejudice and discrimination* (pp. 191–196). McGraw-Hill.

Merriam-Webster. (n.d.). Awareness. In *Merriam-Webster.com dictionary*. https://www.merriam-webster.com/dictionary/awareness

National Academies of Sciences, Engineering, and Medicine. (2017). *Supporting students' college success: The role of assessment of intrapersonal and interpersonal competencies*. The National Academies Press. https://doi.org/10.17226/24697

National Academies of Sciences, Engineering, and Medicine. (2018). *How people learn II: Learners, contexts, and cultures*. The National Academies Press. https://doi.org/10.17226/24783

Neff, K. (2015). *Self-compassion: The proven power of being kind to yourself*. Guilford.

Neff, K., & Germer, C. (2018). *The mindful self-compassion workbook: A proven way to accept yourself, build inner strength, and thrive*. Guilford.

Panksepp, J. (1988). *Affective neuroscience: The foundations of human and animal emotions*. Oxford University Press.

Pereira, C. (2016). Consciousness is quantum computed beyond the limits of the brain: A perspective conceived from cases studied for hydranencephaly. *Neuro-Quantology: An Interdisciplinary Journal of Neuroscience and Quantum Physics, 14*(3), 613–618. https://philpapers.org/archive/PERCIQ.pdf

Robinson, T. L., & Howard-Hamilton, M. F. (2000). *Convergence of race, ethnicity, and gender: The multiple identities in counseling*. Pearson.

Schuh, J. H., Biddix, J. P., Dean, L. A., & Kinzie, J. (2016). *Assessment in student affairs*. Wiley.

Shotten, H., Lowe, S. C., & Waterman, S. J. (Eds.). (2012). *Beyond the asterisk: Understanding native students in higher education*. Stylus.

Suskie, L. (2009). *Assessing student learning: A common sense guide*. Wiley.

Yousey-Elsener, K., Bentrim, E. M., & Henning, G. W. (Eds.). (2015). *Coordinating student affairs divisional assessment*. Stylus.

Zehr, H. (2002). *The little book of restorative justice*. Good Books.

Zerquera, D., Hernández, I., & Berumen, J. (2018). Editor's notes: Introduction to the special issue. In *Assessment and Social Justice: Pushing Through Paradox* (New Directions for Institutional Research, no. 177, pp. 7–14). Jossey-Bass. https://doi.org/10.1002/ir.20253

19

AN INVITATION TO A BEGINNING RATHER THAN THE END

Divya Samuga_Gyaanam+Bheda, Natasha A. Jankowski, and Peter Felten

Throughout the course of this book, readers have been introduced to a myriad of resources, conceptions, and ideas about equity and assessment. At the onset of the publication, an argument was made as to why a book focused on exploring the relationship between equity and assessment is even needed. Chapter authors made the case for assessment activists and provided a foundation and update for readers unfamiliar with the history and literature of equitable assessment in higher education. Further, the placement of equity and assessment within four philosophical lenses was presented as a means to help communicate with each other and those within our institutions as well as understand how equitable assessment work sits outside of the compliance/improvement divide. The authors led readers through an exploration of the role of narratives in assessment as a vehicle for advancing or hindering equity in assessment, reminding us all that it is less about the terminology used to talk about the work of equity in assessment and more about the actions and the stories that reinforce inequities or lift up learning. Different models and approaches to engage in equitable assessment were presented as well, guiding the reader into practice-oriented sections of the book focused on assessment within the classroom, academic programs, student affairs, and across an entire organization designed to serve as examples of equitable assessment from which others can learn. Further, chapters with examples from different institutional types including community colleges and historically Black colleges and universities (HBCUs) and the role of technology in equitable assessment rounded out the practice portion of the book.

Throughout all the chapters, a dual focus was presented on the need to engage in individual work as well as organizational work in advancing equity in assessment—whether through assessment professionals as reflective professionals or as activists committed to the cause of undermining majoritarian, normative regimes. While the authors of this chapter think this book provides an excellent point of entry or continuation to recharge on an equity in assessment journey, it does not claim to provide all the answers, cover all the terrain, or be the end of the conversation. Instead, this edited collection offers an invitation to continue the conversation. The different authors offer ways to understand how to move forward depending on where one sits within an institution and within higher education as a whole. To reshape education as equitable requires not only a village, but a reshaping of the village. It requires, as the three of us argue in this chapter, a shift of what is in focus. It requires a reimagining of the way higher education institutions function to see that equity work is work that cannot be done alone but must be done with others and within communities. There is no checklist or four-step process to attain equity offered in this chapter, instead the three of us invite readers to continue thinking and working together and offer a means to see differently how to engage in equity work.

There are three authors of this chapter in alphabetical order as follows:

- Divya Bheda brings a wealth of expertise from working at various institutions of higher education as an assessment professional but also over a decade of experience in the field of program evaluation and social justice training. The lens she brings of program evaluation, holistic institutional responsiveness, a commitment to student success, and passion for making change happen connects assessment and equity conversations to the larger landscape of higher education, placing this work within the context in which it exists and can thrive organizationally.

- Peter Felten is executive director of the Center for Engaged Learning and professor of history at Elon University. He writes extensively about the lived experiences of undergraduate students, students as partners in learning and teaching, and relationship-rich education. He brings the lens of faculty development to the conversation—a vital partner to any change effort in higher education.

- Natasha Jankowski brings the knowledge of over a decade of examining assessment nationally from her work with the National Institute for Learning Outcomes Assessment (NILOA) along with a focus on learning systems, alignment, and meaningful engagement in making the educational experience more impactful for all who participate—whether faculty, staff, or students.

The Change We Seek

In our author meetings about this chapter, the three of us recognized that higher education needs to work on practices, administration, and systems; or, put another way, assessment professionals need to attend to the micro-, meso-, and macro-levels of our work. Focusing on practices and course/program-level assessment is important, but those are surface level adjustments. These micro-level changes do not critically challenge the macro-level systems and assumptions underlying assessment and higher education more generally. Higher education's current inequities are in no small measure a result of inequitable foundational systems—colleges and universities tend to get the results the system is designed to produce. If systems of higher education are designed to be inequitable, that raises a troubling question for any efforts at reform: Is it possible to tweak our way to equitable assessment by making small changes to micro-level practice and not critically questioning meso- or macro-level systems or assumptions?

The three of us answered that question "yes but no." In many contexts, assessment can become more equitable by tweaking practices, yet in many others significant progress will require systematic change. In some ways, this is the difference between doing equitable assessment and using assessment for equity. Changing assessment practices can make assessment processes more equitable, but may not necessarily enable assessment to be used to further equity. Natasha likes to say "It depends" generally is the right answer to all questions.

The three of us recognize that any call for analyzing and changing both practices and systems (micro and macro) can feel disempowering for many people who are in positions to influence practice but who don't see themselves as capable of systemic or institutional change. Yet assessment can act as a lever in the heavy lifting necessary to make higher education more equitable. So yes, this is hard but essential work, and what is done in day-to-day practice can spark significant change if the assessment lever is applied in the right place at the right time (see chapter 2, this volume, on assessment professionals as activists for a brief fire up to get moving). But that lever can only do the lifting if the system and structures allow it to gain traction and the meso-level of administrative support affirms it, so assessment professionals need to cultivate allies who can help them make change happen. It takes a village to help lift such a heavy load.

As Natasha points out, an important part of system consideration is thinking carefully about the purposes and ends of assessment: What are we really trying to do, become, or document with assessment processes and practices? Is it an end in itself or a means to an end? Engaging in thinking about infusing equity into and fostering equity through assessment challenges us to see our practices and policies as either racist or anti-racist, not benignly neutral and objective. Peter brought to our attention the work of Kathleen Fitzpatrick (2019) writing about "generous thinking" as a radical approach to saving the university. Fitzpatrick (2019) describes generous thinking in part as "working to think *with* rather than *against*" (p. 35) and in part as listening and thinking fundamentally for understanding of other perspectives rather than primarily to critique or argue with texts and people. Her emphasis was on moving away from individual expertise and achievement to ask instead: "What if the expertise that the university cultivated were at its root connected to building forms of collectivity, solidarity, and community both on campus and off?" (p. 44). Fitzpatrick's work aligns with ongoing projects to decolonize higher education and to build more equitable and inclusive systems from the ground up, raising the question: What happens if we try to assess generously?

At this juncture, readers might think, "Oh my, this is a lot to consider and sounds like an ongoing journey of growth and action to advance equity and assessment. Am I ready for this charge or up to this task?" Whether we feel ready or not, our students, our colleagues, our institutions, and our communities *need* us to act. They require us to align our espoused values with our lived ones. Also, the choice to engage in this work or not is one of privilege and Whiteness. As Natasha, a White woman in this work, affirmed in our author meetings, equity in assessment work is not the work of our colleagues of color, but necessarily the work of White folx because the risk is minimal and "more often than not, our privilege does not deplete." Our White colleagues have the power to change systems in ways our colleagues of color often do not. Such positionality requires White colleagues to act and that action can be an invitation. Peter, recognizing his daily lived position of a scholarly, well-established, White, heterosexual man, argued that part of our work in equity is to invite people of color into spaces and opportunities they otherwise would not have been given. It is to notice the absence of faces, voices, and representation. Often, it may require problematizing the conversation, decision, or culture. Sometimes it may mean being a lone dissenter. For those of us with privileged identities, it requires being a connector by serving as the welcoming party for our colleagues of color in this work. If we start to see ourselves and our work through an equity lens, system change is possible.

This book includes various examples from institutions that are trying out different approaches or engaging in the change process of responding to equity in assessment by exploring what may be possible within this space. We offer these examples, not as exemplars for all to follow, but as instances of "visions of the possible" (Shulman, 1999, para. 20) to help readers avoid becoming discouraged by the breadth and depth of the charge of addressing equity. As Peter noted, these examples show that intentional efforts to change are possible, even though the times are challenging and the outcomes are uncertain.

In response to a call from the editors of this book for examples of emerging practices working to address issues of equity, Bethany Alden-Rivers, Shane Williamson, and Kaitlyn Maxwell of the Office of Institutional Effectiveness and the Office of Student Life and Diversity from Lindenwood University provided the following illustrative example. The two offices partnered to create a professional development opportunity for Lindenwood University employees. Open to all faculty and staff, the Certificate in Culturally Responsive Assessment was launched in October 2019 as a way to encourage participants to see differently and explore assessment practices that are inclusive of and responsive to the diverse nature of students at the institution. The certificate was created for three main reasons: (a) colleagues wanted to take part in the emerging national conversation on culturally responsive assessment; (b) funding was available to bring expert guest speakers to campus; and (c) the program's organizers aspired to create a learning experience that would lead to systemic change as opposed to one-time participation. The certificate provided a means to engage participants in a series of activities and personal reflections through a curriculum that was developed through conversations with members of the diversity, equity, and inclusion committee and the assessment committee. In order to earn the certificate, participants must complete a required introductory webinar, two core development opportunities, four focused development opportunities, and draft a 1,000-word reflective account of professional practice that is then peer reviewed. Core development activities used existing opportunities within Lindenwood including the diversity, equity, and inclusion book club, Safe Zone Training, and implicit bias training. Focused development opportunities included facilitated workshops and prerecorded webinars by national experts in culturally responsive assessment. The personal reflection asks participants to articulate the ways in which these professional development experiences have informed their own practice. Despite a disrupted 1st year due to the pandemic, 22 colleagues completed all the requirements for the certificate and more than 35 are in process toward completion. Comments from participants gathered in evaluations of the certificate shared the following:

> I see three areas of practice which will benefit my students directly and Lindenwood as a whole. First, I am recommitted to self-reflection. Second, I am dedicated to a review of my courses, specifically connection of assignments to different groups of students. Finally, I will review student comments and reflections as I look for ways to incorporate student opinion more in program assessment strategies. (Participant B)

> The best part of this experience was feeling like I was truly doing something that mattered. I often get bored and complacent in my current role, and I always left those sessions feeling refreshed, motivated, and re-empowered to make a positive impact. It also brought forth a sense of community. I felt safe in those spaces and often thought "oh yea, these are my people." (Participant C)

In another response to the call from the editors of this book for examples of examining practices differently, Gaelan Lee Benway from the Center for Academic Excellence at Quinsigamond Community College shared the following vignette about the equity and excellence experience which is a yearlong collaborative venture into equity and inclusive excellence that ran for the first time in 2018–2019 and is now in its 3rd year. The project teams faculty and staff together to design and deliver innovative learning experiences to a group of students during the academic year. Quinsigamond Outcomes Research for Excellence (QORE) recruits participants from among new hires, colleagues from minoritized backgrounds, equity-minded workshop attendees, and other campus networks. The project is steered by an equity and excellence street team: QORE plus chairs of the diversity council (governance), diversity caucus, the president's advisory council on equity, the dean and administrative secretary of distance learning, and the center for academic excellence, signaling support from throughout the institution. The goals are to do the following: prepare students for—and provide them with access to—high-quality learning opportunities; ensure that students of color and low-income students participate in the most empowering forms of college learning; value and use the cultural capital of underserved students; and invest in culturally competent practices that lead to the success of underserved students and all students by investing in leadership for equity. Further, supporting equity by paying people for their labor; faculty, both full-time and part-time, are compensated for their time during the summer intensive and assessment work. Staff members must carve time out from their regular duties and negotiate participation as college service with their supervisors. In a modest effort to redress this inequity, all participants receive a letter describing their individual efforts and contributions for their supervisors and personnel files. However, that the difference between faculty and staff compensation was noted and institutional mechanisms of review and hiring were considered speaks to the means by which equity efforts need to take a variety of steps forward to advance the work.

While these two different efforts are highlighted in this chapter (and other examples are highlighted in chapter 4), we want to emphasize that in equitable assessment we should not try to simply apply models from one context into another and expect a positive impact. Those participating and impacted by the processes are the ones whose voices and perspectives must always matter. Equity work is deeply rooted within institutional and structural context. As Divya emphasized in our author conversations, the goal is not "just doing something that feels or seems right or signals commitment, but doing something critically, with intentionality, and humility" that matters. An ongoing willingness to incorporate justice into the design or actual deployment of "equity-work" to ensure no unintentional harm is essential. What equity work requires is a shift in focus.

Shifting the Focus

In order to engage in assessment differently, we need to see things differently. Divya was gracious enough to share a conceptualization of the different spaces and places of equity work pulled from a 2020 AALHE Assessment Conference presentation that was then further developed in a keynote for the University of California Davis assessment conference and thereafter in the IUPUI 2021 conference. She offered three areas to consider in shifting attention including equity arenas, equity actors, and equity actions.

- Equity arenas are spaces and places within which equity can be infused.
- Equity actors are influencers or those to be influenced and can include faculty, staff, students, leaders, community members, and, of course, assessment professionals.
- Equity actions are the actions that can be taken on by any actor based on their agency, allyship, and whether the context is an empowering one.

As we engage in our equity journeys, it may be useful to craft a list of these three areas, such as Table 19.1, where we can outline equity arenas, equity

TABLE 19.1
Equity Positionality Worksheet

Equity Arenas	Equity Actors	Equity Actions

actors, and equity actions to help determine where to focus action and attention at different times throughout the equity journey. We cannot do it all at once, and sometimes, it will be the teaching center that does it, other times the assessment office, and other times, student affairs. The table may serve as a tool for assessment professionals to determine allies and spaces of action, within a unique institutional context. It can even be a table that we make for our own personal journey where the equity actor is ourselves.

However, the table is simply a list of spaces, places, and people if we do not also shift our focus. When Divya was explaining the table to Peter and Natasha, she emphasized that what is key to moving forward is *perceiving or experiencing* differently and *being different*. She said there are *anchors* to our equity work that guide how we delve into and deploy action, how we perceive our roles as actors, and the possibilities/opportunities we see and explore in the different arenas. These anchors are pervasive and foundational elements and include

- relationships and community building;
- communication skills;
- rethinking the use of time, deadlines, and priorities; and
- embodying social justice through interrogating power and identity of self, ultimately leading to activism and solidarity in our efforts.

To help the reader we offer a few examples of what might be in such a table and how the anchors relate. While what is in the table may change, without the anchors of communication, time, social justice, and collaboration, we cannot engage in equity work to the full extent possible. The anchors provide the foundation to change how we see things and our work. It is the positionality and stance—that is, anchors—that makes this table about equity, not simply having equity written in front of each of the header titles.

For instance, within the equity arena of the classroom (whether virtual or not), Divya argued that there are various equity arenas to consider including the syllabus composed of learning outcomes, assignments, references and readings, policies, and resources. When the syllabus is reimagined through the anchors of time and communication, the first class and initial communications with the students can be reimagined. The tone set at the start of the class, the opportunity to cocreate a syllabus with students, an invitation to the students to help those who developed the course see what they cannot or did not see in what has been presented that impacts the students, all become elements worthy of time and discussion. If instead of seeing the class and assessments in focus, the focus shifts to the spaces and environments of educating, the physical learning environment and its connection to assessment can be considered differently. Peter connected with Divya's explanation through Gestalt theory of perception. He shared that there are things we focus upon and while focusing on those elements, other pieces fade into the background. Consider when taking a picture where we focus on a person's face and the area around them blurs out of focus. The anchors act as the focusing agent. The anchors do not change someone's position or make them have to become a different person or a different kind of professional. The same things are in the picture both times. What is changed is what is in focus and because of the focus, what is perceived. What becomes in focus is social justice as the figure and the rest of the image fades to the background. We know everything else is still there in the image, but the faded background is not shaping what we are seeing. Instead, we can see the image in a different way. And once we start to see the work differently, we can help colleagues perceive it differently as well. Much like the image of two faces or a vase, once we can see both, we cannot unsee or unperceive it. Divya described this in our author meetings through the conception of reflexivity.

Reflexivity is a proactive, metacognitive, self-interrogative practice that helps open the curtain and shine light on hidden, unconscious assumptions, values, and norms that we embody, enact, or privilege that impact how reality is perceived and how decisions are assessed, evaluated, and made (Bheda & Jones, 2020). Being reflexive requires seeking the unknown and constantly interrogating the intent, action, and impact of what we do and how we see the world. It is about seeking cognitive dissonance and being comfortable in discomfort. The questions reflexivity explores are—what am I missing here in this context? What are my assumptions about the "right" way of doing things? How are my assumptions leading to a self-fulfilling prophecy in terms of my actions and their impact? Who have I missed or discounted or ignored in considering the impact of my actions? Who has power in my assessment context? Who has voice and who is silenced or marginalized—intentionally or unintentionally?

As Divya shared—when trying to achieve equity through assessment or equity in assessment, an additional concern is the central question of focus: "equity for whom?" Is attention centered on equity for students? Is it equity for colleagues of color? Is it equity for all those made invisible, silenced, marginalized, or oppressed by systems of power? The "who" helps clarify the "why" (why are we engaging in equitable assessment? to what end?) and the "why" should help decide the "what," "how," and "when" of the action. Many times, the focus is only on the "what," "how," and "when" (often compliance-driven). When the focus is on processes, policies, or practices, what is forgotten is to what end and for whom? Without a focus on equity for whom, the depth and rigor of our critical effort is negatively impacted, and our work and ability to authentically engage others in our cause suffers. We may be working to advance equity with one group in one context while unknowingly perpetuating oppression with another. Thus, it behooves us to clarify the "who" and "why" part before undertaking any action and to constantly center it as we engage in action. Table 19.1 provides a tangible means and space to help aid in putting on equity lenses and consider the anchors to perceive or see more clearly what has been in the background and out of focus.

Examples of Seeing Differently in Practice

What might some examples of this approach look like in practice? In our conversations, Natasha raised the example that while a faculty member might go through an exercise of revising an assignment to be more equitable, little will be accomplished if the learning outcome to which the assignment is aligned and was redesigned to support is inequitable and/or if the curriculum is exclusionary. One assignment alone, while a starting point, is not enough to move the needle because it exists within a curricular system as well as an educational system where students have learned to be wary of outlier experiences where they are seen or felt a sense of belonging. Seeing the intersections and moving the background to the foreground can help focus attention on equity work that advances student learning within different parameters. By shifting the focus, new questions emerge on the equitable nature of the readings, course structures, catalog, learning outcome development process, and more.

Divya shared the example of reimagining institutional reward structures and program hiring processes and practices differently—both of which are factors that impact program development and implementation as well as the student experience with the program. Who is involved in the curriculum creation process? Who determines the readings? Who gets a say in suggesting changes or additions? What role is played by student and faculty evaluations? Which faculty have access to funding, flex time, and which have heavier loads and more student advisees? What is the process of hiring and orienting new faculty into the program? All of these are things to consider when equity anchors are utilized to examine practice.

If some of these examples seem ambitious and tangentially connected to assessment, assessment professionals might learn a lesson from a longitudinal study of faculty development initiatives: "Targeting simpler outcomes provides a clear focus for development, but it also carries the message that this development is not really very important—thus making success more difficult to attain" (Condon et al., 2016, p. 120). Equity-building work is not simple. It is complex. As Peter pointed out, research suggests that faculty value educational development *more* when they believe that work is connected to a purpose that they value. If the same is true in assessment, then faculty would value assessment more if they came to see it as a vital tool for equity. In other words, by helping faculty colleagues see that equitable assessment is the goal, they are more likely to commit their time and energy to it. Indeed, faculty assessment fellows who work to shift from compliance to assessment advocacy on issues of equity have demonstrated the importance of articulating bold, meaningful goals for assessment (Hong, 2018). This is the case beyond the academic program too. To engage in equity work is not a solo journey, but one undertaken with a community that engages many allies, supports, and opportunities to help colleagues see differently when equity is brought into focus. In institutions of higher education, there are many learning and experience spaces for all participants—from students and educators in the classroom to students and educators outside the classroom. These various arenas serve as opportunities for action. Arenas inside the classroom in the program and outside the classroom—in student affairs, academic affairs, social events and programming, communications, and so on, impact the ways in which learning unfolds in an institution. Arenas include institutional policies, accreditation endeavors, data collections and analysis, governance, and feedback mechanisms. Strong support for equity is needed from leadership. This support also needs to be pervasive in institutional culture as well. As Natasha highlighted, providing a narrative that aligns equity work to the institutional mission, embedding it in professional development and training that is supported with necessary resources of time and money, can advance equity in assessment.

In a piece on building learning communities through critical pedagogy and translingual practice, Williams (2020) wrote, "The overlooked truth of higher education is that ongoing instructor development is necessary to maintain quality classroom experiences for students and to continually elevate and evolve curricula" (p. 112). Equity work is not possible at scale without institutional support.

Where Do We Go From Here?

As was mentioned at the onset of this chapter, this book is not the end but a beginning. The examples and frames shared offer lenses to think about the places where equity work could reside within policy and practice. The book also serves to remind us, using a metaphor raised by Natasha, that much like nesting dolls, policy and practice operate within assumptions about who students are, what they can do, how they learn, and what counts as evidence of learning. That nesting doll resides inside the specific and unique institutional context, history, and institutional norms that will enable or inhibit equity work from happening. Our own location within an institution shapes the views of what is (and is not) a problem and what changes are possible. Think of examining the nesting dolls with a flashlight and discovering they are composed of prismatic materials, flashing certain shades and lights on different walls. Different things matter to and are seen differently by people within institutions—which is directly tied to different stakeholder roles and viewpoints within the institution.

Values encapsulate all these nesting dolls. Assessment professionals have to be mindful and aware of the intersecting nature of their positions and work. As Natasha explains, assessment professionals should be, ideally, crossing all of the prismatic pieces because assessment professionals sit at the intersection of activity at the institution; they need to be prepared with questions and equity positions for the different actors with whom they intersect. Acting as the conscience of the institution, assessment professionals can continually ask "how are we contributing to equity?" Such a conceptualization would look fundamentally different from the traditional roles of many assessment professionals, and it pushes higher education toward a future that is not yet known. That is something for the field to figure out and this book serves as an invitation to help in the reimagining of assessment.

There are challenges and tensions to all of this, as Natasha constantly reiterates. There are trade-offs and dilemmas, and no easy answers in making this work a reality within the real-world confines of an institution. But great things unfold within institutions of higher education including the ability to suddenly be flexible. In March 2020 in response to COVID-19, institutions pivoted to remote instruction, and embraced the full humanity of students (and faculty and administrators for that matter) to help cope as people and learners in a pandemic. Riding the tidal wave of change, the role of educator can be rethought, becoming comfortable with being uncomfortable and learning to introduce counternarratives into the system. Through integrity and vulnerability, much can be accomplished.

Peter rightly cautions that while the aim is for big goals, the perfect should not be allowed to be the enemy of the good. As higher education professionals, we should critically examine what is within our control and capacity to meaningfully change, and then focus there; even when our lot is constrained there is a little space in which we can play and push for more space. There will be failures and hiccups along the way, but equity in assessment is not an all or nothing game. It is discursive and recursive. Divya states that we can problematize ourselves in this work too and we grow and learn along the way. While the three of us are aware that this work is not quick enough for our students and those living the impact of injustices in a multitude of overlapping ways and spaces, it is always the right time to engage in systemic work.

Peter, in our writing conversations, said that one of his mentors likes to call the faculty development center the pedagogical conscience of the institution, a vital voice for reminding everyone about their ethical commitments in teaching and learning. When applied to assessment, the argument could be made that assessment professionals can be the equity conscience of the institution, given the continuous improvement responsibilities and positionality as a cross functional unit across the institution. Being the equity conscience of the institution means that assessment professionals are always there, always asking, "How is this making us more equitable?"

As authors of this chapter, we are aware that there are some voices in this book and many that are not here. There are many voices that do not have an opportunity to write, participate, or be heard even though they are the knowledge creators and the daily doers of equity work. While we, as authors, tried to live our practice and engage in our own processes of making space for others, there are a great many people *doing* the work who do not have the time to *write* about it. We recognized the irony or rather the hard reality and truth of our current context as we wrote this chapter and reflected on the journey of how this book came to be. Natasha acknowledged that writing a book about equity and assessment during a pandemic and during this time of racial unrest and trauma meant that many equity champions were stretched even thinner as they engaged and continue to engage in the work of healing. We, as authors of this chapter, and contributors to this book, are privileged in that we have been granted a platform and have the bandwidth to write and share our knowledge and perspectives. We will likely reap the benefits of this intellectual effort with further recognition and invitation into new spaces. And if that happens, we hope to live our commitment to equity by shining the light on the work of our colleagues of color and offering them the spotlight. We hope to bring them along with us into these new spaces we enter. We want to affirm that while this is a final chapter, it is not the close but an opening of space for others.

We want to end by reiterating this. You may feel like you have no power, and you can't get someone to do anything—which is why in assessment we often turn to compliance. But we remind you that authority is different from power and that there are many types of power. There is a lot of good trouble assessment professionals can get into, and you have agency. Higher education and society writ large is in need of courageous conversations and vulnerability. Every time you talk about equity, what do you have to lose? As Peter graciously reminded us in the writing of this chapter, almost nobody knows what they are doing with assessment outside the assessment professionals who have expertise in the subject. Why not go into meetings as the experts you are and declare that "equitable assessment is what good assessment looks like" because no one else knows the literature. You have the power and space to agenda set, frame, introduce tools, and claim the space of expertise. There is an acronym floating in the social justice space. Social justice work is being referred to as JEDI work—that is, Justice, Equity, Diversity, and Inclusion work. This acronym makes us smile. After all, there is an inspirational and aspirational element to being a JEDI warrior. We need more JEDI champions in this world. We can be assessment JEDIs. So what are you going to do with this newfound power?

References

Bheda, D., & Jones, A. (2020, Nov 16). FIE TIG week: Reflexivity and the importance of practicing it in evaluation. *AEA365 Blog*. https://aea365.org/blog/fie-tig-week-reflexivity-and-the-importance-of-practicing-it-in-evaluation-by-divya-bheda-alissa-jones/

Condon, W., Iverson, E., Manduca, C., Rutz, C., & Willett, G. (2016). *Faculty development and student learning: Assessing the connections*. Indiana University Press.

Fitzpatrick, K. (2019). *Generous thinking: A radical approach to saving the university*. Johns Hopkins University Press.

Hong, R. (2018). Faculty assessment fellows: Shifting from a culture of compliance to a culture of assessment advocacy. In D. Zerquera, I. Hernández, & J. G. Berumen (Eds.), *Assessment and Social Justice: Pushing Through Paradox* (New Directions for Institutional Research, no. 177, pp. 105–119). Jossey-Bass. https://doi.org/10.1002/ir.20259

Shulman, L. S. (1999). *Visions of the possible: Models for campus support of the scholarship of teaching and learning.* Carnegie Foundation for the Advancement of Teaching and Learning. http://archive.carnegiefoundation.org/publications/elibrary/visions-of-the-possible.html

Williams, C. (2020). "Even though I am speaking Chinglish, I can still write a good essay": Building a learning community through critical pedagogy and translingual practice. In D. C. Maramba & R. T. Teranishi (Eds.), *Transformative practices for minority student success: Accomplishments of Asian American and native American Pacific Islander-Serving institutions* (pp. 101–115). Stylus.

Danielle Acheampong has worked in UCLA's Student Affairs Information and Research Office since 2014 consulting with Student Affairs departments to guide assessment efforts. Through her work, Acheampong seeks to empower staff by supporting the development of assessment skills and confidence. She serves as the 2020–2021 cochair for the ACPA Assessment Institute. Acheampong holds a BA in history from University of Puget Sound, and an MA in museology from the University of Washington. As an audience researcher prior to working in universities, she conducted several studies for museum clients and enjoys bringing unusual perspectives and methods to assessment in higher education.

Gianina R. Baker, PhD, is the acting director of the National Institute for Learning Outcomes Assessment (NILOA), providing leadership and direction on research specific to the assessment of student learning at colleges and universities. Her main research interests include student learning outcomes assessment at minority serving institutions, access and equity issues for underrepresented administrators and students, assessment in athletics, and higher education policy. She holds a PhD in educational organization and leadership with a higher education concentration from the University of Illinois, an MA in human development counseling from Saint Louis University, and a BA in psychology from Illinois Wesleyan University.

Linda Bastone, PhD, is associate provost for faculty affairs at Mercy College (New York). Previously, she was director of the School of Natural and Social Sciences, associate professor of psychology, and codirector of the NIH-funded MARC U-STAR Honors Program at Purchase College, State University of New York (SUNY). As an administrator, teacher, and researcher, Bastone is committed to increasing access and excellence in higher education. She received her BA in psychology and philosophy from the State University of New York at Binghamton and her PhD in social-personality psychology from the City University of New York. She received the SUNY Chancellor's Award for Excellence in Teaching and for Excellence in Community Service.

Kaylan Baxter is a doctoral (PhD) student in the Rossier School of Education at the University of Southern California (USC), research associate in the USC Race and Equity Center, and former affiliate of the Center for Urban Education at USC. Baxter studies how approaches to accountability shape the opportunities, experiences, and outcomes of racially minoritized students, with a focus on community colleges and access-oriented 4-year institutions. Eight years of postsecondary practice, across several units in academic affairs, inform Baxter's research and teaching interests.

Juan G. Berumen, PhD, has a doctorate in education policy studies from Indiana University. Berumen is an experienced social justice advocate, possessing over 15 years as a policy advocate, researcher, and educator in communities and schools. He relies on personal and professional experiences to direct research endeavors and much-needed discussions in educational policy and program analysis that remove systemic barriers and create access and facilitate success for historically marginalized students underrepresented in higher education. Currently, Berumen is an instructor for the Chicano studies program at UC Berkeley and research analyst for the Office of Institutional Effectiveness and Research at Holy Names University.

Divya Bheda (she/her), PhD, is director of education and assessment with Examsoft and an independent consultant. She has over a decade of experience in leading program evaluations, assessments, social justice training, and professional development. Her curricular-assessment-evaluation work has spanned general education, administration, leadership, academic programs and certificates, and student support services. She is passionate about student success and building responsiveness and accountability in higher education in a restorative way. She is a "doer" and always tries to dismantle and unlearn normalized ways of being that are unjust. Through her byline and her work, she'd like to reimagine all aspects of higher education including scholarship.

Eunice Leung Brekke, PhD, is a professor of sociology with Leeward Community College. Brekke's dissertation research *Growing Food, Growing Youth* was a partnership with MAʻO Organic Farms, one of Hawaiʻi's largest independent farms, with a social mission to educate area youth, many who are Native Hawaiian and 1st-generation college students. This partnership has grown to include the development of a Sociology of Food course that is place-based and honors the indigenous values of Hawaiʻi, particularly connection to land and ancestry. Eunice also oversees the assessment of the campus's general education learning outcomes and performs program evaluation for community youth development programs.

Marilee Bresciani Ludvik, PhD, is professor and chair of educational leadership and policy studies at the University of Texas at Arlington. Previously, she was a professor at San Diego State University, and before that was assistant vice president of institutional assessment at Texas A&M University. Ludvik is a certified meditation and yoga instructor. Ludvik's research focuses on using translational neuroscience and mindful compassion practices to inform the design and evaluation of workshops and curriculum to decrease students', faculty, and administrators' stress and anxiety and increase their attention, emotion, and cognitive flexibility, as well as enhance compassion, inquiry, creativity, overall well-being, and career readiness.

Monique Chyba, PhD, is professor of mathematics at University of Hawai'i at Mānoa. Chyba's research expertise lies in optimal control applied to robotics, space exploration, nuclear magnetic resonance, neuroscience, and on data analysis and swarm of multi-agent systems. She is the director of SUPER-M: School and University Partnership for Educational Renewal in Mathematics. The project forges partnerships between UH Mānoa graduate mathematics students and K–12 teachers to design innovative, developmentally appropriate, and engaging activities for K–12 students. Place-based learning is an integral part of her teaching philosophy, immersing students in local culture, and providing opportunities and experiences relevant to their environment.

Lesley D'Souza is a student affairs assessment professional that specializes in storytelling with data. She is the director of strategic storytelling and digital engagement at Western University. Lesley is interested in design thinking in the assessment cycle, and how assessment best practices can broaden to support decolonization. Lesley was cochair for the research, assessment, and evaluation community of practice in the Canadian Association of College and University Student Services and a member of the ACPA Commission for Assessment and Evaluation Directorate. She has an MA in college student personnel from Bowling Green State University and is a mom to two little boys.

Alicia C. Dowd, PhD, is a professor of education, senior scientist, and director of the Center for the Study of Higher Education (CSHE) in the Department of Education Policy Studies at the Pennsylvania State University College of Education. An action researcher, Dowd's scholarship generates knowledge about organizational change toward racial equity in higher education. Her work, which draws on critical theories, cultural historical activity theory, and the experiential knowledge that comes from working directly with college administrators, faculty, and staff as they seek to design equitable institutional practices and policies, informs strategies of equity-minded data use and critical assessment.

Raina Dyer-Barr, PhD, is assistant director for consulting and public engagement for the Office of Community College Research and Leadership (OCCRL) on professional development, evaluation, and consulting inquiries. Her research interests broadly include examining the educational experiences of postsecondary students from underrepresented and/or underserved groups, factors that impact their retention in higher education, and addressing the educational equity gaps that exist in both access and outcomes for members of these populations. She holds a BA in English from the University of California at Los Angeles, and an MA and PhD in educational policy studies from the University of Illinois Urbana Champaign.

Peter Felten, PhD, is executive director of the Center for Engaged Learning, assistant provost for teaching and learning, and professor of history at Elon University. His books include the coauthored *Relationship-Rich Education: How Human Connections Drive Success in College* (Johns Hopkins University Press, 2020), *The Undergraduate Experience* (Jossey-Bass, 2016), and *Engaging Students as Partners in Learning and Teaching* (Jossey-Bass, 2014). He is coeditor of the *International Journal for Academic Development* and a fellow of the Gardner Institute, a foundation that works to advance equity in higher education.

Ciji A. Heiser, PhD, is director for student affairs assessment and effectiveness at Western Michigan University. She coordinates assessment and strategic planning efforts, manages data integration and visualization, and leads evaluation and program review processes. Heiser spent 6 years at The University of North Carolina at Chapel Hill working in assessment and at St. Mary's College of Maryland for international student support. Heiser received her BA in international relations from Bucknell University, MEd from Kent State University, MS in educational research methodology from the University of North Carolina at Greensboro, and PhD in the same program on culturally responsive evaluation and measurement for equity.

Gavin W. Henning, PhD, is professor of higher education and director of the master of higher education administration and doctorate of education programs at New England College. Over his 20+ years in higher education he has been a professor, assessment practitioner, and student affairs administrator. He is past president of ACPA–College Student Educators International, past president of the Council for the Advancement of Standards in Higher Education, and founder of Student Affairs Assessment Leaders (SAAL). He has been recognized for his contributions to student affairs and higher education by receiving ACPA's *Annuit Coeptis* and Diamond Honoree awards.

Ms. Harriet Hobbs is the vice president of institutional effectiveness at Clinton College. Her 21 years of experience include providing leadership for strategic planning, assessment, accreditation, institutional research, teaching and learning, and continuous improvement. She has coauthored multiple articles and given more than 40 conference presentations on the national, regional, and local levels. Her research examines the influence of academic resilience, the effects of noncognitive factors, and equitable assessment practices in higher education.

Natasha A. Jankowski, PhD, is an assessment expert and higher education consultant as well as a lecturer with New England College. She is the former executive director of the National Institute for Learning Outcomes Assessment (NILOA) and previously served as a faculty member and graduate program coordinator for the Department of Education Policy, Organization, and Leadership at the University of Illinois Urbana-Champaign. Her areas of focus include assignment design, transparency, evidence-based storytelling, equity, mapping and alignment of learning, and all things assessment. NILOA was the proud recipient of the ACPA Contribution to Higher Education Award under her leadership.

Royel M. Johnson, PhD, is an associate professor of education and social work at the University of Southern California (USC). He also serves as Director of Student Engagement of the USC Race and Equity Center and is faculty member in the Pullias Center for Higher Education. His research focuses on issues of educational access, equity, and student success. Johnson has more than 40 academic publications including peer-reviewed articles in the *Journal of Higher Education*, *Peabody Journal of Education*, and *Teachers College Record*; and he has been awarded over $5.1 million in grants and contracts. His edited book with Drs. Liliana Garces and Uju Anya, *Racial Equity on College Campuses: Connecting Research and Practice*, was recently published by SUNY Press. For his early career accomplishments, ACPA—College Educators International honored him with their Emerging Scholar award in 2020.

Joseph D. Levy, PhD, serves as the executive director of assessment and accreditation at National Louis University in Chicago, Illinois. Levy earned a BA in English from Baldwin-Wallace College, an MS in student affairs in higher education from Colorado State University, and his EdD in higher education leadership from National Louis University. Experienced with assessment efforts of multiple institutional types, Levy is a member of the Student Affairs Assessment Leaders (SAAL) Board of Directors, leads the applying and leading assessment in student affairs open course, and serves as a coach for the National Institute of Learning Outcomes Assessment (NILOA).

Kaiwipunikauikawēkiu Lipe, PhD, is Native Hawaiian affairs program officer and the director of the Truth, Racial Healing, and Transformation Campus Center, University of Hawai'i at Mānoa. Lipe's work focuses on institutional transformation with a commitment to Indigenous-grounded and equitable futures. She has published on equity and equality from an Indigenous lens and she is also an Obama Foundation Leader for the Asia-Pacific region.

Chiara Logli, PhD, is the institutional assessment specialist at the Honolulu Community College. Previously she served as the assistant director for the East-West Center's Asia Pacific Higher Education Research Partnership, as a Rotary International Fellow in Thailand, as well as a consultant for USAID in Indonesia and CAST/International Baccalaureate Schools worldwide. She also worked for the University of California Berkeley's International House and the University of Santa Barbara's Multicultural Center. She holds a PhD in educational foundations from the University of Hawai'i at Manoa and an MA in political science from the University of Bologna (Italy).

Anne E. Lundquist, PhD, is the managing director for learning and innovation at The Hope Center for College, Community, and Justice at the Lewis Katz School of Medicine at Temple University. She is a White, cisgender, third-generation educated poet, yogi, and social justice advocate who draws on her 30-year career in higher education to help transform higher education into a more effective and equitable sector through research and educational training and services to address student basic needs insecurity. Previously, Lundquist served as assistant vice president for campus strategy at Anthology, director of strategic planning and assessment for the Division of Student Affairs at Western Michigan University, as well as senior student affairs officer at four liberal arts colleges. She holds an MFA in creative writing and a PhD in educational leadership, higher education, from Western Michigan University. She earned her BA in religious studies and English from Albion College.

Peggy L. Maki, PhD, writes, speaks about, and consults with higher education organizations and institutions on the process of assessing student learning, an internally motivated and shared commitment to currently enrolled students' equitable progress toward achieving high-quality learning outcomes. She has consulted at over 610 institutions in the United States and abroad and has written books and articles on assessment for 20+ years. She served as the former American Association for Higher Education's (AAHE) senior scholar on assessment; and has served as a member of several advisory boards and institutes, including currently for the National Institute for Learning Outcomes Assessment (NILOA).

Charmaine Mangram, PhD, is associate professor for the Institute for Teacher Education (Secondary) program at the University of Hawai'i at Mānoa. Mangram studies mathematics teacher professional development for preservice and in-service secondary mathematics teachers and parental engagement in mathematics. She is primarily interested in research that serves to increase access to high quality mathematics education for learners from communities that have been historically marginalized by the U.S. educational system.

Erick Montenegro, PhD, is a fellow with the National Institute for Learning Outcomes Assessment (NILOA) focused on equity-minded assessment practice. Montenegro currently is the senior research associate for The Pell Institute for the Study of Opportunity in Higher Education. Montenegro serves on the board of directors for the Quality Assurance Commons for Higher and Postsecondary Education (QA Commons). As a research analyst for NILOA Montenegro helped launch the national conversation on equity-minded assessment in 2017. He holds a PhD in education policy, organization, and leadership from the University of Illinois at Urbana-Champaign.

Siobhán Ní Dhonacha, PhD, is faculty specialist with the honors program at the University of Hawai'i at Mānoa. Ní Dhonacha teaches and researches experiential learning theory and engagement, writing and oral communication through an interdisciplinary lens, as well as mentoring and advising a diverse student body with a student-centered equity and social justice focus based on the lived principles of an ethics of care philosophy.

Verna F. Orr, PhD, is special assistant for planning and institutional effectiveness at Benedict College, a fellow with the National Institute for Learning Outcomes Assessment (NILOA), and a three-time graduate of Howard University in Washington DC. She also holds a PhD in higher education from the University of Illinois at Urbana-Champaign. She served as cochair of the Historically Black College and University (HBCU) Collaborative for Excellence in Educational Quality Assurance (CEEQA), as well as positions as a research analyst and postdoctoral researcher with

NILOA. She previously served as confidential assistant to the 16th president of Howard University.

Leticia Oseguera, PhD, is an associate professor and senior research associate in the Department of Education Policy Studies and the Center for the Study of Higher Education in the College of Education at the Pennsylvania State University. She received her PhD from the higher education and organizational change program at UCLA. Her research focuses on campus climate and understanding college access and educational opportunities for historically underserved and underrepresented student populations. She has extensive expertise on graduate and undergraduate program evaluation and has published extensively on education policy and student success including STEM program success.

Christine Robinson, PhD, is the executive director of the Office of Assessment and Accreditation (OAA) at the University of North Carolina at Charlotte. The OAA team promotes continuous improvement in student learning, educational practices, and support services, and facilitates an institutional culture of ongoing and systematic self-evaluation and improvement. Her more than 20 years of experience includes collaborating with and leading academic faculty and staff in the assessment of educational practices and programs and institutional effectiveness. She has coauthored multiple articles and two book chapters and given more than 30 conference presentations at 12 national, regional, and local conferences.

Karen Singer-Freeman, PhD, is director of research at the Wake Forest University Center for the Advancement of Teaching. She was previously associate professor of psychology at Purchase College, State University of New York where she was codirector of the MARC U*STAR Honors Program and associate director of the Baccalaureate and Beyond Program, NIH-funded programs for STEM students from underserved groups. She received her BA in psychology and anthropology from the University of Michigan and her PhD in developmental psychology from the University of Minnesota Institute of Child Development. She received the SUNY Chancellor's Award for Excellence in Teaching.

Monica Stitt-Bergh, PhD, is a specialist in the Assessment and Curriculum Support Center with the University of Hawai'i at Mānoa. Stitt-Bergh provides technical support and offers workshops on program- and institution-level learning outcomes assessment, program evaluation, and curriculum development. During the past 5 years, she has assisted in evaluating the campus's efforts to become a Native Hawaiian place of learning for all students. Her classroom experience includes teaching 1st-year writing and social science research methods courses. Stitt-Bergh has published and given conference presentations on learning outcomes assessment in higher education, writing program evaluation, self-assessment, writing-across-the-curriculum, and data visualization.

Kara Plamann Wagoner is an institutional/policy analyst with Kapiʻolani Community College. Always collaborating, Wagoner enjoys being part of a dynamic and insightful team that created an āina (place)-based rubric to accompany the āina-based classes offered on her campus. She is currently earning her PhD in educational psychology at the University of Hawaiʻi at Mānoa, studying theories of learning, as well as measurement, statistics, and evaluation.

Stephanie J. Waterman, PhD, Onondaga, Turtle clan, is an associate professor at the Ontario Institute for Studies in Education/University of Toronto, in leadership, higher, and adult education. She was a long-time cochair for the NASPA: National Association for Student Personnel Administrators Indigenous Peoples Knowledge Community Research and Scholarship Committee and is currently an ACPA-College Student Educators International Senior Scholar. Waterman was awarded the AERA Indigenous Peoples of the Americas SIG 2019 Mike Charleston Award for Distinguished Contributions to Research in Indigenous Education and the 2019 NASPA, Student Affairs Professionals in Higher Education Robert H. Shaffer Award for Outstanding Contribution to Higher Education.

Mary-Ann Winkelmes, PhD, is executive director of the Center for Teaching and Learning at Brandeis University and the founder and principal investigator of the Transparency in Learning and Teaching in Higher Education project (TILTHigherEd.com). From 2013 to 2018 she was a senior fellow at the Association of American Colleges and Universities, director of instructional development and research, and an associate graduate faculty member in the department of history at the University of Nevada, Las Vegas. She also served in leadership roles in teaching and learning centers and faculty development programs at the University of Illinois at Urbana-Champaign, the University of Chicago, and Harvard University.

Eboni M. Zamani-Gallaher, PhD, is professor of higher education/community college leadership and director of the Office for Community College Research and Leadership (OCCRL). She previously served as associate head of the Department of Education Policy, Organization, and Leadership and associate dean of the Graduate College at the University of Illinois at Urbana-Champaign. She serves as the executive director of the Council for the Study of Community Colleges (CSCC). Her teaching, research, and consulting activities largely include psychosocial adjustment and transition of marginalized collegians, transfer, access policies, student development, and services at community colleges.

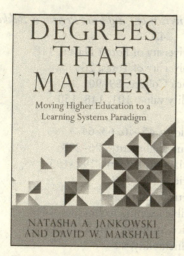

Degrees That Matter

Moving Higher Education to a Learning Systems Paradigm

Natasha A. Jankowski and David W. Marshall

"This book is an important reminder of the necessity for college and university actors to become aware of the critical role they play in the construction of effective learning environments. The authors advocate for a renewed sense of agency where students, faculty, and administrators do not succumb to a culture of compliance. The authors not only ask for a more active and conscious participation in the construction of learning environments, but also for a more honest and public dialogue about the dynamics that work or do not work in higher education institutions. This book is required reading for educational leaders who want to construct creative, caring, and collaborative forms of learning in higher education institutions."—*Teachers College Record*

"Rather than rehashing current debates about the usefulness of higher education, Jankowski and Marshall focus on the heart of the matter, student learning. By rethinking tired conventions, by questioning long held assumptions, and by pointing to the most useful and applicable resources, they offer practical steps for making education more effective and students more successful. Every college or university could stand to benefit from the practical and principled advice this book advances."—*Paul L. Gaston, Trustees Professor, Kent State University*

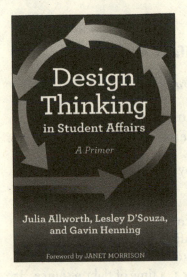

Design Thinking in Student Affairs

A Primer

Julia Allworth, Lesley D'Souza, and Gavin Henning

Foreword by Janet Morrison

Design thinking is an innovative problem-solving framework. This introduction is the first book to apply its methodology to student affairs and, in doing so, points the way to its potentially wider value to higher education as a whole.

With its focus on empathy, which is the need to thoroughly understand users' experiences, design thinking is user-centered, similar to how student affairs is student-centered. Because the focus of design thinking is to design with users, not for users, it aligns well with student affairs practice. In addition, its focus on empathy makes design thinking a more equitable approach to problem-solving than other methods because all users' experiences—not just the experiences of majority or "average" student—need to be understood. Centering empathy in problem-solving processes can be a tool to disrupt higher education systems and practices.

"This book presents a reimagined model of assessment with design thinking, and instantly upon seeing it, you know how needed it is in education today. Focusing upon empathy, ideation, and storytelling throughout the assessment process, the authors of this book present a human-centered approach to engage in assessment of student learning. The design thinking assessment model and key questions remind us that our works sits within a larger context, one that can be infused with equity and act as a tool for decolonizing education."—**Natasha Jankowski,** *Former Executive Director of the National Institute for Learning Outcomes Assessment*

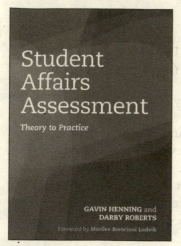